Titles available from boyd & fraser

BASIC Programming
- Applesoft BASIC Fundamentals and Style
- BASIC Fundamentals and Style
- Complete BASIC for the Short Course
- Structured BASIC Fundamentals and Style for the IBM® PC and Compatibles
- Structured Microsoft BASIC: Essentials for Business
- Structuring Programs in Microsoft BASIC

COBOL Programming
- Advanced Structured COBOL: Batch and Interactive
- COBOL: Structured Programming Techniques for Solving Problems
- Comprehensive Structured COBOL
- Fundamentals of Structured COBOL

Database
- A Guide to SQL
- Database Systems: Management and Design

Computer Information Systems
- Applications Software Programming with Fourth-Generation Languages
- Business Data Communications and Networks
- Expert Systems for Business: Concepts and Applications
- Fundamentals of Systems Analysis with Application Design
- Investment Management: Decision Support and Expert Systems
- Learning Computer Programming: Structured Logic Algorithms, and Flowcharting
- Office Automation: An Information Systems Approach

Microcomputer Applications
- An Introduction to Desktop Publishing
- dBASE III PLUS® Programming
- DOS: Complete and Simplified
- Introduction to Computers and Microcomputer Applications
- Macintosh Productivity Tools
- Mastering and Using Lotus 1-2-3®, Release 3
- Mastering and Using Lotus 1-2-3®, Version 2.2
- Mastering and Using WordPerfect® 5.0 and 5.1
- Mastering Lotus 1-2-3®
- Microcomputer Applications: A Practical Approach
- Microcomputer Applications: Using Small Systems Software, Second Edition
- Microcomputer Database Management Using dBASE III PLUS®
- Microcomputer Database Management Using dBASE IV®
- Microcomputer Database Management Using R:BASE System V®
- Microcomputer Productivity Tools
- Microcomputer Systems Management and Applications
- PC-DOS®/MS-DOS® Simplified, Second Edition
- Using Enable®: An Introduction to Integrated Software

Shelly and Cashman Titles
- Computer Concepts with Microcomputer Applications (Lotus 1-2-3® and VP-Planner Plus® versions)
- Computer Concepts
- Essential Computer Concepts
- Learning to Use WordPerfect®, Lotus 1-2-3®, and dBASE III PLUS®
- Learning to Use WordPerfect®, VP-Planner Plus®, and dBASE III PLUS®
- Learning to Use WordPerfect®
- Learning to Use Lotus 1-2-3®
- Learning to Use VP-Planner Plus®
- Learning to Use dBASE III PLUS®
- Computer Fundamentals with Application Software
- Learning to Use SuperCalc®3, dBASE III®, and WordStar® 3.3: An Introduction
- Learning to Use SuperCalc®3: An Introduction
- Learning to Use dBASE III®: An Introduction
- Learning to Use WordStar® 3.3: An Introduction
- BASIC Programming for the IBM Personal Computer
- Structured COBOL: Pseudocode Edition
- Structured COBOL: Flowchart Edition
- RPG II, RPG III, & RPG/400

Order information on page vi.

STRUCTURED MICROSOFT BASIC Essentials for Business

James S. Quasney
John Maniotes
PURDUE UNIVERSITY CALUMET

boyd & fraser publishing company

Credits:

Publisher: Tom Walker
Editor: Donna Villanucci
Director of Production: Becky Herrington
Design/Cover: Ken Russo
Cover Photo: ©David Hughes/Stock Boston
Manufacturing Director: Dean Sherman
Typesetting: Huntington & Black Typography

© 1990 by boyd & fraser publishing
A Division of South-Western Publishing Company
Boston, MA 02116

All rights reserved. No part of this work may be reproduced or used in
any form or by any means—graphic, electronic, or mechanical, including
photocopying, recording, taping, or information and retrieval systems—
without written permission from the publisher.

Manufactured in the United States of America

IBM is a registered trademark of International Business Machines Corporation

Library of Congress Cataloging-in-Publication Data

```
Quasney, James S.
    Structured microsoft BASIC : essentials for business / James S.
  Quasney, John Maniotes.
       p.   cm.
    ISBN 0-87835-452-2
    1. BASIC (Computer program language)  2. Structured programming.
  3. Business--Data processing.   I. Maniotes, John.  II. Title.
  HF5548.4.B3Q37   1990
  005.265--dc20                                             89-17393
                                                                CIP
```

2 3 4 5 6 7 8 9 10 Ki 4 3 2 1 0

Dedication

To our wives: **Linda** and **Mary**
The Quasney tribe: **Lisa**, **Jeff**, **Marci**, **Jodi**, **Amanda**, and **Nikole**
The Maniotes clan: **Dionne**, **Sam**, and **Andrew**

ORDER INFORMATION AND FACULTY SUPPORT INFORMATION

For the quickest service, refer to the map below for the South-Western Regional Office serving your area.

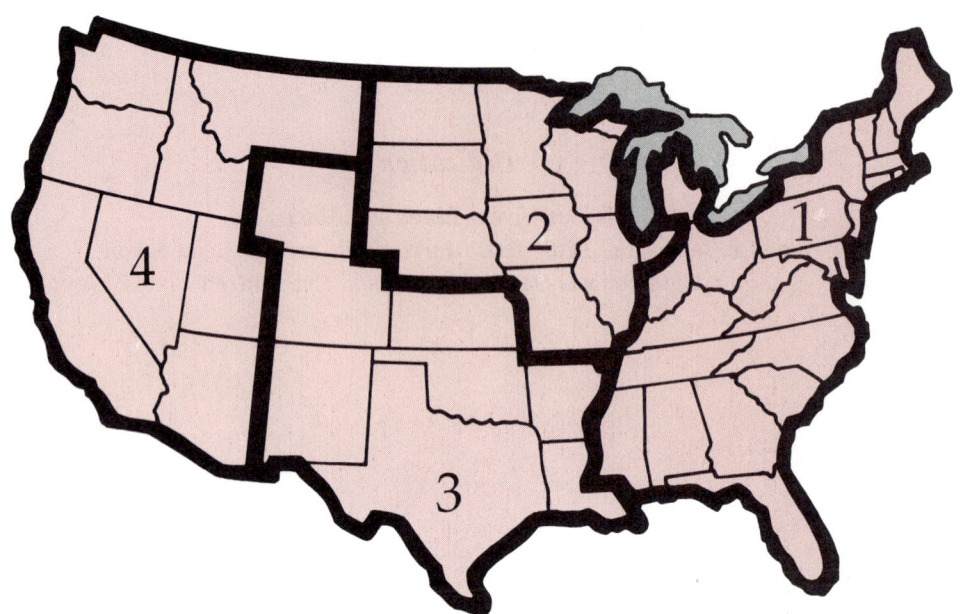

1 ORDER INFORMATION
5101 Madison Road
Cincinnati, OH 45227-1490
General Telephone–513-527-6945
Telephone: 1-800-543-8440
FAX: 513-527-6979
Telex: 214371

FACULTY SUPPORT INFORMATION
5101 Madison Road
Cincinnati, OH 45227-1490
General Telephone–513-527-6950
Telephone: 1-800-543-8444

Alabama	Massachusetts	Pennsylvania
Connecticut	Michigan (Lower)**	Rhode Island
Delaware	Mississippi	South Carolina
Florida	New Hampshire	Tennessee
Georgia	New Jersey	Vermont
Indiana*	New York	Virginia
Kentucky	North Carolina	West Virginia
Maine	Ohio	District of Columbia
Maryland		

*Except for ZIP Code Areas 463, 464. These areas contact Region 2 Office.
**Except for the Upper Peninsula. This area contacts Region 2 Office.

2 ORDER INFORMATION and FACULTY SUPPORT INFORMATION
355 Conde Street
West Chicago, IL 60185
General Telephone–312-231-6000
Telephone: 1-800-543-7972

Illinois	Minnesota	North Dakota
Indiana*	Missouri	South Dakota
Iowa	Nebraska	Wisconsin
Michigan (Upper)**		

*Only for ZIP Code Areas 463, 464. Other areas contact Region 1 office.
**Only for Upper Peninsula. Other areas contact Region 1 office.

3 ORDER INFORMATION
13800 Senlac Drive
Suite 100
Dallas, TX 75234
General Telephone–214-241-8541
Telephone: 1-800-543-7972

FACULTY SUPPORT INFORMATION
5101 Madison Road
Cincinnati, OH 45227-1490
General Telephone–513-527-6950
Telephone: 1-800-543-8444

Arkansas	Louisiana	Texas
Colorado	New Mexico	Wyoming
Kansas	Oklahoma	

4 ORDER INFORMATION and FACULTY SUPPORT INFORMATION
6185 Industrial Way
Livermore, CA 94550
General Telephone–415-449-2280
Telephone: 1-800-543-7972

Alaska	Idaho	Oregon
Arizona	Montana	Utah
California	Nevada	Washington
Hawaii		

CONTENTS

PREFACE — xi

LIST OF PROGRAMMING CASE STUDIES — xvii

■ 1 COMPUTERS AND PROBLEM SOLVING: AN INTRODUCTION — 1

1.1	What Is a Computer?	1
1.2	Computer Hardware	2
1.3	The PC and PS/2 Family	4
1.4	The Stored Program Concept	8
1.5	Computer Software	8
1.6	Problem Solving and Program Development	10
1.7	Test Your BASIC Skills	14
1.8	PC Hands-on Exercises	16

■ 2 MICROSOFT BASIC: AN INTRODUCTION — 19

2.1	Creating a Microsoft BASIC Program	19
2.2	The INPUT Statement	23
2.3	The PRINT and CLS Statements	26
2.4	Documenting a Program — The REM Statement	28
2.5	Getting Aquainted with the PC	30
2.6	Editing Microsoft BASIC Programs	32
2.7	System Commands and Hard-Copy Output	33
2.8	Special Keys	37
2.9	Programming Tips	37
2.10	Test Your BASIC Skills	41
2.11	BASIC Programming Problems	42

3 PROGRAMS WITH CALCULATIONS AND STRINGS 45

3.1	Introduction	**45**
3.2	Constants	**46**
3.3	Variables	**49**
3.4	The LET Statement	**54**
3.5	Expressions	**57**
3.6	Test Your BASIC Skills	**62**
3.7	BASIC Programming Problems	**63**

4 LOOPING AND INPUT/OUTPUT PROCESSING 67

4.1	Introduction	**67**
4.2	The WHILE and WEND Statements	**70**
4.3	The READ, DATA, and RESTORE Statements	**72**
4.4	The PRINT Statement	**78**
4.5	The PRINT USING Statement for Formatted Output	**83**
4.6	The LOCATE Statement	**93**
4.7	Test Your BASIC Skills	**95**
4.8	BASIC Programming Problems	**97**

5 STRUCTURED PROGRAMMING AND DECISION MAKING 101

5.1	Structured Programming	**101**
5.2	The IF Statement	**104**
5.3	Accumulators	**106**
5.4	Implementing the Do-While and Do-Until Logic Structures	**112**
5.5	Implementing the If-Then-Else Structure	**114**
5.6	Pairing of Nested IF Statements	**119**
5.7	Logical Operators	**120**
5.8	Test Your BASIC Skills	**126**
5.9	BASIC Programming Problems	**129**

6 SEQUENTIAL FILE PROCESSING AND THE TOP-DOWN APPROACH — 133

- **6.1** Introduction — 133
- **6.2** Data Files — 133
- **6.3** Sequential File Processing — 134
- **6.4** The Top-Down (Modular) Approach and the GOSUB and RETURN Statements — 150
- **6.5** The ON-GOSUB Statement and Menu-Driven Programs — 155
- **6.6** Control-Break Processing — 164
- **6.7** Test Your BASIC Skills — 171
- **6.8** BASIC Programming Problems — 173

7 FOR LOOPS, ARRAYS, SORTING, AND TABLE PROCESSING — 177

- **7.1** Introduction — 177
- **7.2** The FOR and NEXT Statements — 177
- **7.3** Arrays Versus Simple Variables — 183
- **7.4** Declaring Arrays — 184
- **7.5** Manipulating Arrays — 186
- **7.6** Multi-Dimensional Arrays — 187
- **7.7** Sorting — 189
- **7.8** Searching Tables — 193
- **7.9** Test Your BASIC Skills — 200
- **7.10** BASIC Programming Problems — 202

8 MORE ON STRINGS AND FUNCTIONS — 205

- **8.1** Introduction — 205
- **8.2** String Functions, String Statements, and Special Variables — 205
- **8.3** Numeric Functions — 216
- **8.4** User-Defined Functions — 227
- **8.5** Test Your BASIC Skills — 229
- **8.6** BASIC Programming Problems — 231

9 COMPUTER GRAPHICS AND SOUND 235

9.1	Introduction	235
9.2	Text-Mode Graphics	237
9.3	Medium-Resolution and High-Resolution Graphics	244
9.4	Sound and Music	256
9.5	Test Your BASIC Skills	259
9.6	BASIC Programming Problems	260

APPENDIX A   DEBUGGING TECHNIQUES AND THE ASCII CHARACTER CODES 263

A.1	Debugging Techniques	263
A.2	ASCII Character Codes	266

APPENDIX B   ANSWERS TO THE TEST YOUR BASIC SKILLS EXERCISES (EVEN-NUMBERED) 269

INDEX 277

MICROSOFT BASIC REFERENCE CARD R.1

RESERVED WORDS R.5

STUDENT DISKETTE R.5

PREFACE

ABOUT THIS BOOK

Structured Microsoft BASIC: Essentials for Business is ideally suited for use in an introductory BASIC programming course that utilizes the IBM PC, or IBM PS/2, or compatible system. The text will also meet the needs of instructors teaching an Introductory Data Processing course in which BASIC is a component. *Structured Microsoft BASIC: Essentials for Business* is a perfect complement to the many fine Introductory Computer Information Systems texts on the market today.

OBJECTIVES OF THIS BOOK

The objectives of this book are as follows:

- To acquaint the reader with the correct way to design and write high-quality programs.
- To teach the fundamentals of Microsoft BASIC.
- To teach good problem-solving techniques that can be used in advanced computing and information-processing courses.
- To encourage independent study and help those who are working alone on their own personal computer systems.

LEVEL OF INSTRUCTION

No previous experience with a computer is assumed, and no mathematics beyond the high school freshman level is required. The book is written specifically for the student with average ability, for whom continuity, simplicity, and practicality are characteristics we consider essential. Numerous insights, based on the authors' fifty cumulative years of experience in teaching and consulting in the field of data processing, are implicit throughout the book. For the past fifteen years, we have both taught introductory programming courses using BASIC.

FUNDAMENTAL TOPICS ARE PRESENTED IN DETAIL

Besides introducing students to the correct way to design and write programs by means of structured and top-down techniques, the book presents fundamental topics concerning computers and programming which should be covered in any introductory programming class. These include the stored program concept; getting acquainted with the PC; editing programs; input/output operations; variables and constants; simple and complex computations; the use of functions and subroutines; decision making; the use of counters and running totals; looping and end-of-file tests; counter-controlled loops; the use of logical operators; string manipulation; and graphics. Other essential topics include data validation; table processing; selection; searching; matching; sorting; file processing; and the differences between batch and interactive applications. Every one of these topics is covered in detail in this book.

DISTINGUISHING FEATURES

The distinguishing features of this book include the following:

A Proven Book

This book has evolved over the past decade and is based on the authors' five prior books on BASIC programming. Many instructors who have used our books have shared with us their comments and suggestions for improvement as new programming techniques have been developed. They have done much to shape the contents of this book, which reflects modern programming practices.

Early Presentation of the Structured Programming Approach

Particular attention is given to designing proper programs by means of the three logic structures of structured programming: Sequence, Selection (If-Then-Else and Case), and Repetition (Do-While and Do-Until). A disciplined method for implementing the structured design is adhered to throughout the book.

BASIC Programming Problems with Sample Input and Output

Over 30 challenging field-tested BASIC Programming Problems are included at the end of the chapters. Each of the problems include a statement of purpose, a problem statement, sample input data, and the corresponding output results. Hardcopy and softcopy (Instructor Diskette) solutions to these problems are given in the *Instructor's Manual and Answer Book*.

Student Diskette

The Student Diskette that accompanies this book contains all of the executable programs and data files presented in the text. Students can use this valuable learning aid for the following:

- to select a program that is similar to their solution to a programming assignment (this will save keying time);
- to experiment on their own with developing alternative solutions to the Programming Case Studies presented in the text;
- to access the data files required in the programming assignments; and,
- to store their solutions to programming assignments.

Program names on the Student Diskette are in the form of PRGc-n, where c represents the chapter number and n represents the program number. For example, PRG2-8 refers to the eighth program presented in Chapter 2. Data file names correspond to the names used in the text.

GOTOless Textbook

The GOTO is discussed briefly. All looping is implemented by means of either the WHILE and WEND statements or the FOR and NEXT statements. The GOTO statement is used only to branch forward to a structure terminator when IF statements require more than three physical lines.

Interactive Applications (Menu-Driven Programs)

Although examples of batch processing are presented, the primary emphasis is on interactive processing. The reader is introduced to the INPUT, PRINT, and CLS (Clear Screen) statements early in Chapter 2. The LOCATE statement is presented in Chapter 4 and thereafter is used to build screens. Menu-driven programs are illustrated to familiarize the reader with the type of programming that is proliferating today.

Emphasis on the Program Development Cycle

The program development cycle is presented early in Chapter 1 and is used throughout the book. Good design habits are reinforced, and special attention is given to testing the design before attempting to implement the logic in a program.

Emphasis on Fundamentals and Style

Emphasis is placed on the fundamentals of producing well-written and readable programs. A disciplined style is consistently used in all program examples. Thorough documentation and indention standards illuminate the implementation of the Selection and Repetition logic structures.

Summary of the Microsoft BASIC Language on a Reference Card

A summary of the statements, commands, functions, special variables, special keys, operators, and reserved words can be found on a reference card at the back of the book. This summary is invaluable to the beginning student as a quick reference piece.

Presentation of Programming Case Studies

This book contains 15 completely solved and annotated case studies, illuminating the use of Microsoft BASIC and computer programming in the real world. Emphasis is placed on problem analysis, program design, and an in-depth discussion of the program solution. The program solutions to these Programming Case Studies, as well as all other programs found throughout the book, are available on the Student Diskette in the back of this book.

Program Design Aids

The authors recognize top-down charts and flowcharting as excellent pedagogical aids and as the tools of an analyst or programmer. Hence, many of the Programming Case Studies include top-down charts and program flowcharts to demonstrate programming style, design, and documentation. For the reader's convenience, line numbers have been placed at the top-left corner of the symbols to better illustrate the relationship between the logic diagrams and the program.

Test Your BASIC Skills

A set of short-answer exercises identified as Test Your BASIC Skills appears at the end of each chapter. Over 100 problems, many of which are complete programs, are included for practice. Through the use of these exercises, the reader can master the concepts presented and instructors are afforded a valuable diagnostic tool. Answers for the Test Your BASIC Skills exercises (even-numbered) are included at the end of the book in Appendix B. Answers to the odd-numbered exercises can be found in the *Instructor's Manual and Answer Book*.

Graphics and Sound

Chapter 9 covers the graphics statements and functions in Microsoft BASIC that are central to understanding what can be done with graphics on the PC. Furthermore, the necessary sound and music statements are discussed and are applied to various applications.

ANCILLARY MATERIALS

A comprehensive instructor's support package accompanies *Structured Microsoft BASIC: Essentials for Business*. These ancillaries are available upon request from the publisher.

Instructor's Manual and Answer Book

The *Instructor's Manual and Answer Book* includes the following:

- Lecture outlines for each chapter
- Transparency masters from each chapter of the text
- Chapter-by-chapter objectives and vocabulary lists
- Answers to the odd-numbered Test Your BASIC Skills exercises
- Program solutions to the programming assignments in the book
- Test bank, including true/false, short-answer, fill-in, and multiple-choice questions for quizzes and tests

ProTest: An Easy-to-Use Computerized Test-Generating Package

Boyd & Fraser's state-of-the-art test-generating package, ProTest, has been designed specifically for this book. ProTest is an easy-to-use menu-driven package that is supplied on an IBM PC-compatible diskette. ProTest allows an instructor to create a customized test on the PC in a matter of minutes. The large test bank that accompanies ProTest includes field-tested true/false, multiple-choice, and fill-in questions. A user may also enter his or her own questions into the test bank.

ProTest will run on any IBM PC, IBM PS/2, or compatible system with two floppy-diskette drives or a hard disk.

Instructor Diskette

The Instructor Diskette that accompanies the *Instructor's Manual and Answer Book* includes the solutions to the programming assignments found at the end of Chapters 2 through 9.

ACKNOWLEDGMENTS

We would like to thank and express our appreciation to the many fine and talented individuals who have contributed to the success of this book. We were fortunate to have a group of reviewers whose critical evaluations of our first five BASIC books, *Standard BASIC Programming*; *BASIC Fundamentals and Style*; *Complete BASIC for the Short Course*; *Applesoft BASIC Fundamentals and Style*; and *Structured BASIC Fundamentals and Style for the IBM PC and Compatibles*, were of great value during the preparation of these books. Special thanks again go to Professor James N. Haag, University of San Francisco; Professor R. Waldo Roth, Taylor University; Professor David Bradbard, Auburn University; Professor Donald L. Muench, St. John Fisher College; Professor Jerry Lameiro, Colorado State University; Professors John T. Gorgone and I. Englander of Bentley College; Professor Chester Bogosta, Saint Leo College; Professor John J. Couture, San Diego City College; Professor Syed Shahabuddin, Central Michigan University; Sumit Sircar, University of Texas at

Arlington; Marilyn Markowitz; and James Larson, director of computer services for the Homewood Flossmoor High School District in Homewood, Illinois. We are also very grateful to the following individuals, who reviewed the manuscript for *Structured Microsoft BASIC: Essentials for Business*: Professor Bill Bailey, Casper College; Professor John Monroe, Roberts Wesleyan College; Professor John Ross, Indiana University at Kokomo; and Professor Mick Watterson, Drake University.

The instructional staff of the Information Systems and Computer Programming Department of Purdue University Calumet provided many helpful comments and suggestions, and to them we extend our sincere thanks.

No book is possible without the motivation and support of an editorial staff. Therefore, our final acknowledgment and greatest appreciation are reserved for the following at Boyd & Fraser: Tom Walker, vice president and publisher, for his unfaltering support; Donna Villanucci, development editor, for her organization, suggestions, encouragement, and valuable editorial assistance; and finally, Becky Herrington, director of production, for her creative talents and commitment to quality.

Hammond, Indiana
January 1990

James S. Quasney
John Maniotes

LIST OF PROGRAMMING CASE STUDIES

No.	Case Study	Page
1	Computing an Average	10
2	Determining a Salesperson's Commission	20
3	Tailor's Calculations	45
4A	Finding the Single Discount Rate	55
4B	Finding the Single Discount Rate Using the Top-Down Approach	152
5	Determining the Sale Price	67
6	Determining the Accounts Receivable Balance	90
7A	Weekly Payroll and Summary Report	108
7B	Writing the Weekly Payroll and Summary Report to Auxiliary Storage	139
8	Creating a Sequential File	142
9	Processing a Sequential File	147
10	A Menu-Driven Program	156
11	Sales Analysis Report — Single-Level Control Break	166
12	Deciphering a Coded Message	211
13	Determining the Time It Takes to Double an Investment	218
14	Computer Simulation	225
15	Logo for the Bow-Wow Dog Food Company	238

COMPUTERS AND PROBLEM SOLVING: AN INTRODUCTION

1.1 WHAT IS A COMPUTER?

A **computer** is a machine that can accept data, process the data at high speeds, and give the results of these processes in an acceptable form. A more formal definition of a computer is given by the American National Standards Institute (ANSI), which defines it as a device that can perform substantial computation, including numerous arithmetic and logic operations, without intervention by a human operator.

Computers can handle tedious and time-consuming work and large amounts of data without ever tiring, which makes them indispensable for most businesses. In fact, computers have been among the most important forces in the modernization of business, industry, and society since World War II. Keep in mind, however, that with all their capabilities, computers are merely tools and are not built to think or reason. They extend our intellect, but they do not replace thinking.

Advantages of a Computer

The major advantages of a computer are its speed and accuracy, as well as its ability to store and have ready for immediate recall vast amounts of data. Today's computers can also accept data from anywhere via telephone line or satellite communications. They can generate usable output, like reports, paychecks, and invoices, at a speed of several thousand lines per minute.

Disadvantages of a Computer

Some of the disadvantages of a computer concern obsolescence and on-going costs for training and maintenance. Currently, computer models become technologically obsolete in a matter of a few years. Furthermore, in order for an organization's staff to derive their maximum benefits from a computer, the organization must continually invest in training and maintenance.

1.2 COMPUTER HARDWARE

Computer hardware is the physical equipment of a computer system. The equipment may consist of mechanical, magnetic, optical, electrical, or electronic devices. Although many computers have been built in different sizes, speeds, and costs, and with different internal operations, most of them have the same five basic subsystems, as shown in Figures 1.1 and 1.2.

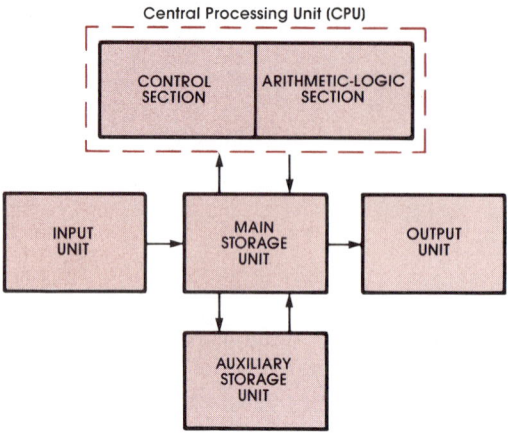

FIGURE 1.1 *Basic structure of a digital computer, where the arrows represent the flow of data.*

Input

An **input unit** is a device that allows **programs** (instructions to the computer) and **data** (like rate of pay, hours worked, and number of dependents) to enter the computer system. This device converts the incoming data into electrical impulses, which are then sent to the other units of the computer. A computer system usually has a **keyboard** for input. Other common input devices include a **joystick** and **mouse**. The keyboard and mouse are shown in Figure 1.2. The diskette unit, which is labelled as auxiliary storage in Figure 1.2, can also serve as an input device.

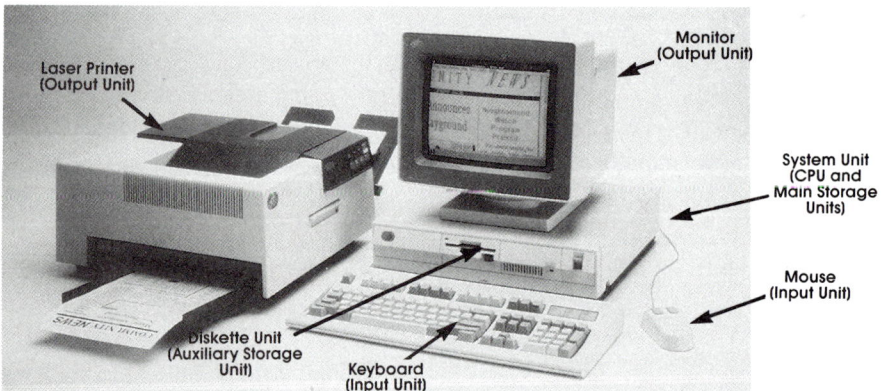

FIGURE 1.2 *The IBM Personal System/2 (PS/2) (Courtesy IBM Corp.).*

Main Storage

After the instructions and data have entered the computer through an input unit, they are stored in the computer's **main storage** unit. Since computers can process vast amounts of data in a short time, and since some can perform millions of calculations in just one second, the storage unit must be able to retain large amounts of data and make any single item rapidly available for processing.

Main storage in a computer is divided into locations called **bytes**, each having a unique **address**. When instructions and data are entered, they are stored in various locations of main storage. The computer leaves data in a storage location until it is instructed to replace it with new data. While a data item is in storage, the computer can "look it up" as often as it is needed without altering that data item. Thus, when data is retrieved from a storage location, the stored contents remain unaltered. When you instruct the computer to put new data in that location, the old data is replaced.

Central Processing Unit (CPU)

The **CPU** controls and supervises the entire computer system and performs the actual arithmetic and logic operations on data, as specified by the written program. The CPU is divided into the **arithmetic-logic section** and the **control section**, as shown in Figure 1.1.

The arithmetic-logic section performs such arithmetic operations as addition, subtraction, multiplication, and division. Depending on the cost and storage capacity of the computer, the speed of the arithmetic section will range from several thousand to many millions of operations per second.

The arithmetic-logic section also carries out the decision-making operations required to change the sequence of instruction execution. These operations include testing various conditions, for example, comparing two characters for equality. The result of these tests causes the computer to take one of two or more alternate paths through the program.

The control section directs and coordinates the entire computer system according to the program developed by the programmer and placed in main storage. The control section's primary function is to analyze and initiate the execution of instructions. This means that it has control over all other subsystems in the computer system.

Auxiliary Storage

The function of the **auxiliary storage unit** is to store data and programs that are to be used over and over again. Common auxiliary storage devices are **magnetic tape drives**, **hard disk drives**, and **diskette drives**.

These auxiliary storage devices can be used to store programs and data for as long as desired. A new program entering the system overwrites the previous program and data in main storage, but the previous program and data may be permanently stored on an auxiliary storage device for recall by the computer.

Output

When instructed by a program, the computer can communicate the results of a program to output units. A computer usually has a **monitor** for output. Other common output devices include a **printer**, a **plotter**, and a **diskette unit**.

The monitor, also called a **video display device**, or **screen**, can be used to display the output results in the form of words, numbers, graphs, or drawings. The monitor is shown in Figure 1.2 on page 2.

1.3 THE PC AND PS/2 FAMILY

In 1981, IBM introduced the IBM Personal Computer (PC), a fully assembled, easy-to-use computer that has become the *de facto* personal computer standard throughout the world.

Since that time, the original PC has undergone many enhancements, and additional models have been produced. These models include the following:

- IBM PC XT
- IBM PCjr
- IBM Portable PC
- IBM Convertible or Laptop
- IBM PC AT (Figure 1.3)
- IBM Personal System/2 (PS/2) (Figures 1.2 and 1.4)

Since 1981, several million IBM PCs and their clones have been manufactured. Currently, there are over one hundred vendors worldwide who provide PC-compatible systems and peripherals.

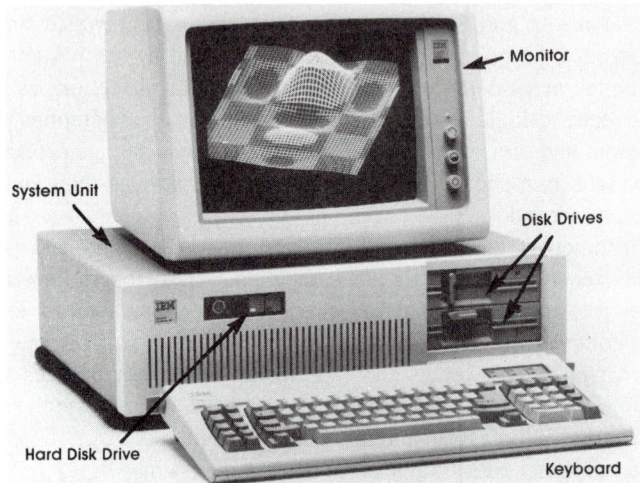

FIGURE 1.3 *The IBM PC AT System (Courtesy IBM Corp.).*

FIGURE 1.4 *The IBM PS/2 System Model 70 (Courtesy IBM Corp.).*

Many accessories and peripheral devices can be connected to the IBM PC and compatibles. This is possible because when IBM introduced the PC, it incorporated expansion slots so that users would be able to add enhancements at will. This "open architecture" has permitted many vendors to manufacture devices that enhance the performance of the PC.

The Keyboard

Figure 1.5 shows the standard IBM PC keyboard. Figure 1.6 shows the enhanced IBM PS/2 keyboard. Both keyboards are similar to that of an ordinary typewriter. A keyboard is an input unit which is used to enter programs and data into the main storage unit. Numeric, alphabetic, and special characters appear in the standard typewriter format on the keyboard.

Note the layout of the function keys, the typewriter keys, and the numeric keypad. These keys will be explained in Chapter 2.

FIGURE 1.5 *The IBM standard keyboard.*

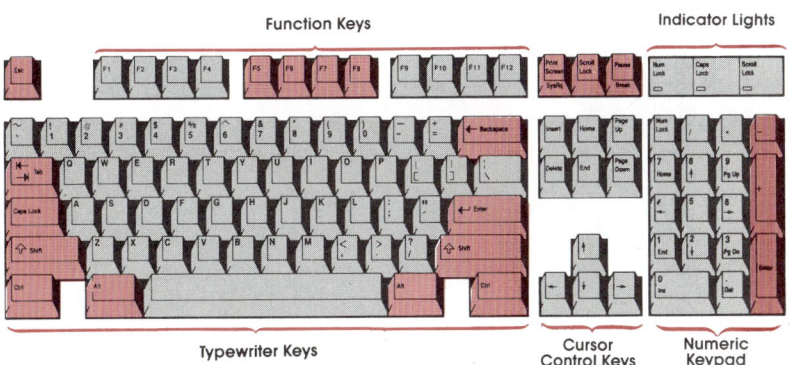

FIGURE 1.6 *The enhanced IBM PS/2 keyboard. Note the different placement of the function and cursor keys in comparison to the IBM standard keyboard in Figure 1.5.*

Monitor

There are two basic types of monitors — monochrome and color. Monochrome monitors come in black and white, green, or amber. Color monitors can display many different colors. Either device can display 40 or 80 characters per horizontal line. There are 25 lines on the screen. See Figures 1.2, 1.3, and 1.4 for examples of monitors.

CPU and Main Storage Unit

All IBM PCs and compatibles contain a 16-bit Intel 8088 CPU, called a microprocessor, which is miniaturized on a **silicon chip**, typically a fraction of an inch long. The IBM PC AT and compatibles contain an Intel 80286 CPU, and the advanced models of the IBM PS/2 and compatibles contain an Intel 80386 or 80486 CPU. Each higher-numbered chip executes programs several times faster than the previous.

The CPU and main storage unit are contained on the system board. Main storage is sometimes called read/write memory, or **RAM**. The PC can contain a minimum of 16K (16,384) bytes of main storage, or RAM. The letter K represents 1,024. Most PCs contain at least 256K bytes of main storage. Additional main storage may be added, up to 640K bytes for the PC and 16 megabytes (16,777,216 bytes) for the PC AT and PS/2.

Read Only Memory (**ROM**) is another form of storage. It is used to store the BASIC interpreter, disk loader, patterns for graphics characters, and so on.

Auxiliary Storage

The IBM PC and compatibles use a 5¼-inch **diskette** for storing and retrieving information. Early PCs used one diskette unit containing a single-sided (SS), single-density (SD) diskette with approximately 160K bytes of storage.

Today, most PCs use one or two diskette units, each containing a double-sided (DS), double-density (DD) diskette with approximately 360K bytes of storage. Hence, on a double-sided diskette, you can file away the contents of at least 125 8½ by 11-inch sheets of paper.

The IBM PS/2 uses 3½-inch diskettes containing 720K bytes. Examples of 5¼-inch and 3½-inch diskettes are shown in Figure 1.7.

FIGURE 1.7 *Diskettes come in both 5¼-inch (left) and 3½-inch (right) sizes. One advantage of the 3½-inch type is its rigid plastic housing, which helps prevent damage to the diskette.*

A 5¼-inch diskette is a thin, circular piece of mylar plastic coated with a magnetic substance, and it comes in a permanent protective jacket. When not in use, the diskette is placed in a sleeve or diskette envelope. Figure 1.8 on the next page shows the various parts of a diskette.

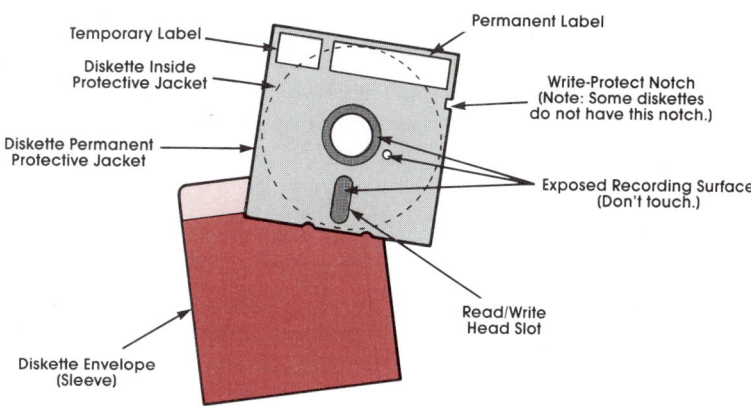

FIGURE 1.8 *The parts of a 5¼-inch diskette (Courtesy IBM Corp.).*

When a diskette is inserted into a disk drive, it is made to spin inside its permanent protective jacket. A read/write head in the disk drive comes into magnetic contact with the recording surface through the slot hole in the diskette's permanent protective jacket (see Figure 1.8).

For additional auxiliary storage, a **hard disk**, containing approximately 20 megabytes (20 million bytes) of storage can be used with a PC. This storage capacity is equivalent to 11,000 double-spaced typewritten pages. As the cost comes down, 40MB, 60MB, and 80MB hard disks are becoming popular.

Network System

Many schools and businesses have opted to install a **network** that allows a printer, a disk drive, and other peripheral devices to be used by many interconnected personal computers. As shown in Figure 1.9, PCs in a network do not always require their own individual diskette drives or printers.

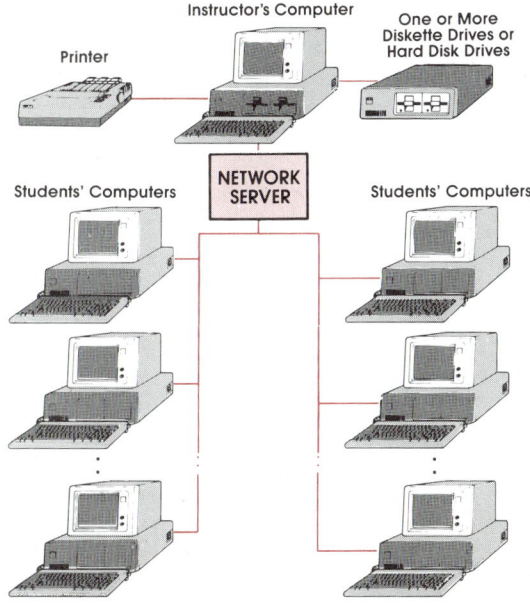

FIGURE 1.9 *A network of personal computers.*

1.4 THE STORED PROGRAM CONCEPT

Before a computer can take action and produce a desired result, it must be given a step-by-step description of the task to be accomplished. The step-by-step description is a series of precise instructions called a **program**. When these instructions are placed in the main storage unit of a computer, they are called the **stored program**. Main storage not only stores data but also stores the instructions that tell the computer what to do with the data. The stored program gives the computer a great deal of flexibility. Without it, the computer's ability to handle tasks would be reduced to that of a desk calculator.

Once the program is in main storage, the first instruction is located and sent to the control section, where it is interpreted and executed. Then the next instruction is located, sent to the control section, interpreted, and executed. This process continues automatically, instruction by instruction, until the program is completed or until the computer is instructed to halt.

In order for the computer to perform still another job, a new program must be stored in main storage. Hence, a computer can easily process a large number of different jobs.

1.5 COMPUTER SOFTWARE

Computer software is a set of programming languages and programs concerned with the operation of a computer system. Some essential computer software comes with the purchase of a computer system. Additional software is either purchased or written by the user in a programming language that the computer understands. Table 1.1 lists some popular software packages and their functions. These packages do not require that you know how to program. They can be purchased at most computer stores that sell personal computer systems.

TABLE 1.1 Some Popular Software Packages and Their Functions

SOFTWARE PACKAGE	FUNCTION
Harvard Presentation Graphics™	A graphics program used to create line graphs, bar graphs, pie charts, and 3-D graphic images.
Microsoft Word™	A word processing program used to write, revise, and edit letters, reports, and manuscripts with efficiency and economy.
Lotus 1-2-3™	An electronic spreadsheet program used to organize data that can be defined in terms of rows and columns. Formulas can be applied to current rows or columns to create new rows and columns of information. Graphic images can be produced on the basis of the data in the spreadsheet. The 1-2-3 refers to the spreadsheet, database, and graphics features of this package.
dBASE III PLUS™ or *dBASE IV*™	A database system used to organize data on an auxiliary storage device. It also allows for the generation of reports and for easy access to the data.

Programming languages are classified as **low-level languages** (like machine language and assembly language) and **high-level languages** (like BASIC, C, Pascal, COBOL, and FORTRAN). Early-generation computers required programmers to program in machine language, and this language was different for each computer manufacturer's system.

Currently, most applications for the PC are programmed in one of the many popular high-level languages listed in Table 1.2. A high-level language is generally machine- or computer-independent; this means that programs written in a high-level language like BASIC can easily be transferred from one computer system to another, with little or no change in the programs.

TABLE 1.2 Some Popular High-Level Languages and Their Appropriate Area of Usefulness

LANGUAGE	AREA OF USEFULNESS
BASIC	**B**eginner's **A**ll-purpose **S**ymbolic **I**nstruction **C**ode is a very simple problem-solving language that is used with personal computers or with terminals in a time-sharing environment. BASIC is used for both business and scientific applications.
C	This high-level language provides easy access to many assembly-language capabilities. C is useful for writing applications packages and systems software, like operating systems.
COBOL	The **CO**mmon **B**usiness **O**riented **L**anguage is an English-like language that is suitable for business data-processing applications. It is especially useful for file and table handling and extensive input and output operations. COBOL is a very widely used programming language.
FORTRAN	**FOR**mula **TRAN**slation is a problem-solving language designed primarily for scientific data processing, engineering, and process-control applications.
Pascal	Pascal, named in honor of the French mathematician Blaise Pascal, is a programming language that allows for the formulations of solutions and data in a form that clearly exhibits their natural structure. It is used primarily for scientific applications and systems programming and to some extent for business data processing.

The Operating System (MS DOS)

The operating system for the PC was designed by the Microsoft Corporation, one of the largest microcomputer software companies in the world. The operating system is called **PC DOS** for the IBM PC and **MS DOS** for the PC compatibles. MS DOS stands for Microsoft Disk Operating System.

This operating system, through a series of enhancements and new versions, has become the standard operating program for all IBM and IBM-compatible personal computer systems. MS DOS is permanently stored on the diskette that is supplied with every PC. This diskette is referred to either as **DOS** or as the **system diskette**.

MS DOS helps to act as an internal "traffic cop" by directing the flow of data into and out of the PC and the peripheral devices (see Figure 1.1 on page 2).

PROGRAMMING CASE STUDY 1: *Computing an Average*

Program 1.1 illustrates a program written in BASIC. It instructs the PC to compute the average of three numbers, 17, 23, and 50.

PROGRAM 1.1

BASIC Program
```
100 ' Program 1.1
110 ' Computing an Average
120 ' *******************
130 AVG = (17 + 23 + 50) / 3
140 PRINT "The average is"; AVG
150 END
```

System Command `RUN`

Displayed Result `The average is 30`

The displayed answer, found below the word RUN, is 30. Even though we are deferring detailed explanations about this program until the next chapter, Program 1.1 gives you some indication of how to instruct a PC to calculate a desired result using BASIC.

■ 1.6 PROBLEM SOLVING AND PROGRAM DEVELOPMENT

Every action the PC is expected to make toward solving a problem must be spelled out in detail in the program. The step-by-step procedures listed in Table 1-3 will help you set up problems for the PC to solve. These procedures make up what is called the **program development cycle**.

Flowcharts

A **program flowchart** is a popular logic tool that is used for showing an algorithm in graphic form. By depicting a procedure for arriving at a solution, a program flowchart also shows how the application or job is to be accomplished.

A programmer prepares a flowchart *before* he or she begins coding the solution in BASIC. Eight basic symbols are used in program flowcharting. They are given in Table 1.4 on page 12 with their respective names and meanings and with some of the BASIC statements that are represented by them.

TABLE 1.3 The Program Development Cycle

STEP	PROCEDURE	DESCRIPTION
1	**Problem Analysis**	Define the problem to be solved precisely, including the form of the input, the form of the output, and a description of the transformation of input to output.
2	**Program Design**	Devise an **algorithm**, or a method of solution, for the computer to use. This method must be a complete procedure for solving the specified problem in a finite number of steps. There must be no ambiguity (no chance that something can be interpreted in more than one way). Develop a detailed logic plan, using **flowcharts**, **pseudocode**, or some other logic tool to describe each step that the PC must perform to arrive at the solution. As far as possible, the flowcharts or pseudocode must describe *what* job is to be done and *how* the job is to be done. Develop good **test data**. As best you can, select data that will test for erroneous input.
3	**Test the Design**	Step by step, go through the flowchart or pseudocode, using the test data as if you were the PC. If the logic plan does not work, repeat steps 1 through 3.
4	**Code the Program**	Code the program in a computer language, like BASIC (see Table 1.2), according to the logic specified in the flowchart or pseudocode. Include program documentation, like comments and explanation, within the program.
5	**Review the Code**	Carefully review the code. Put yourself in the position of the PC and step through the entire program.
6	**Enter the Program**	Submit the program to the PC via a keyboard or other input device.
7	**Test the Program**	Test the program until it is error free and until it contains enough safeguards to ensure the desired result.
8	**Formalize the Solution**	Run the program, using the input data to generate the results. Review, and, if necessary, modify the documentation for the program.

TABLE 1.4 Flowchart Symbols and Their Meanings

SYMBOL	NAME	MEANING
(rectangle)	Process Symbol	Represents the process of executing a defined operation or group of operations which results in a change in value, form, or location of information. Examples: LET, DIM, RESTORE, DEF, and other processing statements. Also functions as the default symbol when no other symbol is available.
(parallelogram)	Input/Output (I/O) Symbol	Represents an I/O function, which makes data available for processing (input) or for displaying (output) of processed information. Examples: READ, INPUT, and PRINT.
(arrows: Left to Right, Right to Left, Top to Bottom, Bottom to Top)	Flowline Symbol	Represents the sequence of available information and executable operations. The lines connect other symbols, and the arrowheads are mandatory only for right-to-left and bottom-to-top flow.
(annotation bracket)	Annotation Symbol	Represents the addition of descriptive information, comments, or explanatory notes as clarification. The vertical line and the broken line may be placed on the left, as shown, or on the right. Example: REM or '.
(diamond)	Decision Symbol	Represents a decision that determines which of a number of alternative paths is to be followed. Examples: IF and ON-GOSUB statements.
(rounded rectangle)	Terminal Symbol	The beginning, the end, or a point of interruption or delay in a program. Examples: STOP, RETURN, and END statements.
(circle)	Connector Symbol	Any entry from, or exit to, another part of the flowchart. Also serves as an off-page connector.
(rectangle with double sides)	Predefined Process Symbol	Represents a named process consisting of one or more operations or program steps that are specified elsewhere. Example: GOSUB.

One rule that is basic to all flowcharts concerns direction. In constructing a flowchart, start at the top (or left-hand corner) of a page. The flow should be top to bottom or left to right. If the flow takes any other course, arrowheads must be used. A plastic template can be obtained from most computer stores or bookstores. This template can be used to help you draw the flowchart symbols. Figure 1.10 shows a flowchart that illustrates the computations required to compute and print the average commission paid to a company's sales personnel and determine the number of male and female sales personnel.

Structured Microsoft BASIC: Essentials for Business   13

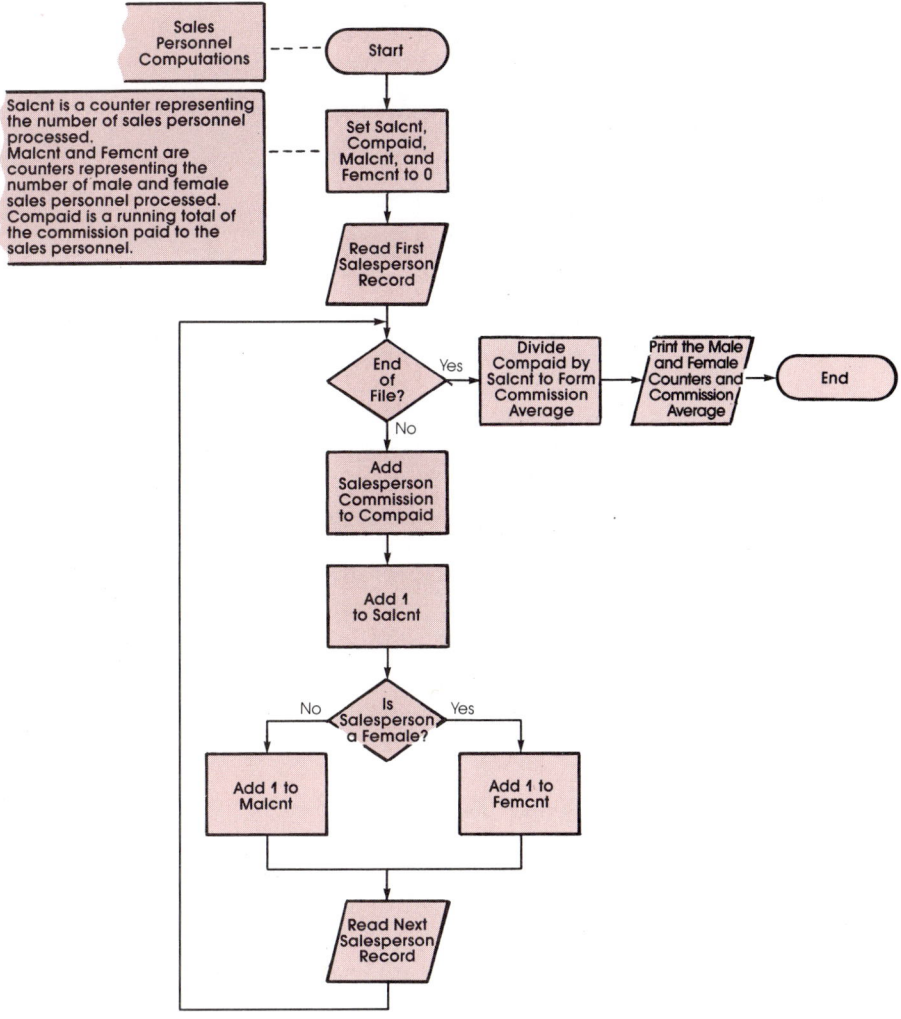

FIGURE 1.10 *Flowchart of the sales personnel computations.*

Pseudocode

Pseudocode is an alternative to program flowcharts which uses standard English and resembles BASIC code. It allows for the logic of a program to be formulated without diagrams or charts. Following are some examples of operations in pseudocode:

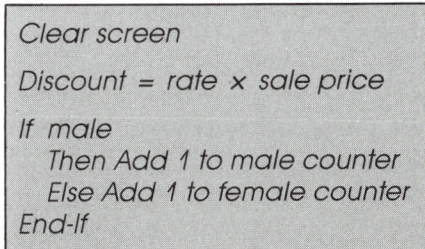

Figure 1.11 shows a pseudocode version of the flowchart solution presented in Figure 1.10.

```
Program: Sales Personnel Computations
Set total commission to 0
Set salesperson counter to 0
Set male counter to 0
Set female counter to 0
Read first salesperson record
Do-While not end-of-file
    Add salesperson commission to total commission
    Add 1 to salesperson counter
    If female
        Then Add 1 to female counter
        Else Add 1 to male counter
    End-If
    Read next salesperson record
End-Do
Commission average = total commission / salesperson counter
Display male and female counters and commission average
End: Sales Personnel Computations
```

FIGURE 1.11 *Pseudocode version of the sales personnel computations.*

Logic tools, like flowcharts and pseudocode, have their strengths and weaknesses. As you solve problems in the later chapters of this book, we suggest you try all of the logic tools, and then choose the one that best suits you. Of course, your instructor may have something to say about the logic tool you use for the required assignments.

■ 1.7 TEST YOUR BASIC SKILLS (Even-numbered answers are in Appendix B.)

1. State three major advantages that computers have over the manual computation of problems.
2. What are the basic subsystems of a computer system? Briefly describe the function of each subsystem.
3. Name the components of the CPU.
4. Name two devices that serve both as input and output devices.
5. Name five personal computer models.
6. What is meant by the term hardware? Software?
7. Construct one flowchart that enables the Mechanical Man to accomplish efficiently the objectives set forth in phases 1 and 2 of Figure 1.12.

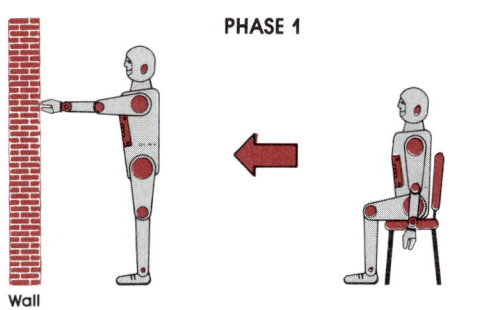
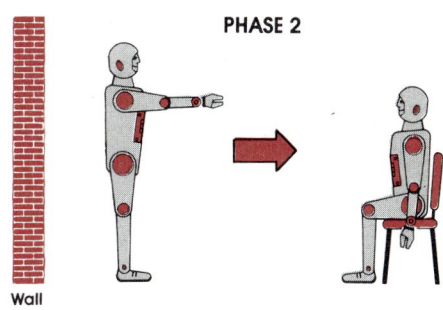

PHASE 1 — The mechanical man is seated at an unknown integer number (0,1,2,...) of steps from the wall. He will stand up and walk forward until he touches the wall with his fingertips. When he is in a seated position with arms raised, his fingertips are aligned with the tips of his shoes.

PHASE 2 — After touching the wall, the mechanical man will return to his chair. Since the chair is too low for him to sense by touch, he can get to it only by going back exactly as many steps as he came forward.

FIGURE 1.12 *The two phases of the Mechanical Man.*

The Mechanical Man possesses the following properties:

- He is restricted to carrying out a limited repertoire of instructions.
- He does *nothing* unless given a specific instruction.
- He must carry out any instructions he is given *one at a time*.
- He understands the following instructions:

  a. Physical Movement:
     1. Stand up (into an erect position without moving feet).
     2. Sit down (into a sitting position without moving feet).
     3. Take one step (forward only; length of steps is always the same, and Mechanical Man can take a step only if he is standing up).
     4. Raise arms (into one fixed position, straight ahead).
     5. Lower arms (into one fixed position, straight down at his sides).
     6. Turn right (in place without taking a step; can be done only if he is standing up; all right turns are 90-degree turns).

  b. Arithmetic:
     1. Add one (to a total that is being developed).
     2. Subtract one (from a total that is being developed).
     3. Record total (any number of totals can be remembered in this way).

  c. Logic: The Mechanical Man can decide what instruction he will carry out next on the basis of answers to the following questions:
     1. Arithmetic results
        a) Is the result positive?
        b) Is the result negative?
        c) Is the result zero?
        d) Is the result equal to a predetermined amount?

     2. Physical status
        a) Are the fingertips of the raised arms touching anything?

8. Construct a flowchart to calculate weekly payroll, using the following rules:

   a. Time and a half is paid for hours worked in excess of 40.
   b. $38.46 is allowed as nontaxable income for each dependent claimed.
   c. The withholding tax is 20 percent of the taxable income.
   d. Assume that end of file is defined as the condition in which the value for the number of hours worked is negative.

   For each employee, input the following information: name; hourly rate of pay; number of hours worked; and, number of dependents.

   For each employee, output the following information: name; gross pay; net pay; and, income tax withheld.

9. Same as problem 7, but use pseudocode to develop the logic that enables the Mechanical Man to accomplish efficiently the objectives shown in Figure 1.12 on the previous page.

■ 1.8 PC Hands-On Exercises

The following exercises are designed to acquaint you with your personal computer system. Consult with your instructor before running these exercises on your PC.

1. Identification of Keys on Keyboard

Find the following important keys on your keyboard. Make a check in the third column as you find each key.

TABLE 1.5 Special Keys on Keyboard

KEY	SYMBOL	CHECK	KEY	SYMBOL	CHECK	KEY	SYMBOL	CHECK
Enter	↵		Print Screen	PrtSc *		Home	7 Home	
Escape	Esc		Capital Lock	Caps Lock		End	1 End	
Tab	⇤ ⇥		Numeral Lock	Num Lock		Insert Key	0 Ins	
Control	Ctrl		Scroll Lock	Scroll Lock		Function Key 1	F1	
Shift	⇧		Alternate	Alt		Delete	• Del	
Backspace	←							

2. Sample Programs

With the assistance of your instructor, obtain and insert into Drive A the diskette titled DOS or the system diskette. Insert into Drive B the diskette titled DOS Supplemental Programs.

See Table 2.5 on page 31, steps 1 to 8, for the initial PC start-up procedure. After the A> prompt appears, enter

   B: (Press the enter key.)

After the B> prompt appears, enter

    `A:BASICA`   (Press the enter key.)

After the system displays the DOS version number and the following prompt:

    `ok`

enter the command

    `RUN "SAMPLES"`   (Press the enter key.)

Follow the self-explanatory instructions that appear on the screen. The DOS Supplemental Programs diskette will display various colors and animation on the screen, and will allow you to interact with the PC.

Try the following sample programs by entering the appropriate letter code:

Code	Sample Programs	Code	Sample Programs
A	Music	E	Donkey
B	Art	G	Ball
D	Circle	H	Colorbar

When you want to terminate a sample program, press the Escape (Esc) key.

3. Formatting a Diskette

When a diskette is purchased, it is blank, (that is, it has nothing recorded on its surface). In order for programs or data to be placed on a diskette, it must first be formatted. Obtain a blank diskette and format it by carefully following the instructions.

1. Boot the PC, using steps 1 through 8 as outlined in Table 2.5 on page 31.
2. Enter the following command to the right of the A>:

    `FORMAT B:`   (Press the Enter key.)

   Be sure to include the colon (:).

3. Insert the diskette to be formatted in the B drive.
4. Press any key.
5. After a short time, the PC will display the number of bytes that are available on the newly formatted diskette and will respond with the following question:

    `Format another (Y/N)?`

   Enter N to quit the FORMAT utility or Y to format another diskette.

DO NOT FORMAT THE STUDENT DISKETTE THAT ACCOMPANIES THIS BOOK.

MICROSOFT BASIC: AN INTRODUCTION

■ 2.1 CREATING A MICROSOFT BASIC PROGRAM

The purpose of this chapter is to explain some of the rules that are common to all BASIC programs and to introduce some fundamental BASIC statements. We will concentrate on "simple" program illustrations, input/output operations, and system commands. Upon successful completion of this chapter, you should be able to develop some elementary programs written in Microsoft (MS) BASIC which will run on an IBM PC or compatible.

General Characteristics of a Microsoft BASIC Program

An MS BASIC program is composed of a sequence of lines. Each line contains a unique **line number** that serves as a label for the statement as shown in Figure 2.1. The line may contain up to 255 characters, although it usually contains considerably fewer.

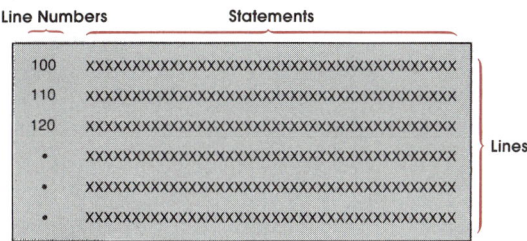

FIGURE 2.1 *The general form of a BASIC program.*

A line begins with a line number and ends when the Enter key is pressed, as indicated by the example below.

Programming Case Study 2, illustrates the composition of an MS BASIC program.

PROGRAMMING CASE STUDY 2: Determining a Salesperson's Commission

Most salespeople work on a commission basis. Their earned commissions are often determined by multiplying their assigned commission rate by the amount of dollar sales. The dollar sales amount is computed by deducting any returned sales from the sum of their weekly sales. Given a biweekly pay period, the earned commission can be determined from the following formula:

Earned Commission = Rate × (Week 1 Sales + Week 2 Sales − Returns)

Let's assume that for the biweekly period, a salesperson's assigned commission rate is 15%, and sales are $1200 the first week, $1500 the second week. The returned sales are $75.

Program 2.1 instructs the PC to compute the earned amount and display it on the screen. The earned commission of 393.75 is just below the **system command** RUN.

PROGRAM 2.1

BASIC Program
```
100 LET COMMISSION = 0.15 * (1200 + 1500 - 75)
110 PRINT COMMISSION
120 END
```
System Command `RUN`

Displayed Result `393.75`

Keywords

There are three lines in this program. The first contains a LET statement. The LET statement consists of the **keyword** LET, a **variable name** COMMISSION, an **equal sign**, four **constants** (0.15, 1200, 1500, and 75), and three **arithmetic operators** (∗, +, and −).

A keyword is a predefined word that has special meaning to MS BASIC. It indicates the type of action to be performed. In Program 2.1, there are three keywords: LET, PRINT, and END. Keywords are also called **reserved words**. See the reference card at the back of this book for a complete list of the MS BASIC keywords.

If a statement does not begin with a keyword and does contain an equal sign, then MS BASIC assumes it is a LET statement. For example, line 100 may be written in the following form:

```
100 COMMISSION = 0.15 * (1200 + 1500 - 75)
```

Even though line 100 does not contain the keyword LET, it is still called a LET statement. It may also be referred to as an **assignment statement**. Except for Program 2.1, in this book all LET statements will be written without the keyword LET.

Variable Names and Constants

In programming, a **variable** is a location in main storage whose value can change as the program is executed. In Program 2.1, the **variable name** COMMISSION references the storage location assigned to it by MS BASIC. Line 100 instructs the PC to complete the arithmetic operations and assign the resulting value of 393.75 to the storage location assigned to COMMISSION. A variable name begins with a letter and may be followed by up to 39 letters, digits, and decimal points. Keywords like LET, PRINT, and END that have special meaning to MS BASIC, may not be used as variable names.

The equal sign in any LET statement means that the value of the variable to the left of the equal sign is to be replaced by the final value of the expression to the right of the equal sign.

Constants, like 0.15, 1200, 1500, and 75, represent ordinary numbers that do not change during the execution of a program. Both constants and variables are covered in detail in Chapter 3.

Arithmetic Operators

The **plus sign** (+) in Program 2.1 signifies addition between the two constants that represent the weekly sales. The **minus sign** (-) indicates subtraction of the returned sales from the sum of the weekly sales. The **asterisk** (*) indicates multiplication between the rate and the actual sales. The seven MS BASIC arithmetic operators are given in Table 2.1. As in mathematics, a set of parentheses is used to override the normal sequence of arithmetic operations.

TABLE 2.1 The Seven Arithmetic Operators

ARITHMETIC OPERATOR	MEANING	EXAMPLES OF USAGE	MEANING OF THE EXAMPLES
^	Exponentiation	2 ^ 3	Raise 2 to the third power, which in this example is 8.
*	Multiplication	60.00 * A1	Multiply the value of A1 by 60.00.
/	Division	H / 10	Divide the value of H by 10.
\	Integer Division	5 \ 3	The integer quotient of 5 divided by 3, which in this example is 1. (Operands are rounded to whole numbers.)
MOD	Modulo	16 MOD 5	The integer remainder of 16 divided by 5, which in this example is 1.
+	Addition	3.14 + 2.9	Add 3.14 and 2.9.
-	Subtraction	S - 35.4	Subtract 35.4 from the value of S.

The PRINT Statement

The second statement in Program 2.1 is called a PRINT statement. PRINT statements instruct the PC to bring a result out from main storage and display it on an output device. The statement causes the PC to display 393.75, the value of COMMISSION. The PRINT statement is covered in detail in Chapter 4.

The END Statement

The last line of Program 2.1 contains the END statement. When executed, the END statement instructs the PC to stop executing the program. While the END statement is not required, it is recommended that you always include one.

Line Numbers

Every line in an MS BASIC program must begin with a unique line number. A line number must be a whole number between 0 and 65529. It must not contain a leading sign, embedded spaces, commas, decimal points, or any other punctuation. Line numbers are used in MS BASIC to

1. indicate the sequence of statement execution;
2. provide control points for branching, a topic discussed in Chapter 3; and
3. add, change, and delete statements within a program.

Many experienced BASIC programmers begin with line number 100 or 1000 and then increase the line number of each new statement by 10. This leaves room to insert up to 9 possible extra statements between the numbers at a later time.

The system command RUN, found just below Program 2.1, instructs the PC to execute the program. It is not part of the program itself and, therefore, does not have a line number. For now, remember that BASIC statements have line numbers and system commands don't.

> ***Line Rule 1:*** A line begins with a line number and ends when the Enter key is pressed. A line may contain up to 255 characters.

> ***Line Rule 2:*** A line number must be be an integer between 0 and 65529. It must not contain a leading sign, embedded spaces, commas, decimal points, or any other punctuation.

> ***Line Rule 3:*** BASIC statements have line numbers; system commands don't.

Some Relationships Between Statements

The PRINT statement in Program 2.1 would display a result of zero if, earlier in the program, we had failed to instruct the PC to assign a value to the variable COMMISSION. In other words, the PC cannot correctly display the value of COMMISSION before it determines this value. Therefore, if Program 2.1 were incorrectly written, as below, the PC would not display the correct results, unless by chance the earned commission were zero.

```
100 PRINT COMMISSION
110 COMMISSION = 0.15 * (1200 + 1500 - 75)   } Invalid
120 END

RUN

 0
```

The following program is incorrect for the same reason:

```
100 PAY = 0.15 * (1200 + 1500 - 75)
110 PRINT COMMISSION                          } Invalid
120 END

RUN

 0
```

The variable COMMISSION in line 110 has not been assigned a value earlier in the above program. The PC will calculate a value of 393.75 for the variable PAY but will display a result of zero. MS BASIC initially assigns all variables in a program a value of zero when the system command RUN is issued.

The correct program can be written as Program 2.1 or as Program 2.2 below.

PROGRAM 2.2

```
100 PAY = 0.15 * (1200 + 1500 - 75)
110 PRINT PAY
120 END
RUN
  393.75
```

Using the variable name PAY is no different from using the variable name COMMISSION, as long as the same name is used consistently. The relationship between output statements, like the PRINT statement, and other statements in a program can now be stated as follows:

> **Output Rule 1:** Every variable appearing in an output statement should have been previously defined in the program.

Although the flexibility of the language permits certain statements to be placed anywhere in a program, logic, common sense, and style dictate where these statements are placed. Style, for our purposes, is defined as disciplined, consistent programming. Discipline and consistency help programmers construct readable, maintainable, and reliable programs.

■ 2.2 THE INPUT STATEMENT

One of the major tasks of any computer program is to integrate the data that is to be processed into the program. In Programs 2.1 and 2.2, the data was included directly in the LET statement in line 100 as constants.

This technique has its limitations. For example, line 100 must be modified each time a new salesperson is processed. An alternative method of integrating the data into the program is shown in Program 2.3 below.

PROGRAM 2.3

```
100 RATE = 0.15       ◄
110 WEEK1 = 1200      ◄───── Data as Constants
120 WEEK2 = 1500      ◄
130 RETURNS = 75      ◄
140 COMMISSION = RATE * (WEEK1 + WEEK2 - RETURNS)
150 PRINT COMMISSION
160 END
RUN
  393.75
```

In this new program, data in the form of constants has been assigned to the variables RATE, WEEK1, WEEK2, and RETURNS. Line 140, used to calculate the earned commission, contains the variables that have been assigned the data in lines 100 through 130. When it executes Program 2.3, the PC must be informed of the numeric values for RATE, WEEK1, WEEK2, and RETURNS before it can calculate a value for COMMISSION. This can be generalized as the following rule:

> **Arithmetic Rule 1:** Every variable appearing to the right of the equal sign in a LET statement should have been previously defined in the program.

This second method of integrating the data into the program has the same limitations as Program 2.1. That is, lines 100 through 130 would have to be modified in order to process a new salesperson. The only advantage of Program 2.3 is that the LET statement itself in line 140 will work for any salesperson.

A third way to integrate data into the program is through the use of the INPUT statement. The INPUT statement provides for assignment of data to variables from a source outside the program during execution. The data is supplied to the program after the command RUN has been entered.

Through the use of the INPUT statement, the solution to Programming Case Study 2 can be made more general for calculating the earned commission for any salesperson, no matter what his or her commission rate, weekly sales, or returned sales. One version of the rewritten program is shown as Program 2.4 below.

PROGRAM 2.4

```
100 INPUT RATE, WEEK1, WEEK2, RETURNS
110 COMMISSION = RATE * (WEEK1 + WEEK2 - RETURNS)
120 PRINT COMMISSION
130 END
RUN                          Data Entered in Response to the
                             Input Prompt
? 0.15, 1200, 1500, 75
 393.75
```

The function of the INPUT statement in line 100 is to display an **input prompt** and suspend execution of the program until data has been supplied. MS BASIC displays a **question mark** (?) for the input prompt. Then it is up to the user to supply the data. It is necessary that the Enter key be pressed following entry of the data.

Once the necessary data has been supplied, line 110 determines the earned commission, line 120 displays the earned commission, and, finally, line 130 terminates the program.

This third way of integrating data into a program, by means of the INPUT statement, is far more efficient than the other two ways, because we can process other sales personnel without modifying statements within the program. For example, to determine the earned commission for three salespeople, we can run the program three times, each time entering different data in response to the input prompt.

It is important that the variables in the INPUT statement and the data supplied in response to the input prompt be separated by commas. A comma is used to establish a **list**, which is a set of distinct elements, each separated from the next by a comma. The comma must be used so that the PC can distinguish how many variables or data elements occur in each list.

It is also important that the user respond with numeric data. For example, if the value 1AB were entered as the last item, rather than 75, then the PC would respond with the following message:

```
Redo from start
```

The same message will appear if too few or too many data items are entered in response to the INPUT statement.

Input Prompt Message

To ensure that the data is entered in the proper sequence, MS BASIC allows for an **input prompt message** to be placed in the INPUT statement. When the PC executes an INPUT statement containing an input prompt message, the message, rather than the question mark, is displayed on the screen. Execution is then suspended until the data is supplied. The following program requests one entry per INPUT statement:

PROGRAM 2.5

```
100 INPUT "Commission rate =====> ", RATE
110 INPUT "Week 1 sales ========> ", WEEK1
120 INPUT "Week 2 sales ========> ", WEEK2
130 INPUT "Return sales ========> ", RETURNS
140 COMMISSION = RATE * (WEEK1 + WEEK2 - RETURNS)
150 PRINT COMMISSION
160 END

RUN

Commission rate =====> 0.15
Week 1 sales ========> 1200
Week 2 sales ========> 1500
Return sales ========> 75
 393.75
```

When line 100 is executed in Program 2.5, the PC displays this input prompt message:

```
Commission rate =====>
```

After displaying the message requesting the commission rate, the PC suspends execution of the program until a response is entered.

If an acceptable response is then entered, the PC displays the next input prompt message and suspends execution again. This process continues until the last INPUT statement has been executed.

After the last data item is entered for line 130, line 140 determines the earned commission. Then line 150 displays the earned commission, and, finally, line 160 terminates the program.

The **quotation marks** surrounding the input prompt message and the comma separating the message from the variable in lines 100 through 130 are required punctuation. If a **semicolon** is used to separate the message from the variable, then a question mark will be displayed immediately after the input prompt message. Here is the rule for determining the placement of the INPUT statement in a program:

> **Input Rule 1:** Every variable appearing in the program whose value is directly obtained through input must be listed in an INPUT statement before it is used elsewhere in the program.

Table 2.2 gives the general form of the INPUT statement.

TABLE 2.2 The INPUT Statement

General Form:	INPUT *variable, . . ., variable* or INPUT *"input prompt message", variable, . . ., variable*
Purpose:	*Provides for the assignment of values to variables from a source external to the program, like the keyboard.*
Keyword Entry:	*Hold down the Alt key and press the I key on your keyboard. (See page 4 of the reference card at the back of this book for a list of all keyword entries using the Alt key.)*
Examples:	

INPUT Statements	Data from an External Source
100 INPUT A	23.5
115 INPUT X, Y, Z	2, 4, 6
300 INPUT A$, B	Gross, -2.73
400 INPUT "Please enter the sales tax: ", T	0.05
500 INPUT "What is your name"; N$	John
600 INPUT "Part number ====> ", P	1289

■ 2.3 THE PRINT AND CLS STATEMENTS

One of the functions of the PRINT statement is to display the values of variables that have been defined earlier in a program. You should understand by now that the following:

```
100 X = 99
110 PRINT X
```

displays 99, which is the value of X, not the letter X. The PRINT statement can also be used to display messages that identify a program result, as shown by line 170 in Program 2.6.

PROGRAM 2.6

```
100 CLS
110 INPUT "Commission rate =====> ", RATE
120 INPUT "Week 1 sales ========> ", WEEK1
130 INPUT "Week 2 sales ========> ", WEEK2
140 INPUT "Return sales ========> ", RETURNS
150 COMMISSION = RATE * (WEEK1 + WEEK2 - RETURNS)
160 PRINT
170 PRINT "Earned commission ===>"; COMMISSION
180 END

RUN

Commission rate =====> 0.15
Week 1 sales ========> 1200
Week 2 sales ========> 1500
Return sales ========> 75

Earned commission ===> 393.75
```

As with the INPUT statement, it is necessary in a PRINT statement to begin and end a message with quotation marks. The quotation marks in a PRINT statement inform MS BASIC that the item to be displayed is a message rather than a variable.

The semicolon following the message in line 170 instructs the PC to keep the **cursor** on the same line instead of positioning it on the next line. The cursor is a movable, blinking marker on the screen which indicates where the next point of character entry, change, or display will be.

MS BASIC displays a numeric value that consists of a sign, the decimal representation, and a **trailing space**. Appearing immediately before the number, the sign is a **leading space** if the number is positive and a leading minus sign if the number is negative. The space following the message displayed by line 170 in Program 2.6 represents the sign of the variable COMMISSION, as shown below:

```
Earned commission ===> 393.75
```

A space here indicates that 393.75 is positive.

Clearing the Screen — The CLS Statement

One of the responsibilities of the programmer is to ensure that the prompt messages and results are meaningful and easy to read. A cluttered screen can make it difficult for you to locate necessary information. To clear the screen, MS BASIC includes the CLS statement, which erases the information on the screen and places the cursor in the upper left corner. The general form of the CLS statement is illustrated in Table 2.3.

TABLE 2.3 *The CLS Statement*

General Form:	CLS
Purpose:	*Erases the information on the first 24 lines of the screen and places the cursor in the upper left corner.*
Example:	100 CLS
Note:	*The 25th line of the screen may be erased with the statement* KEY OFF.

The `CLS` statement is usually one of the first statements to be executed in a program, as it is in Program 2.6. The statement `CLS` may also be entered without a line number. This is called the **immediate mode**. Without a line number, the PC executes the statement as soon as it is entered; it is not made part of the current program. For example, the statement

```
CLS
```

causes the PC to clear the first 24 lines of the screen.

Consider again Program 2.6 which includes the `CLS` statement in line 100. When the RUN command is issued for this program, the PC clears the screen and then displays the input prompt message

```
Commission rate =====>
```

on line 1, column 1. After obtaining a response through the keyboard, the PC displays the next input prompt message on line 2, and the rest of the program is executed.

The `CLS` statement clears the screen, including the image of the program, but it does not clear main storage. After you have entered the RUN command and the output results are displayed, you may again display the program by entering the LIST command. A detailed discussion of the LIST command can be found in Section 2.7.

Line 160 in Program 2.6, which contains a `PRINT` statement without a list, shows how to instruct the PC to display a blank line in order to separate the input prompt messages from the results. A **null (empty) list** like this causes the PRINT statement to display a blank line.

■ 2.4 DOCUMENTING A PROGRAM — THE REM STATEMENT

Documentation is the readable description of what a program or procedure within a program is supposed to do. More often than not, programmers are asked to support the programs they write by means of **internal comments**. Documentation is used to identify programs and clarify parts of a program that would otherwise be difficult for others to understand.

The REM statements in Program 2.7, lines 100 through 140 and lines 160, 210, and 230, are called **remark lines**. The remark line consists of an internal comment, or explanation, intended solely for humans. The keyword REM, when present after a line number, designates the line as a remark line.

PROGRAM 2.7

```
100 REM Program 2.7
110 REM J. S. Quasney
120 REM Determining a Salesperson's Commission
130 REM *************************************
140 REM Clear Screen
150 CLS
160 REM Request Data from Operator
170 INPUT "Commission rate =====> ", RATE
180 INPUT "Week 1 sales ========> ", WEEK1
190 INPUT "Week 2 sales ========> ", WEEK2
200 INPUT "Return sales ========> ", RETURNS
210 REM Calculate the Earned Commission
220 COMMISSION = RATE * (WEEK1 + WEEK2 - RETURNS)
230 REM Display the Earned Commission
240 PRINT
250 PRINT "Earned commission ===>"; COMMISSION
260 END
```

(continued)

```
RUN

Commission rate =====> 0.15
Week 1 sales ========> 1200
Week 2 sales ========> 1500
Return sales ========> 75

Earned commission ===> 393.75
```

REM statements are nonexecutable, which means they have no effect on the results of a BASIC program. Program 2.7, which includes REM statements, and Program 2.6, which does not, both produce the same results. REM statements do take up space in main storage.

MS BASIC permits you to use an **apostrophe** (') as an abbreviation for the keyword REM. MS BASIC also permits the placement of a remark on the right-hand side of a BASIC statement by requiring the insertion of an apostrophe before the comment. The general form for the REM statement is found in Table 2.4 below.

_____TABLE 2.4 The REM Statement_____

General Form:	REM comment
	or
	' comment
Purpose:	*Provides for the insertion of comments in a program.*
Examples:	110 REM J. S. Quasney
	160 REM Determine the Balance Due
	200 REM Program 2.8
	250 '
	300 ' **************************
	310 ' Compute Gross Pay
	320 PRINT ANSWER ' Display result

A general flowchart that corresponds to Program 2.7 is shown in Figure 2.2 on the next page. A flowchart does not have to include a symbol for each statement in the program. For example, the four INPUT statements in Program 2.7 are represented by the single input/output (I/O) symbol "Input Salesperson Data," which follows the "Clear Screen" symbol in the flowchart in Figure 2.2. Furthermore, it is not necessary to include an annotation symbol in the flowchart for every REM statement. For your convenience in following the logic, line numbers have been placed on the top left-hand corner of the symbols in order to illustrate the relationship between the program flowchart and Program 2.7.

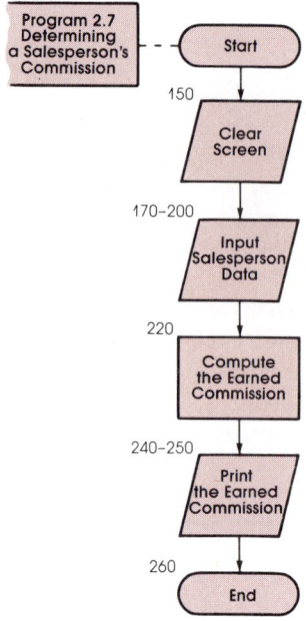

FIGURE 2.2 *A general flowchart for Program 2.7.*

Multiple Statements Per Line

MS BASIC allows you to write multiple statements per line. That is, Program 2.2 can be rewritten as the following:

```
100 ' Program 2.2
110 PAY = 0.15 * (1200 + 1500 - 75) : PRINT PAY : END
```

The statements in line 110 are separated by **colons**. The purpose of the colon is to inform MS BASIC that one statement has ended and a new statement follows on the same line.

Do not precede any statement with a REM statement when using multiple statements per line. MS BASIC considers all characters following the keyword REM or apostrophe (') to be a comment, including the colon. The following entire version of Program 2.2 is a comment line.

```
100 ' Program 2.2 : PAY = 0.15 * (1200 + 1500 - 75) : PRINT PAY : END
```

For the purpose of readability, it is recommended that you use this technique of multiple statements per line sparingly.

■ 2.5 GETTING AQUAINTED WITH THE PC

To enter a BASIC program like Program 2.7 into the PC, you must first familiarize yourself with the procedures for starting up the PC. Table 2.5 presents a step-by-step procedure for getting to the point where you can begin entering a BASIC program. This procedure is sometimes called "booting the PC."

To terminate your session with BASICA, enter the command SYSTEM. The SYSTEM command instructs the PC to return to MS DOS. When the A> or B> sign reappears, raise the load levers on disk drives A and B and carefully remove your diskettes from the disk drive units. Turn the video display device power switch to Off. If using a printer, turn the printer's power switch to Off. Finally, turn the PC's power switch to Off.

TABLE 2.5 Initial PC Start-Up

1. Obtain a diskette titled **DOS**, also known as the **system diskette**, from your instructor. A system diskette contains the operating system (**MS DOS** or **PC DOS**) and **BASICA**. BASICA *is the advanced version of Microsoft BASIC. Also obtain a formatted diskette for storing programs. If the second diskette is new, it must be formatted before proceeding. (See Exercise 3 at the end of Chapter 1 for a discussion on how to format a diskette.)*

2. *Raise (open) the load lever of disk drive A (left or top drive) and insert the system diskette. Lower (close) the load lever of disk drive A. If your PC has a second drive, raise the load lever on disk drive B (right or lower drive) and insert the properly formatted diskette. Lower the load lever of disk drive B.*

3. *Adjust the leg handles at each end of the keyboard, if desired.*

4. *Turn the monitor power switch to On. Adjust the Brightness Control and Contrast Control knobs accordingly.*

5. **Cold Start:** *Turn the PC's power switch to On. After a brief period, the light on disk drive A will come on.*
   Warm Start: *If your PC is initially On, press and hold the Control (Ctrl) and Alt keys, and then press the Del key. Finally, release these three keys. After a brief period of time, the light on disk drive A will come on.*

6. *If using a printer, turn the printer's power switch to On.*

7. *When MS DOS is loaded from the system diskette, it displays the date in a manner similar to this:*
   ```
   Current date is Tue 1-01-1980
   Enter new date:
   ```
   If today's date is September 30, 1992, enter the date as follows: 09-30-1992 *(Press the Enter key.)*

8. *After the date is entered, MS DOS displays the time in a manner similar to this:*
   ```
   Current time is 0:01:23.45
   Enter new time:
   ```
   The time display is in this form: Hours:Minutes:Seconds.Hundredths of a Second
   If the new time is 10:46 a.m., enter 10:46 *(Press the Enter key.)*
   If the new time is 2:34 p.m., enter 14:34 *(Press the Enter key.)*
   Your PC may have a battery-run clock that maintains the date and time when it is not in use. In this case, the date and time are automatically loaded and, therefore, steps 7 and 8 are not required.

9. For a one-diskette drive system or a network system: *When MS DOS displays its prompt (A>), enter the command* BASICA *and press the Enter key. For example,*
   A> BASICA *(Press the Enter key.)*
   ok *(MS BASIC responds that it is ready.)*
   For a two-diskette drive system: *When MS DOS displays its prompt (A>), enter the command* B: *and press the Enter key. For example,*
   A> B: *(Press the Enter key.)*
   When MS DOS displays its prompt (B>), enter the command A:BASICA *and press the Enter key. For example,*
   B> A:BASICA *(Press the Enter key.)*
   ok *(MS BASIC responds that it is ready.)*

10. *You may begin entering your program.*

2.6 EDITING MICROSOFT BASIC PROGRAMS

Microsoft BASIC programs are entered one line at a time into the PC via a keyboard. Pressing the Enter key signals to MS BASIC that a line is complete. During the process of entering a program, you will quickly learn that it is easy to make **keyboard** and **grammatical errors** because of your inexperience with the BASIC language and your unfamiliarity with the keyboard. **Logical errors** can also occur in a program if you have not considered all the details associated with the problem.

Some of these errors can be eliminated if you use coding forms and flowcharts and if you carefully review your design and program before you enter it into the PC. Any remaining errors are resolved by **editing** the BASIC program.

The right side of the keyboard, including the numeric keypad, shown in Figure 2.3 below, contains several keys that are specially designed to aid you in editing BASIC programs. The four arrow keys (←, ↑, →, ↓), also known as the **cursor control keys**, are used to move the cursor on the screen in the indicated direction.

Each time the delete key (Del) is pressed, the PC erases the character located under the cursor.

When pressed, the Insert key (Ins) places the PC in the **insert mode** and allows you to insert characters at the current cursor position. As characters are entered, existing ones are "pushed" to the right. To change back to the **overtype mode**, press any arrow key or the Ins key again.

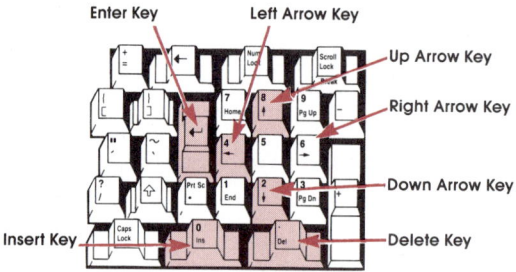

FIGURE 2.3 *The right side of the keyboard, including the numeric keypad.*

Table 2.6 illustrates the features used most commonly in editing a BASIC program. You will find these features both powerful and easy to use.

TABLE 2.6 Commonly Used Features in Editing BASIC Programs

1. Correct an error in the line being keyed before the Enter key is pressed.	Use the ← and → cursor control keys to move to the left and right within a line. You may also insert characters between any two adjacent characters by first pressing the Insert (Ins) key.
	Or,
	Press the Enter key and reenter the entire line.
2. Replace a line in an existing program.	Key in the new statement, using the line number of the line to be replaced.
	Or,
	Use the ↑ or ↓ key to position the cursor on the line to be replaced and follow the instructions in number 1 above. Be sure to press the Enter key when you are finished editing the line.

(continued)

(continued)

3. Insert a new line in an existing program.	Key in the statement, using a line number that will cause MS BASIC to place the statement in the desired sequence.
4. Delete a line in an existing program.	Key in the line number of the line to be deleted and press the Enter key.
5. Delete a sequence of lines.	Enter the system command DELETE, followed by the beginning line number and ending line number separated by a hyphen. For example, DELETE 250-370
6. Copy or move a line.	Use the arrow keys to move the cursor to the line number of the line to be copied or moved. Change the line number to one that will position the line at the desired location and press the Enter key. This will copy the line at the new location. If it is a move operation, use step 4 to delete the unwanted line.
7. Add, delete, or change characters in a line previously entered.	Move the cursor to the line to be edited and follow the instructions in number 1 above. Be sure to press the Enter key when you are finished editing the line.

■ 2.7 SYSTEM COMMANDS AND HARD-COPY OUTPUT

As indicated earlier, two types of instructions are used with MS BASIC. One type consists of BASIC statements, like LET, PRINT, and INPUT. The second type consists of the system commands, like RUN and SYSTEM. Before we discuss system commands, it is important that you understand the concept of a file specification.

File Specifications

Several system commands require the use of a **file specification**. A file specification, also called a **filespec**, is used to identify programs and data files that are placed in auxiliary storage. A filespec is made up of a **device name**, a **file name**, and an **extension**, all included with quotation marks, as shown below.

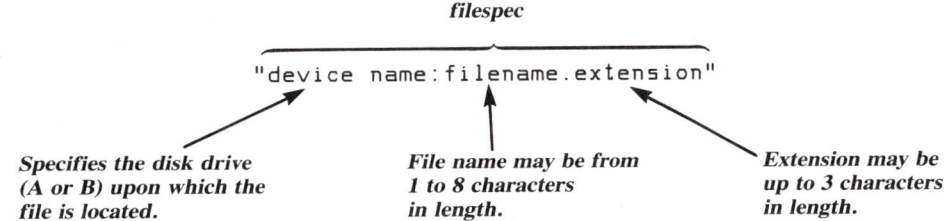

The device name refers to the disk drive, where A identifies the left-hand drive and B identifies the right-hand drive — or the top and bottom drives, respectively. BASIC programs are usually stored on disk drive B. If no device is specified, then the filespec refers to the default drive of the PC at the time of execution. If a device name is included in the file specification, it must be followed by a colon.

File names may be anywhere from 1 to 8 characters in length. Valid characters are uppercase or lowercase A–Z, 0–9, and certain special characters ($ & # @ ! % " ( ) – { } _ / \). If an extension is used, then the file name must be followed by a period. Spaces are not allowed in a file name.

An extension that is up to 3 characters in length may be used to classify a file. Valid characters are the same as for a file name. With MS BASIC, the default extension is BAS. That is, when you use system commands that refer to files, MS BASIC will automatically append an extension of BAS if one is not included. However, it is possible to reference programs without ever using an extension.

Examples of valid filespecs include B:PAYROLL, B:LAB2-1.BAS, Accounts, and S123. The PC does not differentiate between the uppercase and the lowercase characters.

The RUN Command

Perhaps the most important system command for a student programmer is RUN. If this command is not issued, the BASIC program will not be executed.

It is possible to initiate execution at a line number other than the lowest in a program. Whereas the system command RUN instructs the PC to execute the current program in main storage at the lowest line number, the command RUN 200 instructs the PC to execute the program beginning at line 200.

A third form of the RUN command loads and executes a program that is stored in auxiliary storage. RUN "b:lab2-1" causes the PC to load lab2-1 into main storage from drive B and executes lab2-1. At the time the command is issued, the current program in main storage is erased.

The LIST Command

Another useful system command is LIST. It instructs the PC to display all or part of the BASIC program. This command is especially useful in those circumstances where changes have been made to statements in the BASIC program and a new listing of the program is desired. Program 2.8 illustrates the use of the RUN and LIST system commands.

PROGRAM 2.8

```
LIST
100 ' Program 2.8
110 INPUT A, B
120 C = A - B
130 PRINT "The difference is:"; C
140 END

RUN

? 159, 62
The difference is: 97
```

The command LIST can be used to list a program at a point other than the first statement of the program. LIST 130 lists line 130 only. LIST 110-130 lists lines 110 through 130, inclusive. To list from the start of the program through line 120, use LIST-120. Use LIST 120- to list from line 120 to the end of the program.

Holding down the Control (Ctrl) key and pressing the Num Lock key causes the PC to temporarily stop an activity like a program listing. Pressing any key thereafter (except Shift, Break and Ins) causes the PC to continue an activity, like the listing of a program.

Holding down the Control (Ctrl) key and pressing the Break key causes the PC to permanently stop a program listing or program execution.

Listing Program Lines to the Printer

If you have a printer connected to your PC, you may list all or parts of your program to the printer by using the command LLIST. The command LLIST is similar to the LIST command. The only difference is that LIST displays the lines on the screen and LLIST displays the lines on the printer.

The NEW Command

Another command that is of considerable importance is NEW. It instructs the PC to erase or delete the last program that was keyed or loaded into main storage. Without this command, statements from the old program may mix with the statements of the new one.

Table 2.7 summarizes the system commands most often used.

TABLE 2.7 Summary of the Most Often Used System Commands

SYSTEM COMMAND	FUNCTION
LIST	Causes all or part of the BASIC program currently in main storage to be displayed on the screen. The LIST command may also be used to copy lines to a file in auxiliary storage.
LLIST	Causes all or part of the BASIC program currently in main storage to be displayed on the printer.
NEW	Causes the BASIC program currently in main storage to be erased and indicates the beginning of a new program to be created in main storage.
RUN	Causes the BASIC program currently in main storage to be executed. This command may also be used to begin execution at a specified line number of the program in main storage or to load and execute a program from auxiliary storage.
SYSTEM	Causes the PC to permanently exit BASICA and returns control to the operating system MS DOS or PC DOS.

Use of the Function Keys and the KEY Statement

The PC has **function keys**, also called **PF** keys, which are located on the far left side or at the top of the keyboard. See Figures 1.5 and 1.6 on page 5 in Chapter 1. On the IBM standard keyboard they are labeled F1 through F10, as shown in Figure 2.4 below.

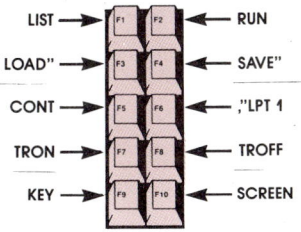

FIGURE 2.4 *The function keys on the left side of the keyboard.*

Each function key is assigned a sequence of characters that is displayed on the 25th line of the screen when the PC is running under BASIC. When you press one of the function keys, its assigned sequence of characters is entered into the PC. For example, if you press F1, the system command LIST is displayed on the screen and is entered into the PC. Pressing F2 is the same as keying in the command RUN and pressing the Enter key.

Besides the function keys, the PC allows you to enter keywords through the use of the Alt key and one of the letter keys. You will recall from Table 2.2, on page 26, that when you hold down the Alt key and press the I key, the keyword INPUT is entered into the PC.

The 25th line on the screen, containing the description of the function keys, can be erased through the use of the KEY statement. For example, 100 KEY OFF instructs the PC to erase the 25th line. To redisplay the line, use the statement 200 KEY ON.

This statement is most frequently used in tandem with the CLS statement to completely clear the screen. For example,

```
300 CLS : KEY OFF   ' Clear Screen
```

The first statement in line 300 clears the first 24 lines. The second statement clears the 25th line. The apostrophe indicates that a comment follows.

Additional System Commands

The system commands summarized in Table 2.7 are the ones most commonly used by BASIC programmers. Additional system commands that you will find useful are listed in Table 2.8.

As described in Table 2.8, the SAVE command allows you to save BASIC programs into auxiliary storage for later use. The LOAD command allows you to load BASIC programs from auxiliary storage into main storage.

TABLE 2.8 Summary of Additional System Commands

SYSTEM COMMAND	FUNCTION
AUTO number, increment	Automatically starts a BASIC line with a line number. Each new line is assigned a systematically incremented line number. Pressing the Control and Break keys terminates the AUTO activity.
FILES "device name:	Lists the names of all programs and data files in auxiliary storage.
KILL "filespec	Deletes a previously stored program or data file from auxiliary storage.
LOAD "filespec	Loads a previously stored program from auxiliary storage into main storage.
NAME "old filespec" AS "new filespec"	Changes the name of a program or data file in auxiliary storage to a new name.
RENUM start,,increment	Renumbers the entire program uniformly.
SAVE "filespec	Saves the current program into auxiliary storage for later use.
TRON	Turns on the program trace feature (see Appendix A).
TROFF	Turns off the program trace feature (see Appendix A).

PC Hard-Copy Output

Most BASIC programmers use a keyboard for input and a video display device for output. In many instances, it is desirable to list the program and the results on a printer. A listing of this type is **hard-copy output**. To obtain a listing on the printer of the program itself, use the system command LLIST.

To obtain a listing of both the program and output results, hold down the Control (Ctrl) key and press the Print Screen (PrtSc) key, and enter the system commands LIST and RUN, as shown below.

>Hold down the Ctrl key and press the PrtSc key.
>LIST
>RUN
>Hold down the Ctrl key and press the PrtSc key again.

When pressed, the Control and Print Screen keys serve as a toggle switch. Pressing the two keys once instructs the PC to direct output to the printer as well as to the screen. Pressing the two keys following the completion of an operation instructs the PC to terminate transmission to the printer.

Sometimes it is desirable to obtain a hard-copy output of exactly what is on the screen. To do this, simply hold down the Shift key and press the PrtSc key. The PC will print the contents of the screen, starting with the lowest line number in the program. This activity can easily be observed by following the movement of the cursor.

■ 2.8 SPECIAL KEYS

In this chapter, you have been introduced to a variety of special keys. Included on page 4 of the reference card at the back of this book is a table of the special keys and their functions. You will find this table useful as you begin entering and executing BASIC programs.

■ 2.9 PROGRAMMING TIPS

Having read the first eight sections of this chapter, you are ready to write your first program to use a PC for solving a problem. At the end of Chapter 2 are several BASIC Programming Problems. Each problem includes a short statement of the problem, suggested input data, and the corresponding output results. Collectively, these items are the **program specifications**. Following the sample BASIC Programming Problem below, we have suggested a step-by-step procedure for solving the problem. You will find this helpful when you begin solving problems on your own. You will also find it helpful to review Section 1.6 on page 10, especially Table 1.3.

Sample BASIC Programming Problem: Computation of State Tax

Problem: Construct a program that will compute the state tax owed by a taxpayer. The state determines the amount of tax owed by taking a person's yearly income, subtracting $500.00 for each dependent, and then multiplying the result by 2%. Use the following formula:

$$\text{Tax} = 0.02 * (\text{Income} - 500 * \text{Dependents})$$

Code the program so that it will request that the taxpayer's income and the number of dependents be entered through the keyboard.

Input Data: Use the following sample input data.

>Taxpayer's income: $73,000.00
>Number of dependents: 8

Output Results: The following results are displayed.

```
Taxpayer's income ========> 73000
Number of dependents ======> 8

State Tax Due ============> 1380
```

The following systematic approach to solving this problem as well as the other BASIC Programming Problems in this textbook is recommended. In essence, this list is the same as the program development cycle in Table 1.3 on page 11.

Step 1: Problem analysis.

Review the program specifications until you thoroughly understand the problem to be solved. Ascertain the form of input, the form of output, and the type of processing that must be performed. For this problem, you should have determined the following.

> **Input**: The program must allow for the user to supply the data through the use of INPUT statements. There are two data items: taxpayer's income and number of dependents.
>
> **Processing**: The formula Tax = 0.02 * (Income − 500 * Dependents) will determine the state tax.
>
> **Output**: The required results include the input prompt messages and the state tax due.

Step 2: Program design.

Develop a method of solution the PC will use. One way to do this is to list the program tasks sequentially. For this exercise, the **program tasks** are as follows:

1. Clear the screen.
2. Prompt the user for the necessary data.
3. Calculate the state tax.
4. Display the state tax.

Once the program tasks have been determined, select the variable names you plan to use in the program solution. Three variable names are required. We will use the following:

INCOME for taxpayer's income
DEPENDENTS for number of dependents
TAX for state tax

Next, draw a program flowchart or write pseudocode that shows how the program will accomplish the program tasks. The flowchart for the sample programming problem is shown in Figure 2.5.

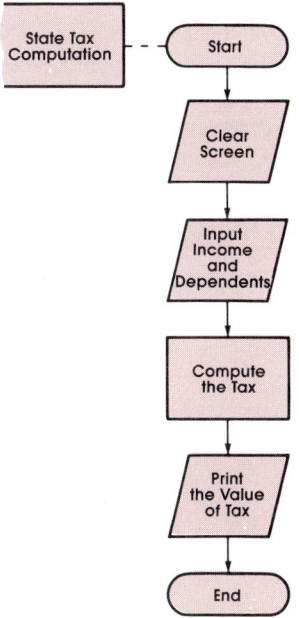

FIGURE 2.5 *A general flowchart for Sample BASIC Programming Problem.*

Step 3: Test the design.

Carefully review the design by stepping through the program flowchart or pseudocode to ensure that it is logically correct.

Step 4: Code the program.

Code the program, as shown in Figure 2.6 below, according to the program design.

```
100 ' CIS 160, DIV. 01, BASIC Programming
110 ' J. S. Quasney
120 ' September 30, 1992
130 ' Sample Basic Programming Problem
140 ' Computation of State Tax
150 ' ***************************************
160 CLS : KEY OFF   ' Clear Screen
170 INPUT "Taxpayer's income =========> ", INCOME
180 INPUT "Number of dependents ======> ", DEPENDENTS
190 ' Calculate Tax
200 TAX = 0.02 * (INCOME - 500 * DEPENDENTS)
210 PRINT
220 PRINT "State tax due ============>"; TAX
230 END
```

FIGURE 2.6 *Program solution for Sample BASIC Programming Problem on coding form.*

Step 5: Review the code.

Carefully review the coding. Put yourself in the position of the PC and step through the program. This is sometimes referred to as **desk checking** your code. Be sure the syntax of each instruction is correct. Check to be sure that the sequence of the instructions is logically correct. **You want to be confident that the program will work the first time it is executed.**

Step 6: Enter the program.

Enter the program into the PC, as shown in the top screen of Figure 2.7. Before starting this step, you should be familiar with the system commands and the method for getting on the PC (see Table 2.5 on page 31).

Step 7: Test the program.

Test the program by executing it, as shown in Figure 2.7. If the input data does not produce the expected results, the program must be reviewed and corrected. (See Appendix A for debugging techniques.)

Step 8: Formalize the solution.

Obtain a **hard copy** (a listing) of the source program (the BASIC code you've written) and the output results. If the program logic was modified in steps 4 through 6, revise the documentation and redraw the program flowchart or rewrite the pseudocode to include the changes.

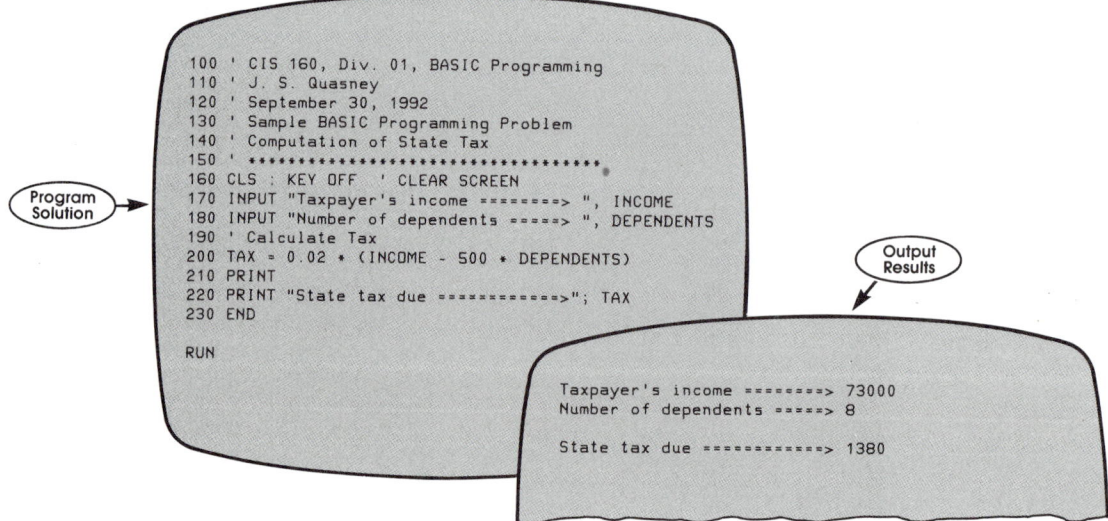

FIGURE 2.7 *Program solution to Sample BASIC Programming Problem entered in the PC and the display from executing the program solution.*

2.10 TEST YOUR BASIC SKILLS (Even-numbered answers are in Appendix B.)

1. Identify the BASIC arithmetic operators for the following:

    a. Addition　　　b. Subtraction　　　c. Multiplication　　　d. Division
    e. Exponentiation　　f. Integer Division　　g. Modulo

2. Put yourself in the place of the PC and record for each line number the current values of W, X, and Y. (**Hint:** The value of a variable does not change until the program instructs the PC to change it.)

    ```
    100 W = 4
    110 X = 2
    120 Y = 6
    130 PRINT Y
    140 W = W + 1
    150 X = W * Y
    160 PRINT X
    170 X = 9
    180 Y = Y - 2
    190 PRINT Y
    200 X = X - 9
    210 PRINT X
    220 END
    ```

Line	W	X	Y	Displayed
100				
110				
120				
130				
140				
150				
160				
170				
180				
190				
200				
210				
220				

3. For each program below, construct a table similar to the one in Exercise 2. Record for each line number the current values of the variables and the results displayed by the PRINT statements.

    a.
    ```
    100 A = 1
    110 B = 3
    120 PRINT A
    130 A = A + 1
    140 B = B - 1
    150 PRINT B
    160 A = A + 1
    170 B = B - 1
    180 PRINT A
    190 END
    ```

    b. A is assigned the value 4 and B is assigned the value 2.
    ```
    100 C = 4
    110 PRINT C
    120 INPUT A, B
    130 C = A \ B + C + 8 MOD 4
    140 A = A - 3
    150 B = C ^ A
    160 PRINT B
    170 END
    ```

    c. A is assigned the value 7 and B is assigned the value 2.
    ```
    100 INPUT A, B
    110 C = A * A
    120 PRINT C
    130 D = A - B
    140 PRINT D
    150 E = 1
    160 PRINT E
    170 D = D - 3
    180 X = E / D
    190 PRINT X
    200 END
    ```

    d. PRINCIPAL is assigned the value 500 and RATE is assigned the value 10.
    ```
    100 INPUT PRINCIPAL, RATE
    110 RATE = RATE / 100
    120 DISCOUNT = PRINCIPAL * RATE
    130 RATE = RATE * 100
    140 ' Display Results
    150 PRINT "Discount rate"; RATE; "%"
    160 PRINT "Price"; PRINCIPAL; "Dollars"
    170 PRINT "Discount"; DISCOUNT; "Dollars"
    180 END
    ```

4. Write LET statements for each of the following:

   a. Assign T the value of 3.
   b. Assign X the value of T less 2.
   c. Assign P the product of T and X.
   d. Triple the value of T.
   e. Assign A the quotient of P divided by X.
   f. Increment X by 1.
   g. Cube the value of R.

5. Fill in the missing word in each of the following:

   a. An output statement must contain the word _____ .
   b. Every BASIC program should contain the _____ statement.
   c. Every LET statement must contain an _____ sign.

6. Describe three techniques presented in Chapter 2 for integrating data into a program.
7. Explain in one sentence the purpose of holding down the Control (Ctrl) key and pressing the Break key.
8. Write a one-sentence explanation of the purpose of each of the following commands: AUTO, FILES, LIST, NEW, RUN, and RENUM.

■ 2.11 BASIC PROGRAMMING PROBLEMS

So that your computer programs are documented properly, you can use the following identification format at the beginning of each BASIC source program:

```
100 ' Department, Course Number, Division, Course Name
110 ' Your Name
120 ' Date
130 ' Problem Number
140 ' A Short Description of the Problem
150 ' **************************************************
```

In line 130, for example, use the comment "Problem 2-1" to represent the first problem in Chapter 2. In line 140, use the title of the problem as the comment.

Upon completion of each problem, turn in to your instructor the following items:

1. a logic diagram in flowchart form or in pseudocode, as required
2. a listing of the source program
3. the output results

Obtain a hard copy (see pages 36 and 37) of your source program and output results. Use meaningful variable names in all the programs. Each major section of the program should be documented with appropriate remark lines.

When you enter a program for the first time, use the AUTO command, which automatically starts a BASIC line with a line number. If additional lines are inserted later, use the RENUM command to begin the program with line 100 or 1000 and increment each line number by 10. Be sure to use the SAVE command to store all program solutions in auxiliary storage in the form of SAVE "LABc-n", where c represents the chapter number and n represents the problem number.

Note: All programming problems in this book include partial or complete sample output results and, when applicable, sample input data. Learn to select good test data to evaluate the logic of your program. Check your design and program against the sample output, and select your own data for additional testing purposes.

1. Computation of a Sum

Purpose: To gain confidence in keying and executing your first BASIC program.

Problem: Key in and execute the following program, which determines the sum of three numbers. Replace the verbiage in lines 100 to 120 with your course identification and name and today's date, as described earlier.

```
100 ' Course Identification
110 ' Your Name
120 ' Today's Date
130 ' Problem 2-1
140 ' Computation of a Sum
150 ' *********************
160 SUM = 25.65 + 13.75 + 15.25
170 PRINT "The sum is"; SUM
180 END
```

Input Data: None.

Output Results: The following results are displayed.

```
The sum is 54.65
```

2. Determining the Selling Price

Purpose: To become familiar with elementary uses of the INPUT, PRINT, and LET statements.

Problem: Merchants are in the retail business to buy goods from producers, manufacturers, and wholesalers and to sell the merchandise to their customers. To make a profit, they must sell their merchandise for more than the cost plus the overhead (taxes, store rent, upkeep, salaries, and so forth). The margin is the sum of the overhead and profit. The selling price is the sum of the margin and cost. Write a program, following the steps outlined in Section 2.9 on page 37, that will determine the selling price of an item that costs $48.27 and has a margin of 25%. Use the following formula:

$$\text{Selling Price} = \left(\frac{1}{1 - \text{Margin}}\right) \times \text{Cost}$$

As an option and to save keying time, develop your solution by loading and modifying the program in Figure 2.7 on page 40 from the Student Diskette in the back of this book. The name of the program is PRG2-9.

Input Data: Use the following data in response to INPUT statements.

Cost: $48.27
Margin: 25%

Output Results: The following results are displayed.

```
What is the cost? 48.27
What is the margin in percent? 25

The selling price is 64.36
```

3. Payroll Problem I: Gross Pay Computations

Purpose: To become familiar with some of the grammatical and logical rules of MS BASIC and to demonstrate the basic concepts of executing an MS BASIC program.

Problem: Construct a program, following the steps outlined in Section 2.9 on page 37, that will clear the screen, then compute and display the gross pay for an employee working 80 hours during a biweekly pay period at an hourly rate of $12.50.

> **Version A:** Insert the data, 80 and 12.50, directly into a LET statement that determines the gross pay.
>
> **Version B:** Assign the data, 80 and 12.50, to variables in LET statements and then compute the gross pay in a separate LET statement.
>
> **Version C:** Enter the data, 80 and 12.50, in response to INPUT statements.

Output Results: The following results are displayed for Versions B and C. For Version A, display only the last line.

```
Hours worked ===> 80
Rate of pay ====> 12.5
Gross pay ======> 1000
```

PROGRAMS WITH CALCULATIONS AND STRINGS

■ 3.1 INTRODUCTION

In Chapter 2, you were introduced to a few simple computer programs that demonstrated some of the grammatical rules of the Microsoft BASIC language. Also presented were examples of programs that interact with the user through the INPUT and PRINT statements. This chapter continues to develop straight-line programs, with more complex computations and manipulation of data.

The focus in this chapter is on constants, variables, expressions, functions, and statements that assign values. This chapter also expands on the type of data that can be assigned to variables by introducing **string values**, examples of which include a word, a phrase, or a sentence. Upon successful completion of this chapter, you will be able to write programs that manipulate string expressions and numeric expressions.

PROGRAMMING CASE STUDY 3: *Tailor's Calculations*

Program 3.1, on the next page, determines the estimated neck, hat, and shoe size of a male customer. The program uses the following formulas:

$$\text{Neck Size} = 3\left(\frac{\text{Weight}}{\text{Waistline}}\right) \quad \text{Hat Size} = \frac{\text{Neck Size}}{2.125} \quad \text{Shoe Size} = 50\left(\frac{\text{Waistline}}{\text{Weight}}\right)$$

Program 3.1 computes the average neck size (15), hat size (7.058824), and shoe size (10) for Mike, who has a 35-inch waistline and weighs 175 pounds. Even though it is not used in the computations, the customer name is requested in the program, because it helps identify the measurements when more than one set of computations is involved.

PROGRAM 3.1

```
100 ' Program 3.1
110 ' Tailor's Computations
120 ' Determine Neck Size, Hat Size and Shoe Size
130 ' ********************************************
140 CLS : KEY OFF  ' Clear Screen
150 INPUT "Customer's first name"; FIRST.NAME$
160 INPUT "Waistline"; WAIST
170 INPUT "Weight"; WEIGHT
180 NECKSIZE = 3 * WEIGHT / WAIST
190 HATSIZE  = NECKSIZE / 2.125
200 SHOESIZE = 50 * WAIST / WEIGHT
210 PRINT
220 PRINT FIRST.NAME$; "'s neck size is"; NECKSIZE
230 PRINT FIRST.NAME$; "'s hat size is"; HATSIZE
240 PRINT FIRST.NAME$; "'s shoe size is"; SHOESIZE
250 END

RUN

Customer's first name? Mike
Waistline? 35
Weight? 175

Mike's neck size is 15
Mike's hat size is 7.058824
Mike's shoe size is 10
```

Program 3.1 contains a sequence of LET statements (lines 180 through 200) with expressions that are more complex than those encountered in Chapter 2. Furthermore, line 150 contains a variable, FIRST.NAME$, that is assigned a string of letters, Mike, rather than a numeric value. The value of FIRST.NAME$ is displayed along with the results because of lines 220 through 240. The following pages introduce some additional formal definitions and special rules for constructing constants, variables, and LET statements, and for manipulating strings.

■ 3.2 CONSTANTS

You will recall from Chapter 2 that constants are values that cannot change during the execution of a program. Two different kinds of constants are valid for use in BASIC programs: **numeric constants** and **string constants**. Numeric constants represent ordinary numbers. A string constant is a sequence of letters, digits, and special characters enclosed in quotation marks. They are used for such nonnumeric purposes as representing an employee name, a social security number, an address, or a telephone number.

Numeric Constants

A numeric constant can have one of the three following forms in MS BASIC:

1. **Integer:** a positive or negative whole number or zero with no decimal point, like –174 or 5903 or 0 or –32768.
2. **Fixed Point:** a positive or negative real number or zero with a decimal point, like 713.1417 or 0.0034 or 0.0 or –35.1 or 1923547463.34.
3. **Floating Point** or **Exponential Form:** A number written as an integer or fixed point constant, followed by the letter D or E and an integer. D or E stands for "times ten to the power." (An explanation of the difference between using a D or an E follows shortly.) Examples are 793E19, 62E–23, 1E0, –2.3D–3, and +12.34789564D+7.

Examples of numeric constants in Program 3.1 are 3, 2.125, and 50, found in lines 180, 190, and 200. A line number like 210 is not considered to be a constant in MS BASIC.

The numeric data items, 35 and 175, entered in response to the INPUT statements in lines 160 and 170, must take the form of numeric constants. This leads to the following rule:

> **Input Rule 2:** Numeric data that is assigned to numeric variables through the use of the INPUT statement must take the form of numeric constants.

A number that is entered in response to the INPUT statement may have as many digits as required, up to a maximum of 38. However, the PC will keep only the number of digits that is specified by the type of variable receiving the value.

Computer Precision

Numeric constants are stored in main storage in one of three forms: integer, single precision, or double precision.

The PC requires 2 bytes of main storage to store an integer constant, 4 bytes to store a single-precision constant, and 8 bytes to store a double-precision constant.

We tell the PC how to store a value, like a numeric constant, by the way we write it. For example, a numeric constant is stored in integer form if it is between −32768 and +32767 and does not contain a decimal point or does include a trailing percent sign (%).

The PC stores a constant in single precision if one of the following is true:

1. it is outside the range for an integer and contains seven or fewer digits;
2. it contains a decimal point and has seven or fewer digits;
3. it is written in exponential form, using E; or
4. it includes a trailing exclamation point (!).

With single precision, the PC maintains seven significant digits.

The PC uses double precision to store a constant if one of the following is true:

1. it has eight or more digits;
2. it is written in exponential form, using D; or
3. it includes a trailing number sign (#).

With double precision, the PC will store up to seventeen digits. With single or double precision, you can represent any number (positive or negative) from 2.9×10^{-39} to 1.7×10^{38}. Table 3.1 on the next page shows several examples of constants as well as the form used by the PC to store them.

TABLE 3.1 Numeric Constants and the Form Used to Store Them

NUMERIC CONSTANT	STORED AS
−128	*Integer*
1	*Integer*
4.923458%	*Integer; stored as the constant 5.*
5125	*Integer*
3E−4	*Single Precision*
1.	*Single Precision*
4.67	*Single Precision*
67.45637681902!	*Single Precision; stored as 67.45638.*
345612	*Single Precision*
3D−4	*Double Precision*
87.3#	*Double Precision*
899045637.87957	*Double Precision*

For the most part, you can let the PC handle the precision with which it stores values, as was done in Chapter 2 and in Program 3.1. *That is, write numeric constants in a BASIC program the same way you would in algebra.* However, you should be aware that it is possible for the BASIC programmer to control both the way a numeric constant is stored and the type of arithmetic the PC will use.

Numeric Constants in Exponential Form

Numeric constants may be written in **exponential form**. This form is similar to **scientific notation**. It is a shorthand way of representing very large and very small numbers in a program. If a result exceeds the precision under which it is stored, the PC displays it in exponential form. For these two reasons, it is useful to have some idea of how to read and write numbers in this form.

With exponential notation, a number, regardless of its magnitude, is expressed as a value between 1 and 10 that is multiplied by a power of 10. For example, 1,500,000 can be expressed as 1.5×10^6 in scientific notation or can be written as an exponential-type constant in the form of 1.5E6. The positive power of 10 in the exponential notation of 1.5×10^6 shows that the decimal point was previously moved 6 places to the left. That is,

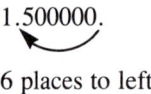

6 places to left

In order to write 1.5×10^6 as an exponential-type constant in a BASIC program, either the letter D (double precision) or E (single precision), which both stand for "times ten to the power," is substituted for the "× 10." Hence, the exponential-type constant may be written as 1.5E6 in single precision or 1.5D6 in double precision.

In the same way, a small number like 0.000000001234 can be expressed as 1.234×10^{-9} or 1.234E−9 or 1.234D−9. The negative power of 10 in 1.234×10^{-9} signifies that the decimal point was moved 9 places to the right, as follows:

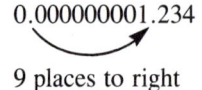

9 places to right

String Constants

A string constant has as its value the string of all characters between surrounding quotation marks. The length of a string constant may be between 0 and 255 characters. A string with a length of zero is a **null string** or an **empty string**. The quotation marks indicate the beginning and end of the string constant and are not considered to be part of the value.

The messages that have been incorporated in INPUT statements to prompt for the required data and in PRINT statements to identify results are examples of string constants. For example, string constants appear in lines 150, 160, and 170 of Program 3.1 on page 46.

String constants can be assigned to variables in a LET statement, as is shown in the following program.

PROGRAM 3.2

```
100 ' Program 3.2
110 ' Examples of String Constants
120 ' ****************************
130 MODEL$ = "Q1937A"
140 PART$ = "12AB34"
150 DESCRIPTION$ = "Nylon, Disc"
160 PRINT "Model number: "; MODEL$
170 PRINT "Part number: "; PART$
180 PRINT "Description: "; DESCRIPTION$
190 END

RUN

Model number: Q1937A
Part number: 12AB34
Description: Nylon, Disc
```

In line 130 of Program 3.2, the variable MODEL$ is assigned the value Q1937A. In line 140, PART$ is assigned the value 12AB34, and in line 150, DESCRIPTION$ is assigned the value Nylon, Disc.

String constants are used in a program to represent values that name or identify a person, place, or thing. They are also used to represent report and column headings and output messages. The ability to manipulate data of this type is important in the field of business data processing. As you will see later in this chapter, MS BASIC also includes string functions for manipulating strings.

■ 3.3 VARIABLES

In Chapter 2, you learned that in programming, a **variable** is a location in main storage whose value can change as the program is executed. In a program, the variable is referenced by a variable name. Variables are declared in a BASIC program by incorporating variable names in statements. For example, the LET statements,

```
100 RANK = 4
110 SCHOOL$ = "Purdue"
```

instruct MS BASIC to set up independent storage areas for RANK and SCHOOL$ as well as the constants 4 and Purdue.

Although it may appear to you that RANK is being assigned the value 4 when you enter the statement through your keyboard, this does not occur until the program is executed. You'll recall from Chapter 1 that a BASIC program must be translated into equivalent machine language instructions before it can be executed. During this translation, the variables and numeric constants of a program are assigned particular storage areas in main storage. Figure 3.1 illustrates the storage areas for RANK and SCHOOL$ before and after execution of lines 100 and 110 in the partial program on the previous page.

	STORAGE FOR VARIABLES		STORAGE FOR CONSTANTS	
Before Execution of Line 100 →	0 RANK	NULL SCHOOL$	4	Purdue
After Execution of Line 100 →	4 RANK	NULL SCHOOL$	4	Purdue
After Execution of Line 110 →	4 RANK	Purdue SCHOOL$	4	Purdue

FIGURE 3.1 *The assignment of values to variables in main storage.*

Unlike a constant, a variable may be redefined (that is, its value may be changed) during the execution of a program. However, its value may remain unchanged in a BASIC program if you so desire.

As with constants, there are two types of simple variables: **numeric** and **string**. A numeric variable may be assigned only a numeric value, and a string variable may be assigned only a string of characters (letters, numbers, and special characters).

When the system command RUN is issued for a program, all numeric variables are assigned an initial value of zero and all string variables are assigned a null value. The LET statement may be used to assign a variable a constant value or the result of a calculation. Variables may also be assigned values through INPUT statements.

Selection of Variable Names

A variable name begins with a letter and may be followed by up to 39 letters, digits, and periods.

If a variable name ends with a dollar sign ($), then MS BASIC establishes a location in main storage to receive a string value. If a variable name does not end with a dollar sign, then MS BASIC establishes a location in main storage to receive a numeric value.

Keywords like, LET, PRINT, and END or any other **reserved word** that has special meaning to MS BASIC may not be used as a variable name. See the reference card at the back of this book for a list of the reserved words. Some examples of numeric and string variable names, invalid if written as given, are listed in Tables 3.2 and 3.3.

TABLE 3.2 Invalid Numeric Variables and the Corresponding Valid Forms

INVALID NUMERIC VARIABLES	TYPE OF ERROR	VALID NUMERIC VARIABLES
1P	*First character must be a letter.*	PAY1 *or* PAY
LET	LET *is a keyword.*	LETS
QUANTITY*	*Special characters other than the period are invalid.*	QUANTITY
FNNUM	*A variable name may not begin with the characters* FN. *(To be discussed in Chapter 8.)*	NUM
RATE$	*A numeric variable must not end with a $.*	RATE

TABLE 3.3 Invalid String Variables and the Corresponding Valid Forms

INVALID STRING VARIABLES	TYPE OF ERROR	VALID STRING VARIABLES
EMP.NAME	*Appended dollar sign necessary.*	EMP.NAME$
WIDTH$	WIDTH *is a keyword.*	WIDE$
LAST NAME$	*Blank character not permitted within a variable name.*	LAST.NAME$

When you compose variable names, make them as meaningful as possible. It is far easier for a person to read the various statements in a program if meaningful names are used. For example, let's assume that the formula for gross pay is given by

Gross Pay = Rate × Hours

The following statement may represent the formula in a BASIC program:

    150 A = B * C

However, it is more meaningful to write

    150 G = R * H

It is even more meaningful to say

    150 GROSS = RATE * HOURS

Some BASIC programmers apply the period to group variable names, as shown below:

Group name. Specific name

For example, if several variable names are needed to describe data in an employee record, then EMP may be used as the group name. The part of the variable name that follows the period differentiates between the variable names that begin with the group name, as shown here:

    EMP.NUMBER$
    EMP.NAME$
    EMP.ADDRESS$
    EMP.SALARY
    EMP.CODE$

Develop a style for choosing meaningful variable names for a program. During the program design stage, establish guidelines for how variable names will be selected, and rigorously follow these guidelines when coding the program. Of course, you must abide by the rules that may restrict or enhance the ways you construct variable names.

Declaring Variable Types

The name of a variable determines whether it is string or numeric, and, if numeric, what its precision is.

As the last character in a variable name, the dollar sign ($) declares that the variable will represent a string. If the dollar sign is absent at the end of the variable name, then the variable is declared to be numeric. As with numeric constants, numeric variables may be declared type integer, single precision, or double precision.

If there is no trailing special character in a variable name, then MS BASIC defines it as single precision. Variable names like SUM, EMP.SALARY, and PRODUCT are single-precision numeric variables. All of the numeric variables used thus far in this book have been of this type.

You may also declare a variable to be single precision explicitly by appending an exclamation point (!) to the variable name. Variable names like NUMBER!, MEAN!, and ASSESSMENT! are examples of explicitly declared single-precision variables. Also see the third and fourth examples in Table 3.4.

Single-precision variables can store up to 7 significant digits. If a value being assigned to a single-precision variable contains 8 or more digits, the system will round it to 7. For this reason, the 7th digit may not always be exact. The numeric values that may be assigned to a single-precision variable are restricted to the range (positive or negative) 2.9×10^{-39} to 1.7×10^{38}.

An integer variable is declared by ending the variable name with a percent sign (%). The first two examples in Table 3.4 illustrate integer-type variables. Integer variables take up less space in main storage and for that reason are often used in programs to count the number of times something has occurred. Integer variables can hold only an integer value that is between −32,768 and +32,767. If you assign an integer variable a noninteger value, MS BASIC will round the noninteger value to an integer. For example,

```
100 GPA% = 3.7
```

results in GPA% being assigned the value 4.

TABLE 3.4 Declaring the Type of Numeric Variable

NUMERIC VARIABLE	DECLARED TYPE
CODE%	*Integer*
POINT%	*Integer*
DEVIATION	*Single Precision*
ERROR!	*Single Precision*
SPECS#	*Double Precision*
WEIGHT#	*Double Precision*

Assigning Values to String Variables Using the INPUT Statement

The following program requests that string data be entered in response to the INPUT statements.

PROGRAM 3.3

```
100 ' Program 3.3
110 ' Entering String Data in
120 ' Response to the INPUT Statement
130 ' ******************************
140 INPUT "Model number: ", MODEL$
150 INPUT "Part number: ", PART$
160 INPUT "Description: ", DESCRIPTION$
170 PRINT
180 PRINT "The model number is "; MODEL$
190 PRINT "The part number is "; PART$
200 PRINT "The description is "; DESCRIPTION$
210 END
RUN

Model number: "Q1937A"        ⎫   Quoted String Data
Part number: "345123"         ⎬ ← Entered in Response to the
Description: "Nylon, Disc"    ⎭   Program's INPUT Statements

The model number is Q1937A
The part number is 345123
The description is Nylon, Disc
```

In Program 3.3, the string variables MODEL$, PART$, and DESCRIPTION$ are assigned quoted strings, following the rules for string constants. In general, surrounding a string with quotation marks is optional when an INPUT statement is used to assign the string to a string variable, but there are certain exceptions. Examine the output from Program 3.3 when unquoted strings are entered along with one quoted string, in contrast to the original output, in which all three strings were quoted:

```
RUN

Model number: Q1937A          ⎫
Part number: 345123           ⎬ ← Unquoted Strings
Description: "Nylon, Disc"    ← Quoted String

The model number is Q1937A
The part number is 345123
The description is Nylon, Disc
```

The first two string data items, Q1937A and 345123, are entered as unquoted strings. The third data item Nylon, Disc is entered within quotes because it contains an embedded comma. Quotation marks are necessary only if one of the following two characteristics is true of the string data item:

1. either the string contains leading or trailing spaces, or
2. the string contains a comma or colon.

The following rule summarizes the assignment of string data items through the use of the INPUT statement.

> **Input Rule 3:** String data that is assigned to string variables through the use of the INPUT statement may be entered with or without surrounding quotation marks, provided the string contains no leading or trailing spaces or embedded commas or colons. If the string contains leading or trailing spaces or embedded commas or colons, it must be surrounded with quotation marks.

Displaying String Variables

MS BASIC does not add leading or trailing spaces when it displays a string value. Therefore, when a semicolon is used as the separator between string items in a PRINT statement, a space should be included to separate the displayed values. Line 180 of the following partial program includes a space that follows the word is in the string constant. This causes the PC to display the value of MODEL$ one space after the word is.

```
180 PRINT "The model number is "; MODEL$
 .
 .
 .
RUN
The model number is Q1937A
```

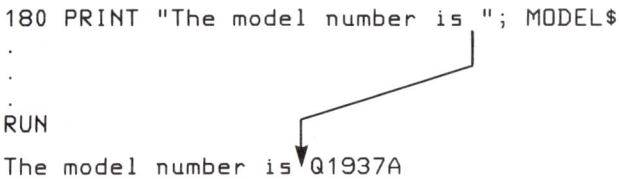

■ 3.4 THE LET STATEMENT

The LET statement in MS BASIC is used to assign a value to a variable. The general form of the LET statement is given in Table 3.5. Each LET statement consists of the optional keyword LET, followed by a variable, followed by an equal sign, and then by an expression.

TABLE 3.5 The LET Statement

General Form:	LET *numeric variable* = *numeric expression* or LET *string variable* = *string expression*
Purpose:	*Causes the evaluation of the expression, followed by the assignment of the resulting value to the variable to the left of the equal sign.*

Examples:	`100 LET PERIMETER = 2 * SIDE1 + 2 * SIDE2`
	 `150 LET Q = (B + A) / 2 - Q + R`
	 `200 COUNT = COUNT + 1`
	 `250 OPPOSITE = -OPPOSITE`
	 `300 ARRAY.1(Y, 4) = 0`
	 `350 DESCRIPTION$ = "PLIER"`
	 `400 HYPOTENUSE = (BASE ^ 2 + HEIGHT ^ 2) ^ (1/2)`
	 `450 P(I) = C(K) + P(J)`
	 `500 E = M * C^2`
	 `550 NUMBER$ = PREFIX$ + "0520"`

Note:	The keyword LET *is optional.*

The execution of the LET statement is not a one-step process for the PC. The execution of a LET statement requires two steps: evaluation of the expression and assignment of the result to the variable to the left of the equal sign.

Although the equal sign is employed in MS BASIC, it does not carry all the properties of the equal sign in mathematics. For example, the equal sign in MS BASIC does not allow for the symmetric relationship. That is, 100 LET A = B cannot be written as 100 B = LET A.

The equal sign in MS BASIC can best be described as meaning "is replaced by." Therefore,

```
160 INTEREST = PRINCIPAL * RATE * TIME / 360
```

means that the old value of INTEREST is replaced by the value determined from the expression to the right of the equal sign.

PROGRAMMING CASE STUDY 4A: Finding the Single Discount Rate

Program 3.4, on the next page, determines the single discount rate that is equal to the series of discount rates of 40%, 20%, and 10%, using the following formula:

$$\text{Rate} = 1 - (1 - \text{rate}_1)(1 - \text{rate}_2)(1 - \text{rate}_3) \ldots (1 - \text{rate}_n)$$

where Rate is the single discount rate, and rate_1, rate_2, ..., rate_n is the series of discount rates. The number of factors of $(1 - \text{rate}_n)$ that are used to determine the single discount rate is dependent on the number of discounts. Program 3.4 is written to find the single discount rate for a series of three discount rates.

After the three discount rates are assigned their decimal values in Program 3.4, line 180 determines the value of the single discount from the expression found to the right of the equal sign. Specifically, the expression is evaluated and the final value 0.568 is assigned to the variable RATE. Line 200 displays the value for RATE before the program ends.

PROGRAM 3.4

```
100 ' Program 3.4
110 ' Finding the Single Discount Rate
120 ' *********************************
130 CLS : KEY OFF  ' Clear Screen
140 PRINT "Enter in Decimal Form:"
150 INPUT "           First Discount ======> ", RATE1
160 INPUT "           Second Discount =====> ", RATE2
170 INPUT "           Third Discount ======> ", RATE3
180 RATE = 1 - (1 - RATE1) * (1 - RATE2) * (1 - RATE3)
190 PRINT
200 PRINT "Single Discount ================>"; RATE
210 END

RUN

Enter in Decimal Form:
           First Discount ======> 0.40
           Second Discount =====> 0.20
           Third Discount ======> 0.10

Single Discount ================> .568
```

When dealing with rates that usually occur in percent form, it is often preferable to have the program accept the data and display the results in percent form. Program 3.5 shows how you can write a solution to Programming Case Study 4A that accomplishes this task.

PROGRAM 3.5

```
100 ' Program 3.5
110 ' Finding the Single Discount Rate
120 ' *********************************
130 CLS : KEY OFF  ' Clear Screen
140 PRINT "Enter in Percent Form:"
150 INPUT "           First Discount ======> ", RATE1
160 INPUT "           Second Discount =====> ", RATE2
170 INPUT "           Third Discount ======> ", RATE3
180 RATE1 = RATE1 / 100
190 RATE2 = RATE2 / 100
200 RATE3 = RATE3 / 100
210 RATE = 1 - (1 - RATE1) * (1 - RATE2) * (1 - RATE3)
220 RATE = 100 * RATE
230 PRINT
240 PRINT "Single Discount ================>"; RATE; "%"
250 END

RUN

Enter in Percent Form:
           First Discount ======> 40
           Second Discount =====> 20
           Third Discount ======> 10

Single Discount ================> 56.8 %
```

In Program 3.5, the INPUT statements (lines 150 through 170) prompt the user to enter the discount rates in percent form. In lines 180 through 200, the rates are changed from percent form to decimal form by dividing RATE1, RATE2, and RATE3 by 100. The single discount is then determined by line 210. Line 220 replaces the assigned value of RATE (0.568) with 100 times RATE. In other words, line 220 changes the value of RATE from decimal form to percent form. Line 240 then displays the value of RATE. The string constant % that is found at the end of line 240 helps identify the result as a percent value.

Program 3.5 includes two concepts that many student programmers have difficulty understanding. The first is that the same variable — RATE1, for example, in line 180 — can be found on both sides of an equal sign. The second concerns the reuse of a variable that had been assigned a value through computations in an earlier LET statement. In Program 3.5, RATE1, RATE2, and RATE3 are reused in line 210 after having been assigned values in earlier LET statements. At the end of this chapter, you will find several exercises that will help you understand these important concepts.

■ 3.5 EXPRESSIONS

Expressions may be either numeric or string. **Numeric expressions** consist of one or more numeric constants, numeric variables, and numeric function references, all of which are separated from each other by parentheses and arithmetic operators.

The seven valid arithmetic operators and examples of their use are shown in Table 2.1 on page 21. They include exponentiation (^), multiplication (*), division (/), integer division (\), modulo (MOD), addition (+), and subtraction (−).

You'll recall that exponentiation is the raising of a number to a power. For example, 4 ^ 2 is equal to 16, and 3 ^ 4 is equal to 81. In programming, the asterisk (*) means "times" and the slash means "divided by." Therefore, 8 * 4 is equal to 32, and 8 / 4 is equal to 2. For addition and subtraction, the traditional signs are used.

Two arithmetic operators that may be unfamiliar to you are the backslash (\) and MOD. The backslash instructs the PC first to round the dividend and the divisor to integers and then to truncate any decimal portion of the quotient. For example, 5 \ 3 is equal to 1, and 6.8 \ 3.2 is equal to 2.

The modulo operator returns the integer remainder of integer division. For example, 34 MOD 6 is equal to 4, and 23 MOD 12 is equal to 11.

String expressions consist of one or more string constants, string variables, and string function references separated by the **concatenation operator** (+), which combines two strings into one. No other operators are allowed in string expressions.

A programmer must be concerned with both the formation and the evaluation of an expression. It is necessary to consider what an expression is, as well as what constitutes validity in an expression, before it is possible to write valid BASIC statements with confidence.

Formation of Numeric Expressions

The definition of a numeric expression dictates the manner in which it is to be validly formed. For example, it may be perfectly clear to you that the following invalid statement has been formed to assign A twice the value of B.

```
100 A = 2B    ' Invalid Statement
```

However, the PC will reject the statement, because a constant and a variable within the same expression must be separated by an arithmetic operator. The statement can validly be written as follows:

```
100 A = 2 * B
```

Evaluation of Numeric Expressions

Formation of complex expressions involving several arithmetic operations can sometimes create problems. For example, consider the following statement:

```
100 A = 8 / 4 / 2
```

Does this assign a value of 1 or 4 to A? The answer depends on how the PC evaluates the expression. If the PC completes the operation 8 / 4 first and then completes 2 / 2, the expression yields the value 1. If the PC completes the second operation, 4 / 2, first and then completes 8 / 2, it yields 4.

The PC follows the normal algebraic rules. Therefore, the expression 8 / 4 / 2 yields a value of 1.

The order in which the operations in an expression is evaluated is given by the following rule:

> **Precedence Rule 1:** Unless parentheses dictate otherwise, reading from left to right in a numeric expression, all exponentiations are performed first, then all multiplications and/or divisions, then all integer divisions, then all modulo arithmetic, and finally all additions and/or subtractions.

The expression below yields the value of 1.41, as follows:

```
(2 - 3 * 4/5)^2 + 5/(4 * 3 - 2^3) = (2 - 3 * 4 / 5)^2 + 5 / (4 * 3 - 8)
                                  = (2 - 2.4)^2 + 5 / (12 - 8)
                                  = (-0.4)^2 + 5 / 4
                                  = 0.16 + 5 / 4
                                  = 0.16 + 1.25
                                  = 1.41
```

Use parentheses freely when in doubt as to the formation and evaluation of a numeric expression. For example, if you wish to have the PC divide 8 * D by 3 ^ P, the expression may correctly be written as 8 * D / 3 ^ P, but you may also write it as (8 * D) / (3 ^ P) and feel more certain of the result.

For more complex expressions, MS BASIC allows parentheses to be contained within other parentheses. When this occurs, the parentheses are said to be **nested**. In this case, MS BASIC evaluates the innermost parenthetical expression first and then goes on to the outermost parenthetical expression.

Table 3.6 gives examples of the MS BASIC equivalent of some algebraic statements. Study each example carefully. Two of the most common errors student programmers make are surrounding the wrong part of an expression with parentheses and not balancing the parentheses. Be sure that an expression has as many closed parentheses as open parentheses.

TABLE 3.6 MS BASIC Equivalent Statements

ALGEBRAIC STATEMENTS	EQUIVALENT LET STATEMENTS
$H = \sqrt{X^2 + Y^2}$	130 H = (X ^ 2 + Y ^ 2) ^ 0.5
$S = AL^P K^{1-P}$	170 S = A * L ^ P * K ^ (1 - P)
$Q = \dfrac{-b + \sqrt{b^2 - 4ac}}{2a}$	220 Q = (-B + (B ^ 2 - 4 * A * C) ^ 0.5) / (2 * A)
$A = F\left[\dfrac{r}{(1+r)^n - 1}\right]$	350 A = F * (R / (((1 + R) ^ N) - 1))
$P = \sqrt[3]{(x-p)^2 + y^2}$	600 P = ((X - P) ^ 2 + Y ^ 2) ^ (1 / 3)
$Z = \dfrac{ab}{x + \sqrt{x^2 - a^2}}$	810 Z = A * B / (X + (X ^ 2 - A ^ 2) ^ 0.5)

This order of operations is sometimes called the **rules of precedence**, or the **hierarchy of operations**. The meaning of these rules can be made clear with some examples. For instance, the expression 18 / 3 ^ 2 + 4 * 2 is evaluated as follows:

```
18 / 3 ^ 2 + 4 * 2 = 18 / 9 + 4 * 2
                   = 2     + 4 * 2
                   = 2     + 8
                   = 10
```

If you had trouble following the logic behind this evaluation, use this technique: Whenever a numeric expression is to be evaluated, "look" or "scan" from *left to right* five different times, applying Precedence Rule 1. On the first scan, every time you encounter an ^ operator, you perform exponentiation. In this example, 3 is raised to the power of 2, yielding 9.

On the second scan, moving from left to right again, every time you encounter the operators * and /, perform multiplication and division. Hence, 18 is divided by 9, yielding 2, and 4 and 2 are multiplied, yielding 8.

On the third scan, from left to right, perform all integer division. On the fourth scan, from left to right, perform all modulo arithmetic. (In this example, there is no integer division or modulo arithmetic.)

On the fifth scan, moving again from left to right, every time you detect the operators + and –, perform addition and subtraction. In this example, 2 and 8 are added to form 10.

The expression below yields the value of –2.73, as follows:

```
2 - 3 * 4/5 ^ 2 + 5/4 * 3 - 2 ^ 3 = 2 - 3 * 4/25 + 5/4 * 3 - 8   (at end
                                                                  of first scan)
                                  = 2 - 0.48 + 3.75 - 8          (at end of
                                                                  second scan)
                                  = -2.73                        (at end of fifth scan)
```

Note that the above expression is similar to the one on page 58 but without the parentheses.

The Use of Parentheses in Numeric Expressions

Parentheses may be used to change the order of operations. In MS BASIC, parentheses are normally used to avoid ambiguity and to group terms in a numeric expression; they do not imply multiplication. The order in which the operations in an expression containing parentheses is evaluated is given in the following rule:

> ***Precedence Rule 2:*** When parentheses are inserted into an expression, the part of the expression within the parentheses is evaluated first, and then the remainder of the expression is evaluated according to Precedence Rule 1.

String Expressions

The ability to process strings of characters is an essential part of any programming language that is to be used for business applications. Letters, words, names, and a combination of letters and numbers can play an important role in generating readable reports and easing communication between non-technical personnel and the computer.

In MS BASIC, string expressions include string constants, string variables, string function references, and a combination of the three, separated by the concatenation operator (+). Consider the following program:

PROGRAM 3.6

```
100 ' Program 3.6
110 ' Examples of String Expressions
120 ' *****************************
130 CLS : KEY OFF   ' Clear screen
140 INPUT "Area code ===============> ", AREA.CODE$
150 INPUT "Local number ============> ", LOCAL$
160 TEMP$ = AREA.CODE$
170 COMMENT$ = "Telephone number "
180 NUMBER$ = AREA.CODE$ + "-" + LOCAL$
190 PRINT
200 PRINT COMMENT$; "========> "; NUMBER$
210 PRINT "Area code ===============> "; TEMP$
220 END
RUN

Area code ===============> 219
Local number ============> 844-0520

Telephone number ========> 219-844-0520
Area code ===============> 219
```

Examples of string expressions in Program 3.6 include the following:

1. the string variable AREA.CODE$ in line 160, which is assigned to TEMP$;
2. the string constant `Telephone number` in line 170, which is assigned to COMMENT$; and
3. the string expression AREA.CODE$ + "-" + LOCAL$ in line 180, which is assigned to NUMBER$.

In line 180, the plus sign is the concatenation operator. When strings are concatenated, they are joined in the order in which they are found. The result is a single string. The value of NUMBER$, which is displayed by line 200, is illustrated in the output results of Program 3.6.

Use of LEFT$, LEN, MID$, and RIGHT$ String Functions

Although concatenation is the only valid string operation, MS BASIC includes functions that allow for additional string manipulation. The most often used string functions are presented in Table 3.7; other string functions are presented in Chapter 8.

TABLE 3.7 Some Common String Functions

LEFT$(X$, N)	*Returns the leftmost N characters of the string argument X$.*
LEN(X$)	*Returns the number of characters in the value associated with the string argument X$.*
MID$(X$, P, N)	*Returns N characters of the string argument X$ beginning at P.*
RIGHT$(X$, N)	*Returns the rightmost N characters of the string argument X$.*

Where X$ is a string expression, and N and P are numeric expressions.

PROGRAM 3.7

```
100 ' Program 3.7
110 ' Example of Referencing String Functions
120 ' ****************************************
130 CLS : KEY OFF    ' Clear screen
140 ' ****** Request Telephone Number *******
150 INPUT "Complete telephone number =====> ", NUMBER$
160 AREA.CODE$ = LEFT$(NUMBER$, 3)
170 PREFIX$ = MID$(NUMBER$, 5, 3)
180 LOCAL$ = RIGHT$(NUMBER$, 4)
190 COUNT = LEN(NUMBER$)
200 PRINT
210 PRINT "Area code =============> "; AREA.CODE$
220 PRINT "Prefix ================> "; PREFIX$
230 PRINT "Last four digits ======> "; LOCAL$
240 PRINT "Character count in "; NUMBER$; " =====>"; COUNT
250 END

RUN

Complete telephone number =====> 219-844-0520

Area code =============> 219
Prefix ================> 844
Last four digits ======> 0520
Character count in 219-844-0520 =====> 12
```

In Program 3.7, the function LEFT$ in line 160 assigns the three leftmost characters of NUMBER$ to AREA.CODE$. AREA.CODE$ is assigned the string 219. In line 170, the MID$ function assigns 3 characters beginning with the fifth character 8 in NUMBER$ to PREFIX$. PREFIX$ is assigned the string 844. In line 180, the function RIGHT$ assigns the last four characters of NUMBER$ to LOCAL$. LOCAL$ is assigned the string 0520. Finally, in line 190, the numeric variable COUNT is assigned a value equal to the number of characters in NUMBER$. COUNT is assigned the numeric value 12.

3.6 Test Your Basic Skills (Even-numbered answers are in Appendix B.)

1. Which arithmetic operation is performed first in the following numeric expressions?

   a. `9 / 5 * 6`
   b. `X - Y + A`
   c. `3 * (A + 8)`
   d. `(X * (2 + Y)) ^ 2 + Z ^ (2 ^ 2) - 6 MOD 3`
   e. `X / Y \ Z`
   f. `(B ^ 2 - 4 * A * C) / (2 * A)`

2. Evaluate each of the following:

   a. `4 * 5 * 3 / 6 - 7 ^ 2 / 3`
   b. `(2 - 4) + 5 ^ 2`
   c. `12 \ 6 / 2 + 7 MOD 3 + 3`

3. Calculate the numeric value for each of the following valid numeric expressions if A = 3, B = 4, C = 5, W = 3, T = 4, X = 1, and Y = 2.

   a. `(A + B / 2) + 6.2`
   b. `(A / (C + 1) * 4 - 5) / 2 + ( 4 MOD 3 \ 3)`
   c. `3 * (A ^ B) / C`
   d. `X + 2 * Y * W / 3 - 7 / (T - X / Y) - W ^ T`

4. Which of the following are invalid variables in Microsoft BASIC? Why?

   a. `A`
   b. `SALE!`
   c. `INT`
   d. `P.1#`
   e. `39`
   f. `PRINT`
   g. `7F`
   h. `FOR$`
   i. `Q$`
   j. `Q9%`

5. Consider the valid programs below. What is displayed if each program is executed?

   a.
   ```
   100 ' Exercise 3.5a
   110 A = 2.5
   120 B = 4 * A / 2 * A + 5
   130 PRINT B
   140 B = 4 * A / (2 * A + 5)
   150 PRINT B
   160 A = -A
   170 PRINT A
   180 A = -A
   190 PRINT A
   200 END
   ```

   b. Assume SEED is assigned the value 1.
   ```
   100 ' Exercise 3.5b
   110 INPUT "Enter seed number ===> ", SEED
   120 SEED = SEED * (SEED + 1)
   130 PRINT SEED
   140 SEED = SEED * (SEED + 1)
   150 PRINT SEED
   160 SEED = SEED * (SEED + 1)
   170 PRINT SEED
   180 SEED = SEED * (SEED + 1)
   190 PRINT SEED
   200 END
   ```

6. Write a valid LET statement for each of the following algebraic statements.

   a. $q = (d + e)^{1/3}$
   b. $d = (A^2)^{3.2}$
   c. $b = \dfrac{20}{6 - S}$
   d. $Y = a_1 x + a_2 x^2 + a_3 x^3 + a_4 x^4$
   e. $h = X + \dfrac{X}{X - Y}$
   f. $S = 19.2 X^3$
   g. $V = 100 - (2/3)^{100 - B}$
   h. $t = \sqrt{76{,}234/(2.37 + D)}$
   i. $V = 0.12340005 M - \left[\dfrac{(0.123458)^3}{M - N} \right]$
   j. $Q = \dfrac{(F - M1000)^{2B}}{4M} - \dfrac{1}{E}$

7. If necessary, insert parentheses so that each numeric expression results in the value indicated.

   a. 8 / 2 + 2 + 12 --> 14
   b. 8 ^ 2 - 1 --> 8
   c. 3 / 2 + 0.5 + 3 ^ 1 --> 5
   d. 12 MOD 5 \ 2 + 1 ^ 2 + 1 * 2 * 3 / 4 - 3 / 2 --> 0
   e. 12 - 2 - 3 - 1 - 4 --> 10
   f. 7 * 3 + 4 ^ 2 - 3 / 13 --> 22
   g. 3 * 2 - 3 * 4 * 2 + 3 --> -60
   h. 3 * 6 - 3 + 2 + 6 * 4 - 4 / 2 ^ 1 --> 33

8. Which of the following are invalid LET statements?

   a. 100 X = 9 / B(A + C)
   b. 200 X + 5 = Y
   c. -40 X = 17
   d. 750 P = 4 * 3 -+6
   e. 260 FOR = 4
   f. 290 X = -X * (((1 + R) ^ 2 - N) ^ 2 + (2 + X)
   g. 300 GET Q = R ^ S ^ Q ^ T
   h. 400 P = +4
   i. 500 G = 4(-2 + A)
   j. 600 X = X + 1

9. Calculate the numerical value for each of the following validly formed LET statements if $A = 2$ and $B = 3$.

   a. 100 D = (A ^ 6 / A * B) - (8 * B / 4)
      110 D = D + 1

   b. 100 E1 = A * B
      110 E1 = A ^ (6 / E1)
      120 E2 = B * 8
      130 E3 = 4 + 1
      140 E2 = E2 / E3
      150 A = E1 - E2

10. Repeat Exercise 9 for the case where the value of A is 1 and the value of B is 2.

3.7 BASIC PROGRAMMING PROBLEMS

1. Computing the Six-Month Dow-Jones Average

Purpose: To become familiar with entering data items in response to an INPUT statement; declaring integer, single-precision, and double-precision variables; and calculating an average.

Problem: Construct a program to input the end-of-month Dow-Jones closings for the last six months; compute the average in various precision modes from these six numbers; and print the average.

>   **Version A:** Perform all inputs, computations, and outputs in single-precision mode.
>   **Version B:** Perform all inputs, computations, and outputs in double-precision mode.
>   **Version C:** Perform all inputs, computations, and outputs in integer mode.

Input Data: Use the following sample data: 2259.45, 2133.45, 2209.53, 2199.98, 2211.91, 2231.41

Output Results: The following results are displayed.

>   **For Version A (Single Precision):**
>
>   ```
>   Last six-month closings: 2259.45, 2133.45, 2209.53, 2199.98, 2211.91, 2231.41
>   The six-month Dow-Jones average is 2207.622
>   ```
>
>   **For Version B (Double Precision):**
>
>   ```
>   Last six-month closings: 2259.45, 2133.45, 2209.53, 2199.98, 2211.91, 2231.41
>   The six-month Dow-Jones average is 2207.621666666667
>   ```

For Version C (Integer Precision):

```
Last six-month closings: 2259.45, 2133.45, 2209.53, 2199.98, 2211.91, 2231.41
The six-month Dow-Jones average is 2208
```

2. Maturity Value of an Investment Converted Quarterly

Purpose: To become familiar with the concepts associated with arithmetic operations; with parentheses in expressions; and with the use of INPUT, LET, and PRINT statements.

Problem: Write a program to determine the maturity value of an investment of P dollars for N years at I percent converted quarterly. Use the following formula:

$$S = P\left(1 + \frac{I}{M}\right)^{NM}$$

where S = maturity value
 P = investment
 I = nominal rate of interest
 N = time of years
 M = number of conversions per year

Input Data: Use the following sample data in response to the appropriate INPUT statements.

Investment:	$10,500
Interest:	11.5%
Time:	4 years 6 months
Conversions:	4

(**Hint:** The program must include a statement to change the rate from percent form to decimal form. See Program 3.5 on page 56 or PRG3–5 on the Student Diskette.)

Output Results: The following results are displayed.

```
Please enter the:
        Investment ============> 10500
        Nominal rate in % ====> 11.5
        Time in years ========> 4.5
        No. of Conversions ===> 4
Maturity value ==============> $ 17489.05
```

3. Payroll Problem II: Federal Withholding Tax Computations

Purpose: To become familiar with executing a program for several sets of data.

Problem: Modify Payroll Problem I in Chapter 2 on page 44 (BASIC Programming Problem 3) to accept by means of INPUT statements an employee number, number of dependents, hourly rate of pay, and hours worked during a biweekly pay period. Use the following formulas to compute the gross pay, federal withholding tax, and net pay:

1. Gross pay = hours worked × hourly rate of pay
2. Federal withholding tax = 0.2 × (gross pay − dependents × 38.46)
3. Net pay = gross pay − federal withholding tax

Execute the program for each employee described on the next page under the Input Data for this problem. Have the program clear the screen before accepting any data.

Input Data: Use the following sample data.

Employee Number	Number of Dependents	Hourly Rate of Pay	Hours Worked
123	2	$12.50	80
124	1	8.00	100
125	1	13.00	80
126	2	4.50	20

Output Results: The following results are displayed for employee number 123.

```
Employee number ============> 123
Number of dependents =======> 2
Hourly rate of pay =========> 12.50
Hours worked ===============> 80

Gross pay ==================> 1000
Federal withholding tax ===> 184.616
Net pay ====================> 815.3841
```

LOOPING AND INPUT/OUTPUT PROCESSING

■ 4.1 INTRODUCTION

The programs discussed in the previous chapters are classified as **straight-line programs**. Up to this point, therefore, we have not utilized the complete power of the PC; essentially, we have used it as a high-speed calculator. However, the power of a PC is derived both from its speed and its ability to do repetitive tasks. In regard to the second of these two capabilities, one of the purposes of this chapter is to introduce you to the WHILE and WEND statements. These two statements allow you to instruct the PC to loop and repeat a task in a program.

The programs developed in Chapters 2 and 3 also processed only small amounts of data. In this chapter we will present a technique for integrating data into a program through the use of the READ and DATA statements. The READ and DATA statements are usually preferred over the INPUT statement when a program has to process large amounts of data that are part of the program itself.

The third topic to be discussed in this chapter is the generation of tabular reports. To write programs that can produce meaningful information in a form that is easy to read and understand, you need to know more about the PRINT statement. You will also learn about the PRINT USING and LOCATE statements, which give you even more control over the output than the PRINT statement does.

Upon successful completion of this chapter, you will be able to write programs that can process data that is part of the program itself, and you will be able to generate more readable reports. Furthermore, you will be able to write programs that can repeat the same task over and over.

PROGRAMMING CASE STUDY 5: Determining the Sale Price

Program 4.1, on page 69, computes the discount amount and sale price for each of a series of products. The discount amount is determined from the following formula:

$$\text{Discount Amount} = \frac{\text{Discount Rate}}{100} \times \text{Original Price}$$

The sale price is determined from the formula:

Sale Price = Original Price − Discount Amount

The product data includes the product number, the original price, and the discount rate, as shown below:

	Product Number	Original Price	Discount Rate in Percent
	112841A	$115.00	14
	213981B	100.00	17
	332121A	98.00	13
	586192X	88.00	12
Trailer	714121Y	43.00	8
Record →	EOF	0	0

The flowchart that corresponds to Program 4.1 is given is Figure 4.1.

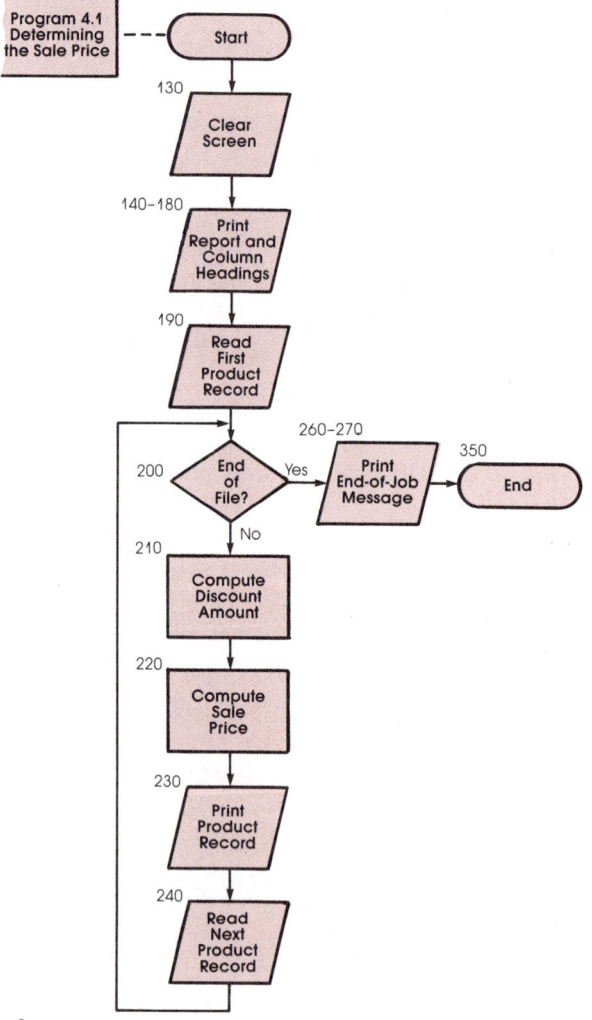

FIGURE 4.1 *Flowchart for Program 4.1.*

PROGRAM 4.1

```
100 ' Program 4.1
110 ' Determining the Sale Price
120 ' *************************
130 CLS: KEY OFF   ' Clear Screen
140 PRINT TAB(21); "Determine the Sale Price"
150 PRINT
160 PRINT "Product", "Original", "Discount", "Discount", "Sale"
170 PRINT "Number", "Price", "Rate in %", "Amount", "Price"
180 PRINT
190 READ PRODUCT$, ORIGINAL.PRICE, RATE
200 WHILE PRODUCT$ <> "EOF"
210    DISCOUNT = RATE / 100 * ORIGINAL.PRICE
220    SALE.PRICE = ORIGINAL.PRICE - DISCOUNT
230    PRINT PRODUCT$, ORIGINAL.PRICE, RATE, DISCOUNT, SALE.PRICE
240    READ PRODUCT$, ORIGINAL.PRICE, RATE
250 WEND
260 PRINT
270 PRINT "End of Report"
280 ' ******Data Follows*******
290 DATA 112841A, 115, 14
300 DATA 213981B, 100, 17
310 DATA 332121A,  98, 13
320 DATA 586192X,  88, 12
330 DATA 714121Y,  43,  8
340 DATA EOF,       0,  0   : ' This is the Trailer Record
350 END

RUN
```

```
                  Determine the Sale Price

Product       Original      Discount      Discount      Sale
Number        Price         Rate in %     Amount        Price

112841A       115           14            16.1          98.9
213981B       100           17            17            83
332121A        98           13            12.74         85.26
586192X        88           12            10.56         77.44
714121Y        43            8             3.44         39.56

End of Report
```

In Program 4.1, the PRINT statement in line 140 includes the TAB function, which specifies that the report heading is to begin exactly in column 21. The two PRINT statements in lines 160 and 170 and the one in line 230 contain a **comma separator** after each string constant or variable, instead of the semicolon separator used in previous programs. The use of the comma separator in PRINT statements causes the PC to produce output that is automatically positioned in a tabular format. These concepts are described in detail in Section 4.4.

Lines 190 and 240 contain READ statements that instruct the PC to assign values to PRODUCT$, ORIGINAL.PRICE, and RATE from the sequence of data created from DATA statements that begin at line 290. Note that this data is part of Program 4.1 itself. The rules regarding the READ and DATA statements are presented in Section 4.3.

Following the first READ statement in line 190, lines 200 through 250 establish a **While loop**. In looping, a control statement, like the WEND statement in line 250, automatically returns control to the corresponding WHILE statement in line 200. The WHILE statement is the first of a series of statements that are executed repeatedly as long as PRODUCT$ does not equal the value EOF. When PRODUCT$ does equal the value EOF, the WHILE statement in line 200 transfers control to line 260. One execution of the While loop is called a **pass** or **iteration**. Note that the statements within the loop, lines 210 through 240, are indented by three spaces for the purpose of readability.

Program 4.1 contains two READ statements, located in lines 190 and 240. The first READ statement, in line 190, is executed only once and is referred to as a *primary read*. The other READ statement, in line 240, is executed in each pass through the While loop. Although many programming styles exist, the programming style of using two READ statements and a While loop will be employed often in this book.

■ 4.2 THE WHILE AND WEND STATEMENTS

By now, the potential of the WHILE and WEND statements should be apparent. In Program 4.1, after the first three values in line 290 are read by the READ statement in line 190, the WHILE statement in line 200 tests to see whether or not PRODUCT$ is equal to the value EOF. Since PRODUCT$ is equal to 112841A, execution continues with line 210 and the data describing the first product is processed. At the bottom of the While loop, line 240 reads the next three data values. These newly read values for PRODUCT$, ORIGINAL.PRICE, and RATE replace the three original values in the main storage unit. The PC then executes the WEND statement in line 250. The WEND statement automatically returns control to its corresponding WHILE statement in line 200.

As a result, the PC again tests to see whether it has read the trailer record represented by line 340. Since the READ statement only assigned the second set of data items the previous time it was executed, another pass on the While loop is made. The PC continues this looping operation until all the values in the DATA statements have been read by the READ statement in line 240 and all the computations and output have been completed.

The general forms for the WHILE and WEND statements are shown in Tables 4.1 and 4.2.

As illustrated in the flowchart in Figure 4.1, the WHILE statement is represented in a flowchart by the diamond-shaped symbol. The long flowline that exits the I/O symbol at the bottom of the flowchart and enters just above the diamond-shaped symbol represents the branch called for by the WEND statement.

TABLE 4.1 The WHILE Statement

General Form:	WHILE condition
Purpose:	*Causes the statements between* WHILE *and* WEND *to be executed repeatedly while the condition is true. When the condition is false, control transfers to the line that follows the corresponding* WEND *statement.*
Keyword Entry:	*Hold down the Alt key and press the W key on your keyboard.*
Examples:	100 WHILE COUNT = 0 200 WHILE EMP.NAME$ <> "EOF" 300 WHILE SIDE1 + SIDE2 < 5 400 WHILE EMP.NUMBER$ > "000000" 500 WHILE DISCOUNT >= 500 600 WHILE AMOUNT <= 125.25

TABLE 4.2 The WEND Statement

General Form:	WEND
Purpose:	Identifies the end of a While loop. Automatically transfers control to the corresponding WHILE statement.
Examples:	500 WEND
	700 WEND

With regard to the placement of the WHILE and WEND statements in a program, the WHILE statement *must* have a lower line number than the corresponding WEND statement.

Testing for the End of File

Lines 290 through 330 in Program 4.1 contain data for only five products. The sixth product in line 340 is the **trailer record**. It represents the end of file and is used to determine the point at which all the valid data has been processed. To incorporate an end-of-file test, a variable must be selected and a trailer record added to the data. In Program 4.1, the authors selected the product number as the test for end of file and the data value EOF. Since it guards against reading past end of file, the trailer record is also called the **sentinel record**. The value EOF is called the **sentinel value** and is clearly distinguishable from all the rest of the data assigned to PRODUCT$. This sentinel value is the same as the string constant that is found in line 200.

After the READ statement in line 240 assigns PRODUCT$ the value EOF, the WEND statement returns control to the WHILE statement. Since PRODUCT$ is equal to the value EOF, the WHILE statement causes the PC to branch forward to line 260, which follows the corresponding WEND statement. Line 270 then displays the message End of Report and line 350 causes the PC to terminate execution of the program. Lines 260 through 270 are also referred to as an **end-of-file routine**.

Three other points about establishing a test for end of file in a While loop are worthy of note:

1. It is important that the trailer record contain enough values for all the variables in the READ statement. In Program 4.1, if we added only the sentinel value EOF to line 340, there would not be enough data to fulfill the requirements of the three variables in the READ statement. We arbitrarily assigned zero values to each.

2. The While loop requires the use of two READ statements. The first READ statement (line 190) reads the first product record before the PC enters the While loop. The second READ statement, found at the bottom of the While loop (line 240), causes the PC to read the next data record. This READ statement reads the remaining data records, one at a time, until there are no more data records left. Note that if the first record contains the product EOF, the WHILE statement will immediately transfer control to the statement below the corresponding WEND statement.

3. Program 4.1 can process any number of products simply by placing each one in a DATA statement prior to the trailer record.

Conditions

In line 200 of Program 4.1, the WHILE statement contains the **condition**

```
PRODUCT$ <> "EOF"
```

The condition is made up of two expressions and a **relational operator**. The condition specifies a relationship between expressions that is either true or false. If the condition is true, execution continues with the line that follows the WHILE statement. If the condition is false, control is transferred to the line that follows the corresponding WEND statement.

The PC makes a comparison between the two operators on the basis of the relational operator. Table 4.3 lists the six valid relational operators in MS BASIC.

TABLE 4.3 Relational Operators Used in Conditions

RELATIONS	MATH SYMBOL	BASIC SYMBOL	EXAMPLES
Equal To	=	=	200 WHILE CODE$ = "1"
Less Than	<	<	300 WHILE GROSS < 1000
Greater Than	>	>	400 WHILE RATE > 0.05
Less Than Or Equal To	≤	<= or =<	500 WHILE TAX <= 250
Greater Than Or Equal To	≥	>= or =>	600 WHILE COUNT >= 10
Not Equal To	≠	<> or ><	700 WHILE NAME$ <> "End"

There are several important points to watch for in the application of conditions. For example, it is invalid to compare a numeric expression to a string expression. The following is invalid:

```
500 WHILE DOLLARS$ > 100      ' Invalid
```

Furthermore, the condition should ensure termination of the loop. If a logical error like

```
240 WHILE 3 > 1
     .
     .
     .
300 WEND
```

— *This condition is always true.*

is not detected, a never-ending loop develops. The endless program execution cannot be stopped except by manual intervention, such as holding down the Control key and pressing the Break key on your PC keyboard.

■ 4.3 THE READ, DATA, AND RESTORE STATEMENTS

In Section 4.1, the READ and DATA statements were briefly introduced. This section will illustrate the rules of the READ, DATA, and RESTORE statements and will give further examples of their use, as well as explain their limitations.

The DATA Statement

The DATA statement provides for the creation of a sequence of data items for use by the READ statement. The general form of the DATA statement and some examples are given in Table 4.4.

TABLE 4.4 The DATA Statement

General Form:	DATA data item, . . ., data item where each **data item** is either a numeric constant or a string constant.
Purpose:	*Provides for the creation of a sequence of data items for use by the* READ *statement.*
Examples (*with* READ *statements*):	

	`110 DATA 2, -3.14, 0.025, -95`
	`120 READ A, B, C, D2`
	`-----------------------------------------`
	`130 DATA 0.24E33, 0, -2.5D-12, 1.23, 2.46, 5`
	`140 READ E, F, G(J), X#, Y, Z%`
	`-----------------------------------------`
	`150 DATA 15, , ",", YES, "2 + 7 = ", NO, 2.2, ""`
	`160 READ H, A$, B$(3), C$, D$, E$, I, F$`

Note:	*In line 160 of the last example, A$ and F$ are both assigned the null character.*

The DATA statement consists of the keyword DATA, followed by a list of data items that are separated by mandatory commas. The data items may be numeric or string and are formulated according to the following rules:

> **DATA Rule 1:** Numeric data items that are placed in a DATA statement must be formulated as numeric constants.

> **DATA Rule 2:** String data items that are placed in a DATA statement may be formulated with or without surrounding quotation marks, provided the string contains no trailing or leading blanks or embedded commas or colons. A string that contains a trailing or leading blank or an embedded comma or colon must be surrounded with quotation marks.

> **DATA Rule 3:** The apostrophe (') may not be used in a DATA statement to signify a comment. A comment may be placed at the end of a DATA statement by preceding the keyword REM or apostrophe (') with a colon (:).

Data items from all DATA statements in a program are collected in main storage into a single **data-sequence holding area**. The order in which the data items appear in the DATA statements determines their order in the single data sequence (see Figure 4.2 on the next page). In other words, the ordering of the data items is based on two considerations: the ascending line numbers of the DATA statements, and the order from left to right of the data items within each DATA statement.

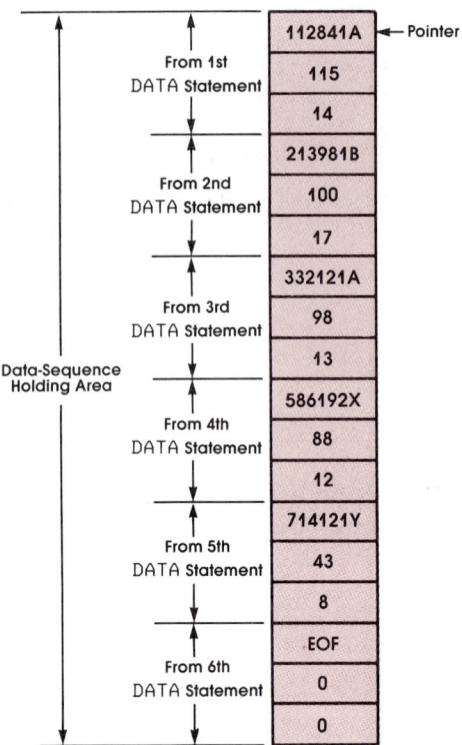

FIGURE 4.2 *The order of data items as represented in main storage from the sequence of DATA statements in Program 4.1, lines 290 to 340.*

The number of data items that can be represented in a DATA statement depends not only on the type of problem but also on the programming style that is adopted by the programmer. Some programmers prefer to write one DATA statement for each data item, like this:

```
110 DATA 310386024
120 DATA JOE NIKOLE
130 DATA -3.85
140 DATA -1E-15
150 READ SOC.SEC$, EMP.NAME$, AMOUNT, STANDARD
```

Others prefer to write as many data items in a DATA statement as there are variables in the READ statement that refers to that DATA statement. For example, the previous DATA and READ statements can be rewritten in this way:

```
140 DATA 310386024, JOE NIKOLE, -3.85, -1E-15
150 READ SOC.SEC$, EMP.NAME$, AMOUNT, STANDARD
```

The DATA statement, like the REM statement, is a nonexecutable statement; that is, if the execution of a program reaches a line that contains a DATA statement, it proceeds to the next line with no other effect. The convention used in this book is to place all DATA statements at the end of programs as shown in Programs 4.1 and 4.2.

The READ Statement

The READ statement provides for the assignment of values to variables from a sequence of data items created from DATA statements. The general form of the READ statement is given in Table 4.5. The READ statement consists of the keyword READ, followed by a list of variables that are separated by mandatory commas. The variables may be numeric or string variables.

TABLE 4.5 The READ Statement

General Form:	READ *variable*, . . ., *variable* where each **variable** is either a numeric variable or a string variable.
Purpose:	*Provides for the assignment of values to variables from a sequence of data items created from DATA statements.*
Examples *(with DATA statements):*	See Table 4.4.

The READ statement causes the variables in its list to be assigned specific values, in order, from the data sequence that is formed by all of the DATA statements. In order to visualize the relationship between the READ statement and its associated DATA statement, think of a **pointer** that is associated with the data-sequence holding area, as shown in Figure 4.2. When a program is first executed, this pointer points to the first data item in the data sequence. Each time a READ statement is executed, the variables in the list are assigned specific values from the data sequence, beginning with the data item indicated by the pointer, and the pointer is advanced one value per variable, in a downward fashion, to point beyond the data used.

Program 4.2 illustrates the data-sequence holding area and pointer for a program that contains multiple READ and DATA statements. The pointer *initially* points to the location of 565.33 in the holding area. When line 150 is executed, the value of 565.33 is assigned to the variable MON.SAL; the pointer is advanced to the location of the next value, 356.45, which is assigned to the variable TUES.SAL; and the pointer is advanced to the location of the next value, 479.56. When line 160 is executed, the variable WED.SAL is assigned the value of 478.56, THUR.SAL the value of 756.23, and FRI.SAL the value of 342.23.

As this assignment occurs, the pointer advances one value per variable to point to a location beyond the data used, which is recognized by the PC as the end of the data-sequence holding area.

PROGRAM 4.2

```
100 ' Program 4.2
110 ' Determining the Average Daily Sales
120 ' with Multiple READ and
130 ' Multiple DATA Statements
140 ' ***********************************
150 READ MON.SAL, TUES.SAL
160 READ WED.SAL, THUR.SAL, FRI.SAL
170 AVERAGE = (MON.SAL + TUES.SAL + WED.SAL + THUR.SAL + FRI.SAL) / 5
180 PRINT MON.SAL, TUES.SAL
190 PRINT WED.SAL, THUR.SAL, FRI.SAL
200 PRINT "The average is"; AVERAGE
210 ' ********** Data Follows **********
220 DATA 565.33, 356.45, 478.56
230 DATA 756.23, 342.23
240 END
```

(continued)

```
RUN

 565.33          356.45
 478.56          756.23         342.23
The average is 499.76
```

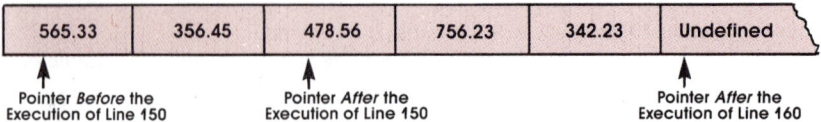

Pointer *Before* the Execution of Line 150
Pointer *After* the Execution of Line 150
Pointer *After* the Execution of Line 160

In Program 4.2, the PC is unable to calculate AVERAGE correctly until it has the value of MON.SAL, TUES.SAL, WED.SAL, THUR.SAL, and FRI.SAL. The READ statement should occur somewhere *before* the LET statement in the program. This example can be generalized to give the following:

> ***READ Rule 1:*** Every variable that appears in the program whose value is directly obtained by a READ should be listed in a READ statement before it is used elsewhere in the program.

While the placement of the DATA statements in a program is immaterial, the placement of the READ statement is important. Furthermore, more than one DATA statement may be used to satisfy one READ statement, and more than one READ statement may be satisfied from one DATA statement.

> ***READ Rule 2:*** A program that contains a READ statement must also have at least one DATA statement.

If the number of data items to be assigned to the variables of a READ statement is insufficient, a diagnostic message appears, as shown in Program 4.3. However, excessive data items are ignored, as shown in Program 4.4.

PROGRAM 4.3

```
100 ' Program 4.3
110 ' Insufficient Data Items
120 ' in a DATA Statement
130 ' **********************
140 READ A, B, C, D
150 PRINT A, B, C, D
160 ' **** Data Follows *****
170 DATA 1, 2, 3
180 END

RUN

Out of DATA in 140
```

PROGRAM 4.4

```
100 ' Program 4.4
110 ' Excessive Data Items
120 ' in a DATA Statement
130 ' ********************
140 READ A, B, C
150 PRINT A, B, C
160 ' *** Data Follows ***
170 DATA 1, 2, 3, 4, 5
180 END

RUN

 1              2              3
```

Finally, the type of data item in the data sequence must correspond to the type of variable to which it is to be assigned. If they do not agree, then the error message `Syntax error` displays.

> **READ Rule 3:** Numeric variables in READ statements require numeric constants as data items in DATA statements, and string variables require quoted strings or unquoted strings as data.

The RESTORE Statement

Usually data items from a DATA statement are processed by a READ statement only once. If you want the PC to read all or some of the same data items later in the program, you must use the RESTORE statement to reset the pointer in the data-sequence holding area.

The RESTORE statement allows the data in a given program to be reread as often as is necessary by other READ statements. The general form of the RESTORE statement, with examples, is given in Table 4.6. The RESTORE statement consists of the keyword RESTORE, optionally followed by a line number. If no line number follows the keyword RESTORE, then the next READ statement accesses the first data item in the first DATA statement. If a line number follows RESTORE, the next READ statement accesses the first data item in the DATA statement that is referenced by the specified line number.

TABLE 4.6 The RESTORE Statement

General Form:	RESTORE line number where **line number** is optional.
Purpose:	Allows the data items in DATA statements to be reread. If no line number follows the keyword RESTORE, then the next READ statement accesses the first data item in the first DATA statement. If a line number follows RESTORE, the next READ statement accesses the first data item in the DATA statement referenced by the specified line number.
Examples:	500 RESTORE 600 RESTORE 450

The RESTORE statement causes the pointer to be moved back to a specified area in the data-sequence holding area. This is done so that the next READ statement executed will read the data from that point in the sequence once again.

The `RESTORE` statement is generally used when it is necessary to perform several types of computations on the same data items.

4.4 THE PRINT STATEMENT

The execution of the `PRINT` statement generates a string of characters for transmission to an external source like a monitor. The `PRINT` statement is commonly used to display the results from computations, to display headings and labeled information, and to plot points on a graph. In addition, the `PRINT` statement allows you to control the spacing and the format of the desired output.

The general form of the `PRINT` statement is given with examples in Table 4.7. The `PRINT` statement consists of the keyword `PRINT` followed by an optional list of **print items**, separated by mandatory commas or semicolons or spaces. The print items may be numeric or string constants, variables, expressions, or null items. In addition, the print items may include useful function references, like the `MID$` function described in Chapter 3.

Print Zones and Print Positions

The most common use of the `PRINT` statement is to output values that have been defined earlier in a program. Every sample program presented thus far has included a `PRINT` statement. Listing items separated by commas within a `PRINT` statement, like the following:

```
230     PRINT PRODUCT$, ORIGINAL.PRICE, RATE, DISCOUNT, SALE.PRICE
```

causes the values of PRODUCT$, ORIGINAL.PRICE, RATE, DISCOUNT, and SALE.PRICE to be displayed on a *single* line. MS BASIC displays the five values in **print zones**.

There are five print zones per line. Each print zone has 14 positions, for a total of 70 positions per line. The **print positions** are numbered consecutively from the left, starting with position 1, as shown in Figure 4.3.

TABLE 4.7 The PRINT Statement

General Form:	PRINT *item pm item pm . . . pm item* where each **item** is a constant, variable, expression, function reference, or null and each **pm** is a comma, semicolon, or space.
Purpose:	*Provides for the generation of labeled and unlabeled output or of output in a consistent tabular format from the program to the screen.*
Keyword Entry:	*Press the question mark (?) key or simultaneously the Alt and P keys on your keyboard.*

Examples:	`100 PRINT`
	`150 PRINT EMP.NAME$`
	`200 ? AMOUNT, CODE$`
	`250 PRINT COUNT; DISCOUNT, EMPLOYEE$; NUMBER`
	`300 PRINT SEX.CODE$; " "; TIME; " "; MARITAL.STATUS$`
	`350 PRINT HEIGHT, WEIGHT; RACE$; JOB(8);`
	`400 PRINT "X = "; X, "Y = "; Y`
	`450 PRINT "The answer is $"; H,`
	`500 PRINT TAB(10); (X + Y) / 4, INT(A)`
	`550 ? ,, AREA, 10, 20`
	`600 PRINT "The interest rate is"; I; "%"`
	`650 PRINT X; " "; 2 * X; " "; 3 * X; " "; 4 * X`
	`700 PRINT A B C`

Note:	*One or more spaces between print items has the same effect as the semicolon.*

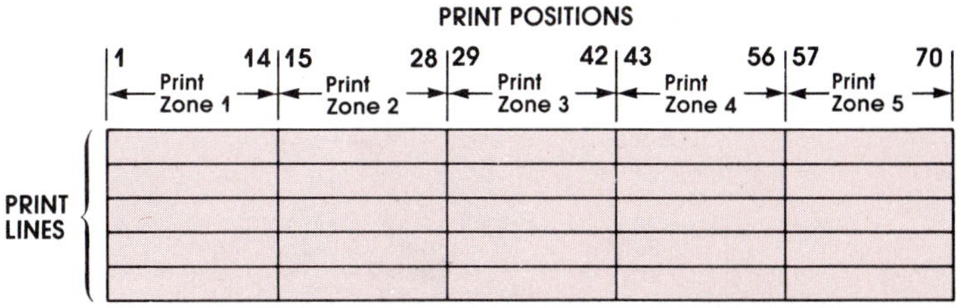

FIGURE 4.3 *In the 80-column display mode, the print line is divided into five print zones.*

Representation of Numeric Output

Numeric constants, variables, expressions, and function references are evaluated to produce a string of characters consisting of a sign, the decimal representation of the number, and a trailing space. The sign is a leading space if the number is positive and is a leading minus sign if the number is negative.

Representation of String Output

String constants, variables, expressions, and functions are displayed without any leading or trailing spaces. For example, when the following line,

```
200 PRINT "BAS"; "IC"
```

is executed, the PC displays BASIC in print positions 1 through 5. Unlike the way it treats numeric output, the PC does not insert a trailing space following the string constants in the output.

Use of the Comma Separator

Punctuation marks like the comma, semicolon, and space are placed between print items. In this section, the role of the comma, or **comma separator**, is examined. As illustrated in Figure 4.4, on the next page, the comma separator allows you to produce output that is automatically positioned in tabular format. Each PRINT statement executed displays one line of information, *unless* one of the following two conditions is true:

1. the number of print zones required by the PRINT statement exceeds five (see Figure 4.4, line 270), or
2. the PRINT statement ends with a punctuation mark, like a comma or semicolon (see Figure 4.4, lines 190, 200, and 280).

PROGRAM 4.5

```
100 ' Program 4.5
110 ' Use of the Comma Separator
120 ' *****************************
130 X = -10
140 Y = -2.3
150 Z = -369.246
160 A = -1.234
170 B = -999.999
180 C = -4.56789E-12

190 PRINT "Column 1", "Column 2",
200 PRINT "Column 3", "Column 4",
210 PRINT "Column 5"
220 PRINT X
230 ? X, Y
240 PRINT X,  , Y, Z, -3 * 2
250 PRINT X,  , ,  , Y
260 PRINT X, Y, Z, A, B
270 PRINT X, Y, Z, A, B, X, Y

280 PRINT X, Y
290 PRINT Z, A
300 PRINT C, C, C, C, C
310 PRINT  , "End", "of", "Report"
320 END
```

RUN

1 Print Zone 1	14|15 Print Zone 2	28|29 Print Zone 3	42|43 Print Zone 4	56|57 Print Zone 5 70|
Column 1	Column 2	Column 3	Column 4	Column 5
-10				
-10	-2.3			
-10		-2.3	-369.246	-6
-10				-2.3
-10	-2.3	-369.246	-1.234	-999.999
-10	-2.3	-369.246	-1.234	-999.999
-10	-2.3			
-10	-2.3	-369.246	-1.234	
-4.56789E-12	-4.56789E-12	-4.56789E-12	-4.56789E-12	-4.56789E-12
	End	of	Report	

FIGURE 4.4 *The effect of commas with numeric and string expressions in PRINT statements.*

Use of the Semicolon and Space Separators

In this section, we will examine the identical role of the **semicolon** and **space separators** in the PRINT statement. Whereas the comma separator allows you to tab to the next print zone, the semicolon or space does not. Instead, the semicolon or space in a PRINT statement causes the display of the value immediately to the right of the preceding one. The semicolon or space enables you to display more than five items per line. Use of the semicolon or space is referred to as displaying values in a **packed** or **compressed format**. (Compare the compressed format in Figure 4.5 with the tabular format in Figure 4.4.)

Program 4.6, as illustrated in Figure 4.5, shows the use of the semicolon and space separators. Whereas each numeric value displayed is preceded by a leading sign and a trailing space, string values are displayed with no spaces separating them (see line 180).

In line 190, all five print items are separated by the semicolon, and the values are all displayed within the first 20 print positions. Line 200 shows the use of the space separator in place of the semicolon separator. In line 210, the keyword PRINT is followed by a comma separator, which causes the value of A, the first print item, to be displayed beginning in print zone 2.

If a PRINT statement ends with a semicolon, as in line 240, the first item in the next PRINT statement (line 250) displays on the same line in compressed form.

Creating Blank Lines

If a PRINT statement contains a null list, then a blank line results. For example,

```
200 PRINT
```

contains no print items and results in the display of a blank line. Line 240 in Program 4.6 displays two blank lines before the values of A, B, and C are displayed.

PROGRAM 4.6

```
100 ' Program 4.6
110 ' Use of the Semicolon and Space Separators
120 ' *****************************************
130 A = -10
140 B = -20
150 C = -30
160 D = -40
170 E = -50
180 PRINT "The"; "value"; "of"; "A"; "is"; A
190 PRINT A; B; C; D; E
200 PRINT "The " "value " "of " "A " "is " A
210 PRINT , A; " "; B; " "; C; " "; D; " "; E
220 PRINT "The value of A is "; A
240 PRINT : PRINT : PRINT A, B; C;
250 PRINT D, E
260 END
RUN
```

1 14	15 28	29 42
Print Zone 1	Print Zone 2	Print Zone 3
ThevalueofAis-10		
-10 -20 -30 -40 -50		
The value of A is -10		
	-10 -20 -30	-40 -50
The value of A is -10		
-10	-20 -30 -40	-50

FIGURE 4.5 *The effect of semicolons and spaces with numeric and string expressions in PRINT statements.*

Use of the TAB Function

Thus far, PRINT statements have contained the comma, semicolon, and space as separators among numeric and string expressions in order to display the values of these expressions in a readable format with correct spacing. Compact and exact spacing of output results can also be achieved by the use of the TAB and SPC functions.

The TAB function is used in the PRINT statement to specify the exact print positions for the various output results on a given line. Use of the TAB function as follows,

```
140  PRINT TAB(21); "Determine the Sale Price"
```

causes the string to be displayed beginning in exactly print position 21. The form of the TAB function is

    TAB(numeric expression)

where the numeric expression, the argument, may be a numeric constant, a variable, an expression, or a function reference. The value of the argument determines the position on the line of the next character to be displayed. The TAB function may be used in a PRINT, LPRINT, and PRINT #n statement. The LPRINT statement is discussed shortly, and the PRINT #n statement is discussed in Chapter 6. The rules on the next page summarize the use of the TAB function.

> **TAB Rule 1:** The argument must evaluate to an integer between 1 and 255.

> **TAB Rule 2:** A decimal argument is rounded to the nearest integer.

> **TAB Rule 3:** Backspacing is not permitted with the TAB function.

Displaying Spaces — The SPC Function

The SPC function is similar to the space bar on a typewriter. It may be used in a PRINT statement to insert spaces between print items. The form of the SPC function is

    SPC(numeric expression)

Consider the following:

    240 PRINT "Column 1"; SPC(3); "Column 2"; SPC(5); "Column 3"

The SPC(3) causes the insertion of three spaces between Column 1 and Column 2. The SPC(5) inserts five spaces between Column 2 and Column 3. The spaces inserted between displayed results are often called **filler**. The SPC function may be used any number of times in the same statement. However, it may be used only in a PRINT, LPRINT, or PRINT #n statement.

Calculations within the PRINT Statement

MS BASIC permits calculations to be made within the PRINT statement. For instance, the sum, difference, product, quotient, modulo, and exponentiation of two numbers, like 4 and 2, may be made in the conventional way by using LET statements or by using the PRINT statement, as in Program 4.7.

PROGRAM 4.7

```
100 ' Program 4.7
110 ' Calculations Within a PRINT Statement
120 ' ************************************
130 PRINT 4 + 2; SPC(4); 4 - 2; SPC(4); 4 * 2
140 PRINT 4 / 2; SPC(4); 4 \ 2; SPC(4); 4 MOD 2; SPC(4); 4 ^ 2
150 END

RUN
 6     2     8
 2     2     0      16
```

Using the Immediate Mode

As described earlier in Chapter 2, MS BASIC has an immediate mode of operation, which permits your PC to act as a powerful desk calculator. When you are in the immediate mode, BASIC statements like the PRINT statement can be executed individually, without being incorporated into a program. You merely enter the keyword PRINT, followed by any numeric expression. As soon as you press the Enter key, the PC immediately computes and displays the value of the expression. Line numbers are not used in the immediate mode.

The following example of calculating a complex expression uses the immediate mode of MS BASIC:

```
PRINT (2 - 3 * 4 / 5) ^ 2 + 5 / (4 * 3 - 2 ^ 3)
 1.41
```

The value displayed is 1.41. This expression was previously computed in Section 3.5, on page 58, to illustrate the effect of parentheses and the rules of precedence with respect to the evaluation of numeric expressions.

MS BASIC also allows you to use the immediate mode to **debug** programs. For example, if a fatal error occurs, the PRINT statement can be used to display the values of variables used in the program that terminates. It is important that no other commands be issued between the time the program stops and the time the PRINT statement is entered. See Appendix A for a discussion of debugging a program that has errors.

The LPRINT Statement

While the PRINT statement displays results on the screen, the LPRINT statement prints the results on the printer. Everything that has been presented with respect to the PRINT statement in this chapter applies to the LPRINT statement as well. Obviously, to use this statement you must have a printer attached to your PC.

■ 4.5 THE PRINT USING STATEMENT FOR FORMATTED OUTPUT

The PRINT USING statement is far more useful than the PRINT statement in exactly controlling the format of a program's output. In section 4.4, you were introduced to the comma, the semicolon, the space and the TAB and SPC functions for print-control purposes. For most applications, these print-control methods will suffice. However, when you are confronted with generating readable reports for non-technical personnel, more control over the format of the output is essential. The PRINT USING statement gives you the desired capabilities to display information according to a predefined format instead of the free format provided by the PRINT statement. Through the use of the PRINT USING statement, you can do the following:

1. Specify the exact image of a line of output.
2. Force decimal-point alignment when displaying numeric tables in columnar format.
3. Control the number of digits that are displayed for a numeric result.
4. Specify that commas be inserted into a number. (Starting from the units position of a number and progressing toward the left, digits are separated into groups of three by a comma.)
5. Specify that the sign status of the number be displayed along with the number (+ or blank if positive, – if negative).
6. Assign a fixed or floating dollar sign ($) to the number displayed.
7. Force a numeric result to be displayed in exponential notation.
8. **Left-** or **right-justify** string values in a formatted field (i.e., align the leftmost or rightmost characters, respectively).
9. Specify that only the first character of a string be displayed.
10. Round a value automatically to a specified number of decimal digits.

The general form of the PRINT USING statement is given with examples in Table 4.8.

TABLE 4.8 The PRINT USING Statement

General Form:	PRINT USING *string expression; list* where ***string expression*** (sometimes called the ***descriptor field*** or ***format field***) is either a string constant or a string variable, and ***list*** is a list of items to be displayed in the format specified by the descriptor field.
Purpose:	*Provides for controlling exactly the format of a program's output to the screen by specifying an image to which that output must conform.*
Keyword Entry:	*Hold down the Alt key and press the P key for the keyword* PRINT. *Hold down the Alt key and press the U key for the keyword* USING.
Examples:	150 PRINT USING "The answer is #,###.##"; COST 200 PRINT USING "## divided by # is #.#"; NUM, DEN, QUOT 300 FORMAT.1$ = "Total cost =======> $$,###.##-" 310 PRINT USING FORMAT.1$; TOTAL 350 FORMAT.2$ = "**,###.##" 360 PRINT USING FORMAT.2$; CHECK; 900 PRINT USING "\ \"; CUST.NAME$ 950 PRINT USING "!, !, \ \"; FIRST$, MIDDLE$, LAST$ 975 PRINT USING "Example _##"; NUMBER 999 PRINT USING "#.##^^^^"; DIS.1, DIS.2, DIS.3, DIS.4

Declaring the Format of the Output

To control the format of the displayed values, the PRINT USING statement is employed in conjunction with a string expression that specifies exactly the image to which the output must conform. The string expression is placed immediately after the words PRINT USING in the form of a string constant or string variable. If the format is described by a string variable, then the string variable must be assigned the format by a LET statement before the PRINT USING statement is executed in the program. Consider the following two methods:

Method 1:

```
100 ' Format Specified as a String in the PRINT USING Statement
110 PRINT USING "Employee ### has earned $$,###.##"; CLOCK, SALARY
```

Method 2:

```
100 ' Format Specified Earlier and Assigned to a String Variable
110 FORMAT$ = "Employee ### has earned $$,###.##"
       .
       .
       .
170 PRINT USING FORMAT$; CLOCK, SALARY
```

In Method 1, the string following the keywords PRINT USING in line 110 instructs the PC to display the values of CLOCK and SALARY, using the format found in that statement. In Method 2, the string constant has been replaced by the string variable FORMAT$, which was assigned the desired format in line 110. If CLOCK is equal to 000105 and SALARY is equal to 4563.20, then the results displayed from the execution of line 110 in Method 1 or line 170 in Method 2 are as follows:

```
Employee 105 has earned $4,563.20
```

Format Symbols

Table 4.9 includes the format symbols that are available with MS BASIC. One or more consecutive format symbols appearing in a string expression is a **descriptor field**, or **format field**.

TABLE 4.9 Format Symbols

SYMBOL	FUNCTION	EXAMPLES
#	Grouped number signs define a numeric descriptor field and cause the display of a numeric value in integer form.	# ### ####
.	The period is used for decimal-point placement. A decimal point in a numeric descriptor field causes the display of a numeric value in fixed point form.	###. ###.## .###
,	The comma is used for automatic-comma placement. A comma in front of a decimal point in a numeric descriptor field causes the display of a numeric value with commas displayed to the left of the decimal point every three significant digits.	#,###,### ###,###.## ######,.##
^ ^ ^ ^	Four consecutive circumflexes to the right of a numeric descriptor field causes the display of a value in exponential notation (D or E format).	##^^^^ #.###^^^^ -##.###^^^^
+	A single plus sign to the left or right of a numeric descriptor field causes the display of a numeric value with a sign (plus or minus) immediately before or after the number.	+##,###.## ###+ #,###.##+
-	A single minus sign to the right of a numeric descriptor field causes the display of negative numbers with a trailing minus sign and positive numbers with a trailing space.	##.##- ###- ###,###.##-
$	A single leading dollar sign in a numeric descriptor field causes the display of a fixed dollar sign in that position, followed by a numeric value. (Note: The dollar sign may be substituted for any valid BASIC character listed in Table A.1 in Appendix A. Format symbols must be preceded by the underscore character.)	$### $##.## $#,###.##+
$ $	Two leading dollar signs in a numeric descriptor field cause the display of a single dollar sign immediately to the left of the first significant digit of a numeric value.	$$##.## $$###.##- $$,###.##
* *	Two leading asterisks in a numeric descriptor field cause the display of a numeric value with leading spaces, filled with asterisks, to the left of the numeric value.	**###.### **,###.## **.##

(continued)

(continued)		
**$	*Two leading asterisks followed by a single dollar sign in a numeric descriptor field combine the effects of the previous two symbols. These symbols (**$) cause the display of a numeric value with leading spaces filled with asterisks, followed by a floating dollar sign immediately to the left of the numeric value.*	**$######## **$#,###.##+
&	*The ampersand causes the display of a complete string value left-justified.*	&
!	*The exclamation point causes the display of the first character of a string value.*	!
_	*The underscore causes the display of the next character in the descriptor field as if the character were a string constant. Any of the format symbols in this table can be displayed as a string constant.*	_& _! _# #_# _$$##.##_#
\n spaces\	*Two backslashes separated by n spaces cause the display of a string of characters left-justified and equal in length to 2 plus the number of spaces (n).*	\\ \ \ \ \ \ \

The Number Sign Symbol

The number sign (#) is the format symbol that is used to define a numeric descriptor field. Grouped number signs indicate exactly how many positions are desired in a numeric result during output. A number sign reserves space for a digit or sign. For example, in a numeric result,

        #   indicates one position;
      ##   indicates two positions;
   ####   indicates four positions; and
####.##   indicates seven positions, one of which is the decimal point and two of which are to the right of the decimal point.

It is your responsibility to ensure that enough number signs are in the descriptor field to fit the output results into the prescribed format.

Consider the following example, where A = 10, B = −11, C = 12.75, and D = 4565:

```
100 ' Format Specified Earlier and Assigned to a String Variable
110 FORMAT$ = "   ####        ####      ##        ###"
    .
    .
    .
190 PRINT USING FORMAT$; A, B, C, D
```

The results that are displayed from the above sequence, where ƀ represents a blank character, are as follows:

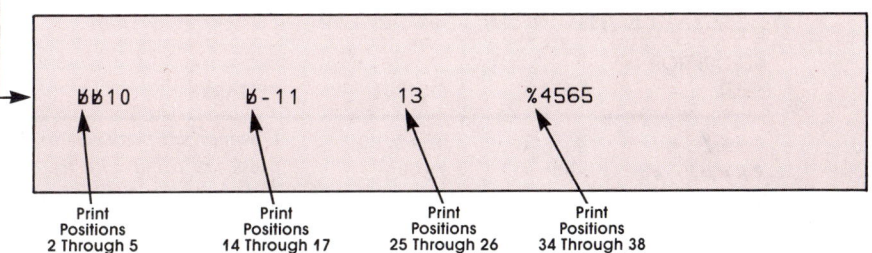

Table 4.10 summarizes the use of the number sign in the previous sample program.

TABLE 4.10 Use of the Number Sign (#) in a Descriptor Field

DESCRIPTOR FIELD	DATA	OUTPUT	REMARKS
####	10	ƀƀ10	Right-justify the digits in the field with leading spaces. Note the floating minus sign.
####	−11	ƀ−11	
##	12.75	13	The data is displayed rounded to an integer, since only integers are specified by the descriptor field.
###	4565	%4565	Since the data is too large for the specified descriptor field, the value is displayed but is preceded by a percent sign (%) to indicate that an insufficient number of positions were reserved for this descriptor field.

If the string expression referenced in a PRINT USING statement contains fewer descriptor fields than print items in the list, MS BASIC reuses the string expression. For example, when the following line is entered in the immediate mode,

```
    PRINT USING "##   "; -5, -7, -9
```

the PC displays

```
    -5    -7    -9
```

The Decimal Point (Period) Symbol

The period (.) in a numeric descriptor field places a decimal point in the output record at that character position in which it appears, and the format of the numeric result is aligned with the position of the decimal point. When number signs (#) precede the decimal point in a descriptor field, any leading zeros appearing in the data are replaced by spaces, except for a single leading zero immediately preceding the decimal point.

When number signs follow the decimal point, unused positions to the right of the decimal point are filled with trailing zeros. When the data contains more digits to the right of the decimal point than the descriptor field allows, the data is displayed rounded to the limits of the descriptor field.

Table 4.11 illustrates the use of the decimal point in various descriptor fields.

TABLE 4.11 Use of the Decimal Point (.) in a Descriptor Field

DESCRIPTOR FIELD	DATA	OUTPUT	REMARKS
####.##	217.5	ƀ217.50	Unspecified positions to the right of the decimal point are filled with trailing zeros.
#####.##	-40	ƀƀ-40.00	
#####.##	23.458	ƀƀƀ23.46	Data is rounded.
####.##	0.027	ƀƀƀ0.03	The last leading zero before the decimal point is not suppressed.

The Comma Symbol

A comma (,) to the left of the decimal point in a numeric descriptor field places a comma to the left of every third digit that is to the left of the decimal point. A comma specifies a digit position within the descriptor field. If there are fewer than four significant digits to the left of the decimal point, the PC displays a space in place of the comma symbol. Table 4.12 illustrates the use of the comma in various descriptor fields.

If the descriptor field that contains a comma has too few number signs, the comma is replaced by a digit.

TABLE 4.12 Use of the Comma (,) in a Descriptor Field

DESCRIPTOR FIELD	DATA	OUTPUT	REMARKS
#,###	4000	4,000	Comma displayed.
#,###,###	999999	ƀƀ999,999	Comma displayed.
#,###.##	-30.5	ƀƀ-30.50	Space displayed for comma when leading digits are blank.
########,.##	9876543.21	9,876,543.21	Comma in front of a decimal point in descriptor field.

Formatted Character String Output

Descriptor fields for string values are defined in terms of the ampersand (&), two backslashes (\\), the exclamation point (!), or the underscore (_), rather than the number sign (#). Table 4.9 summarizes these four symbols.

As a descriptor field, the ampersand represents a variable-length string field. The number of positions used to display the string is dependent on the internal size of the string. The ampersand indicates the beginning position in which the string is displayed, and expansion is to the right in the line.

The exact number of positions to use for displaying a string value can be specified by using two backslashes separated by zero or more spaces. The number of positions in the descriptor field, including the two backslashes, indicate how many positions are to be used to display the string value. The string value is aligned in the descriptor field left-justified. If the internal value of the string contains fewer characters than the descriptor field, the string value is filled with spaces on the right in the print line. If the internal value of the string contains more characters than the descriptor field, the string value is truncated on the right. Table 4.13 summarizes the use of the backslash, and Program 4.8 gives examples of its use.

TABLE 4.13 Use of the Backslash (\) in a Descriptor Field

DESCRIPTOR FIELD	NUMBER OF SPACES BETWEEN BACKSLASHES	DATA	OUTPUT	REMARKS
\ \	3	ABCDE	ABCDE	Size of descriptor field and string value the same.
\ \	1	ABCDE	ABC	The last two characters are truncated.
\\	0	ABCDE	AB	The last three characters are truncated.
\ \	6	ABCDE	ABCDEbbb	Three spaces are appended to the right of the string value in the print line.

PROGRAM 4.8

```
100 ' Program 4.8
110 ' Use of Two Backslashes in a Descriptor Field
120 ' *********************************************
130 CLS : KEY OFF   ' Clear Screen
140 PRINT      "Name      Address       City-State     Zip Code"
150 PRINT      "----      -------       ----------     --------"
160 FORMAT$ = "\      \ \       \ \         \ \          \       \"
170 READ CUST.NAME$, CUST.STREET$, CUST.CITY$, CUST.ZIP$
180 PRINT USING FORMAT$; CUST.NAME$, CUST.STREET$, CUST.CITY$, CUST.ZIP$
190 ' ************** Data Follows **************
200 DATA Jones J., 451 W 45th, "Munster, IN", 46321-0452
210 END

RUN

Name      Address       City-State     Zip Code
----      -------       ----------     --------
Jones J.  415 W 45th    Munster, IN    46321-0452
```

Study closely the method used in lines 140 through 160 in Program 4.8 to align the fields. The string constants in lines 140 and 150 are purposely started six positions to the right of the keyword PRINT so that the column headings align with the string constant in line 160. This technique will be used throughout this book.

The LPRINT USING Statement

Like the LPRINT statement, the LPRINT USING statement prints the results on the printer. Everything that has been presented with respect to the PRINT USING statement also applies to the LPRINT USING statement. This statement gives you the capacity to print results according to a predefined format on the printer.

PROGRAMMING CASE STUDY 6: Determining the Accounts Receivable Balance

This problem and its program solution incorporate much of the information discussed so far in this chapter, including the following useful techniques for formatting a report:

1. Align the detail lines with the column headings.
2. Force decimal-point alignment.
3. Control the number of digits displayed in a result.
4. Specify that commas and decimal points are to be appropriately displayed in numeric results.

Problem: Ron's Family Discount House would like its PC to generate a management report for the accounts receivable balance for a monthly billing period. The following formula is used to determine the balance:

End of Month Balance = Beginning of Month Balance −
Payments + Purchases − Credits +
Service Charge on Ending Unpaid Balance

The following formula is used to compute the service charge:

Service Charge = 19.5% Annually on the Unpaid Balance
or
= 0.01625 ∗ (Beginning of Month Balance −
Payments − Credits) per Month

The input data for each customer includes customer number, beginning-of-month balance, payments, purchases, and credits. The following accounts receivable data is to be processed:

Customer Number	Beginning Balance	Payments	Purchases	Credits
14376172	$1,112.32	$35.00	$56.00	$ 0.00
16210987	30.00	30.00	15.00	0.00
18928384	125.50	25.00	0.00	12.50
19019293	120.00	12.00	12.00	23.00
19192929	10.00	7.00	2.50	1.50
EOF	0	0	0	0

The program should generate a report that includes report and column headings and a line of information for each customer. Each line is to include the five values read for each customer, the service charge, and end-of-month balance as described on the **printer spacing chart** shown in Figure 4.6. Lines 1 through 4 of the printer spacing chart define the report and column headings. Line 6 defines the **detail line** that is displayed for each record processed: the row of Xs on line 6 describes an area for a string value, and the groups of 9s, with commas and decimal points, describe areas for numeric values. Finally, line 8 describes the end-of-job message.

```
1                        Accounts Receivable Balance
2
3 Customer  Begin                    Pur-                 Service   Ending
4 Number    Balance    Payment       chases    Credit     Charge    Balance
5
6 XXXXXXXX  9,999.99   9,999.99   9,999.99  9,999.99    999.99    9,999.99
7
8 End of Report
```

FIGURE 4.6 Output for Program 4.9, designed on a printer spacing chart.

Following are a list of the program tasks; a program solution; and a discussion of the program solution.

Program Tasks

The following program tasks correspond to Program 4.9.

1. Initialization

   a. Clear the screen.
   b. Display report and column headings described on the printer spacing chart in Figure 4.6.
   c. In a string expression, define the detail line described on the printer spacing chart in Figure 4.6.

2. Process File

   a. Read an accounts receivable record; use the following variable names:

      CUSTOMER$: Customer Number
      BEG.BAL: Beginning Balance
      PAYMENTS: Payments
      PURCHASES: Purchases
      CREDITS: Credits

   b. Use a WHILE statement to establish a loop. The condition within the WHILE statement should allow the loop to be executed as long as CUSTOMER$ does not equal the sentinel value EOF.

      (1) Compute the unpaid balance from this formula:
          UNPAID.BAL = BEG.BAL - PAYMENTS - CREDITS
      (2) Compute the service charge from this formula:
          SERV.CHARGE = 0.01625 * UNPAID.BAL

(3) Compute the end-of-month balance from this formula:
END.BAL = UNPAID.BAL + PURCHASES + SERV.CHARGE
(4) Employ the PRINT USING statement to display the seven values pertaining to the customer.
(5) Read the next accounts receivable record.

3. Wrap-up — display the message End of Report.

Program Solution   The following program corresponds to the preceding program tasks.

PROGRAM 4.9

```
100 ' Program 4.9
110 ' Determining the Accounts Receivable Balance
120 ' *********************************************
130 CLS : KEY OFF   ' Clear Screen
140 PRINT    "           Accounts Receivable Balance"
150 PRINT
160 PRINT    "Customer  Begin                Pur-              Service  Ending"
170 PRINT    "Number    Balance  Payment    chases   Credit    Charge   Balance"
180 FORMAT$="\        \  #,###.##  #,###.##  #,###.##  #,###.##    ###.##  #,###.##"
190 PRINT
200 READ CUSTOMER$, BEG.BAL, PAYMENTS, PURCHASES, CREDITS
210 WHILE CUSTOMER$ <> "EOF"
220    UNPAID.BAL  = BEG.BAL - PAYMENTS - CREDITS
230    SERV.CHARGE = .01625 * UNPAID.BAL
240    END.BAL     = UNPAID.BAL + PURCHASES + SERV.CHARGE
250    PRINT USING FORMAT$; CUSTOMER$, BEG.BAL, PAYMENTS, PURCHASES,
                   CREDITS, SERV.CHARGE, END.BAL
260    READ CUSTOMER$, BEG.BAL, PAYMENTS, PURCHASES, CREDITS
270 WEND
280 PRINT
290 PRINT "End of Report"
300 ' ************** Data Follows **************
310 DATA 14376172, 1112.32, 35,   56,    0
320 DATA 16210987,      30, 30,   15,    0
330 DATA 18928384,   125.5, 25,    0, 12.5
340 DATA 19019293,     120, 12,   12,   23
350 DATA 19192929,      10,  7,  2.5,  1.5
360 DATA EOF,            0,  0,    0,    0
370 END
RUN
                Accounts Receivable Balance

Customer  Begin                Pur-              Service  Ending
Number    Balance  Payment    chases   Credit    Charge   Balance

14376172 1,112.32    35.00     56.00     0.00    17.51  1,150.83
16210987    30.00    30.00     15.00     0.00     0.00     15.00
18928384   125.50    25.00      0.00    12.50     1.43     89.43
19019293   120.00    12.00     12.00    23.00     1.38     98.38
19192929    10.00     7.00      2.50     1.50     0.02      4.02

End of Report
```

Discussion of the Program Solution

When the RUN command is issued for Program 4.9, the PC clears the screen and then executes the PRINT statements (lines 140 through 170 and 190) that display the report and column headings. Line 180 assigns FORMAT$ the descriptor field for the detail line described on the printer chart in Figure 4.6. FORMAT$ is referenced later by the PRINT USING statement in line 250. Note that line 250 extends beyond 80 columns. When keying in a line that exceeds 80 characters, hold down the Control (Ctrl) key and press the Enter key to advance the cursor to the next physical line.

In line 200, the READ statement causes the PC to read the first record found in line 310. Since the first record is not the end of file, the WHILE statement in line 210 passes control to line 220 and customer 14376172 is processed.

After the second record is read, the WEND statement in line 270 instructs the PC to loop back to line 210 to test for end of file. The second record is processed and displayed before the PC reads the next record. This process continues until all of the accounts receivable records have been processed. When the trailer record is read, control passes to line 280. After the message End of Report is displayed, Program 4.9 is terminated by line 370.

The report shows that through the use of the PRINT USING statement in line 250, Program 4.9 displays all monetary values rounded to the nearest cent, with decimal points aligned and right-justified below the column headings. The customer number, which is defined as a string item, is displayed left-justified. The significance of taking the time to lay out the report on a printer spacing chart should be apparent in Programming Case Study 6. Once the printer spacing chart is complete, the format of the report can be copied directly into the program, as shown in lines 140 through 180.

With the output techniques discussed thus far in this chapter, you can now begin to dress up the output. Programmers often forget that most people who use the results of computer-generated reports are unfamiliar with computers and are confused by poorly formatted output. You now have the capacity in MS BASIC to produce high-quality reports that are meaningful and easy to read.

■ 4.6 THE LOCATE STATEMENT

The LOCATE statement may be used to position the cursor on the screen. It may also be used to change the shape of the cursor from a block to an underscore or vice versa. MS BASIC defines the screen as having 25 rows and 80 columns. The LOCATE statement can position the cursor precisely on any one of the two thousand print positions on the screen.

The general form of the LOCATE statement is shown in Table 4.14 on the next page. The values that follow the keyword LOCATE are called **parameters**.

TABLE 4.14 The LOCATE Statement

General Form:	LOCATE row, column, cursor where **row** represents the row and is a numeric expression between 1 and 25; **column** represents the column and is a numeric expression between 1 and 80; and **cursor** is a numeric expression equivalent to 0 or 1. Zero makes the cursor a block and 1 makes the cursor an underscore or vice versa.
Purpose:	Positions the cursor precisely on the screen. May also be used to change the shape of the cursor from a block to an underscore.
Keyword Entry:	Hold down the Alt key and press the L key.
Examples:	100 LOCATE 5, 10 200 LOCATE 1, 1 300 KEY OFF : LOCATE 25, 4 400 LOCATE 7 500 LOCATE , 50 600 LOCATE 4, 6, 0 700 LOCATE , , 1

In Table 4.14, line 100 moves the cursor to column 10 on line 5. It makes no difference whether the cursor is above or below line 5 or to the right or left of column 10; when line 100 is executed, the cursor is moved to the specified location.

Line 200 moves the cursor to the home position: leftmost column on line 1. The cursor is located at column 4 on line 25 following the execution of line 300 in Table 4.14. It is important that the KEY OFF statement be executed to clear line 25 before the LOCATE statement is executed.

One of the interesting characteristics of line 25 is that unlike the other 24 lines, it does not scroll. For this reason, line 25 is often used to display messages that are of a more permanent nature. Line 400 in Table 4.14 moves the cursor directly up or down to the same column on line 7. In line 500, the row is left blank, and in this case, the PC moves the cursor to column 50 of the current line. When the parameters row, column, or cursor in the LOCATE statement are left blank, the PC uses the current value.

Line 600 of Table 4.14 causes the PC to position the cursor in column 6 of line 4. Furthermore, the third parameter, zero, instructs the PC to make the cursor a block. With line 700, the cursor remains at the current position and is made an underscore.

4.7 TEST YOUR BASIC SKILLS (Even-numbered answers are in Appendix B.)

1. Consider the valid programs listed below. What is displayed if each program is executed?

   a.
   ```
   100 ' Exercise 4.1a
   110 ' MPG Comparison
   120 READ CAR.MODEL$, MILES, GALLONS
   130 WHILE CAR.MODEL$ <> "EOF"
   140     MPG = MILES / GALLONS
   150     PRINT "Car model ===> "; CAR.MODEL$
   160     PRINT "Miles ========>"; MILES
   170     PRINT "Gallons =====>"; GALLONS
   180     PRINT "Mpg =========>"; MPG
   190     PRINT
   200     READ CAR.MODEL$, MILES, GALLONS
   210 WEND
   220 PRINT "Job Finished"
   230 ' *** Data Follows ***
   240 DATA A,   1275, 41.7
   250 DATA B,    685, 23.2
   260 DATA C,   1650, 62.5
   270 DATA EOF, 0,    0
   280 END
   ```

   b.
   ```
   100 ' Exercise 4.1b
   110 READ X, Y
   120 WHILE X <> -1
   130     PRINT "Old value of X ="; X
   140     PRINT "Old value of Y ="; Y
   150     T = X
   160     X = Y
   170     Y = T
   180     PRINT "New value of X ="; X
   190     PRINT "New value of Y ="; Y
   200     PRINT
   210     READ X, Y
   220 WEND
   230 LOCATE 13, 7 : PRINT "Job Finished"
   240 ' *** Data Follows ***
   250 DATA 4, 6
   260 DATA 3, 7
   270 DATA -1, 0
   280 END
   ```

   c.
   ```
   100 ' Exercise 4.1c
   105 ' Nested While Loops
   110 CLS : KEY OFF   ' Clear Screen
   120 ROW = 0
   130 WHILE ROW < 10
   140     ROW = ROW + 1
   150     COLUMN = 0
   160     WHILE COLUMN < 40
   170         COLUMN = COLUMN + 1
   180         LOCATE ROW, COLUMN : PRINT "*"
   190     WEND
   200 WEND
   210 END
   ```

   d.
   ```
   100 ' Exercise 4.1d
   110 ' Displaying Hi!
   120 CLS : KEY OFF   ' Clear Screen
   130 ROW = 12
   140 COLUMN = 31
   150 CURSOR = 0
   160 WHILE ROW < 20
   170     COLUMN = COLUMN + 4
   180     LOCATE ROW , COLUMN, CURSOR : PRINT "Hi!"
   190     ROW = ROW + 1
   200 WEND
   210 END
   ```

2. Which of the following statements are true?

   a. Backspacing on the same line is permissible with the TAB function.
   b. It is invalid to have a DATA statement without a READ statement in a program.
   c. Every program must have a PRINT statement.
   d. It is invalid to have a WHILE statement with a higher line number than its corresponding WEND statement in a program.
   e. It is invalid to have more data items in a DATA statement than are required by a READ statement.
   f. The LOCATE statement is used to position the cursor vertically and horizontally on the screen.
   g. The RESTORE statement instructs the system to execute the program beginning at the lowest line number.
   h. It is valid to have two adjacent commas in a DATA statement.
   i. The LOCATE statement is used to clear a specific position on the screen.

3. Write a single PRINT statement to compute and display:

   a. $\sqrt{Y}$ b. $\sqrt[3]{Y}$ c. $\sqrt[4]{Y}$

4. Write a PRINT USING statement that includes the string constant for the purpose of displaying the message The amount is followed by the value of AMOUNT. Include a numeric descriptor field with the following characteristics:

   a. five digit positions, two to the right of the decimal point;
   b. a floating dollar sign;
   c. a sign status to the right of the number; and
   d. three or more check protection asterisks.

5. Determine whether the conditions below are true or false, given the following: CREDIT.UNION = 25, INS.DED = 20, and SALARY = 900

   a. CREDIT.UNION >= 25
   b. SALARY / INS.DED < CREDIT.UNION
   c. INS.DED = CREDIT.UNION - 5
   d. SALARY <> 800
   e. 875 + CREDIT.UNION <= SALARY
   f. INS.DED > 20

6. Write a sequence of statements that will clear the screen and display the value 6 in print position 6 of line 6.

7. Write a program that will generate the following graphic output. Use the LOCATE statement to position the upper-leftmost asterisk in column 33 of line 8.

   ```
   * * * * * * * * * * * *
   *  B  A  S  I  C  *
   B  L              N  B
   A     E     R        A
   S           A        S
   I     E     R        I
   C  L              N  C
   *  B  A  S  I  C  *
   * * * * * * * * * * * *
   ```

8. For each of the following descriptor fields and corresponding data, indicate what the computer displays. Use the letter ƀ to indicate the space character.

	Descriptor Field	Data	Result		Descriptor Field	Data	Result
a.	###	25		b.	#,###.##	38.4	
c.	$$,###.##-	-22.6		d.	$#,###.##-	425.89	
e.	**#,###.##	88.756		f.	#,###.#	637214	
g.	##.##-	3.975		h.	###.##	-123.8	
i.	##,###.###	12.6143		j.	##.##^^^^	265.75	
k.	!	ABCD		l.	&	ABCD	
m.	\\ (zero spaces)	ABCD		n.	\ \ (2 spaces)	ABCD	

4.8 BASIC PROGRAMMING PROBLEMS

1. Inflation Gauge

Purpose: To become familiar with gauging inflation and the use of the WHILE, WEND, READ, DATA, and PRINT statements.

Problem: Write a program to read today's current price, the previous price, and the number of weeks between price quotes. Compute the sample annual inflation rate and the expected price of the item one year from today's current price. For each item processed, display the item, current price, computed annual inflation rate, and expected price in one year. (**Hint:** Use Programming Case Study 5 on page 67 or PRG4-1 on the Student Diskette as a guide to solving this problem.)

Input Data: Prepare and use the following sample data.

Item	Current Price	Previous Price	Number of Weeks
1 doz. eggs	$0.93	$0.92	13
1 lb. butter	2.59	2.50	15
1 gal. milk	1.92	1.85	18
1 loaf bread	1.10	1.07	6

Output Results: The following results are displayed.

```
              Inflation Gauge Report
              Current      Inflation      Expected
Item          Price        Rate in %      Price in 1 Yr
----          -------      ---------      -------------

1 doz. eggs   .93          4.301071       .97
1 lb. butter  2.59         12.04632       2.902
1 gal. milk   1.92         10.5324        2.122222
1 loaf bread  1.1          23.63634       1.36

Job Finished
```

Alternative Formatted Output Results: Employ the PRINT USING statement to align the decimal points and display all numeric results to the nearest hundredth place, right-justified under their column headings.

2. Determining the Eventual Cash Value of an Annuity

Purpose: To become familiar with the LOCATE statement; INPUT statement; looping; the hierarchy of operations in a complex LET statement; and building a screen for data entry.

Problem: An annuity, or installment plan, is a series of payments made at equal intervals of time. Examples of annuities are pensions and premiums on life insurance. More often than not, the interest conversion period is unequal to the payment interval. The following formula determines the eventual cash value of an annuity of R dollars paid per year in P installments for N years at an interest rate of J percent converted M times a year.

$$S = R \left[\frac{\left(1 + \frac{J}{M}\right)^{MN} - 1}{P\left[\left(1 + \frac{J}{M}\right)^{M/P} - 1\right]} \right]$$

where S = eventual cash value
  R = payment per year
  P = number of installments per year
  N = duration of the annuity in years
  J = nominal interest rate
  M = conversions per year

Write a program to determine the eventual cash value of an annuity. After processing the first annuity, loop back to process the next annuity. Use the INPUT statement to accept data items.

Prior to processing the first annuity, clear the screen and use the LOCATE statement to center the instructions and messages. After the results for the first set of data are displayed, request that the operator enter Y to process another set of data and N to terminate the program. If Y is entered, request the operator to enter the next set of data.

Input Data: Prepare and use the following sample data.

Description	Set 1	Set 2	Set 3
Payment per year	$2000	$3000	$4000
Installments per year	12	12	12
Time in years	20	20	20
Interest rate in %	13	14	15
Conversions per year	2	4	6

Output Results: The results shown below are displayed for set 1. Begin the screen title on line 5, column 25. After that, skip a line between each line displayed. Skip three lines prior to the last line. When the operator requests that the program terminate, clear the screen and display an appropriate message. The Eventual Cash Value for sets 2 and 3 are $318,119.80 and $492,591.70.

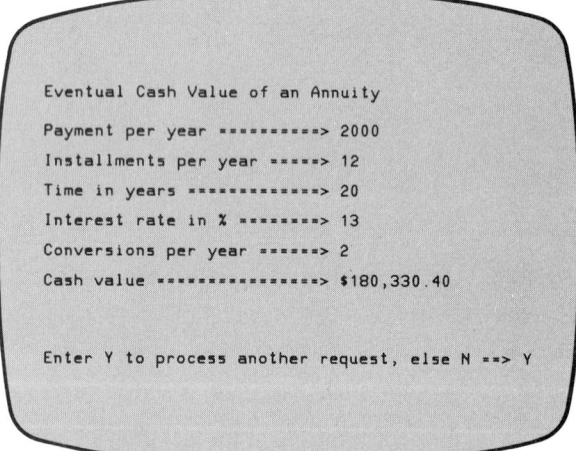

3. Payroll Problem III: Biweekly Payroll Report

Purpose: To become familiar with looping and the use of the PRINT USING, READ, and DATA statements.

Problem: Modify Payroll Problem II in Chapter 3 on page 64 (BASIC Programming Problem 3) to generate a report with column headings and a line of information for each employee. Each line is to include employee number, gross pay, federal withholding tax, and net pay. (**Hint:** Use Programming Case Study 6 on page 90 or PRG4-9 on the Student Diskette as a guide to solving this problem.)

Input Data: Use the sample data found in Payroll Problem II. Add a trailer record. Select your own sentinel value.

Output Results: The following results are displayed.

```
                Biweekly Payroll Report
    Employee
     Number     Gross Pay      Fed. Tax     Net Pay
    --------    ----------     --------     -------
       123       1,000.00       184.62      815.38
       124         800.00       152.31      647.69
       125       1,040.00       200.31      839.69
       126          90.00         2.62       87.38

    End of Payroll Report
```

STRUCTURED PROGRAMMING AND DECISION MAKING

5.1 STRUCTURED PROGRAMMING

It is appropriate at this time to introduce some important concepts related to **structured programming**.

Structured programming is a methodology according to which all program logic can be constructed from a combination of the following three basic logic structures:

1. **Sequence.** The most fundamental of the logic structures, it provides for two or more actions to be executed in the order in which they appear as shown in Figure 5.1 on the next page.
2. **If-Then-Else** or **Selection.** Provides a choice between two alternative actions.
3. **Do-While** or **Repetition.** Provides for the repeated execution of a loop.

The following are two common extensions to these logic structures:

4. **Do-Until** or **Repeat-Until.** An extension of the Do-While logic structure.
5. **Case.** An extension of the If-Then-Else logic structure, in which the choice includes more than two alternatives.

So far in this book, the Sequence and Do-While logic structures have been used, even though they have not been identified by their formal names.

The use of structured programming offers definite advantages. Computer professionals have found that when it is applied correctly in the construction of programs, structured programming yields the following benefits:

1. Programs are more readable.
2. Less time is spent debugging, testing, and modifying the program.
3. The programmer's productivity is increased.
4. The quality, reliability, and efficiency of the program are improved.

Clearly, there are important payoffs in the use of structured programming.

Logic Structures

In the previous chapter, the programs performed precisely the same computation for every set of data items that was processed. In some applications, it is not always desirable to process each set of data items in exactly the same way. For example, in a program that computes gross pay, some employees may be eligible for overtime (the number of hours they worked in a given week is greater than 40), while others may not. Therefore, in a payroll computation, a decision must be made concerning which of two gross pay formulas to use.

The sequential flow of control used in previous programs and shown in Figure 5.1 is not sufficient to solve problems that involve **decision making.** To develop an algorithm that requires deviation from sequential control, we need another logic structure. This new structure, called If-Then-Else, is shown in Figure 5.2.

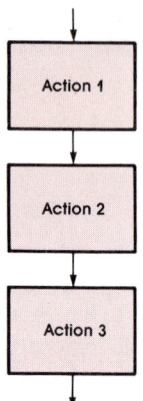

FIGURE 5.1 *Sequence structure.*

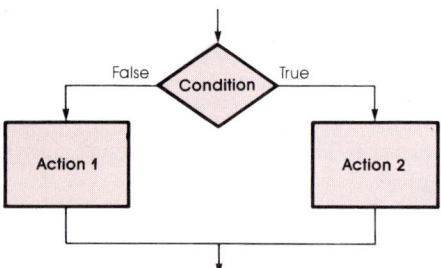

FIGURE 5.2 *If-Then-Else structure.*

The flowchart representation of a decision is the diamond-shaped symbol. One flowline will always be shown entering the decision symbol, and two lines will always be shown leaving the decision symbol. A condition that must be either true or false is written within the decision symbol. Such a condition asks, for example, whether two variables are equal or whether an expression is within a certain range. If the condition is true, one path is taken; if not, the other path is taken.

To instruct the PC to select actions on the basis of the values of variables, as illustrated in Figure 5.2, MS BASIC includes the IF statement. This chapter presents a number of examples to illustrate how IF statements are used to implement If-Then-Else structures.

An extension of the If-Then-Else structure, in which selection of one of many alternatives is based on a condition is referred to as the Case structure. The Case structure is illustrated in Figure 5.3.

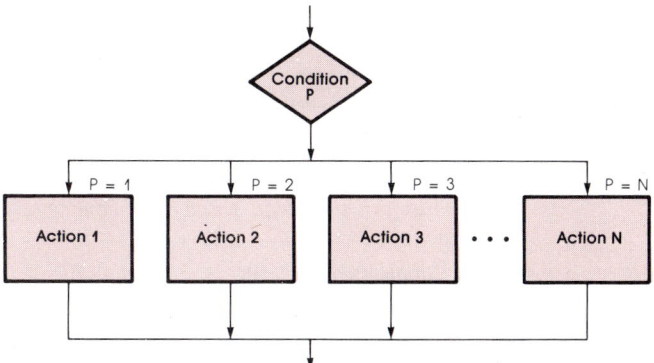

FIGURE 5.3 *Case structure.*

As we saw in Chapter 4 with looping, it is necessary to include within the repeatedly executed process a decision to terminate the loop after a sufficient number of repetitions has occurred. Most computer professionals agree that the decision to terminate a loop should be located at the very top or very bottom of the loop. A loop that has the termination decision at the top is called a Do-While structure (see Figure 5.4). All of the loops presented in Chapter 4 were of this variety.

A loop that has the termination decision at the bottom is called a Do-Until structure (see Figure 5.5). The major difference between the two structures lies in the minimum number of times the loop may be executed. With the Do-While structure, where the decision is at the top of the loop, it is possible that the body of the loop may be executed zero times. With the Do-Until structure, the body of the loop is always executed at least once.

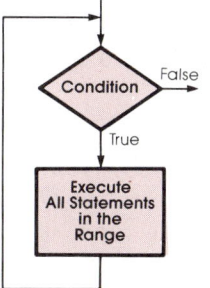 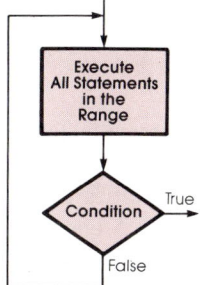

FIGURE 5.4 *Do-While structure.*   **FIGURE 5.5** *Do-Until structure.*

5.2 THE IF STATEMENT

The IF statement is commonly regarded as one of the most powerful statements in MS BASIC. The major function of this statement is to perform selection. The IF statement is used to let a program choose between two alternative paths, as illustrated earlier in Figure 5.2. The general form of the IF statement is given in Table 5.1.

TABLE 5.1 The IF Statement

General Form:	IF *condition* THEN *clause* ELSE *clause* or IF *condition* THEN *clause* where **condition** *is a relationship that is either true or false, and* **clause** *is a statement, series of statements (separated by colons), or a line number.*
Purpose:	If the condition is true, the PC executes the statement or series of statements following the keyword THEN. If the condition is false, the PC executes the statement or series of statements following the keyword ELSE. If the clause executed is a line number, then the PC continues execution at that line number.
Keyword Entry:	For the keyword THEN, hold down the Alt key and press the T key on your keyboard. For the keyword ELSE, hold down the Alt key and press the E key on your keyboard.

Examples:	100 IF TAX >= 0
	    THEN SWITCH = 0
	
	200 IF GEN$ = "M"
	    THEN PRINT "MR." + NAME$: MAL = MAL + 1
	    ELSE PRINT "MS." + NAME$: FEM = FEM + 1
	
	300 IF EDUC$ <> "13" THEN 310 ELSE 350
	
	400 IF 2 * A * B <= 0
	    THEN PRINT A : READ A : ACNT = ACNT + 1
	    ELSE PRINT B : READ B : BCNT = BCNT + 1
	
	500 IF MAR.STAT = "M"
	    THEN MARRIED = MARRIED + 1
	    ELSE SINGLE = SINGLE + 1
	
	600 IF J > 5
	    THEN IF J < 10 THEN PRINT E
	                     ELSE PRINT G

As indicated in Table 5.1, the IF statement is used to specify a decision. The condition appears between the keywords IF and THEN. As with the WHILE statement in Chapter 4, the condition specifies a relationship between expressions which is either true or false. The relationship is a comparison between one numeric expression and another or between one string expression and another. In determining whether or not a condition is true, the PC first determines the single value of each expression in the condition and then evaluates them both with respect to the relational operator. Table 4.3 in Chapter 4, on page 72, lists the six relational operators that are used to indicate the type of comparison.

If the condition in the IF statement is true, the PC acts upon the THEN clause. If the condition is false, the PC acts upon the ELSE clause. If the selected clause is a line number, then control transfers to the stated line number. If the selected clause is a statement or a series of statements, then following execution of the clause, control passes to the next numbered line following the IF statement. If a selected THEN or ELSE clause is null, control transfers to the next numbered line following the IF statement.

The following partial flowchart illustrates the use of the If-Then-Else structure to resolve a gross pay computation in which employees are paid a fixed rate per hour for hours worked less than or equal to 40 and time and a half for hours worked greater than 40.

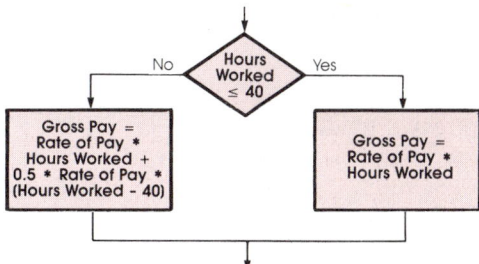

The gross pay computation illustrated in the partial flowchart may be written as follows:

```
3400 ' ********** Compute Gross Pay - Style 1 **********
3410 IF HOURS <= 40
        THEN GROSS = HOURS * RATE
        ELSE GROSS = HOURS * RATE + 0.5 * RATE * (HOURS - 40)
3420
```

Line 3410 selects a LET statement to compute the gross pay (GROSS). If hours worked (HOURS) is less than or equal to 40, the gross pay is computed by means of the LET statement following THEN. If the condition, HOURS <= 40, is false, then the gross pay is computed by means of the LET statement following ELSE. In either case, control passes to line 3420.

Note the programming style that was used to write the Gross Pay Computation Module. The THEN and ELSE clauses are on separate lines without line numbers. Furthermore, for the sake of readability, the keywords THEN and ELSE are indented three spaces in relation to the keyword IF. This programming style will be used to write most of the IF statements in this book.

The gross pay computation could also have been written with the following programming style:

```
3400 ' ********** Compute Gross Pay - Style 2 **********
3410 IF HOURS<=40 THEN GROSS=HOURS*RATE ELSE GROSS=HOURS*RATE+0.5*RATE*(HOURS-40)
3420
```

This style of cramming the characters is valid but somewhat awkward to read and is not recommended in practice.

Logical Versus Physical Lines

MS BASIC differentiates between a **logical line** and a **physical line**. A logical line is composed of a line number that is followed by one or more physical lines that have no line numbers. Each logical line may contain up to 255 characters (254 plus the Enter key). Each physical line, except for the last, contains 80 characters. The last physical line contains the exact number of characters displayed and the Enter key. Therefore, a logical line may have a maximum of four physical lines. The last physical line may have up to 15 characters.

To terminate a physical line with fewer than 80 characters displayed, hold down the Ctrl key and press the Enter key. This combination of keys causes the PC to fill the remainder of the physical line with blank characters and to move the cursor to column 1 of the next physical line. You end the last physical line by pressing the Enter key. Consider again the first version of line 3410, presented on the previous page:

Hold down the Ctrl key and press the Enter key.

```
One      ⎧ 3410 IF HOURS <= 40
Logical  ⎨      THEN GROSS = HOURS * RATE
Line     ⎩      ELSE GROSS = HOURS * RATE + 0.5 * RATE * (HOURS-40)
```

Press the Enter key.

Comparing Numeric Expressions

If the condition in an IF statement includes two numeric expressions, the comparison is based on the algebraic values of the two expressions. That is, the PC evaluates not only the magnitude of each resultant expression but also its sign.

Comparing String Expressions

If the condition in an IF statement includes two string expressions, the PC evaluates the two strings from left to right, one character at a time. Two string expressions are considered equal if they are of the same length and contain an identical sequence of characters. As soon as one character in an expression is different from the corresponding character in the other expression, the comparison stops and the PC decides which expression has a lower value, generally on the basis of numerical and alphabetical order. In other words, the PC evaluates two string expressions the same way you would.

■ 5.3 ACCUMULATORS

Most programs require **accumulators**, which are used to develop totals. Accumulators are numeric variables that are initialized to a value of zero prior to the start of a loop, then incremented within the loop, and then manipulated or displayed following the loop. Although the PC automatically initializes numeric variables to zero, good programming practice demands that this be done in the program. There are two types of accumulators: counters and running totals. Both types are discussed in the sections that follow.

Counters

A **counter** is an accumulator that is used to count the number of times some action or event is performed. For example, appropriately placed within a loop, the statement

```
240 EMP.COUNT = EMP.COUNT + 1
```

causes the counter EMP.COUNT to increment by 1 each time a record is read. Associated with a counter is a statement placed prior to the loop which initializes the counter to some value. In most cases the counter is initialized to zero.

Running Totals

A **running total** is an accumulator that is used to sum the different values that a variable is assigned during the execution of a program. For example, appropriately placed within a loop, the statement

```
250 CMPY.SALARY = CMPY.SALARY + EMP.SALARY
```

causes CMPY.SALARY (company monthly salary) to increase by the value of EMP.SALARY. The accumulator CMPY.SALARY is called a running total. If a program is processing an employee file and the variable EMP.SALARY is assigned the employee's monthly salary each time a record is read, then variable CMPY.SALARY in line 250 below represents the running total of the monthly salaries paid to all the employees in the file. As with a counter, a running total must be initialized to some predetermined value.

Consider the following partial program, which includes both counters and a running total. Assume that each time a record is read, EMP.SALARY is assigned the employee's monthly salary.

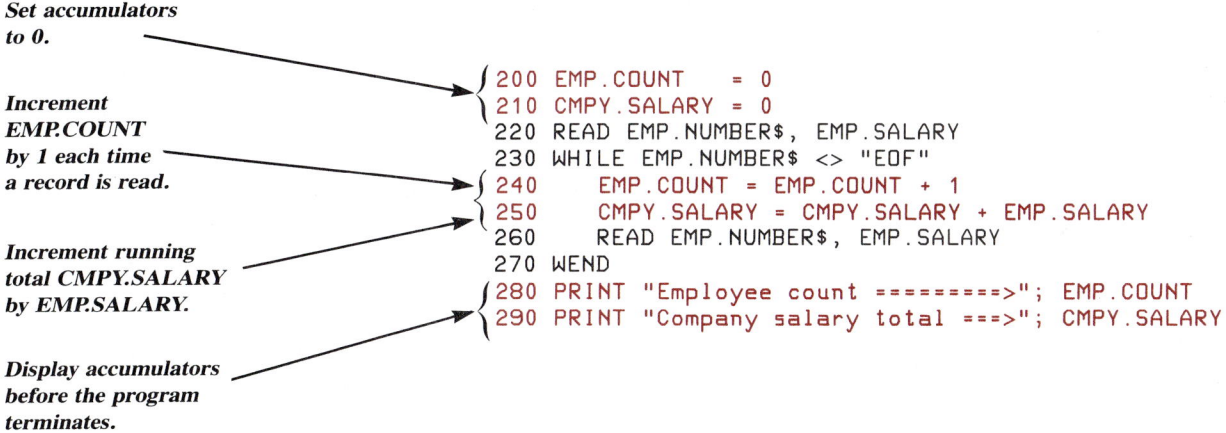

Set accumulators to 0.

Increment EMP.COUNT by 1 each time a record is read.

Increment running total CMPY.SALARY by EMP.SALARY.

Display accumulators before the program terminates.

```
200 EMP.COUNT    = 0
210 CMPY.SALARY = 0
220 READ EMP.NUMBER$, EMP.SALARY
230 WHILE EMP.NUMBER$ <> "EOF"
240    EMP.COUNT = EMP.COUNT + 1
250    CMPY.SALARY = CMPY.SALARY + EMP.SALARY
260    READ EMP.NUMBER$, EMP.SALARY
270 WEND
280 PRINT "Employee count =========>"; EMP.COUNT
290 PRINT "Company salary total ===>"; CMPY.SALARY
```

Lines 200 and 210 initialize the accumulators to zero. Each time a record is read, line 240 increments EMP.COUNT by 1. Line 250 increments the company monthly salary running total (CMPY.SALARY) by the employee's monthly salary (EMP.SALARY). Finally, lines 280 and 290 display the values of EMP.COUNT and CMPY.SALARY.

PROGRAMMING CASE STUDY 7A: Weekly Payroll and Summary Report

The following example incorporates both a counter and a running total, as well as some of the concepts discussed earlier in this section.

Problem: A payroll application requires that the employee number, the hours worked, the rate of pay, and the gross pay be displayed for each of the following employees.

Employee Number	Hours Worked	Rate of Pay
124	40	$5.60
126	56	5.90
128	38	4.60
129	48.5	6.10

Also, the total gross pay, the total number of employees, and the average gross pay for this payroll are to be displayed. The required report is described on the printer spacing chart shown in Figure 5.6.

```
              Weekly Payroll Report

Employee No.    Hours      Rate     Gross Pay

    XXX         999.9      99.99    99,999.99

Total Gross Pay ========> $$,999.99
Number of Employees ====>     999
Average Gross Pay ======> $$,999.99

End of Payroll Report
```

FIGURE 5.6 *Output for Case Study 7A designed on a printer spacing chart.*

The gross pay is determined by multiplying the hours worked by the hourly rate of pay. Overtime (hours in excess of 40) is paid at 1.5 times the hourly rate.

Following are the program tasks in outline form; a flowchart; a program solution; and a discussion of the program solution.

Program Tasks Consider the following program tasks.

1. Initialization

   a. Initialize a counter (EMP.COUNT) and running total (TOTAL.GROSS) to zero. Use the counter to determine the total number of employees processed. Use the running total to determine the total gross pay.
   b. Clear the screen.
   c. Initialize the report format — assign the heading lines, the detail line, and the total lines, described in Figure 5.6, to string variables.
   d. Display the report and column headings.

2. Process File

   a. Read an employee record. Use the following variable names for the employee record:

   EMP.NUMBER$: Employee Number
   EMP.HOURS: Employee Hours
   EMP.RATE: Employee Hourly Rate

   b. Use a WHILE statement to establish a loop for processing the employee records until EMP.NUMBER$ equals the value EOF. If end of file, transfer control to line 340. If not end of file, do the following:
      (1) Determine the gross pay and increment accumulators.
         (a) Increment the counter EMP.COUNT by 1.
         (b) Compute the employee overtime (EMP.OVERTIME).
         (c) Determine the gross pay (EMP.GROSS). If EMP.OVERTIME is less than or equal to zero, use this formula:

   EMP.GROSS = EMP.HOURS * EMP.RATE

   If EMP.OVERTIME is greater than zero, use this formula:

   EMP.GROSS = EMP.HOURS * EMP.RATE + 0.5 * EMP.RATE * EMP.OVERTIME

         (d) Increment the running total (TOTAL.GROSS) by the employee gross pay (EMP.GROSS).
      (2) Display an employee record.
      (3) Read the next employee record.

3. Wrap-up

   a. Compute the average employee gross pay (AVERAGE.GROSS).
   b. Display the accumulators (TOTAL.GROSS and EMP.COUNT) and average employee gross pay (AVERAGE.GROSS).
   c. Display an end-of-job message.

110 CHAPTER FIVE — STRUCTURED PROGRAMMING AND DECISION MAKING

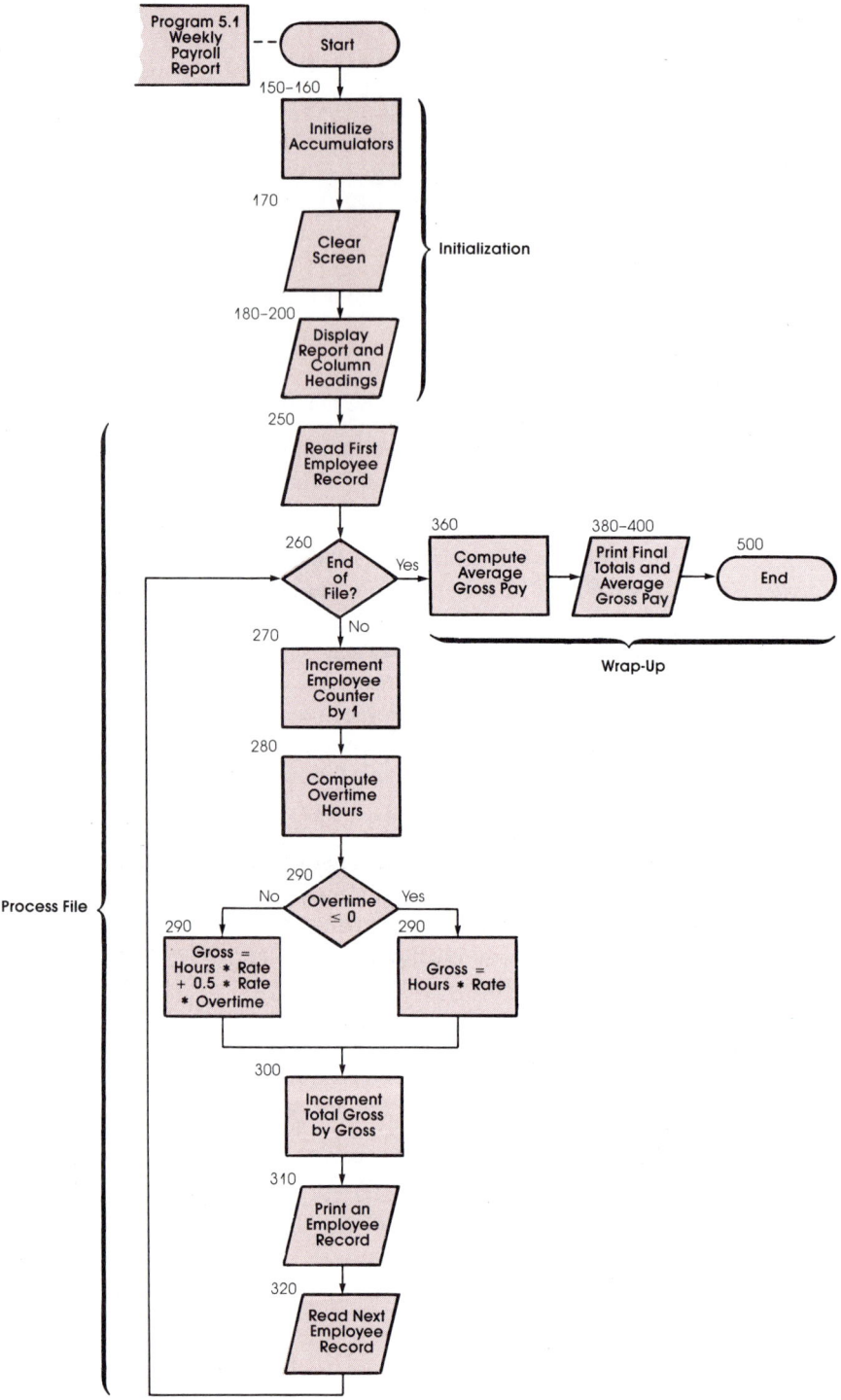

FIGURE 5.7 General flowchart for Program 5.1.

Program Solution   The following program corresponds to the preceding tasks and to the flowchart in Figure 5.7.

PROGRAM 5.1

```
100 ' Program 5.1
110 ' Weekly Payroll and Summary Report
120 ' ********************************
130 '
140 ' ******** Initialization *********
150 EMP.COUNT   = 0
160 TOTAL.GROSS = 0
170 CLS : KEY OFF   ' Clear Screen
180 PRINT       "           Weekly Payroll Report"
190 PRINT
200 PRINT     "Employee No.   Hours     Rate     Gross Pay"
210 FORMAT$ = "     \ \        ###.#     ##.##     ##,###.##"
220 PRINT
230 '
240 ' ********* Process File **********
250 READ EMP.NUMBER$, EMP.HOURS, EMP.RATE
260 WHILE EMP.NUMBER$ <> "EOF"
270    EMP.COUNT    = EMP.COUNT + 1
280    EMP.OVERTIME = EMP.HOURS - 40
290    IF EMP.OVERTIME <= 0
          THEN EMP.GROSS = EMP.HOURS * EMP.RATE
          ELSE EMP.GROSS = EMP.HOURS * EMP.RATE + .5 * EMP.RATE * EMP.OVERTIME
300    TOTAL.GROSS = TOTAL.GROSS + EMP.GROSS
310    PRINT USING FORMAT$; EMP.NUMBER$, EMP.HOURS, EMP.RATE, EMP.GROSS
320    READ EMP.NUMBER$, EMP.HOURS, EMP.RATE
330 WEND
340 '
350 ' ************ Wrap-up ************
360 AVERAGE.GROSS = TOTAL.GROSS / EMP.COUNT
370 PRINT
380 PRINT USING "Total Gross Pay =========> $$,###.##"; TOTAL.GROSS
390 PRINT USING "Number of Employees ====>     ###";    EMP.COUNT
400 PRINT USING "Average Gross Pay ======> $$,###.##"; AVERAGE.GROSS
410 PRINT
420 PRINT "End of Payroll Report"
430 '
440 ' ********** Data Follows *********
450 DATA 124, 40,    5.60
460 DATA 126, 56,    5.90
470 DATA 128, 38,    4.60
480 DATA 129, 48.5, 6.10
490 DATA EOF,  0,    0
500 END
RUN
            Weekly Payroll Report

Employee No.   Hours     Rate     Gross Pay

    124        40.0      5.60      224.00
    126        56.0      5.90      377.60
    128        38.0      4.60      174.80
    129        48.5      6.10      321.77

Total Gross Pay =========> $1,098.17
Number of Employees ====>     4
Average Gross Pay ======>   $274.54

End of Payroll Report
```

Discussion of the Program Solution

The solution to the Weekly Payroll and Summary Report, as represented by the flowchart in Figure 5.7 and the corresponding Program 5.1, includes a few significant points that did not appear in previous programs. They are as follows:

1. A counter (EMP.COUNT) and a running total (TOTAL.GROSS) are used. Both are initialized to zero (lines 150 and 160) and are incremented each time an employee record is read. The counter is used to keep track of the total number of employees and is incremented in line 270. The running total is used to sum the gross pay and is incremented by the individual employee gross pay in line 300.
2. A decision is made in line 290 to determine which one of the two formulas is to be used to compute the gross pay. If EMP.OVERTIME is less than or equal to zero, the PC uses the THEN clause. If EMP.OVERTIME is greater than zero, the PC uses the ELSE clause.
3. Line 360 involves calculating an average that is based on the total gross pay (TOTAL.GROSS) and the number of employees (EMP.COUNT).
4. By calculating the overtime in line 280 and assigning it to the variable EMP.OVERTIME, we are able to eliminate the recomputation of this value. Whenever a value is required several times in a program, it is better to compute it once and assign it a variable that can be referenced later, as in line 290, than to recompute it every time it is needed.

■ 5.4 IMPLEMENTING THE DO-WHILE AND DO-UNTIL LOGIC STRUCTURES

In designing and implementing a loop, think carefully about where to place the decision to terminate the loop. As mentioned earlier, most computer professionals recommend that the decision to terminate should be at the very top or very bottom of the loop.

If, in the design of a solution, the decision to terminate is at the top of the loop (Do-While), then use the WHILE and WEND statements to implement the loop. The program flowchart in Figure 5.7 on page 110 has the decision to terminate at the very top of the loop. It is the same logic structure that we used in Chapter 4. In each case, we used the WHILE and WEND statements to implement the loop.

Keep in mind that with the Do-While loop, the body of the loop may not be executed at all. This would be the case, for example, if the first DATA statement in a program contained the trailer record.

If, in the design of a solution, the decision to terminate is at the bottom of the loop (Do-Until), then you can only simulate the Do-Until structure in MS BASIC; there is no UNTIL statement. Simulating a Do-Until structure may be accomplished through the use of the WHILE, WEND, LET, and IF statements. The LET statement, located just before the WHILE statement, assigns the variable in the condition of the WHILE statement a value that ensures that the body of the loop is executed at least once. The IF statement tests the actual condition and assigns a value to the variable tested in the WHILE statement. The value assigned by the IF statement determines whether the While loop should terminate.

To illustrate a Do-Until structure and its implementation in BASIC, consider the flowchart in Figure 5.8 and Program 5.2. The program computes and displays the sum of the first 100 integers.

By assigning MORE$ a value of "Yes" in line 160, we ensure that the body of the loop is executed at least once because of the condition in the WHILE statement in line 170. The minimum number of times the body of a loop may be executed is the key difference between a Do-While and Do-Until structure.

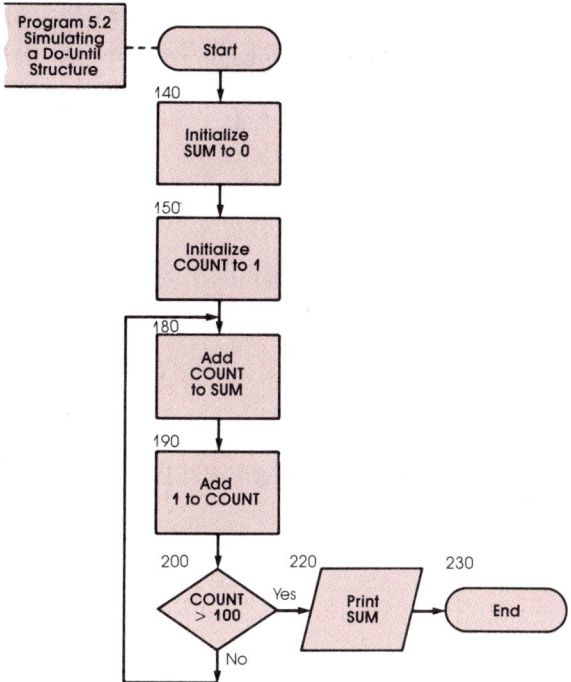

FIGURE 5.8 *A flowchart for Program 5.2.*

PROGRAM 5.2

```
100 ' Program 5.2
110 ' Simulating a Do-Until Structure
120 ' Using WHILE, WEND, LET, and IF Statements
130 ' *****************************************
140 SUM = 0
150 COUNT = 1
160 MORE$ = "YES"
170 WHILE MORE$ = "YES"
180    SUM = SUM + COUNT
190    COUNT = COUNT + 1
200    IF COUNT > 100
          THEN MORE$ = "NO"
210 WEND
220 PRINT "The sum is"; SUM
230 END

RUN

The sum is 5050
```

5.5 IMPLEMENTING THE IF-THEN-ELSE STRUCTURE

This section describes the various forms of the If-Then-Else structure and the use of IF statements to implement them in MS BASIC.

Simple Forms of the If-Then-Else Structure

Consider the If-Then-Else structure in Figure 5.9 and the corresponding methods of implementing the logic in MS BASIC. Assume that REG$ represents a person's voter-registration status. If REG$ is equal to the value Y, the person is registered to vote. If REG$ does not equal Y, the person is not registered to vote. REG.CNT and NREG.CNT are counters that are incremented as specified in the flowchart.

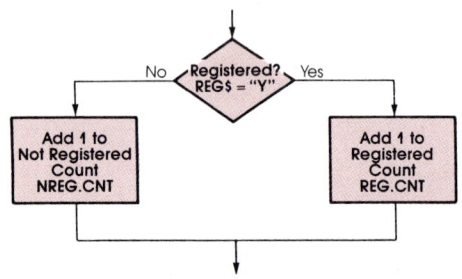

Method 1: Using a single IF statement.

```
200 IF REG$ = "Y"
        THEN REG.CNT  = REG.CNT  + 1
        ELSE NREG.CNT = NREG.CNT + 1
210
```

Method 2: Using two IF statements.

```
200 IF REG$ = "Y"
        THEN REG.CNT  = REG.CNT  + 1
210 IF REG$ <> "Y"
        THEN NREG.CNT = NREG.CNT + 1
```

FIGURE 5.9 *Implementation of the If-Then-Else structure, with alternative processing for the true and false cases.*

In the first method of solution shown in Figure 5.9, an IF statement resolves the logic indicated in the partial flowchart. Line 200 compares REG$ to the value Y. If REG$ is equal to Y, then REG.CNT is incremented by 1 in the THEN clause. If REG$ does not equal Y, NREG.CNT is incremented by 1 in the ELSE clause. Regardless of the counter incremented, control passes to line 210, the next numbered line following line 200. Line 210 is said to be the **structure terminator**, since both the true and false tasks pass control to this line.

In method 2, REG$ is compared to the value Y twice. In line 200, if REG$ is equal to Y, then the counter REG.CNT is incremented by 1. In line 210, the counter NREG.CNT is incremented by 1 if REG$ does not equal Y.

Although both methods are valid, and both satisfy the If-Then-Else structure, the first method is more efficient, as it involves fewer lines of code, less execution time, and less main storage. Therefore, the first method is recommended over the second.

As shown in Figures 5.10, 5.11, and 5.12, the If-Then-Else structure can take on a variety of appearances. In Figure 5.10, there is a task only if the condition is true.

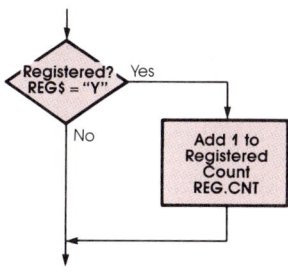

Method 1: Using an `IF` statement with no `ELSE` clause.

```
200 IF REG$ = "Y"
       THEN REG.CNT = REG.CNT + 1
210
```

Method 2: Using an `IF` statement with a null `ELSE` clause.

```
200 IF REG$ = "Y"
       THEN REG.CNT = REG.CNT + 1
       ELSE
210
```

FIGURE 5.10 *Implementation of an If-Then-Else structure with alternative processing for the true case.*

In Figure 5.10, the first method is preferred over the second, since it is more straightforward and involves fewer lines of code. Note that the second method involves a null `ELSE` clause.

The If-Then-Else structure in Figure 5.11 illustrates the incrementation of the counter NREG.CNT when the condition is false.

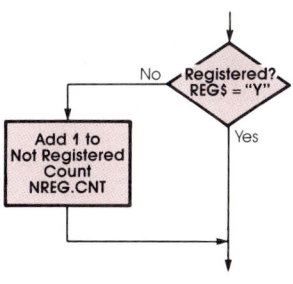

Method 1: Negating the condition in the decision symbol and using an `IF` statement.

```
200 IF REG$ <> "Y"
       THEN NREG.CNT = NREG.CNT + 1
210
```

Method 2: Using an `IF` statement with a null `THEN` clause.

```
200 IF REG$ = "Y"
       THEN
       ELSE NREG.CNT = NREG.CNT + 1
210
```

FIGURE 5.11 *Implementation of an If-Then-Else structure with alternative processing for the false case.*

In method 1, the relation in the condition that is found in the partial flowchart has been negated. The condition REG$ = "Y" has been modified to read REG$ <> "Y" in the BASIC code. Negating the relation is usually preferred when additional tasks must be done as a result of the condition being false. In method 2, the relation is the same as in the decision symbol. When the condition REG$ = Y is true, the null THEN clause simply passes control to line 210. Either method is acceptable. Some programmers prefer always to include both a THEN and an ELSE clause, even when one of them is null. On the other hand, some prefer to negate the condition rather than include a null clause.

The If-Then-Else structure in Figure 5.12 includes alternative tasks for both the true and false cases. Each task is made up of several statements.

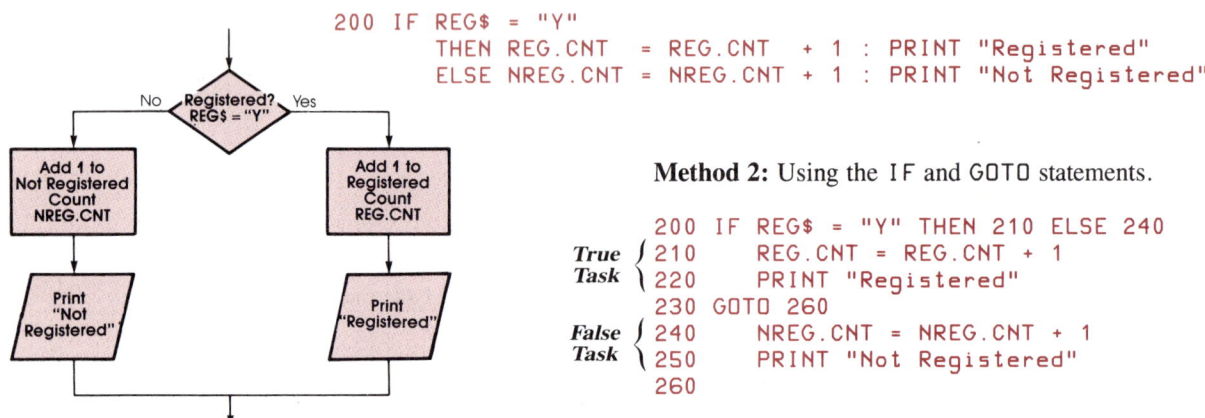

FIGURE 5.12 *Implementation of an If-Then-Else structure with several statements for both the true and false cases.*

In method 1 of Figure 5.12, if the condition REG$ = "Y" is true, the two statements in the THEN clause are executed. If the condition is false, the two statements in the ELSE clause are executed.

In method 2, the IF and GOTO statements are used to implement the If-Then-Else structure. If the condition is true, control passes to line 210 and the true task is executed. At the conclusion of the true task, the GOTO 260 in line 230 transfers control to line 260, thereby branching forward past the false task (lines 240 and 250). If the condition in line 200 is false, control passes to line 240 and the false task is executed. In either case, control continues at line 260, the structure terminator.

Although both methods satisfy the If-Then-Else structure, the first method is more straightforward and involves fewer lines of code. Therefore, for this example, the first method is recommended over the second method. However, since MS BASIC allows for only 255 characters in a line, method 2 should be used when many physical lines are involved in the THEN or ELSE clause.

GOTO — A Dangerous Four-Letter Word

As with most programming languages, MS BASIC includes the infamous GOTO statement. The general form of the GOTO statement is given in Table 5.2.

TABLE 5.2 The Unconditional GOTO Statement

General Form:	GOTO line number
Purpose:	Causes the execution of the program to be continued at the specified line number.
Keyword Entry:	Hold down the Alt key and press the G key.
Examples:	240 GOTO 300 570 GOTO 630

The GOTO statement may be used to transfer control up or down to any line in a program. In other words, you can instruct the PC to jump around from one routine to another in a program. It is a statement that should be avoided unless all other means fail. We introduce it at this juncture in the book as a means to implement certain If-Then-Else structures that have multiple statements in the true or false task. This is the only situation that requires the use of the GOTO statement in MS BASIC.

Nested Forms of the If-Then-Else Structure

A nested If-Then-Else structure is one in which the action to be taken for the true or false case includes yet another If-Then-Else structure. The second If-Then-Else structure is considered to be nested or layered within the first.

Study the partial program that corresponds to the nested If-Then-Else structure in Figure 5.13.

```
200 IF AGE >= 18 THEN 210 ELSE 230
210     IF REG$ = "Y"
            THEN REG.CNT  = REG.CNT  + 1 : PRINT "Registered"
            ELSE ELIG.CNT = ELIG.CNT + 1 : PRINT "Eligible and Not Registered"
220 GOTO 240
230     NELIG.CNT = NELIG.CNT + 1 : PRINT "Not Eligible to Register"
240
```

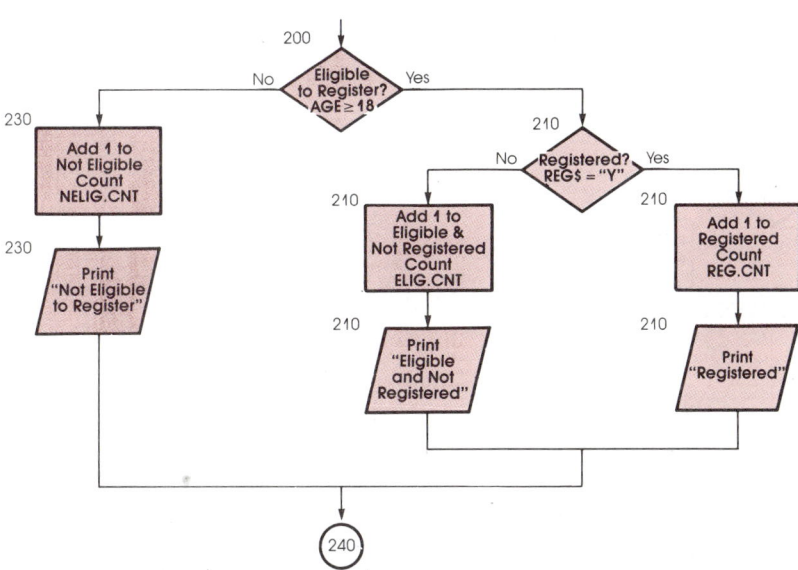

FIGURE 5.13 Implementation of a nested If-Then-Else structure.

In Figure 5.13, if the condition AGE >= 18 is true, the true task is executed and control passes to line 210. If the condition is false, the ELSE clause in line 230 is executed. The true task contains a second IF statement, which corresponds to the inner If-Then-Else structure in the flowchart. Note in Figure 5.13 that only one of the three alternative tasks is executed for each record processed. Regardless of the path taken, control eventually passes to the structure terminator in line 240.

If-Then-Else structures can be nested to any depth, but readability decreases as nesting increases. Consider the nested structure in Figure 5.14 and the corresponding implementation in MS BASIC. Figure 5.14 contains three nests of If-Then-Else structures and six counters. The counters can be described in the following manner:

NE.MALE: totals the number of males not eligible to register
NE.FEM: totals the number of females not eligible to register
NR.MALE: totals the number of males who are old enough to vote but have not registered
NR.FEM: totals the number of females who are old enough to vote but have not registered
NVOTE: totals the number of individuals who are eligible to vote but did not vote
VOTE: totals the number of individuals who voted

In the partial BASIC program in Figure 5.14, line 200 corresponds to the decision at the very top of the flowchart. Line 210 handles the true case to the right in the flowchart. Line 230 fulfills the false case to the left in the flowchart. Incorporating the logic and concepts found in Figure 5.14 into a complete program is left as an exercise for you at the end of this chapter (see BASIC Programming Problem 3 on page 131).

```
200 IF AGE >= 18 THEN 210 ELSE 230
210     IF REG$ = "Y"
            THEN IF VOTE$ = "Y" THEN VOTE = VOTE + 1      ELSE NVOT    = NVOTE + 1
            ELSE IF SEX$  = "F" THEN NR.FEM = NR.FEM + 1 ELSE NR.MALE = NR.MALE + 1
220 GOTO 240
230     IF SEX$ = "F"
            THEN NE.FEM  = NE.FEM + 1
            ELSE NE.MALE = NE.MALE + 1
240
```

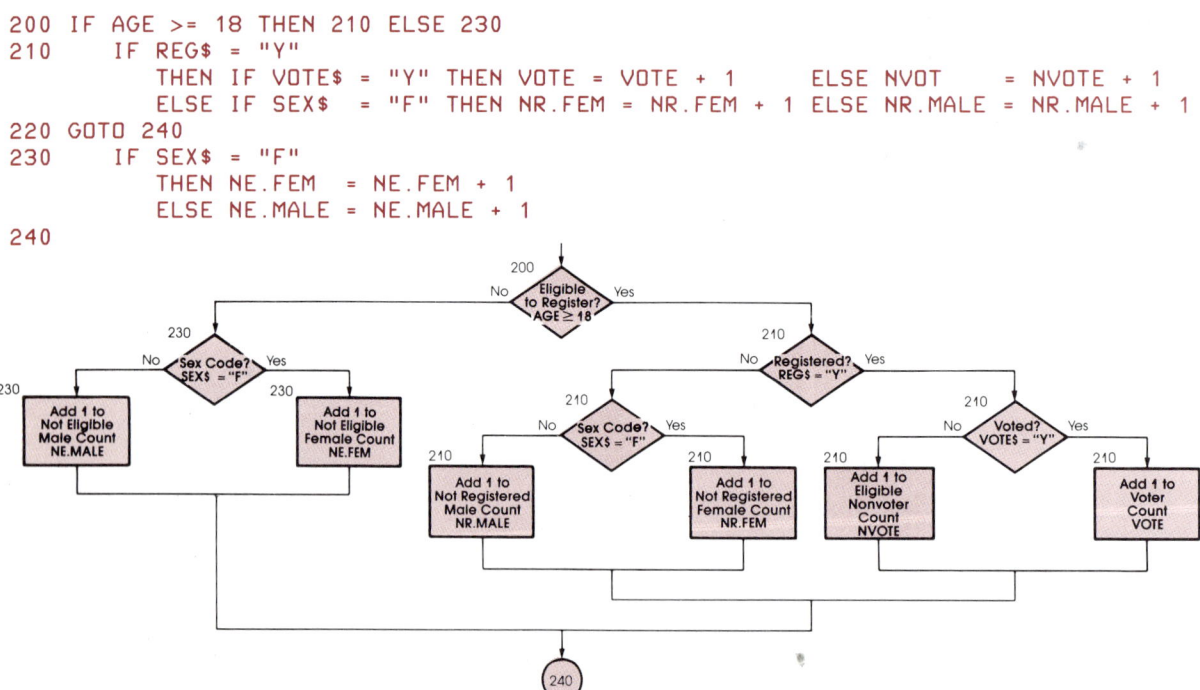

FIGURE 5.14 *Implementation of a nested If-Then-Else structure with several layers.*

PAIRING OF NESTED IF STATEMENTS

Line 210 of Figure 5.14 is called a **nested** IF statement. A nested IF statement is one in which another IF statement immediately follows the keyword THEN or ELSE. In the following statement, two ELSEs follow two IFs:

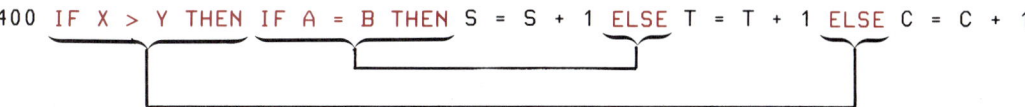

The relationship between a specific IF-THEN and the ELSE to which it is paired can be determined by the following rule:

> **Nested IF Rule 1:** Each ELSE is matched with the closest previous unmatched IF-THEN.

In line 400, reading from left to right, the first ELSE belongs to IF A = B THEN. The second ELSE is paired with IF X > Y THEN.

If X is greater than Y, the condition A = B is evaluated. If A equals B, S is incremented by 1. If X is greater than Y and A does not equal B, T is incremented by 1. If X is not greater than Y, C is incremented by 1.

It is not necessary that a nested IF statement have as many ELSE clauses as THEN clauses. For example, the statement

```
550 IF X = Y
        THEN IF A = B
                THEN IF C = D THEN T = T + 1 ELSE S = S + 1
```

contains three THEN clauses and one ELSE clause. The ELSE belongs to IF C = D THEN. Therefore, if all three conditions are true, the counter T is incremented by 1. If the first two conditions are true and the third condition is false, S is incremented by 1 and control passes to the next numbered line following 550. If either of the first two conditions is false, control passes to the next numbered line following 550.

On the other hand, it is invalid to have more ELSE clauses than THEN clauses in a single nested IF statement. Thus, the following nested IF statement is invalid:

```
750 IF S > T
        THEN PRINT A
        ELSE PRINT B ELSE PRINT C
```
Invalid Owing to Unbalanced ELSE

Nested IF statements tend to increase the complexity of a program significantly. This is especially true if more than two IF statements are located within the same IF statement. If the number exceeds two, we suggest that you use logical operators or consider breaking up the nested IF statement as shown in Figures 5.13 and 5.14.

5.7 LOGICAL OPERATORS

In many instances, a decision to execute one alternative or another is based upon two or more conditions. In previous examples that involved two or more conditions, we tested each condition in a separate decision statement. In this section, we will discuss combining conditions within one decision statement by means of the logical operators AND, OR, XOR, EQV, and IMP. When two or more conditions are combined by these logical operators, the expression is called a **compound condition**. The logical operator NOT allows you to write a condition in which the truth value is **complemented**, or reversed.

The NOT Logical Operator

A condition made up of two expressions and a relational operator is sometimes called a **relational expression**. A relational expression that is preceded by the logical operator NOT forms a condition that is false when the relational expression is true. If the relational expression is false, then the condition is true. Consider the following IF statements:

Method 1: Using the NOT logical operator.

```
700 IF NOT A > B
       THEN READ A
```

Method 2: Using other relations to complement.

```
700 IF A <= B
       THEN READ A
```

Method 3: Using a null THEN.

```
700 IF A > B
       THEN
       ELSE READ A
```

If A is greater than B (the relational expression is true), then the condition NOT A > B is false. If A is less than or equal to B (the relational expression is false), then the condition is true. All three methods are equivalent; however, methods 1 and 2 are preferred.

Because the logical operator NOT can increase the complexity of the decision statement significantly, use it sparingly. As illustrated in Table 5.3, with MS BASIC you may write the complement, or reverse, of a condition by using other relations.

TABLE 5.3 Use of Other Relations to Complement a Condition

CONDITION	COMPLEMENT OF CONDITION	
	METHOD 1	METHOD 2
A = B	A <> B	NOT A = B
A < B	A >= B	NOT A < B
A > B	A <= B	NOT A > B
A <= B	A > B	NOT A <= B
A >= B	A < B	NOT A >= B
A <> B	A = B	NOT A <> B

The following rule summarizes the use of the logical operator NOT.

> **Logical Operator Rule 1:** The logical operator NOT requires that the relational expression be false for the condition to be true. If the relational expression is true, then the condition is false.

The AND Logical Operator

The AND operator requires that both conditions be true for the compound condition to be true. Consider the following IF statements:

Method 1: Using the AND logical operator.

```
200 IF SEX$ = "M" AND AGE > 20
        THEN PRINT EMP.NAME$
210
```

Method 2: Using nested IF statements.

```
200 IF SEX$ = "M"
        THEN IF AGE > 20
                THEN PRINT EMP.NAME$
210
```

If SEX$ is equal to the value M and AGE is greater than 20, then EMP.NAME$ is displayed before control passes to line 210. If either one of the conditions is false, then the compound condition is false and control passes to line 210 without EMP.NAME$ being displayed. Although both methods are equivalent, method 1 is more efficient, more compact, and more straightforward than method 2.

Like a single condition, a compound condition can be only true or false. To determine the truth value of the compound condition, the PC must evaluate and assign a truth value to each individual condition. Then the truth value is determined for the compound condition.

For example, if X equals 4 and Y$ equals "1", the PC evaluates the following compound condition in the manner shown:

```
300 IF X = 3 AND Y$ = "1" THEN PRINT "True"
       1. false   2. true
           3. false
```

The PC first determined the truth value for each condition, then concluded that the compound condition was false because of the AND operation.

A compound condition can be made up of several conditions separated by AND operators. The flowchart in Figure 5.15 indicates that all three variables (T1, T2, and T3) must equal zero to increment COUNT by 1. Line 3400 in Figure 5.15 illustrates the use of a compound condition to implement the logic. The AND operator requires that all three conditions be true for COUNT to be incremented by 1. If any one of the three conditions is false, control is transferred to line 3410 and COUNT is not incremented by 1.

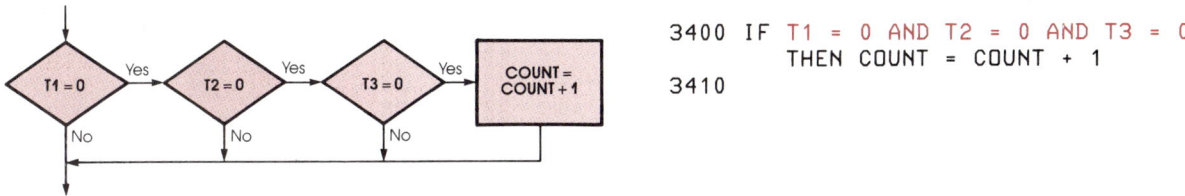

```
3400 IF T1 = 0 AND T2 = 0 AND T3 = 0
        THEN COUNT = COUNT + 1
3410
```

FIGURE 5.15 *Use of two AND operators.*

The following rule summarizes the use of the logical operator AND:

> ***Logical Operator Rule 2:*** The logical operator AND requires that all conditions be true for the compound condition to be true.

The OR Logical Operator

The OR operator requires that only one of the two conditions be true for the compound condition to be true. If both conditions are true, the compound condition is also true. The use of the OR operator is illustrated below.

Method 1: Using the OR logical operator.
```
500 IF DIV = 0 OR EXPO > 1E30
          THEN PRINT "WARNING" : END
510
```

Method 2: Using two IF statements.
```
500 IF DIV = 0
          THEN PRINT "WARNING" : END
505 IF EXPO > 1E30
          THEN PRINT "WARNING" : END
510
```

In line 500 of method 1, if either DIV equals 0 or EXPO is greater than 1E30, the THEN clause is executed. If both conditions are true, the THEN clause is also executed. If both conditions are false, the THEN clause is bypassed and control passes to the next numbered line. Method 2 employs two IF statements to resolve the same problem. Again, both methods are equivalent. However, method 1 is more straightforward than method 2.

Figure 5.16 illustrates a partial flowchart and the use of two OR operators to implement it.

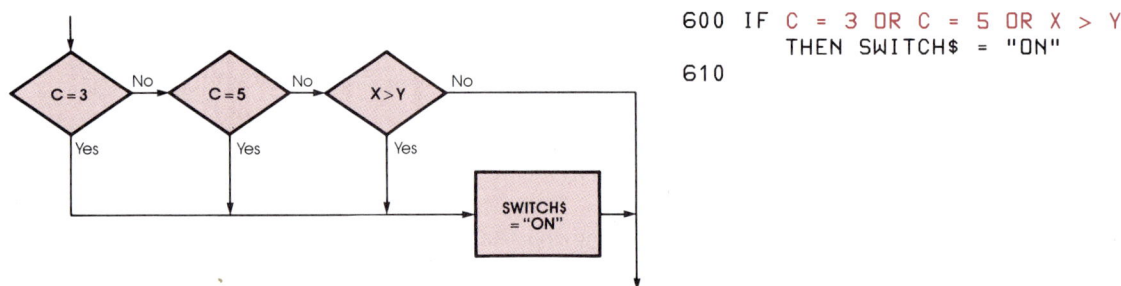

```
600 IF C = 3 OR C = 5 OR X > Y
          THEN SWITCH$ = "ON"
610
```

FIGURE 5.16 *Use of two OR operators.*

As with the logical operator AND, the truth values of the individual conditions in line 600 of Figure 5.16 are first determined, then the truth values for the conditions containing the logical operator OR are evaluated. For example, if C equals 4, X equals 4.9, and Y equals 4.8, the following condition is true:

```
      C = 3   OR   C = 5   OR   X > Y   THEN SWITCH$ = "ON"
      ‾‾‾‾‾        ‾‾‾‾‾        ‾‾‾‾‾
     1. false    2. false     3. true
           ‾‾‾‾‾‾‾‾‾‾‾‾‾‾
              4. false
           ‾‾‾‾‾‾‾‾‾‾‾‾‾‾‾‾‾‾‾‾‾‾‾‾‾‾‾‾
                       5. true
```

In line 600, the PC first evaluates the individual conditions (steps 1, 2, and 3). The first and second conditions are false and the third condition is true. Next, the PC evaluates the leftmost OR (step 4). Since the truth values of the first two conditions are false, the truth value of C = 3 OR C = 5 is also false.

Finally, the PC evaluates the truth value of the condition resulting from step 4 and the condition resulting from step 3 for the rightmost logical operator OR. Since the condition resulting from step 3 has a truth value of true, the entire condition is determined to be true.

The following rule summarizes the use of the logical operator OR:

> **Logical Operator Rule 3:** The logical operator OR requires that *only one* of the conditions be true for the compound condition to be true. If both conditions are true, the compound condition is also true.

The Logical Operators XOR, EQV, and IMP

Three logical operators that are not used very often but are a part of MS BASIC are XOR (exclusive OR), EQV (equivalence), and IMP (implication).

The XOR operator requires that one of the two conditions be true for the compound condition to be true. If both conditions are true, the compound condition is false. For example, if C = 3 and D = 4, then the following compound condition is false.

```
C = 3 XOR D > 3
```
1. true 2. true
3. false

The EQV operator requires that both conditions be true or both conditions be false for the compound condition to be true. For example, if C = 4 and D = 3, then the following compound condition is true.

```
C = 3 EQV D > 3
```
1. false 2. false
3. true

The IMP operator requires that both conditions be true or both conditions be false or the first condition be false and the second condition be true for the compound condition to be true. For example, if C = 4 and D = 5, then the following compound condition is true.

```
C = 3 IMP D > 3
```
1. false 2. true
3. true

Truth Tables

Truth tables for the six logical operators discussed in this section are summarized in Table 5.4 on the next page. A summary of the order of precedence of all MS BASIC operators, including arithmetic, relational, and logical, can be found on page 4 of the reference card in the back of this book.

TABLE 5.4 Truth Tables for Logical Operators Where A and B Represent Conditions, T Represents True, and F Represents False

LOGICAL OPERATOR NOT			LOGICAL OPERATOR XOR		
VALUE OF A	VALUE OF NOT A		VALUE OF A	VALUE OF B	VALUE OF A XOR B
T	F		T	T	F
F	T		T	F	T
			F	T	T
			F	F	F

LOGICAL OPERATOR AND			LOGICAL OPERATOR EQV		
VALUE OF A	VALUE OF B	VALUE OF A AND B	VALUE OF A	VALUE OF B	VALUE OF A EQV B
T	T	T	T	T	T
T	F	F	T	F	F
F	T	F	F	T	F
F	F	F	F	F	T

LOGICAL OPERATOR OR			LOGICAL OPERATOR IMP		
VALUE OF A	VALUE OF B	VALUE OF A OR B	VALUE OF A	VALUE OF B	VALUE OF A IMP B
T	T	T	T	T	T
T	F	T	T	F	F
F	T	T	F	T	T
F	F	F	F	F	T

Combining Logical Operators

Logical operators can be combined in a decision statement to form a compound condition. The formation of compound statements that involve more than one type of logical operator can create problems unless you fully understand the order in which the PC evaluates the entire condition. Consider the following decision statement:

```
800 IF X > Y OR T = D AND H < 3 OR NOT Y = R
       THEN COUNT = COUNT + 1
```

Does the PC evaluate operators from left to right or right to left or one type of operator before another?

The order of evaluation is a part of what is called the **rules of precedence**. Just as we have rules of precedence for arithmetic operations (Chapter 3, pages 58 and 59), we also have rules of precedence for logical operators.

> ***Precedence Rule 3:*** Unless parentheses dictate otherwise, reading from left to right, conditions containing arithmetic operators are evaluated first; then those containing relational operators; then those containing NOT operators; then those containing AND operators; then those containing OR or XOR operators; then those containing EQV operators; and finally those containing IMP operators.

The compound condition found earlier in line 800, then, is evaluated as follows. Assume that D = 3, H = 3, R = 2, T = 5, X = 3, and Y = 2:

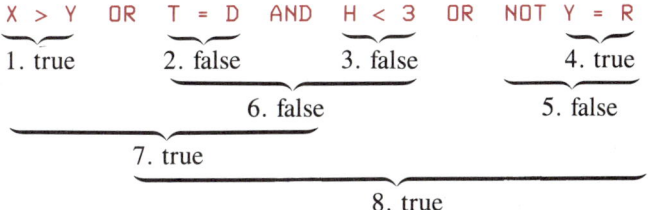

If you have trouble following the logic behind this evaluation, use this technique: Applying the rules of precedence, look or scan from *left to right* four different times. On the first scan, determine the truth value of each condition that contains a relational operator. On the second scan, moving from left to right again, evaluate all conditions that contain NOT operators. Y = R is true and NOT Y = R is false. On the third scan, moving again from left to right, evaluate all conditions that contain AND operators. T = D is false, as is H < 3; therefore, T = D and H < 3 is false. On the fourth scan, moving from left to right, evaluate all conditions that contain OR operators. The first OR yields a truth value of true. The second OR yields, for the entire condition, a final truth value of true.

Using Parentheses with Compound Conditions

Parentheses may be used to change the order of precedence. In MS BASIC, parentheses are normally used to avoid ambiguity and to group conditions with a desired logical operator. When there are parentheses in a compound condition, the PC evaluates that part of the compound condition within the parentheses first and then continues to evaluate the remaining compound condition according to the rules of precedence. For example, suppose variable C (below) has a value of 6 and D has a value of 3. Consider the compound condition:

```
    C = 7    AND    D < 4    OR    D <> 0
    1. false         2. true         3. true
           4. false
                  5. true
```

Following the order of precedence for logical operators, the compound condition yields a truth value of true. If parentheses surround the latter two conditions in the compound condition, then the OR operator is evaluated before the AND condition, and the compound condition yields a truth value of false, as shown below:

```
    C = 7    AND    (D < 4    OR    D <> 0)
    4. false         1. true         2. true
                            3. true
              5. false
```

Parentheses may be used freely when the evaluation of a compound condition is in doubt. For example, if you wish to evaluate the compound condition

```
C > D AND S = 4 OR X < Y AND T = 5
```

you may incorporate it into a decision statement as it stands. You may also write it as

```
(C > D AND S = 4) OR (X < Y AND T = 5)
```

and feel more certain of the outcome of the decision statement.

■ 5.8 TEST YOUR BASIC SKILLS (Even-numbered answers are in Appendix B.)

1. Consider the valid programs below. What is displayed if each program is executed?

   ```
   a. 100 ' Exercise 5.1a          b. 100 ' Exercise 5.1b
      110 I = 1                       110 READ X, Y
      120 WHILE I <= 2                120 WHILE X > 0
      130   J = 1                     130   IF X = Y AND Y >= 10
      140   WHILE J <= 2                        THEN PRINT "Both Conditions Are True"
      150     K = 1                   140   IF X = Y XOR Y >= 10
      160     WHILE K <= 2                      THEN PRINT "Only One of the Two Conditions Is True"
      170       PRINT I, J, K         150   IF NOT X = Y AND NOT Y >= 10
      180       K = K + 1                       THEN PRINT "Neither Condition Is True"
      190     WEND                    160   READ X, Y
      200     J = J + 1               170 WEND
      210   WEND                      180 PRINT "End of Job"
      220   I = I + 1                 190 ' ********* Data Follows **********
      230 WEND                        200 DATA 3, 5, 8, 10, 15, 15, 4, 4, -1, 0
      240 END                         210 END
   ```

2. Write a BASIC statement that will initialize X to 0 and another that will initialize T to 10. Also, write additional BASIC statements that will consecutively increment these variables by the following amounts:

   a. 1   b. 7   c. 2   d. double each value   e. minus 1

3. Determine the truth value of the compound conditions below, given the following:

   Employee number (E) = 500   Tax (T) = $60
   Salary (S) = $700   Insurance deduction (I) = $40
   Job code (J) = 1

   a. E < 400 OR J = 1   b. S = 700 AND T = 50
   c. S - T = 640 AND J = 1   d. T + I = S - 500 OR J = 0
   e. NOT J < 0   f. NOT S > 500 AND NOT T > 80
   g. NOT (J = 1 OR T = 60)   h. J = 1 XOR E >= 500
   i. I <> 40 EQV S > 500   j. S = 700 IMP T = 60
   k. S < 300 AND I < 50 OR J = 1   l. S < 300 AND (I < 50 OR J = 1)
   m. NOT (NOT J = 1)

4. Determine the value of Q that will cause the condition in the IF statements below to be true.

   a. `100 IF Q > 8 OR Q = 3`
      `    THEN LET Z = Z / 10`

   b. `110 IF Q + 10 >= 7 AND NOT Q < 0`
      `    THEN PRINT "THE ANSWER IS "; A`

   c. `120 IF Q / 3 < 9`
      `    THEN COUNT = COUNT + 1`

   d. `130 IF Q <> 3 XOR Q = 3`
      `    THEN SUM = SUM + AMT`

5. Assume that P and Q are simple conditions. The following logical equivalences from mathematics are known as DeMorgan's laws:

   > `NOT (P OR Q)` is equivalent to `NOT P AND NOT Q`
   > `NOT (P AND Q)` is equivalent to `NOT P OR NOT Q`

   Use DeMorgan's laws to find a logical equivalent for each of the following:

   a. `NOT(P OR (NOT Q))`
   b. `NOT((NOT P) OR Q)`
   c. `NOT(NOT P AND Q)`
   d. `NOT((NOT P) AND (NOT Q))`

6. Construct partial programs for each of the following logic structures:

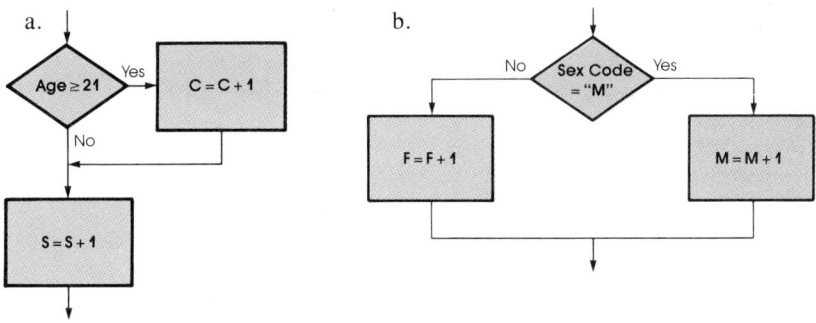

7. Construct partial programs for each of the logic structures found below and on the next page.

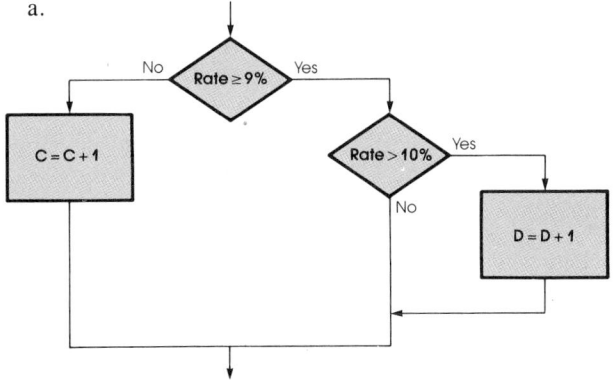

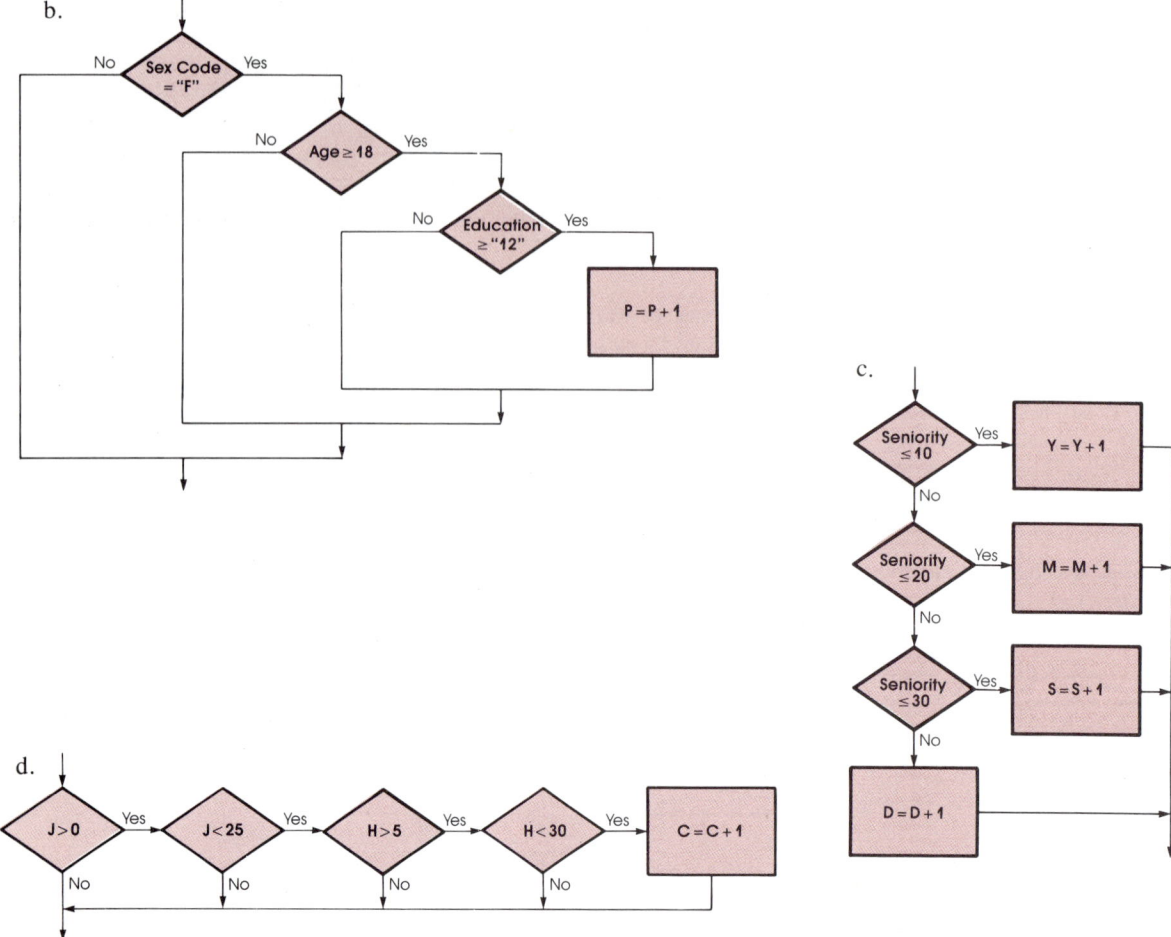

8. Write a program that determines the number of negative values N, number of zero values Z, and number of positive values P in the following data set: 4, 2, 3, –9, 0, 0, –4, –6, –8, 3, 2, 0, 0, 8, –3, 4. Use the sentinel value –1E37 to test for the end of file.
9. Given the four variables W, X, Y, and Z, with previously defined values, write a sequence of IF statements to increment the variable COUNT by 1 if all four variables have the exact value of 100. If one or more variables have a different value, execute line 300 instead.
10. The sequence of Fibonacci numbers begins with 1, 1 and continues endlessly, each number being the sum of the preceding two:

    1, 1, 2, 3, 5, 8, 13, 21, 34, ...

Construct a program to compute the first X numbers of the sequence where the value of X is entered in response to an INPUT statement.
11. Given two positive valued variables, A and B, write a sequence of statements to assign the variable with the larger value to GREATER and the variable with the smaller value to SMALLER. If A and B are equal, assign either one to EQUAL.

12. The values of three variables U, V, and W are positive and not equal to each other. Using IF statements, determine which has the smallest value and assign this value to SMALL.
13. The symbol N! represents the product of the first N positive integers: $N! = N * (N - 1) * (N - 2) * \ldots * 1$. When a result is defined in terms of itself, we call it a **recursive definition**. Construct a program that will accept from the keyboard a positive integer and compute its factorial. The recursive definition is as follows: If $N = 1$, then $N! = 1$; otherwise $N! = N(N - 1)!$. For example, $5! = 5 * 4 * 3 * 2 * 1 = 120$.
14. Write a partial program to set $A = -1$ if C and D are both zero; set $A = -2$ if neither C nor D is zero; and set $A = -3$ if either, but not both, C or D is zero.
15. In each of the following compound conditions, indicate the order of evaluation by the PC. (See the examples on page 125. Beginning with 1, use numbers to show the order of evaluation.)

    a. S > 0 OR A > 0 OR T > 0
    b. S > 0 AND A > 0 AND NOT T > 0

■ 5.9 BASIC PROGRAMMING PROBLEMS

1. Employee Average Yearly Salary

Purpose: To illustrate the concepts of counter and running total initialization; counter and running total incrementation; looping; and testing for the last value in a set of data.

Problem: Construct a program to read, count records, accumulate salaries, and display a sequence of data consisting of employee numbers and salaries for various employees in a payroll file. After the sentinel value (EOF) is processed, display the total number of employees and the average yearly salary of all the employees processed. (Hint: See Program 5.1 on page 111 or PRG5-1 on the Student Diskette.)

Input Data: Prepare and use the following sample data in DATA statements.

Employee Number	Employee Salary
123	$16,000
148	8,126
184	14,800
196	17,400
201	18,950
EOF	0

Output Results: The following results are displayed.

```
Employee    Employee
Number      Salary
--------    --------
   123      16,000.00
   148       8,126.00
   184      14,800.00
   196      17,400.00
   201      18,950.00

Number of Employees ===>   5
Average Salary ========> $15,055.20
```

2. Voter Analysis

Purpose: To become familiar with nested If-Then-Else structures.

Problem: Construct a program that will clear the screen, analyze a citizen file, and generate the following totals. (**Hint:** See Figure 5.14 on page 118.)

1. number of males not eligible to register
2. number of females not eligible to register
3. number of males who are old enough to vote but have not registered
4. number of females who are old enough to vote but have not registered
5. number of individuals who are eligible to vote but did not vote
6. number of individuals who did vote
7. number of records processed

Input Data: Prepare and use the following sample data in DATA statements.

Number	Age in Years	Sex Code	Registered	Voted
1614	18	F	N	N
1321	21	M	N	N
1961	33	M	Y	Y
1432	46	F	Y	Y
1721	25	M	Y	Y
1211	16	M	N	N
1100	38	F	Y	Y
4164	34	M	Y	N
2139	19	M	Y	N
8647	25	F	Y	Y
9216	13	M	N	N
7814	15	F	N	N

Output Results: The following results are displayed.

```
Voter Analysis

Males Not Eligible to Register ===================> 2
Females Not Eligible to Register =================> 1

Males Old Enough to Vote but Not Registered =====> 1
Females Old Enough to Vote but Not Registered ===> 1

Individuals Eligible to Vote but Did Not Vote ===> 2
Individuals that Voted ==========================> 5

Total Number of Records Processed ===============> 12

End of Report
```

3. Stockbroker's Commission

Purpose: To become familiar with the If-Then-Else structure and with methods used to determine a stockbroker's commission.

Problem: Write a program that will read a stock transaction and determine the stockbroker's commission. Each transaction includes the following data: the stock name, price per share, number of shares involved, and the stockbroker's name.

The stockbroker's commission is computed in the following manner: if price per share P is less than or equal to $40.00, the commission rate is $0.15 per share; if P is greater than $40.00, the commission rate is $0.25 per share; and if the number of shares sold is less than 125, the commission is 1.5 times the rate per share.

Each line of output is to include the stock transaction data set and the commission paid the stockbroker. Test the stock name for the EOF. Display the total commission earned. (**Hint**: See Program 5.1 on page 111 or PRG5-1 on the Student Diskette.)

Input Data: Prepare and use the following sample data in DATA statements.

Stock Name	Price per Share	Number of Shares	Stockbroker Name
Crane	$32.50	200	Baker, G.
FstPa	17.50	100	Smith, J.
GenDyn	56.25	300	Smith, A.
Harris	40.00	125	Lucas, M.
BellCd	48.00	160	Soley, K.
BellHow	22.00	300	Jones, D.

Output Results: The following results are displayed.

```
                Stockbroker's Commission
Stock      Price         Number       Stockbroker
Name       Per Share     Of Shares    Name           Commission
-----      ---------     ---------    -----------    ----------
Crane       32.50          200        Baker, G.         30.00
FstPa       17.50          100        Smith, J.         22.50
GenDyn      56.25          300        Smith, A.         75.00
Harris      40.00          125        Lucas, M.         18.75
BellCd      48.00          160        Soley, K.         40.00
BellHow     22.00          300        Jones, D.         45.00

Total Commission Earned                               $231.25

End of Report
```

4. Payroll Problem IV: Bi-Weekly Payroll Computations with Time and a Half for Overtime

Purpose: To become familiar with decision making and with some payroll concepts.

Problem: Modify Payroll Problem III in Chapter 4, on page 99 (BASIC Programming Problem 3), to include the following conditions.

1. Overtime (hours worked > 80) is paid at 1.5 times the hourly rate.
2. Federal withholding tax is determined in the same manner as indicated in Payroll Problem III. However, assign a value of $0.00 if the gross pay is less than the product of the number of dependents and $38.46.
3. After processing the employee records, display the total gross pay, federal withholding tax, and net pay.

(**Hint:** See Program 5.1 on page 111 or PRG5-1 on the Student Diskette.)

Input Data: Use the sample data found in Payroll Problem II in Chapter 3, on page 64 (BASIC Programming Problem 3). Modify the data representing employee 126 so that the number of dependents equals 9.

Output Results: The following results are displayed.

```
                Biweekly Payroll Report
    Employee
    Number       Gross Pay       Fed. Tax        Net Pay
    --------     ---------       --------        -------
      123         1,000.00         184.62         815.38
      124           880.00         168.31         711.69
      125         1,040.00         200.31         839.69
      126            90.00           0.00          90.00

    Total Gross Pay ========>  3,010.00
    Total Withholding Tax ==>    553.23
    Total Net Pay ==========>  2,456.77

    End of Payroll Report
```

SEQUENTIAL FILE PROCESSING AND THE TOP-DOWN APPROACH

■ 6.1 INTRODUCTION

In the first five chapters of this book, we emphasized the importance of integrating data into the program. You learned that data may be entered into a program through the use of the LET statement, the INPUT statement, or the READ and DATA statements. This chapter presents a fourth method for entering data — the use of data files. With data files, the data is stored in auxiliary storage rather than in the program itself. This technique is used primarily for dealing with large amounts of data.

This chapter also presents the top-down (modular) approach to solving problems. The top-down approach is a usefull methodology for solving larger and more complex problems than those presented in earlier chapters. Included in the presentation are the GOSUB, ON-GOSUB, and RETURN statements.

The ON-GOSUB statement may be used to implement the Case structure, (see Figure 5.3 on page 103). As we shall see later in this chapter, the Case structure is commonly used with **menu-driven programs**. A menu-driven program is one in which a **menu** or series of menus is used to guide an operator through a multifunction interactive program. The menu itself lists the functions that a program or a section of a program can perform.

At the conclusion of this chapter, you should be able to design programs that write reports to auxiliary storage, build data files, and process data files. You will also be able to write menu-driven programs and solve problems by first breaking them into smaller and more manageable subproblems.

■ 6.2 DATA FILES

In previous chapters, program development was emphasized. Of equal concern are the organization and processing of data in the form of files. This is especially true in a business environment for the following three reasons:

1. Business applications, such as payroll, billing, order entry, and inventory, involve the processing of extensive amounts of data.
2. Data must be continually updated if management reports are to be useful.
3. The same data is often required for several applications, such as payroll, personnel, pension plans, and insurance reporting.

Computer manufacturers have applied a great deal of effort toward the development of both hardware, like auxiliary storage devices, and software, like **file-handling statements**, in order to deal directly with the organization and processing of large amounts of data.

In programs in previous chapters, the LET statement, the INPUT statement, or the READ and DATA statements were used to enter data into the PC. A more efficient and convenient method of organizing data is to store it on an auxiliary storage device, like a diskette or hard disk, and keep it separate from the programs that will process the data. Data stored in this fashion is a **file**, a group of related records. The number of records making up a file may range from just a few to thousands or millions. Each record within the file contains related data items (fields).

MS BASIC includes a set of file-handling statements that allow a user to do the following:

1. create new data files;
2. define the data files to be used by a program;
3. open an existing file;
4. read data from a file;
5. write data to a file;
6. test for the end of file; and
7. close a file.

File Organization

File organization is a method of arranging records on an auxiliary storage device. MS BASIC provides for two types of file organization: sequential and random.

A file that is organized sequentially is called a **sequential file** and is limited to sequential processing. This means that the records can be processed only in the order in which they are placed in the file. Conceptually, a sequential file is identical to the use of DATA statements within a BASIC program. For example, the fourteenth data item in a DATA statement of a BASIC program cannot be processed until the previous thirteen data items have been read. Similarly, the fourteenth record in a sequential file cannot be processed until after the previous thirteen records have been read.

Sequential organization can also be used to write reports to auxiliary storage instead of to an external device, such as a screen or a printer. Once the report is in auxiliary storage, it can be displayed at any time and as often as needed. Writing reports to auxiliary storage is a common practice, especially with programs that generate multiple reports. In such programs, each report is written to a separate file.

A file that is organized randomly is called a **random file** or a **relative file**. The sequence of processing a random file has no relationship to the sequence in which the records are stored in it. If the tenth record in a file is required by a program, the record can be directly accessed without reading the previous nine records. However, the program must indicate to the PC the location of the record relative to the beginning of the file. For example, to access the tenth record instead of the third or forth record, the program must explicitly indicate to the PC that the tenth record is requested for processing.

■ 6.3 SEQUENTIAL FILE PROCESSING

This section presents the file-handling statements required to create and process sequential files. Also, sample programs are presented to illustrate the following:

1. how reports can be written to auxiliary storage instead of to the screen or to the printer;
2. how to build sequential files that other programs can process; and
3. how reports can be generated from data that is located in sequential files.

Opening Sequential Files

Before any existing file can be read from or written to, it must be opened by the OPEN statement. When executed, the OPEN statement carries out the following five basic functions:

1. It requests the PC to allocate a **buffer**. A buffer is a part of main storage through which data is passed between the program and auxiliary storage.
2. It identifies by name the file to be processed.
3. It indicates whether the file is to be read from or written to.
4. It assigns the file a filenumber.
5. It sets the pointer to the beginning of the file or to the end of the file.

The general form of the OPEN statement is shown in Table 6.1.

TABLE 6.1 The OPEN Statement for Sequential Files

General Form:	OPEN *filespec* FOR *mode* AS *#filenumber*
	where **filespec** *is the name of the file;*
	mode *is one of the following:*
	INPUT *specifies sequential input mode, where the* pointer *is positioned at the beginning of the file;*
	OUTPUT *specifies sequential output mode, where the* pointer *is positioned at the beginning of the file;*
	APPEND *specifies sequential output mode, where the* pointer *is positioned to the end of the file; and*
	filenumber *is a numeric expression whose value is between 1 and the maximum number of files allowed (3 by default). The filenumber is associated with the file (**filespec**) for as long as it is open. The filenumber may be used by other file-handling statements to refer to the specific file.*
Keyword Entry:	Hold down the Alt key and press the O key on your keyboard.
Purpose:	*Allows a program to read records from or write records to a sequential file.*
Examples:	500 OPEN "B:EMPLOYEE.DAT" FOR INPUT AS #1 600 OPEN "PAYROLL.LIS" FOR OUPUT AS #2 700 OPEN "ACCOUNTS.DAT" FOR APPEND AS #3 800 OPEN FILESPEC$ FOR INPUT AS #3
Note:	*MS BASIC provides for a second general form for the* OPEN *statement:* OPEN *mode, #filenumber, filespec*
	(This second general form is less contemporary than the general form specified at the top of this table, and will therefore not be used in this book.)

As described in Table 6.1, a sequential file may be opened for input, output, or append. Line 500 in the examples section of Table 6.1 opens an existing file EMPLOYEE.DAT for input as filenumber 1. The file is located on the B drive. Since EMPLOYEE.DAT is opened for input, the program can only read records from it. An attempt to write a record to EMPLOYEE.DAT will result in the following diagnostic message:

```
Bad file number
```

If an attempt is made to open a nonexistent file for input, the following diagnostic message displays:

```
File not found
```

Line 600 in Table 6.1 opens PAYROLL.LIS on the default drive for output. Since PAYROLL.LIS is opened for output, the program can only write records to the sequential file.

Opening a sequential file for output always creates a new file. If, for example, PAYROLL.LIS already exists, then it is deleted before it is opened. Since there are never any records in a newly opened file, the data pointer is positioned at the beginning of the file.

In the third example in Table 6.1, line 700 opens ACCOUNTS.DAT on the default drive for appending records to the end of the file. If ACCOUNTS.DAT exists, the data pointer is positioned after the last record. If ACCOUNTS.DAT does not exist, the PC creates ACCOUNTS.DAT and positions the data pointer at the beginning of the file.

The append mode (APPEND) should be used in the OPEN statement whenever records are added to a sequential file. For example, with an order-entry application, it may be desirable to maintain a weekly customer-order file. Orders entered on a daily basis are appended to those which have been previously entered. At the end of the week, the customer-order file will contain the orders for the week in the sequence entered.

The following rules summarize the use of the OPEN statement.

> **OPEN Rule 1:** A sequential file must be opened before it can be read from or written to.

> **OPEN Rule 2:** A program can only read records from a sequential file that has been opened for input.

> **OPEN Rule 3:** A sequential file must already exist if it is opened for input.

> **OPEN Rule 4:** A program can only write records to a sequential file that has been opened for output or append.

> **OPEN Rule 5:** A filenumber can be assigned to only one sequential file at a time.

Closing Sequential Files

When a program is finished reading or writing to a file, it must close the file with the CLOSE statement. The CLOSE statement terminates the association between the file and the filenumber assigned in the OPEN statement and deallocates the part of main storage that is assigned to the buffer. If a file is being written to, the CLOSE statement ensures that the last record is transferred from the buffer in main storage to auxiliary storage.

The general form of the CLOSE statement is shown in Table 6.2.

TABLE 6.2 The CLOSE Statement

General Form:	CLOSE *or* CLOSE #filenumber$_1$, ..., #filenumber$_n$
Purpose:	*Terminates the association between a filenumber and a file that was established in a previously executed* OPEN *statement.* *If the file is opened for output or append, the* CLOSE *statement ensures that the last record is transferred from main storage to auxiliary storage.* *If no filenumbers follow the keyword* CLOSE, *then all opened files are closed.*
Examples:	600 CLOSE #1, #2, #3 700 CLOSE #1 800 CLOSE #2, #1 900 CLOSE

The CLOSE statement terminates access to a file. For example,

    4600 CLOSE #2, #3

causes the files assigned to filenumbers 2 and 3 to be closed. Any other files previously opened by the program remain open.

Following the close of a specified file, the filenumber may be assigned again to the same file or to a different file by an OPEN statement. The following rule summarizes the CLOSE statement.

> ***CLOSE Rule 1:*** A file must be opened before it can be closed.

Writing Reports to a Sequential File

The PRINT #n and PRINT #n, USING statements are used to write reports to sequential files. Once it has been written to a file, a report can be displayed or printed as often as desired without the program being reexecuted. The general forms of the PRINT #n and PRINT #n, USING statements are shown on the next page in Tables 6.3 and 6.4, respectively.

The PRINT #n and PRINT #n, USING statements work in exactly the same way as the PRINT and PRINT USING statements except that information is written to a sequential file in auxiliary storage rather than to the screen. For example, the statement

    500 PRINT A, B, C

displays the values of the variables A, B, and C on the screen in print zones 1, 2, and 3. Similarly, the statement

    500 PRINT #1, A, B, C

creates and transmits a record image to the sequential file, assigned to filenumber 1, with the values of the variables A, B, and C beginning in zones 1, 2, and 3 of the record.

TABLE 6.3 The PRINT #n Statement

General Form:	PRINT #n, item pm item pm ... pm item
	where **n** is a filenumber assigned to a file defined in an OPEN statement; **item** is a constant, variable, expression, function reference, or null; and **pm** is a punctuation mark such as a comma, semicolon, or space.
Purpose:	Provides for the generation of labeled and unlabeled output or of output in a consistent tabular format from the program to a sequential file in auxiliary storage.
Keyword Entry:	Press the question mark (?) key or hold down the Alt key and press the P key on your keyboard.
Examples:	100 PRINT #1, 200 PRINT #2, EMP.NAME$, AGE, WEIGHT 300 PRINT #1, TAB(10); "Total Sales ======>"; TOTAL 400 PRINT #2, X + Y/4, C * B 500 PRINT #3, Q1TAX, Q2TAX, Q3TAX, Q4TAX 600 PRINT #2, SUM;
Note:	One or more spaces between the print items have the same effect as the semicolon. The print items may be numeric or string.

TABLE 6.4 The PRINT #n, USING Statement

General Form:	PRINT #n, USING string expression; list
	where **n** is a filenumber assigned to a file defined in an OPEN statement; **string expression** (sometimes called the descriptor field or format field) is either a string constant or a string variable; and **list** is a list of items to be displayed in the format specified by the descriptor field.
Purpose:	Provides for controlling exactly the format of a program's output to a sequential file by specifying an image to which that output must conform.
Keyword Entry:	Hold down the Alt key and press the P key for the keyword PRINT. Hold down the Alt key and press the U key for the keyword USING.
Examples:	550 PRINT #3, USING "The answer is #,###.##"; COST 600 PRINT #2, USING "## divided by # is #.#"; NUM, DEN, QUOT 650 FORMAT1$ = "Total cost ========> $$,###.##-" 700 PRINT #7, USING FORMAT1$; TOTAL 750 FORMAT2$ = "**,###.##" 760 PRINT #1, USING FORMAT2$; CHECK; 800 PRINT #2, USING "\ \"; CUST.NAME$ 850 PRINT #3, USING "!, !, \ \"; FIRST$, MIDDLE$, LAST$ 905 PRINT #4, USING "Example _##"; NUMBER 950 PRINT #9, USING "#.##^^^^"; DIS1, DIS2, DIS3, DIS4
Note:	For more information on the descriptor field, see Table 4.9 on page 85.

PROGRAMMING CASE STUDY 7B: *Writing the Weekly Payroll and Summary Report to Auxiliary Storage*

In Chapter 5, the Weekly Payroll and Summary Report (Programming Case Study 7A) was introduced. In the solution (Program 5.1 on page 111), the PRINT and PRINT USING statements displayed the report on the screen. In the following modified solution, the report is written to a sequential file in auxiliary storage. Program 6.1 is identical to Program 5.1 except for some minor comments and the inclusion of the following:

1. line 173, which displays a message on the screen indicating that the report is being written to auxiliary storage;
2. line 176, which opens for output the sequential file REPORT.LIS on the B drive;
3. inclusion of filenumber 1 in each PRINT and PRINT USING statement writing the report;
4. line 423, which closes REPORT.LIS; and
5. lines 426 and 429, which display end-of-job information on the screen.

Program Solution   The following program writes the weekly payroll and summary report to auxiliary storage.

PROGRAM 6.1

```
100 ' Program 6.1
110 ' Writing the Weekly Payroll and Summary Report
113 ' to Auxiliary Storage
116 ' Report File Name = REPORT.LIS
120 ' ******************************************
130 '
140 ' *************** Initialization ***************
150 EMP.COUNT   = 0
160 TOTAL.GROSS = 0
170 CLS : KEY OFF   ' Clear Screen
173 LOCATE 10, 20 : PRINT "Writing Payroll Report to Auxiliary Storage..."
176 OPEN "REPORT.LIS" FOR OUTPUT AS #1
180 PRINT #1, "          Weekly Payroll Report"
190 PRINT #1,
200 PRINT #1, "Employee No.   Hours     Rate     Gross Pay"
210 FORMAT$ = "     \   \       ###.#     ##.##    ##,###.##"
220 PRINT #1,
230 '
240 ' *************** Process File ***************
250 READ EMP.NUMBER$, EMP.HOURS, EMP.RATE
260 WHILE EMP.NUMBER$ <> "EOF"
270     EMP.COUNT    = EMP.COUNT + 1
280     EMP.OVERTIME = EMP.HOURS - 40
290     IF EMP.OVERTIME <= 0
           THEN EMP.GROSS = EMP.HOURS * EMP.RATE
           ELSE EMP.GROSS = EMP.HOURS * EMP.RATE + .5 * EMP.RATE * EMP.OVERTIME
300     TOTAL.GROSS = TOTAL.GROSS + EMP.GROSS
310     PRINT #1, USING FORMAT$; EMP.NUMBER$, EMP.HOURS, EMP.RATE, EMP.GROSS
320     READ EMP.NUMBER$, EMP.HOURS, EMP.RATE
330 WEND
340 '
```

(continued)

```
350 ' **************** Wrap-up ******************
360 AVERAGE.GROSS = TOTAL.GROSS / EMP.COUNT
370 PRINT #1,
380 PRINT #1, USING "Total Gross Pay ========> $$,###.##"; TOTAL.GROSS
390 PRINT #1, USING "Number of Employees ====>    ###";    EMP.COUNT
400 PRINT #1, USING "Average Gross Pay ======> $$,###.##"; AVERAGE.GROSS
410 PRINT #1,
420 PRINT #1, "End of Payroll Report"
423 CLOSE #1
426 LOCATE 12, 20 : PRINT "Report Stored Under File Name REPORT.LIS"
429 LOCATE 14, 20 : PRINT "End of Job"
430 '
440 ' *************** Data Follows ***************
450 DATA 124, 40,   5.60
460 DATA 126, 56,   5.90
470 DATA 128, 38,   4.60
480 DATA 129, 48.5, 6.10
490 DATA EOF, 0,    0
500 END
```

Discussion of the Program Solution

When the RUN command is issued for Program 6.1, the information shown in Figure 6.1 is displayed on the screen to inform the operator that the report is being written to a sequential file in auxiliary storage under the name REPORT.LIS on the default drive.

```
Writing Payroll Report to Auxiliary Storage...

Report Stored Under File Name REPORT.LIS

End of Job
```

FIGURE 6.1 *The display from the execution of Program 6.1.*

The report written to auxiliary storage by Program 6.1 is illustrated in Figure 6.2

```
             Weekly Payroll Report

  Employee No.   Hours     Rate    Gross Pay

       124       40.0      5.60     224.00
       126       56.0      5.90     377.60
       128       38.0      4.60     174.80
       129       48.5      6.10     321.77

  Total Gross Pay ========> $1,098.17
  Number of Employees ====>        4
  Average Gross Pay ======>   $274.54

  End of Payroll Report
```

FIGURE 6.2 *Results of Program 6.1 written to auxiliary storage under the file name REPORT.LIS and displayed with the MS DOS command TYPE.*

Flowchart of the OPEN and CLOSE Statements

The I/O symbol is used to represent the OPEN and CLOSE statements. Therefore, the flowchart symbol below on the left represents the OPEN statement in line 176 of Program 6.1, and the flowchart symbol on the right represents the CLOSE statement in line 423 of Program 6.1.

Writing Data to a Sequential File

In Program 6.1, the PRINT #n and PRINT #n, USING statements were employed to write a report to a sequential file in auxiliary storage. To write data to a sequential file, we use the WRITE #n statement which writes data in a format required by the INPUT #n statement. The format requirement is similar to that of the READ and DATA statements — all data items are separated by commas. The WRITE #n statement also surrounds all string data items with quotation marks to ensure no loss of leading or trailing blanks.

The following WRITE #n statement writes a record in the format required by the INPUT #n statement.

```
500 WRITE #2, EMP.NAME$, AGE, CODE$, SENIORITY
```

The WRITE #n statement in line 500 causes a comma to be placed between the data items. Quotation marks are placed around the values of EMP.NAME$ and CODE$ and a carriage return character <cr> is appended to the last data item written to form the record. For example, if EMP.NAME$ = John Smith, AGE = 46, CODE$ = 3, and SENIORITY = 12, then line 500 transmits the following record to the sequential file assigned to file number 2:

```
"John Smith",46,"3",12<cr>
```
⬅ *Record Transmitted to Filenumber 2 by Line 500*

Note that the string values are delimited with the quotation marks and that the usual leading and trailing spaces surrounding positive numbers are compressed out.

The general form of the WRITE #n statement is given in Table 6.5.

TABLE 6.5 The WRITE #n Statement

General Form:	WRITE #n, list of variables
	where **n** is a filenumber assigned to a sequential file opened for output.
Purpose:	*Writes data items separated by commas to a sequential file in auxiliary storage.*
Examples:	1000 WRITE #1, COST, MARGIN, PRICE
	2000 WRITE #2, AMOUNT, DESCRIPTION$

PROGRAMMING CASE STUDY 8: Creating a Sequential File

Problem: The PUC Company has requested that a sequential file (INVNTORY.DAT) be created from the inventory data below. The data must be written in a format that is consistent with the INPUT #n statement. Use a series of LOCATE and INPUT statements to display the screen design shown in Figure 6.3.

In the following inventory data, each line represents an inventory record.

Stock Number	Warehouse Location	Description	Unit Cost	Selling Price	Quantity on Hand
C101	1	Roadhandler	97.56	125.11	25
C204	3	Whitewalls	37.14	99.95	140
C502	2	Tripod	32.50	38.99	10
S209	1	Maxidrill	88.76	109.99	6
S416	2	Normalsaw	152.55	179.40	1
S812	2	Router	48.47	61.15	8
S942	4	Radialsaw	376.04	419.89	3
T615	4	Oxford-Style	26.43	31.50	28
T713	2	Moc-Boot	24.99	29.99	30
T814	2	Work-Boot	22.99	27.99	56

Following are a list of the program tasks in outline form; a program solution; and a discussion of the program solution.

Program Tasks

1. Initialization

   a. Set record count (RECORD.COUNT) to zero.
   b. Clear the 25th line of the screen.
   c. Open the file INVNTORY.DAT for output as filenumber 1.

2. Build File

   a. Assign CONTROL$ the value Y.
   b. Establish a While loop that executes until CONTROL$ does not equal Y or y. Do the following within this loop:
      (1) Clear the screen and display a screen title.
      (2) Request and accept STOCK$, LOCATION$, DESC$, COST, PRICE, and QUANTITY.
      (3) Request the operator to enter Y to add the record, else N. Assign the entry to ADDREC$.
      (4) If ADDREC$ equals Y or y, use the WRITE #n statement to write the record to INVNTORY.DAT and add 1 to RECORD.COUNT.
      (5) Request the operator to enter Y to add another record, else N. Assign the entry to CONTROL$.

3. Wrap-up

   a. Close the file.
   b. Clear the screen and display a message indicating that the file creation is complete.
   c. Display the number of records (RECORD.COUNT) written to INVNTORY.DAT.

Structured Microsoft BASIC: Essentials for Business   **143**

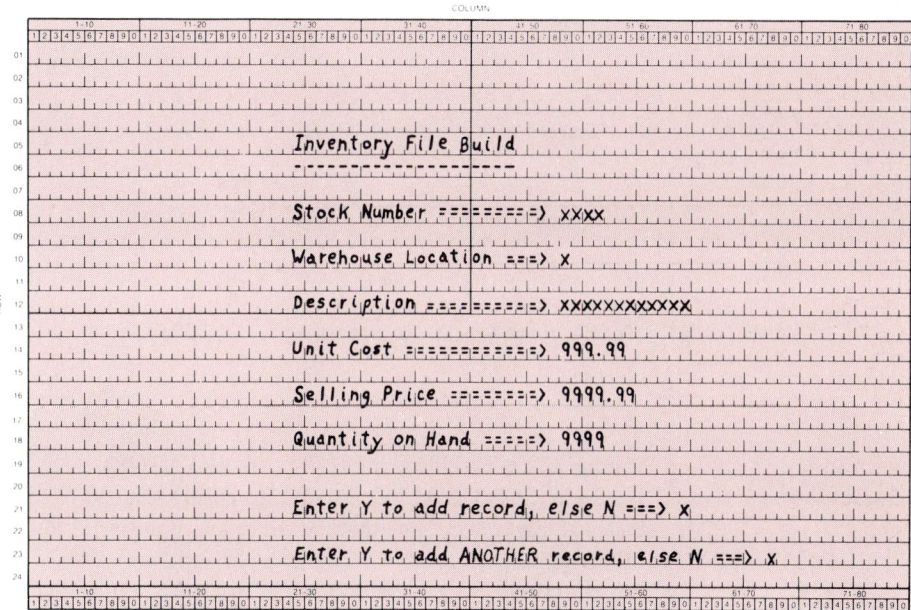

FIGURE 6.3 *The screen design for requesting operator entry of inventory records for Program 6.2.*

Program Solution   The following program corresponds to the preceding tasks.

PROGRAM 6.2

```
100 ' Program 6.2
110 ' Creating a Sequential File
120 ' Output File Name = INVNTORY.DAT
130 ' *******************************
140 '
150 ' ******** Initialization *******
160 RECORD.COUNT = 0
170 KEY OFF   ' Clear 25th line
180 OPEN "INVNTORY.DAT" FOR OUTPUT AS #1
190 '
200 ' ********** Build File *********
210 CONTROL$ = "Y"
220 WHILE CONTROL$ = "Y" OR CONTROL$ = "y"
230     CLS   ' Clear Screen
240     LOCATE  5, 25 : PRINT "Inventory File Build"
250     LOCATE  6, 25 : PRINT "--------------------"
260     LOCATE  8, 25 : INPUT "Stock Number ==========> ", STOCK$
270     LOCATE 10, 25 : INPUT "Warehouse Location ===> ", LOCATION$
280     LOCATE 12, 25 : INPUT "Description ==========> ", DESC$
290     LOCATE 14, 25 : INPUT "Unit Cost ============> ", COST
300     LOCATE 16, 25 : INPUT "Selling Price ========> ", PRICE
310     LOCATE 18, 25 : INPUT "Quantity On Hand =====> ", QUANTITY
320     LOCATE 21, 25
```

(continued)

```
330     INPUT "Enter Y to add record, else N ===> ", ADDREC$
340     IF ADDREC$ = "Y" OR ADDREC$ = "y"
            THEN WRITE #1, STOCK$, LOCATION$, DESC$, COST, PRICE, QUANTITY:
                 RECORD.COUNT = RECORD.COUNT + 1
350     LOCATE 23, 25
360     INPUT "Enter Y to add ANOTHER record, else N ===> ", CONTROL$
370 WEND
380 '
390 ' *********** Wrap-up ***********
400 CLOSE #1
410 CLS   ' Clear Screen
420 LOCATE 10, 15 :PRINT "Creation of Sequential File Is Complete"
430 LOCATE 14, 15
440 PRINT "Total Number of Records in INVNTORY.DAT ===>"; RECORD.COUNT
450 END
```

Discussion of the Program Solution

When Program 6.2 is executed, line 180 opens INVNTORY.DAT for output as filenumber 1. Line 210 assigns CONTROL$ the value Y to ensure that the While loop (lines 220 through 370) executes at least once. Note that the condition in the WHILE statement in line 220 is true if CONTROL$ equals Y or y.

Within the While loop, the LOCATE, PRINT, and INPUT statements in lines 240 through 330 cause the display shown in Figure 6.4. If the operator enters a Y or y in response to the INPUT statement in line 330, then line 340 writes the record to INVNTORY.DAT and RECORD.COUNT is incremented by 1. If the operator does not enter a Y or y, then the record showing on the screen is not added to the file. The last INPUT statement in the While loop (line 360), requests that the user enter a Y or N, depending on whether there are any more records to add.

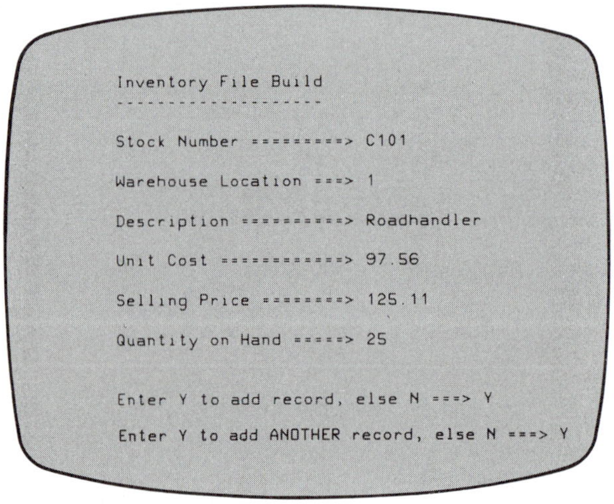

```
Inventory File Build
--------------------

Stock Number ==========> C101

Warehouse Location ===> 1

Description ==========> Roadhandler

Unit Cost ============> 97.56

Selling Price ========> 125.11

Quantity on Hand =====> 25


Enter Y to add record, else N ===> Y

Enter Y to add ANOTHER record, else N ===> Y
```

FIGURE 6.4 *The display after the first record is entered due to the execution of Program 6.2.*

Figure 6.5 shows the format of the data written to INVNTORY.DAT by Program 6.2.

```
"C101","1","Roadhandler",97.56,125.11,25
"C204","3","Whitewalls",37.14,99.95,140
"C502","2","Tripod",32.5,38.99,10
"S209","1","Maxidrill",88.76,109.99,6
"S416","2","Normalsaw",152.55,179.4,1
"S812","2","Router",48.47,61.15,8
"S942","4","Radialsaw",376.04,419.89,3
"T615","4","Oxford-Style",26.43,31.5,28
"T713","2","Moc-Boot",24.99,29.99,30
"T814","2","Work-Boot",22.99,27.99,56
```

FIGURE 6.5 *A listing of INVNTORY.DAT created by Program 6.2.*

Line 400 in Program 6.2 closes INVNTORY.DAT. This ensures that the last record entered by the operator is moved from the buffer to the file in auxiliary storage. Figure 6.6 shows the display due to lines 410 through 440 of Program 6.2.

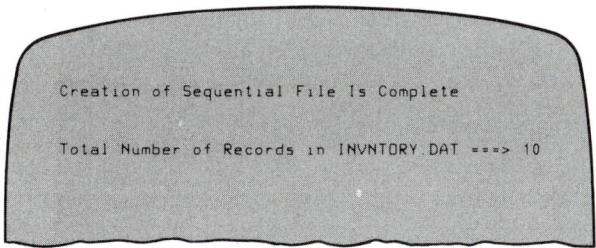

FIGURE 6.6 *The end-of-job display due to the execution of Program 6.2.*

The INPUT #n Statement

The INPUT #n statement is used to read data from a sequential file that has been created by using the WRITE #n statement. The statement is the same as the READ statement except that it reads data from a file instead of from DATA statements. Line 190 in the following partial program reads six data items from the sequential file INVNTORY.DAT.

```
190 OPEN "INVNTORY.DAT" FOR INPUT AS #1
    .
    .
320 INPUT #1, STOCK$, LOCATION$, DESC$, COST, PRICE, QUANTITY
```

For data to be read from a sequential file, the following must be true:

1. The file must already exist.
2. The file must be opened for input.
3. The data items in the file must be separated by a comma or by a carriage return character (<cr>).

The general form of the INPUT #n statement is shown in Table 6.6.

TABLE 6.6 The INPUT #n Statement

General Form:	INPUT #n, list of variables
	where **n** is a filenumber assigned to a sequential file opened for input.
Purpose:	Reads data items from a sequential file in auxiliary storage and assigns them to variables.
Keyword Entry:	Hold down the Alt key and press the I key on your keyboard.
Examples:	300 INPUT #1, SUM, FIX, DESC$, PRICE
	400 INPUT #2, AMOUNT
	500 INPUT #3, CODE$, SALARY, TAX, DEPENDENTS

The INPUT #n statement causes the variables in its list to be assigned specific values, in order, from the data sequence found in the sequential file assigned to filenumber n. In order to visualize the relationship between the INPUT #n statement and the associated file, think of a pointer associated with the data items, as discussed in Chapter 4. When the OPEN statement is executed, this pointer references the first data item in the data-sequence holding area. Each time an INPUT #n statement is executed, the variables in the list are assigned values from the data-sequence holding area, beginning with the data item that is indicated by the pointer, and the pointer is advanced one value per variable. Hence, the pointer points to the next data item to be assigned when the INPUT #n statement is executed.

The following rules summarize the material discussed in this section.

> **Input Rule 4:** Before the INPUT #n statement is executed, the filenumber n must be assigned to a sequential file that is opened for input.

> **Input Rule 5:** Numeric variables in INPUT #n statements require numeric constants as data items, and string variables require strings as data.

The EOF Function

When a sequential file that was opened for output is closed, the PC automatically adds an end-of-file mark after the last record written to the file. Later, when the same sequential file is opened for input, you can use the EOF(n) function to test for the end-of-file mark. The n indicates the filenumber assigned to the file in the OPEN statement.

If the EOF function senses the end-of-file mark, it returns a value of –1 (true). Otherwise, it returns a value of 0 (false). The EOF function can be used to control a While loop. For example, consider the partial program at the top of the next page.

```
190 OPEN "INVNTORY.DAT" FOR INPUT AS #1
     .
     .
     .
300 ' ********** Process File *********
310 WHILE NOT EOF(1)
320     INPUT #1, STOCK$, LOCATION$, DESC$, COST, PRICE, QUANTITY
330     TOTAL.COST  = COST  * QUANTITY
340     TOTAL.PRICE = PRICE * QUANTITY
350     GRAND.TOTAL.COST  = GRAND.TOTAL.COST  + TOTAL.COST
360     GRAND.TOTAL.PRICE = GRAND.TOTAL.PRICE + TOTAL.PRICE
370     LPRINT USING FORMAT$; STOCK$, DESC$, COST, PRICE,
                          QUANTITY, TOTAL.COST, TOTAL.PRICE
380     LPRINT
390 WEND
```

In line 310, the EOF(1) function is used to control the While loop (lines 310 through 390). Each time line 310 is executed, the PC checks to see whether the data pointer is pointing to the end-of-file mark in INVNTORY.DAT.

When using the EOF function, it is important to organize your program so that the test for the end of file precedes the execution of the INPUT #n statement. Therefore, note in the previous partial program that only one INPUT #n statement is employed, and that this statement is placed inside at the top of the While loop as line 320. This is different from our previous programs, which employed two READ statements — one prior to the While loop and one at the bottom of the While loop.

The logic exhibited by the While loop also works when the file is empty (i.e., when the file contains no records). If the INVNTORY.DAT file is empty, line 190 in the partial program above will still open the file for input. However, when line 310 is executed, the EOF function immediately detects the end-of-file mark on the empty file, thereby causing the While loop to pass control to the statement following line 390.

The following rule summarizes the placement of the EOF function in a program.

EOF Function Rule 1: The EOF function should test for the end-of-file mark prior to the execution of an INPUT #n statement.

PROGRAMMING CASE STUDY 9: *Processing a Sequential File*

Problem: INVNTORY.DAT was created by Program 6.2; the contents of the sequential file are shown in Figure 6.5 on page 145.

For each record in INVNTORY.DAT, the following is to be printed on the printer by means of the LPRINT and LPRINT USING statements:

1. stock number
2. description
3. unit cost
4. selling price
5. quantity on hand
6. total item cost of a stock item (unit cost times quantity on hand)
7. total selling price of a stock item (selling price times quantity on hand)

Print the report title and column headings at the top of the page and print the inventory records on every other line (in other words, double-space the report). Print the total inventory cost and the total inventory selling price after all records have been processed.

The printer spacing chart in Figure 6.7 illustrates the design of the report to be printed.

```
                          Inventory Analysis

                                                            Total
Stock                  Unit  Selling  Quantity  Total      Selling
No.    Description     Cost  Price    on Hand   Item Cost  Price
----   -----------     ------ -------  --------  ---------  --------
XXXX   XXXXXXXXXX     999.99 9999.99    9999    99,999.99  99,999.99

Totals                                          999,999.99 999,999.99

Job Complete
```

FIGURE 6.7 *The output for Program 6.3, designed on a printer spacing chart.*

Following are the program tasks, in outline form; a program solution; and a discussion of the program solution.

Program Tasks

1. Initialization

   a. Set grand total cost (GRAND.TOTAL.COST) and grand total price (GRAND.TOTAL.PRICE) to zero.
   b. Clear the screen.
   c. Open the file INVENTORY.DAT for input as filenumber 1.
   d. Print the report title and column headings.
   e. Align the detail and total line formats below the report title and column headings.

2. Process File — establish a While loop that executes until the EOF function detects the end-of-file mark in INVNTORY.DAT. Do the following within the loop:

   a. Use the INPUT #n statement to read an inventory record. Use the same variable names found in the WRITE #n statement in line 340 of Program 6.2. (Consistent use of variable names between programs referencing the same file is not necessary, but it is good programming practice.)
   b. Compute the total cost (TOTAL.COST) and total price (TOTAL.PRICE). The total cost is determined by multiplying the unit cost by the quantity on hand. The total price is determined by multiplying the selling price by the quantity on hand. Increment the grand total cost (GRAND.TOTAL.COST) by the total cost and increment the grand total price (GRAND.TOTAL.PRICE) by the total price.
   c. Use the LPRINT USING statement to print the inventory record. Use an empty LPRINT statement to double-space.

3. Wrap-up

   a. Close INVNTORY.DAT.

b. Print the grand total cost (GRAND.TOTAL.COST) and grand total price (GRAND.TOTAL.PRICE).
c. Print an end-of-job message to conclude the report.

Program Solution — The following program employs the printer spacing chart in Figure 6.7 and corresponds to the preceding program tasks.

PROGRAM 6.3

```
100 ' Program 6.3
110 ' Processing a Sequential Data File
120 ' Input File Name = INVNTORY.DAT
130 ' ********************************
140 '
150 ' ********* Initialization ********
160 GRAND.TOTAL.COST  = 0
170 GRAND.TOTAL.PRICE = 0
180 CLS : KEY OFF   ' Clear Screen
190 OPEN "INVNTORY.DAT" FOR INPUT AS #1
200 LPRINT      "                    Inventory Analysis"
210 LPRINT
220 LPRINT      "                                                           Total"
230 LPRINT "Stock                    Unit Selling Quantity Total     Selling"
240 LPRINT "No.   Description        Cost Price   On Hand  Item Cost Price"
250 LPRINT "----- ------------       ---- -------  --------  --------- -------"
260 FORMAT$ ="\   \   \        \ ###.## ####.##    #### ##,###.## ##,###.##"
270 TOT.L1$ ="Totals                                     ###,###.## ###,###.##"
280 TOT.L2$ ="Job Complete"
290 '
300 ' ********* Process File *********
310 WHILE NOT EOF(1)
320    INPUT #1, STOCK$, LOCATION$, DESC$, COST, PRICE, QUANTITY
330    TOTAL.COST  = COST * QUANTITY
340    TOTAL.PRICE = PRICE * QUANTITY
350    GRAND.TOTAL.COST  = GRAND.TOTAL.COST  + TOTAL.COST
360    GRAND.TOTAL.PRICE = GRAND.TOTAL.PRICE + TOTAL.PRICE
370    LPRINT USING FORMAT$; STOCK$, DESC$, COST, PRICE,
                        QUANTITY, TOTAL.COST, TOTAL.PRICE
380    LPRINT
390 WEND
400 '
410 ' ************ Wrap-up ************
420 CLOSE #1
430 LPRINT
440 LPRINT USING TOT.L1$; GRAND.TOTAL.COST, GRAND.TOTAL.PRICE
450 LPRINT
460 LPRINT TOT.L2$
470 END
```

Discussion of the Program Solution — When the RUN command is issued for Program 6.3, the report illustrated in Figure 6.8 on the next page is printed on the printer. The following points should be noted concerning the program solution represented by Program 6.3.

1. In line 190, the OPEN statement opens INVNTORY.DAT for input as filenumber 1. The remaining file-handling statements, lines 320 and 420, and the EOF function in line 310, reference INVNTORY.DAT by specifying the filenumber 1.

2. The While loop, lines 310 through 390, processes records until the end-of-file mark is detected by the EOF function.
3. Even though the warehouse location is not manipulated or displayed by Program 6.3, it is necessary to include a variable (LOCATION$) that represents the warehouse location in the list of the INPUT #n statement (line 320), since the data item is part of the record. You cannot be selective and input from a sequential file only those data items which you plan to manipulate or display. All data items within the record must be assigned to variables in the INPUT #n statement.

```
                        Inventory Analysis

                                                           Total
    Stock                Unit  Selling  Quantity  Total    Selling
    No    Description    Cost  Price    On Hand   Item Cost Price
    ----- -----------    ----  -------  --------  --------- -------
    C101  Roadhandler    97.56  125.11      25    2,439.00   3,127.75

    C204  Whitewalls     37.14   99.95     140    5,199.60  13,993.00

    C502  Tripod         32.50   38.99      10      325.00     389.90

    S209  Maxidrill      88.76  109.99       6      532.56     659.94

    S416  Normalsaw     152.55  179.40       1      152.55     179.40

    S812  Router         48.47   61.15       8      387.76     489.20

    S942  Radialsaw     376.04  419.89       3    1,128.12   1,259.67

    T615  Oxford-Style   26.43   31.50      28      740.04     882.00

    T713  Moc-Boot       24.99   29.99      30      749.70     899.70

    T814  Work-Boot      22.99   27.99      56    1,287.44   1,567.44


    Totals                                       12,941.77  23,448.00

    Job Complete
```

FIGURE 6.8 *The report generated by Program 6.3.*

■ 6.4
THE TOP-DOWN (MODULAR) APPROACH AND THE GOSUB AND RETURN STATEMENTS

It is appropriate that we introduce you to a programming methodology called **top-down** or **modular programming**. The objective of top-down programming is to break down a problem into smaller and more manageable subproblems. In other words, to solve a problem top-down, you divide and conquer.

The idea of solving a problem by dividing it into subproblems is not new. In his *Discourse on Method*, written some three hundred years before the first computer was built, René Descartes made this very same point. In essence, he said that the resolution of a problem can be achieved if a person (1) divides each of the difficulties into as many parts as possible, and (2) thinks in an orderly fashion, beginning with those matters which are simplest and easiest to understand and gradually working toward those which are more complex.

The Top-Down Chart

A graphic representation of the top-down approach is called a **top-down chart**, which is also known as a **hierarchy chart** or a **VTOC — Visual Table of Contents**. Figure 6.9 represents a top-down chart in which the problem or task presented in Programming Case Study 4A on page 55 in Chapter 3 is broken down into subtasks. The overall task and each of the subtasks are represented by a process symbol with a short description written inside it. The top-down chart is read from top to bottom, and in general from left to right.

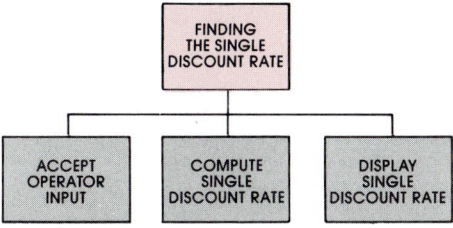

FIGURE 6.9 *A top-down chart for the problem presented in Programming Case Study 4A.*

A top-down chart differs from a program flowchart in that it does not show decision-making logic or flow of control. A program flowchart shows *procedure*, but a top-down chart shows *organization*. A top-down chart allows you to concentrate on defining *what* needs to be done in the program before deciding *how* and *when* it is to be done, which is represented in a program flowchart or by pseudocode.

A top-down chart is very similar to a company's organization chart; each subtask carries out a function for its superior. Think of the higher-level subtasks as vice presidents of the organization, who perform the controlling functions of that organization. The top-down chart in Figure 6.9 resembles a small company in that there is only one level below the president. As a company grows and becomes more complex, additional levels are appended to the organizational chart to carry out the tasks for that organization. Likewise, as problems become larger and more complex, additional levels are appended to the top-down chart.

Implementing a Top-Down Design — Internal Subroutines (Modules)

Once the larger, more complex problem has been decomposed into smaller pieces, a solution to each subtask can be designed, coded, and tested independently. The group of statements that is associated with a single programming task within a BASIC program is called an **internal subroutine** or a **module**.

An internal subroutine is executed only if referenced (*called*) by an explicit instruction from some other part of the program, as illustrated in Figure 6.10. Following execution of the internal subroutine, control passes back to the statement that immediately follows the instruction that activated the subroutine.

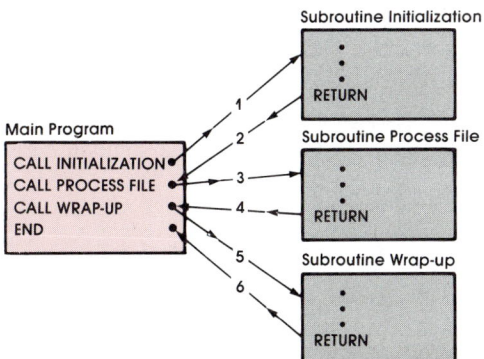

FIGURE 6.10 *A conceptual view of control transferring to an internal subroutine and eventually returning to the statement that immediately follows the instruction that activated the subroutine.*

The GOSUB and RETURN Statements

In BASIC, a subroutine is called by a GOSUB statement. The keyword GOSUB is immediately followed by a line number to which control is transferred. The last statement executed in a subroutine must be the RETURN statement. The RETURN statement returns control to the next executable statement following the corresponding GOSUB statement. A subroutine, therefore, can exit only through a RETURN statement. When a GOSUB statement is executed,

1. the main program calls or transfers control to the subroutine;
2. the called subroutine executes and performs a particular or recurring task for the main program; and
3. the RETURN statement of the subroutine transfers control back to the first executable statement following the GOSUB that referenced it.

The general forms for the GOSUB and RETURN statements are shown in Tables 6.7 and 6.8.

TABLE 6.7 The GOSUB Statement

General Form:	GOSUB *line number* where the line number represents the first line of a subroutine.
Purpose:	Causes control to transfer to the subroutine that is represented by the specified line number. Causes the location of the next executable statement following the GOSUB to be retained.
Examples:	1250 GOSUB 1600 1900 GOSUB 2000

TABLE 6.8 The RETURN Statement

General Form:	RETURN
Purpose:	Causes control to transfer from the subroutine back to the first executable statement immediately following the GOSUB statement that referenced it.
Example:	1700 RETURN
Note:	The RETURN statement may be followed by a line number. (This option is not used in this book.)

PROGRAMMING CASE STUDY 4B: *Finding the Single Discount Rate Using the Top-Down Approach*

Consider the following top-down approach to Programming Case Study 4A, Finding the Single Discount Rate, on page 55 in Chapter 3. The solution corresponds to the top-down chart in Figure 6.9 on page 151.

PROGRAM 6.4

Main Module
```
1000 ' Program 6.4
1010 ' Finding the Single Discount Rate
1020 ' ***********************************************
1030 ' *                Main Module                  *
1040 ' ***********************************************
1050 GOSUB 2000    ' Call Accept Operator Input
1060 GOSUB 3000    ' Call Compute Single Discount Rate
1070 GOSUB 4000    ' Call Display Single Discount Rate
1080 END
1090 '
```

Three Sub-routines
```
2000 ' ***********************************************
2010 ' *             Accept Operator Input           *
2020 ' ***********************************************
2030 CLS : KEY OFF   ' Clear Screen
2040 PRINT "Enter in Percent Form:"
2050 INPUT "          First Discount ======> ", RATE1
2060 INPUT "          Second Discount ======> ", RATE2
2070 INPUT "          Third Discount ======> ", RATE3
2080 RETURN
2090 '
3000 ' ***********************************************
3010 ' *          Compute Single Discount Rate       *
3020 ' ***********************************************
3030 RATE1 = RATE1 / 100
3040 RATE2 = RATE2 / 100
3050 RATE3 = RATE3 / 100
3060 RATE = 1 - (1 - RATE1) * (1 - RATE2) * (1 - RATE3)
3070 RATE = 100 * RATE
3080 RETURN
3090 '
4000 ' ***********************************************
4010 ' *          Display Single Discount Rate       *
4020 ' ***********************************************
4030 PRINT
4040 PRINT "Single Discount ================>"; RATE; "%"
4050 RETURN
4060 ' ************** End of Program **************
RUN

Enter in Percent Form:
          First Discount ======> 40
          Second Discount ======> 20
          Third Discount ======> 10

Single Discount ================> 56.8 %
```

When the RUN command is issued for Program 6.4, the GOSUB statement in line 1050 transfers control to the Accept Operator Input Module, which begins at line 2000. This module clears the screen and accepts the three discounts. The RETURN statement in line 2080 returns control to line 1060. Line 1060 represents the next executable statement following the GOSUB in the Main Module, which referenced the Accept Operator Input Module.

The GOSUB in line 1060 calls the Compute Single Discount Rate Module, which begins at line 3000. Once the single discount RATE has been determined, the RETURN statement in line 3080 returns control to line 1070 in the Main Module. Line 1070, in turn, transfers control to the Display Single Discount Rate Module. Following the display of the single discount RATE, the RETURN statement in line 4050 returns control to line 1080 of the Main Module. The END statement in line 1080 halts the execution of the program.

Note also that by placing the END statement in line 1080, we prevent the Accept Operator Input Module from being executed again.

Prior to Program 6.4, all programs used the END statement as the *physical* end of the program. In Program 6.4, the END statement, line 1080, is used to indicate the *logical* end of the program and line 4060, a remark line, is used to indicate the physical end of the program. MS BASIC does not require a physical END statement.

Flowchart Representation of GOSUB, RETURN, and Referenced Subroutine

The GOSUB statement, which calls the subroutine, is represented by the **predefined process symbol**, which was defined in Table 1.4 on page 12. The predefined process symbol consists of a set of vertical lines within the rectangle and indicates that the program steps of the subroutine are specified elsewhere. In Figure 6.11, the first subroutine is represented by the flowchart to the right of the Main Module, and the RETURN statement is represented by the terminal symbol.

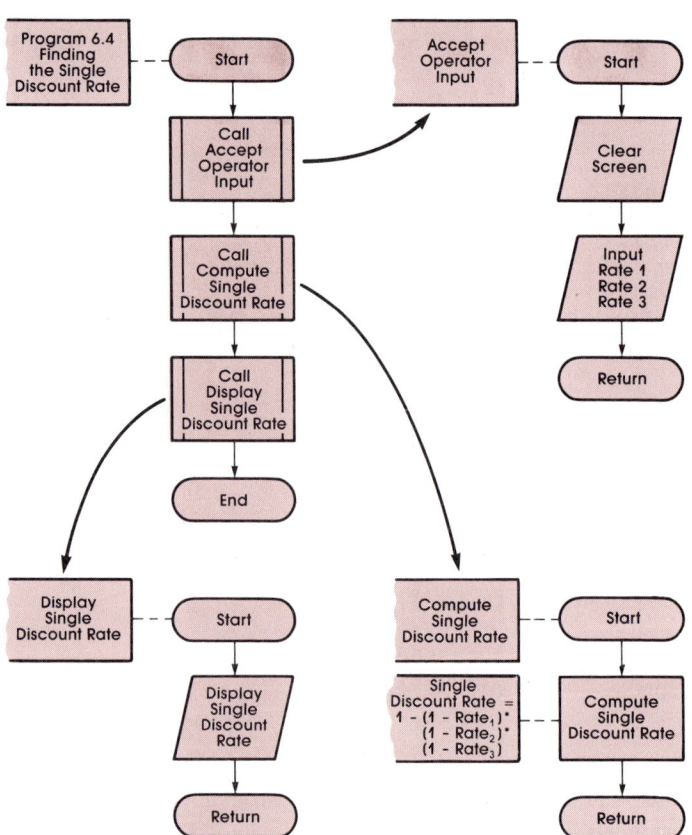

FIGURE 6.11 *General flowcharts for the Main Module and subroutines for Program 6.4.*

6.5 THE ON-GOSUB STATEMENT AND MENU-DRIVEN PROGRAMS

The GOSUB statement is defined as an unconditional subroutine call, because each time such a statement is executed, control is always transferred to the specified subroutine. In contrast, the ON-GOSUB statement allows for selected subroutine calls. Depending on the current value of the numeric expression that is associated with this statement, control will be transferred to one of two or more subroutines.

The ON-GOSUB statement can be used to implement an extension of the If-Then-Else structure, in which selection of one of many alternatives is based on an integer test. This extended version of the If-Then-Else structure is called the Case structure; it is illustrated in Figure 5.3 on page 103.

The condition in the ON-GOSUB statement may be a numeric variable or a numeric expression (never a string variable or string expression). The condition is placed between the keywords ON and GOSUB. Depending on the value of the condition, control transfers to one of several subroutines that are defined by line numbers appearing in a list that follows the keyword GOSUB. The general form of the ON-GOSUB statement is given in Table 6.9.

TABLE 6.9 The ON-GOSUB Statement

General Form:	ON numeric expression GOSUB $lineno_1, lineno_2, \ldots, lineno_n$
Purpose:	Causes control to transfer to the subroutine represented by the selected line number, where n is the current value of the numeric expression. Also causes the location of the next statement following the ON-GOSUB to be retained.
Examples:	1300 ON CODE GOSUB 2000, 3000, 4000, 5000 1500 ON AGE / 10 + 1 GOSUB 2500, 3500, 2500, 2500, 3500 1750 ON A MOD B GOSUB 1850, 1950, 2050, 2050, 2050
Note:	Non-integer values are rounded. If the value of the numeric expression is 0 or greater than the number of line numbers (but less than or equal to 255), execution continues with the next statement following the ON-GOSUB.
	If the value of the numeric expression is less than 0 or greater than 255, the program is terminated following the display of the message Illegal function call.

When the ON-GOSUB statement is executed, control transfers to one of the subroutines that are represented by the line numbers in the list following the keyword GOSUB. Commas are mandatory punctuation in the list of line numbers in the ON-GOSUB statement. The PC reads the line numbers in the ON-GOSUB statement from left to right, beginning with the first one in the list. If the value of the condition is 1, then control is transferred to the first line number in the list; if 2, then control is transferred to the second line number; and so on. Consider the following example.

```
1200 ON CODE GOSUB 2300, 2300, 2300, 2400, 2400, 2500, 2300, 2600
```

            Condition   List of line numbers representing subroutines to which control is transferred depending on the value of the condition.

If the value of CODE is 1 at the instant of the execution of line 1200, control will be transferred to line number 2300. The same thing will take place whenever CODE has the integer value of 2, 3, or 7. When CODE is equal to 4 or 5, control will pass to the subroutine that is represented by line 2400. When CODE is equal to 6, control will pass to the subroutine that begins at line number 2500. Finally, when CODE is equal to 8, control will be transferred to the subroutine at line number 2600.

The numeric expression in an `ON-GOSUB` statement is evaluated and rounded to obtain an integer whose value is then used to select a line number from the list following the keyword GOSUB. Consider the following example:

```
3000 ON A * B - C / D + E GOSUB 3200, 3400, 3600
```

If the value of the expression A * B − C / D + E is 2.64, it will be rounded to an integer value of 3 and control will be transferred to line number 3600, which is the subroutine represented by the third line number in the list following the `GOSUB`.

It is easy to see why programmers use the `ON-GOSUB` statement. An `ON-GOSUB` statement is used when the design of a program includes a Case structure (see Figure 5.3 on page 103) and the condition in the decision symbol can be equated to an integer test. Programming Case Study 10 illustrates a major use of the `ON-GOSUB` statement.

The BEEP Statement

When executed, the `BEEP` statement causes the PC's speaker to beep for a quarter of a second; several successive `BEEP` statements produce a constant beeping sound. For example, the following statement causes the PC to beep for one second.

```
220 BEEP : BEEP : BEEP : BEEP
```

The `BEEP` statement is often used in validation routines to alert the operator that something is wrong. The general form of the `BEEP` statement is given in Table 6.10.

TABLE 6.10 The BEEP Statement

General Form:	BEEP
Purpose:	*Causes the PC's speaker to beep for a quarter of a second.*
Examples:	100 BEEP
	200 BEEP : BEEP : BEEP : BEEP : BEEP : BEEP

PROGRAMMING CASE STUDY 10: A Menu-Driven Program

It is not at all uncommon for programs to have multiple functions. A **menu**, which is a list of the functions that a program can perform, is often used to guide an operator through a multifunction program. We call a program that displays a menu of functions a **menu-driven program**. Such a program displays a menu like the one illustrated on the screen layout form in Figure 6.12. The operator can then choose the desired function from the list by entering a corresponding code. Once the request is satisfied, the program again displays the menu. As illustrated in Figure 6.12, one of the codes (in this case 7) terminates execution of the program.

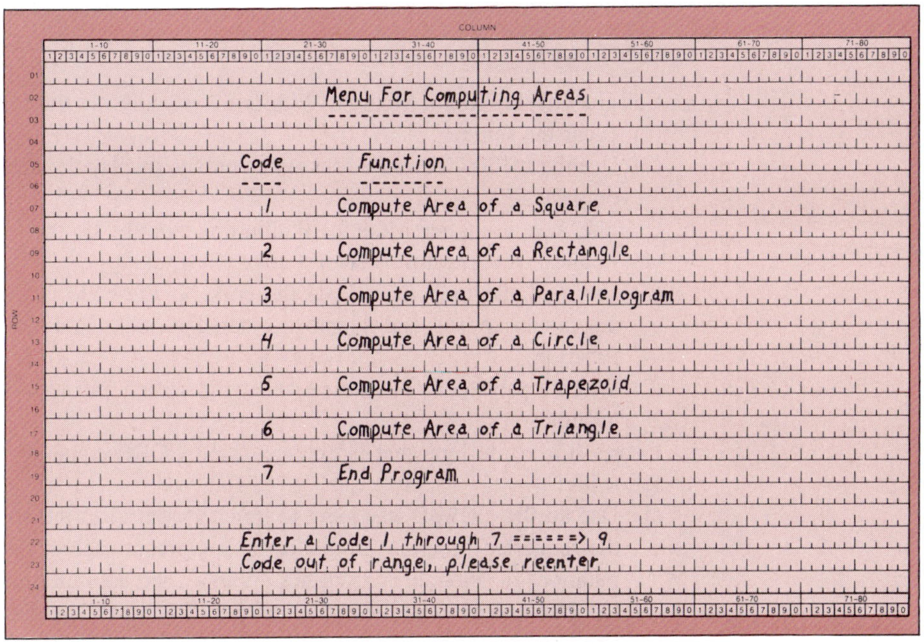

```
                              COLUMN
              Menu For Computing Areas
              ---------------------

         Code      Function
         ----      --------
          1        Compute Area of a Square

          2        Compute Area of a Rectangle

          3        Compute Area of a Parallelogram

          4        Compute Area of a Circle

          5        Compute Area of a Trapezoid

          6        Compute Area of a Triangle

          7        End Program


              Enter a Code 1 through 7 ======> 9
              Code out of range, please reenter
```

FIGURE 6.12 *A menu of program functions designed on a screen layout form.*

Problem: A menu-driven program is to compute the area of a square, rectangle, parallelogram, circle, trapezoid, and triangle. The program should display the menu shown in Figure 6.12. Once a code is entered, the program must do a range check to ensure that the code corresponds to one of the menu functions. After the selection of the proper function, the program should prompt the operator for the necessary data, compute the area, and display it accordingly. The displayed results are to remain on the screen until the Enter key on the keyboard is pressed. After that, the program should display the menu again.

Use the following formulas for the areas:

1. Area of a square: $A = S * S$, where S is the length of a side of the square.
2. Area of a rectangle: $A = L * W$, where L is the length and W is the width of the rectangle.
3. Area of a parallelogram: $A = B * H$, where B is the length of the base and H is the height of the parallelogram.
4. Area of a circle: $A = 3.141593 * R * R$, where R is the radius of the circle.
5. Area of a trapezoid: $A = \dfrac{H(B1 + B2)}{2}$, where H is the height, B1 is the length of the primary base, and B2 is the length of the secondary base of the trapezoid.
6. Area of a triangle: $A = \dfrac{B * H}{2}$, where B is the base and H is the height of the triangle.

Following is a list of the program tasks that correspond to the top-down chart; the top-down chart itself (Figure 6.13 on page 159); a program solution; and a discussion of the program solution.

Program Tasks   The following program tasks correspond to the top-down chart in Figure 6.13.

1. Process Request
   a. Call the Display Menu Module. Within this module, do the following:
      (1) Clear the screen.
      (2) Use the `LOCATE` and `PRINT` statements to display the menu shown in Figure 6.12 on page 157.
   b. Call the Accept a Code Module. Within this module, do the following:
      (1) Request the operator to enter a code (CODE).
      (2) Use a While loop to validate the code. If the code is invalid, beep the speaker, display an appropriate diagnostic message, and again ask the operator to select a function.
      (3) When a valid code is entered, clear the screen and return to the Process Request Module.
   c. Establish a While loop that is executed until CODE equals 7. Within the loop, do the following:
      (1) Use an `ON-GOSUB` statement to transfer control to the subroutine that carries out the requested function. In this case, implement each of the six different area computations in separate subroutines. Within each subroutine, do the following:
         (a) Use one or more `INPUT` statements to request the data.
         (b) Compute the area.
         (c) Display the results.
         (d) Prior to returning to the Process Request Module, call a subroutine (Return to Menu) to beep the speaker in order to alert the operator to press the Enter key. Use the following prompt message to redisplay the menu:

            `Press Enter key to return to the menu...`

      (2) Call the Display Menu Module described in step 1a.
      (3) Call the Accept a Code Module described in step 1b.

2. Wrap-up
   a. Clear the screen.
   b. Display a pleasant message prior to terminating the program.

The general flowchart of the Process Request Module in Figure 6.13 illustrates the six independent functions of Program 6.5. Each subroutine reference includes its own input, processing, and output statements.

Program Solution   Program 6.5 at the bottom of the next page corresponds to the top-down chart in Figure 6.13 and the preceding tasks. The red-colored symbols in Figure 6.13 are implemented in Program 6.5 as modules. The grey-colored symbols represent subtasks that have been moved into their superior modules in Program 6.5

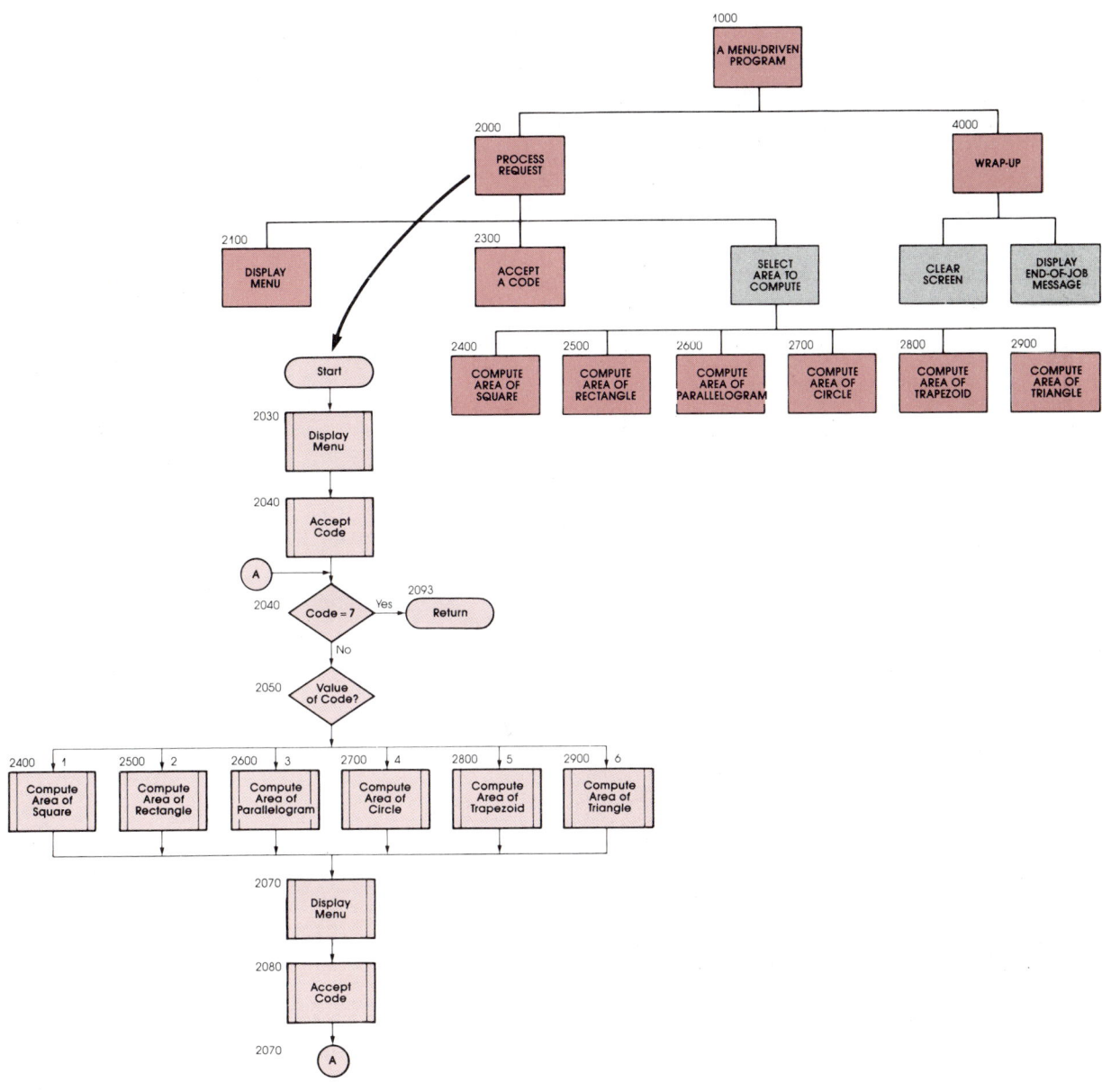

FIGURE 6.13 *A top-down chart and general flowchart for the Process Request Module for Program 6.5.*

PROGRAM 6.5

```
1000 ' Program 6.5
1010 ' A Menu-Driven Program
1020 ' ************************************************************
1030 ' *                    Main Module                           *
1040 ' ************************************************************
1050 GOSUB 2000   ' Call Process Request
1060 GOSUB 4000   ' Call Wrap-up
1070 END
```

(continued)

```
2000 ' ****************************************************************
2010 ' *                       Process Request                        *
2020 ' ****************************************************************
2030 GOSUB 2100   ' Call Display Menu
2040 GOSUB 2300   ' Call Accept a Code
2050 WHILE CODE <> 7
2060    ON CODE GOSUB 2400, 2500, 2600, 2700, 2800, 2900   ' Call Compute Area
2070    GOSUB 2100   ' Call Display Menu
2080    GOSUB 2300   ' Call Accept a Code
2090 WEND
2093 RETURN
2095 '
2100 ' ****************************************************************
2110 ' *                        Display Menu                          *
2120 ' ****************************************************************
2130 CLS : KEY OFF   ' Clear Screen
2140 LOCATE  2, 27 : PRINT "Menu for Computing Areas"
2150 LOCATE  3, 27 : PRINT "------------------------"
2160 LOCATE  5, 19 : PRINT "Code     Function"
2170 LOCATE  6, 19 : PRINT "----     --------"
2180 LOCATE  7, 19 : PRINT "  1      Compute Area of a Square"
2190 LOCATE  9, 19 : PRINT "  2      Compute Area of a Rectangle"
2200 LOCATE 11, 19 : PRINT "  3      Compute Area of a Parallelogram"
2210 LOCATE 13, 19 : PRINT "  4      Compute Area of a Circle"
2220 LOCATE 15, 19 : PRINT "  5      Compute Area of a Trapezoid"
2230 LOCATE 17, 19 : PRINT "  6      Compute Area of a Triangle"
2240 LOCATE 19, 19 : PRINT "  7      End Program"
2250 RETURN
2260 '
2300 ' ****************************************************************
2310 ' *                        Accept a Code                         *
2320 ' ****************************************************************
2330 LOCATE 22, 19 : INPUT "Enter a Code 1 through 7 ======> ", CODE
2340 WHILE CODE < 1 OR CODE > 7
2350    BEEP : BEEP : BEEP : BEEP
2360    LOCATE 23, 19 : PRINT "Code out of range, please reenter"
2370    LOCATE 22, 52 : PRINT SPC(10)
2380    LOCATE 22, 52 : INPUT "", CODE
2390    LOCATE 23, 19 : PRINT SPC(40)
2392 WEND
2394 CLS
2396 RETURN
2398 '
2400 ' ****************************************************************
2410 ' *                   Compute Area of a Square                   *
2420 ' ****************************************************************
2430 LOCATE 5, 24 : PRINT "Compute Area of a Square"
2440 LOCATE 8, 24 : INPUT "Length of Side of Square ====> ", SIDE
2450 AREA = SIDE * SIDE
2460 LOCATE 10, 24 : PRINT "Area of Square ===============>" ; AREA; "Square Units"
2470 GOSUB 3000   ' Call Return to Menu
2480 RETURN
2490 '
2500 ' ****************************************************************
2510 ' *                  Compute Area of a Rectangle                 *
2520 ' ****************************************************************
2530 LOCATE  5, 24 : PRINT "Compute Area of a Rectangle"
2540 LOCATE  8, 24 : INPUT "Length of Rectangle =====> ", LONG
2550 LOCATE 10, 24 : INPUT "Width of Rectangle ======> ", WIDE
2560 AREA = LONG * WIDE
2570 LOCATE 12, 24 : PRINT "Area of Rectangle =======>"; AREA; "Square Units"
2580 GOSUB 3000   ' Call Return to Menu
2590 RETURN
2595 '
```

(continued)

```
2600 ' ****************************************************************
2610 ' *              Compute Area of a Parallelogram                 *
2620 ' ****************************************************************
2630 LOCATE  5, 24 : PRINT "Compute Area of a Parallelogram"
2640 LOCATE  8, 24 : INPUT "Base of Parallelogram =====> ", BASE
2650 LOCATE 10, 24 : INPUT "Height of Parallelogram ===> ", HEIGHT
2660 AREA = BASE * HEIGHT
2670 LOCATE 12, 24 : PRINT "Area of Parallelogram =====>"; AREA; "Square Units"
2680 GOSUB 3000   ' Call Return to Menu
2690 RETURN
2695 '
2700 ' ****************************************************************
2710 ' *                  Compute Area of a Circle                    *
2720 ' ****************************************************************
2730 LOCATE  5, 24 : PRINT "Compute Area of a Circle"
2740 LOCATE  8, 24 : INPUT "Radius of Circle =====> ", RADIUS
2750 AREA = 3.141593 * RADIUS * RADIUS
2760 LOCATE 10, 24 : PRINT "Area of Circle =======>"; AREA; "Square Units"
2770 GOSUB 3000   ' Call Return to Menu
2780 RETURN
2790 '
2800 ' ****************************************************************
2810 ' *                Compute Area of a Trapezoid                   *
2820 ' ****************************************************************
2830 LOCATE  5, 24 : PRINT "Compute Area of a Trapezoid"
2840 LOCATE  8, 24 : INPUT "Primary Base of Trapezoid =====> ", BASE1
2850 LOCATE 10, 24 : INPUT "Secondary Base of Trapezoid ===> ", BASE2
2860 LOCATE 12, 24 : INPUT "Height of Trapezoid ===========> ", HEIGHT
2870 AREA = HEIGHT * (BASE1 + BASE2) / 2
2880 LOCATE 14, 24 : PRINT "Area of Trapezoid =============>";AREA; "Square Units"
2890 GOSUB 3000   ' Call Return to Menu
2893 RETURN
2895 '
2900 ' ****************************************************************
2910 ' *                 Compute Area of a Triangle                   *
2920 ' ****************************************************************
2930 LOCATE  5, 24 : PRINT "Compute Area of a Triangle"
2940 LOCATE  8, 24 : INPUT "Base of Triangle =====> ", BASE
2950 LOCATE 10, 24 : INPUT "Height of Triangle ===> ", HEIGHT
2960 AREA = BASE * HEIGHT / 2
2970 LOCATE 12, 24 : PRINT "Area of Triangle =====>"; AREA; "Square Units"
2980 GOSUB 3000   ' Call Return to Menu
2990 RETURN
2995 '
3000 ' ****************************************************************
3010 ' *                        Return to Menu                        *
3020 ' ****************************************************************
3030 BEEP : BEEP : BEEP : BEEP
3040 LOCATE 20, 24 : INPUT "Press Enter key to return to menu...", A$
3050 RETURN
3060 '
4000 ' ****************************************************************
4010 ' *                           Wrap-up                            *
4020 ' ****************************************************************
4030 CLS
4040 LOCATE 12, 24 : PRINT "End of Program - Have a Nice Day!"
4050 RETURN
4060 ' ******************** End of Program ********************

RUN
```

Discussion of the Program Solution

When Program 6.5, is first executed, line 1050 calls the Process Request Module. In this module, line 2030 calls the Display Menu Module.

In the Display Menu Module, line 2130 clears the screen, and lines 2140 through 2240 display the menu illustrated in Figure 6.14 on page 162. The last line of Figure 6.14 is displayed by line 2330 of the Accept a Code Module. Assume that function 3 is selected, as shown in the lower right corner of Figure 6.14.

When the Enter key is pressed, lines 2340 through 2392 validate the code. Once a valid code is entered, line 2394 again clears the screen before control is returned to the Process Request Module.

Since CODE is not equal to 7, the WHILE statement in line 2050 allows control to pass to the ON-GOSUB statement in line 2060. With CODE equal to 3, control passes to the Compute Area of a Parallelogram Module (lines 2600 through 2695). Figure 6.15, for example, shows a base of 10 units and a height of 4 units to have been entered, which results in an area of 40 square units for the parallelogram. The subroutine (Return to Menu) called by line 2680 allows the operator to view the results on the screen for as long as he or she wishes. Note that the speaker is beeped four times (this produces one constant beep that lasts for a second). Once the Enter key is pressed in response to line 3040, the PC returns control to line 2070 and again displays the menu shown in Figure 6.14.

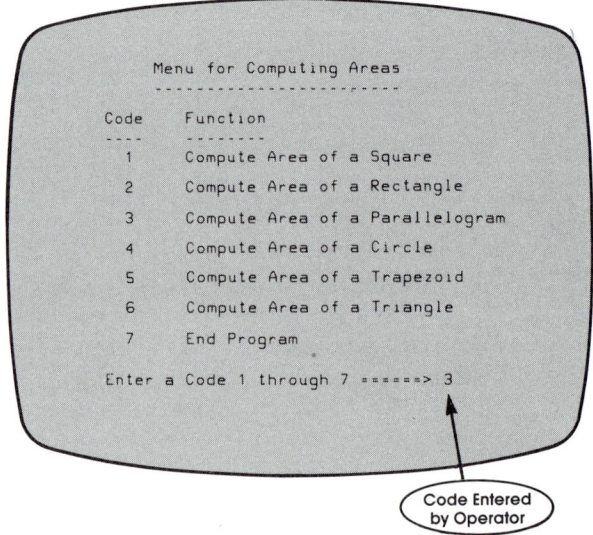

FIGURE 6.14 *The menu displayed by the Display Menu and Accept Code Modules in Program 6.5.*

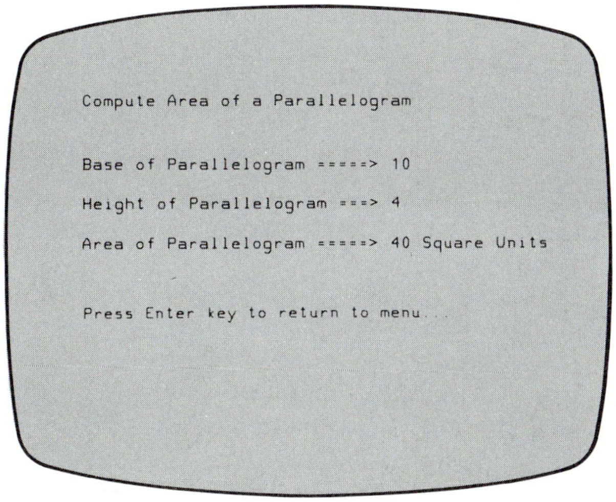

```
            Compute Area of a Parallelogram

       Base of Parallelogram =====> 10
       Height of Parallelogram ===> 4

       Area of Parallelogram =====> 40 Square Units


       Press Enter key to return to menu...
```

FIGURE 6.15 *The display from the selection of code 3 (Compute Area of a Parallelogram).*

Figure 6.16 shows an out-of-range code, which causes the PC to beep before displaying a diagnostic message. The beeping and the display of the diagnostic message are due to lines 2350 and 2360. Line 2370 is used to refresh that part of the screen where the incorrect code is displayed so that another code may be entered. After a valid code is entered in response to line 2380, the screen is again cleared by line 2394 and control is returned to the Process Request Module.

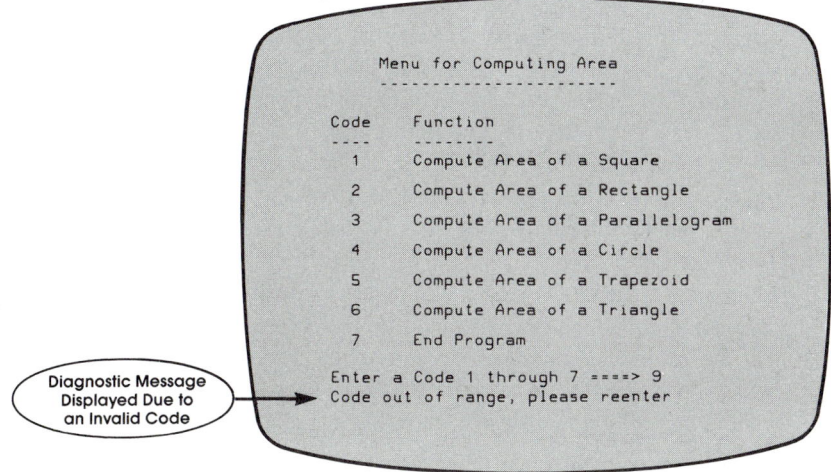

FIGURE 6.16 *Diagnostic message displayed by line 2360, owing to the invalid code 9.*

If the operator enters a code of 5 to compute the area of a trapezoid with a primary base of 18, a secondary base of 9, and a height of 5, the display shown in Figure 6.17 occurs.

```
Compute Area of a Trapezoid

Primary Base of Trapezoid =====> 18

Secondary Base of Trapezoid ===> 9

Height of Trapezoid ===========> 5

Area of Trapezoid =============> 67.5 Square Units

Press Enter key to return to the menu...
```

FIGURE 6.17 *The display from the selection of code 5 (Compute Area of a Trapezoid).*

To terminate execution of Program 6.5, a code of 7 is entered. Line 1060 in the Main Module calls upon the Wrap-up Module, which displays an appropriate message before line 1070 terminates execution of the program.

The preceding problem could have been solved by replacing the ON-GOSUB statement with a series of consecutive IF statements. Usually, however, when a series of three or more integer tests are to be performed in succession, the ON-GOSUB statement is the better alternative.

■ 6.6 CONTROL-BREAK PROCESSING

Most businesses today are divided into smaller units for the purpose of better management. A retail company that is doing business on a national scale may have several levels of management, with the levels headed by such people as a district manager, a store manager, and a department manager. To evaluate the performance of the units within each level, managerial reports are generated, showing summaries or minor totals for each subunit. For example, a sales analysis report that is generated for the manager of a company often shows a summary sales total for each district within the company as well as a grand sales total for the company.

Programs that are written to generate levels of subtotals use a technique involving **control fields** and **control breaks**. A control field contains data that is to be compared from record to record. A control break occurs when the data in the control field changes.

A control break may be used to display a summary line each time a selected data item, common to all records in the file, changes value. The variable that is assigned to the selected data item is called the **control variable**. For this technique to work successfully, it is essential that the records be processed in sequence, according to the data item that determines the break. For example, to generate the Sales Analysis Report shown in Figure 6.18, all the records that belong to district 1 must precede all the district 2 records.

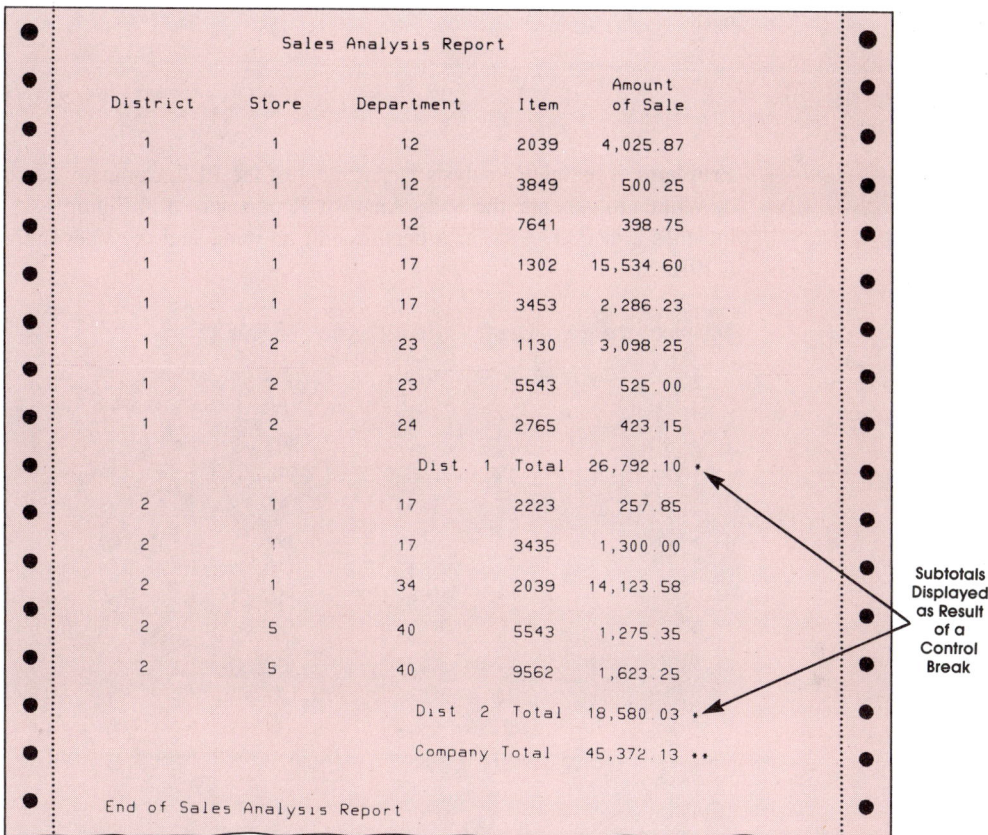

FIGURE 6.18 *Sales Analysis Report (report with a single-level control break).*

With the sales records in sequence, the program solution can check each sales record to see whether it is the first record of a new district. If the sales record represents an item from the *old* district (i.e., if the current item and the previous one belong to the same district), then selected contents of that record are displayed, and the PC adds the sales amount for that item to a district sales accumulator.

When a sales record that belongs to a *new* district is read, a control break occurs and the current value of the district sales accumulator is displayed. In addition, asterisks are usually displayed to the right of the totals to indicate a summary. One asterisk indicates the lowest level, two asterisks the next level, and so on. Before processing the sales record that caused the control break, the PC must add the district sales to the company sales total, which is displayed after all records in the file have been processed.

Furthermore, the control variable must be assigned the value of the next district number before the processing of the record is resumed. Finally, the variable that is used to sum the district sales must be reset to zero after each control break so that it can be used to sum the sales for the next district.

The following Programming Case Study pertains to generating the report found in Figure 6.18.

PROGRAMMING CASE STUDY 11: Sales Analysis Report — Single-Level Control Break

Problem: The Sales Analysis Department of the PUC Company has requested that a program be written to generate the Sales Analysis Report shown in Figure 6.18. Each record in the file includes a district, a store, a department, an item, and the sales amount, as shown in Figure 6.19A.

District	Store	Dept.	Item	Amt. of Sale	
1	1	12	2039	$ 4,025.87	"1","1","12","2039",4025.87
1	1	12	3849	500.25	"1","1","12","3849",500.25
1	1	12	7641	398.75	"1","1","12","7641",398.75
1	1	17	1302	15,534.60	"1","1","17","1302",15534.6
1	1	17	3453	2,286.23	"1","1","17","3453",2286.23
1	2	23	1130	3,098.25	"1","2","23","1130",3098.25
1	2	23	5543	525.00	"1","2","23","5543",525
1	2	24	2765	423.15	"1","2","24","2765",423.15
2	1	17	2223	257.85	"2","1","17","2223",257.85
2	1	17	3435	1,300.00	"2","1","17","3435",1300
2	1	34	2039	14,123.58	"2","1","34","2039",14123.58
2	5	40	5543	1,275.35	"2","5","40","5543",1275.35
2	5	40	9562	1,623.25	"2","5","40","9562",1623.25
		(A)			(B)

FIGURE 6.19 (A) The sales data in ascending sequence by department within store within district. (B) A listing of the sales data stored in SALES.DAT.

The sales records are located in the data file SALES.DAT in ascending sequence by district, as illustrated in Figure 6.19B. A data file like SALES.DAT may be created by a program that is similar to Program 6.2. Note that although the first four data items in each record of SALES.DAT are numeric, we have stored them as string values because we do not plan to do arithmetic on them.

The data items within each sales record are to be printed on the printer. Also to be printed are the sales total for each district before a new district is processed and the final sales total for the company after all sales records have been processed. At the top of the new page, print the report title, and column headings as illustrated in Figure 6.18.

Following are a top-down chart and a general flowchart of the Process File Module (Figure 6.20 on page 168); a list of the program tasks in outline form; a program solution; and a discussion of the program solution.

Program Tasks

The following program tasks correspond to the top-down chart in Figure 6.12 on pages 168 and 169.

1. Initialization

    a. Two running totals are necessary. Set DIST.TOTAL (district sales accumulator) and CMPY.TOTAL (company sales accumulator) to zero.
    b. Clear the screen.
    c. Display a message instructing the operator to set the paper to the top of the page in the printer.
    d. Open the sequential data file SALES.DAT for input.
    e. Print report and column headings.

2. Process File, if not end of file

    a. Use the INPUT #n statement to read the first sales record in SALES.DAT. Use the following variable names:

       DIST$:   District
       STORE$:   Store
       DEPT$:   Department
       ITEM$:   Item Number
       AMOUNT: Amount of Sale

    b. Assign the control variable, DIST.CTRL$, the value of DIST$. (This assignment is often called "priming the pump," since it sets DIST.CTRL$ equal to the first district.)
    c. Call the Process a Sales Record Module. Within this module, do the following:
        (1) Increment the district sales accumulator (DIST.TOTAL) by the amount of the sale (AMOUNT).
        (2) Print the five data values described in step 2a. Double-space the detail lines.
    d. Establish a While loop that executes repeatedly until the end-of-file mark is reached. Use the EOF function to control the While loop. Within the While loop, do the following:
        (1) Read the next sales record in SALES.DAT.
        (2) Test for a control break. If DIST$ (district of sales record just read) does not equal DIST$.CTRL$ (district being processed), then call the Process a District Control Break Module. This module must do the following:
            (a) Increment the company sales accumulator (CMPY.TOTAL) by the district sales accumulator (DIST.TOTAL).
            (b) Print the district sales accumulator (DIST.TOTAL).
            (c) Set the control variable (DIST.CTRL$) equal to the new district (DIST$).
            (d) Initialize the district sales accumulator (DIST.TOTAL) to zero.
        (3) Call the Process a Sales Record Module described in step 2c.
    e. Following the While loop, call the Process a District Control Break Module described in step 2d(2). This call ensures that the last district total is processed.

3. Wrap-up

    a. Close SALES.DAT.
    b. Print the company sales accumulator (CMPY.TOTAL) and an end-of-job message.
    c. Display an end-of-job message on the screen.

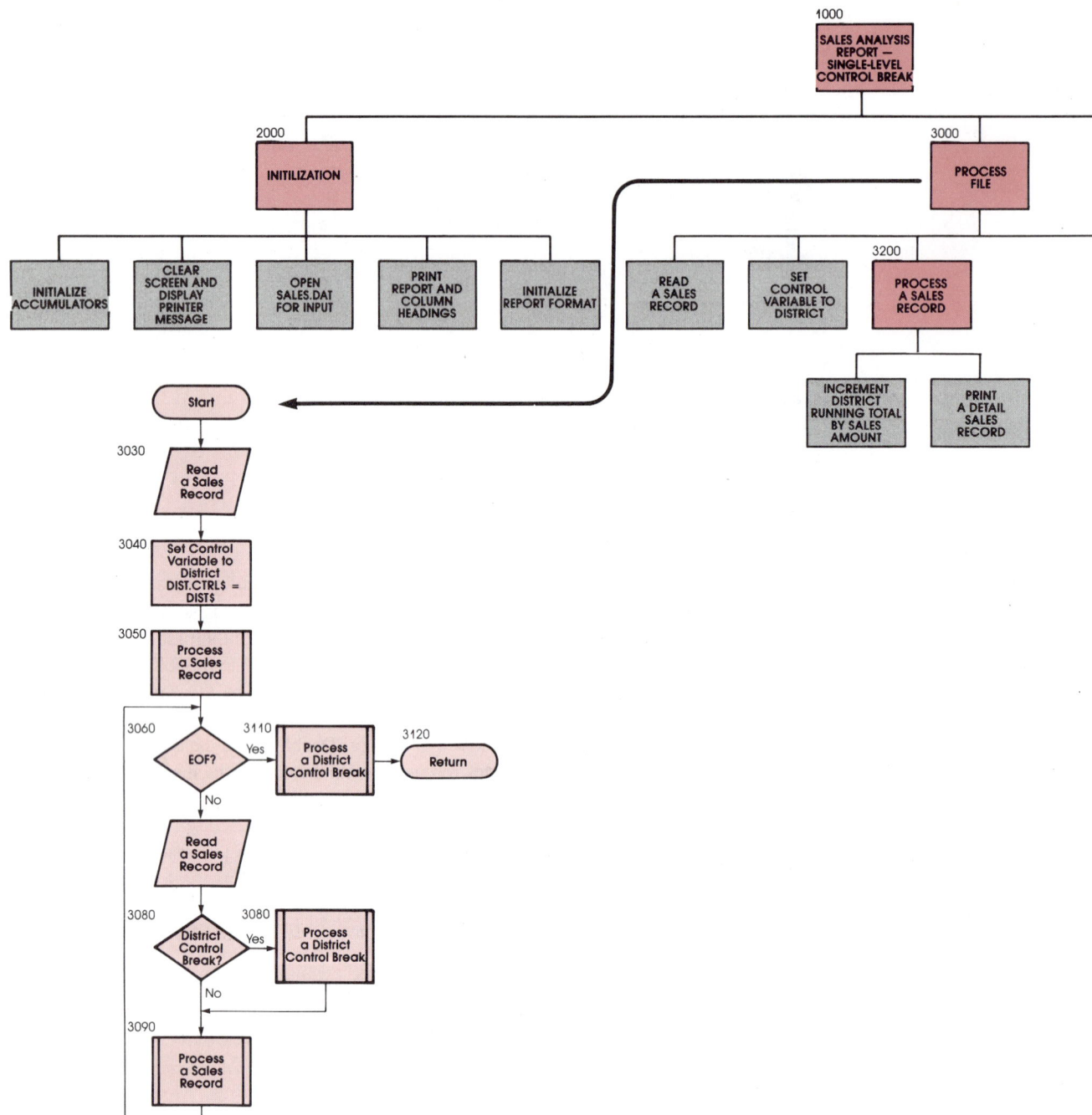

FIGURE 6.20 *A top-down chart and a general flowchart of the process file module for Program 6.6.*

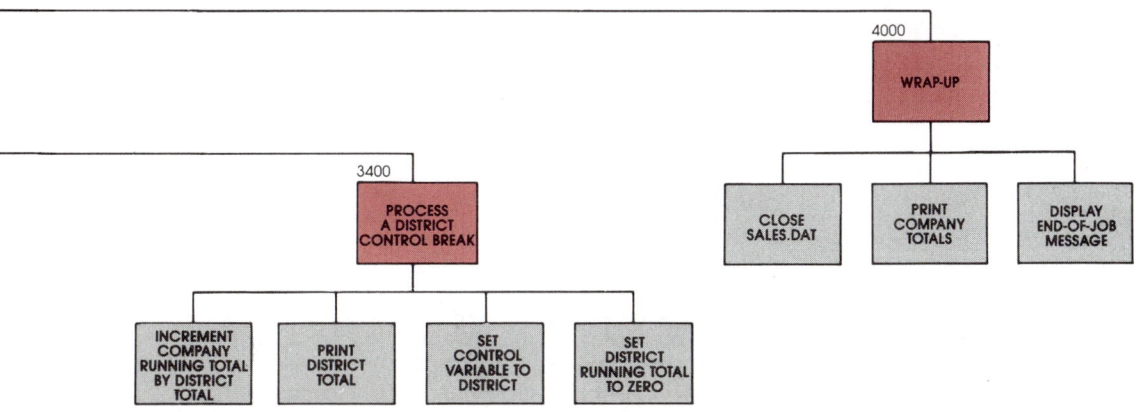

Program Solution The following program corresponds to the preceding program tasks and to the top-down chart in Figure 6.20.

PROGRAM 6.6

```
1000 ' Program 6.6
1010 ' Sales Analysis Report -- Single Level Control Break
1020 ' Input File Name = SALES.DAT
1030 ' ****************************************************
1040 ' *                    Main Module                   *
1050 ' ****************************************************
1060 GOSUB 2000    ' Call Initialization
1070 IF NOT EOF(1)
        THEN GOSUB 3000    ' Call Process File
1080 GOSUB 4000    ' Call Wrap-up
1090 END
1100 '
2000 ' ****************************************************
2010 ' *                   Initialization                 *
2020 ' ****************************************************
2030 DIST.TOTAL = 0
2040 CMPY.TOTAL = 0
2050 CLS : KEY OFF   ' Clear Screen
2060 LOCATE 10, 20
2070 PRINT "Set the paper in the printer to the top of page."
2080 LOCATE 12, 20
2090 INPUT "Press the Enter key when the printer is ready...", CONTROL$
2100 OPEN "SALES.DAT" FOR INPUT AS #1
2110 LPRINT       "             Sales Analysis Report"
2120 LPRINT       "                                               Amount"
2130 LPRINT       "District     Store     Department      Item    Of Sale"
2140 DETL.LN$ = "    \\         \\          \\           \ \    ##,###.##"
2150 TOT.L1$  = "                                Dist. \\ Total ###,###.## *"
2160 TOT.L2$  = "                                Company Total ####,###.## **"
2170 TOT.L3$  = "End of Sales Analysis Report"
2180 RETURN
2190 '
```

(continued)

```
3000 ' *************************************************
3010 ' *                 Process File                  *
3020 ' *************************************************
3030 INPUT #1, DIST$, STORE$, DEPT$, ITEM$, AMOUNT
3040 DIST.CTRL$ = DIST$
3050 GOSUB 3200      ' Call Process a Sales Record
3060 WHILE NOT EOF(1)
3070    INPUT #1, DIST$, STORE$, DEPT$, ITEM$, AMOUNT
3080    IF DIST$ <> DIST.CTRL$
            THEN GOSUB 3400  ' Call Process a District Control Break
3090    GOSUB 3200   ' Call Process a Sales Record
3100 WEND
3110 GOSUB 3400      ' Call Process a District Control Break
3120 RETURN
3130 '
3200 ' *************************************************
3210 ' *             Process a Sales Record            *
3220 ' *************************************************
3230 DIST.TOTAL = DIST.TOTAL + AMOUNT
3240 LPRINT USING DETL.LN$; DIST$, STORE$, DEPT$, ITEM$, AMOUNT
3250 LPRINT
3260 RETURN
3270 '
3400 ' *************************************************
3410 ' *         Process a District Control Break      *
3420 ' *************************************************
3430 CMPY.TOTAL = CMPY.TOTAL + DIST.TOTAL
3440 LPRINT USING TOT.L1$; DIST.CTRL$, DIST.TOTAL
3450 LPRINT
3460 DIST.CTRL$ = DIST$
3470 DIST.TOTAL = 0
3480 RETURN
3490 '
4000 ' *************************************************
4010 ' *                   Wrap-up                     *
4020 ' *************************************************
4030 CLOSE #1
4040 LPRINT USING TOT.L2$; CMPY.TOTAL
4050 LPRINT : LPRINT : LPRINT TOT.L3$
4060 LOCATE 14, 20 : PRINT "Job Complete"
4070 RETURN
4080 '
4090 ' *************** End of Program ******************
```

Discussion of the Solution

When the RUN command is issued for Program 6.5, the PC prints the report shown in Figure 6.18 on page 165. Note the following important points regarding the control break process in Program 6.5.

1. In the Initialization Module, lines 2030 and 2040 initialize the district and company accumulators.
2. The Process File Module is called by line 1070 only if SALES.DAT is not empty. The IF statement is required in line 1070 because the first statement in the Process File Module (line 3030) is the INPUT #n statement.
3. In the Process File Module, line 3030 reads the first record. Line 3040 sets the control variable (DIST.CTRL$) equal to the first district (DIST$). Line 3050 causes the first sales record to be processed.

The WHILE statement in line 3060 tests to determine whether there are any records left in SALES.DAT. Within the While loop, line 3070 reads the next record. Line 3080 compares the district of the most recently read sales record DIST$ to the control variable DIST.CTRL$. If they are different, a control break has occurred and the Process a District Control Break Module is called. Whether or not a control break occurs, line 3090 processes the sales record last read by line 3070.

Following the processing of a record, line 3100 returns control to the WHILE statement in line 3060. When the end-of-file mark is finally detected, the WHILE statement transfers control to line 3110, and the totals for the last district in the file are processed.

4. In the Process a District Control Break Module, the four requirements for processing a control break are fulfilled in the following way:
    a. Line 3430 increments the company sales accumulator (CMPY.TOTAL) by the district sales accumulator (DIST.TOTAL).
    b. Lines 3440 through 3450 print the value of the district sales accumulator. Note that line 3440 uses the control variable (DIST.CTRL$) rather than the variable DIST$ to print the district number. Can you explain why we don't print DIST$?
    c. Line 3460 assigns the control variable (DIST.CTRL$) the value of the new district.
    d. Line 3470 sets the district sales accumulator (DIST.TOTAL) to zero.
5. In the Wrap-up Module, the company sales total (CMPY.TOTAL) is printed.

■ 6.7 TEST YOUR BASIC SKILLS (Even-numbered answers are in Appendix B.)

1. Consider the valid program listed below and to the right, then explain its function. Assume that the values in the table below and to the left are entered in response to the INPUT statements in the program.

Stock Item	Selling Price	Discount Code
138	$ 78.56	2
421	123.58	3
617	475.65	2
812	23.58	1
917	754.56	4
eof		

```
100 ' Exercise 6.1
110 CLS : KEY OFF   ' Clear Screen
120 OPEN "EX61A.DAT" FOR OUTPUT AS #1
130 INPUT "Stock Item ======> ", ITEM$
140 WHILE ITEM$ <> "eof"
150     INPUT "Selling Price ===> ", PRICE
160     INPUT "Discount Code ===> ", CODE$
170     WRITE #1, ITEM$, PRICE, CODE$
180     INPUT "Stock Item ======> ", ITEM$
190 WEND
200 CLOSE #1
210 PRINT : PRINT "Job Complete"
220 END
```

2. Fill in the blanks in the following sentences:

   a. The _____ statement with a mode of _____ or _____ must be executed before a PRINT #n, PRINT #n, USING, or WRITE #n statement is executed.
   b. The _____ statement with a mode of _____ must be executed before an INPUT #n statement is executed.
   c. A file can be opened as often as required, provided it is _____ before each subsequent open.
   d. The _____ function is used to test for the end-of-file mark with a sequential file.
   e. When records are to be added to the end of a sequential file, the _____ mode is used in the OPEN statement.

3. Explain the purpose of the EOF function. Also indicate where it should be located in a program in relation to the INPUT #n statement.
4. A program is to read records from one of three sequential files, SALES1.DAT, SALES2.DAT, and SALES3.DAT. The three files are stored on the diskette in the B drive. Write three OPEN statements that would allow the program to read records from any of the three sequential files.
5. Construct a WRITE #n statement that would write the values of A, B, X$, and D to a sequential file in the format required by the INPUT #n statement.
6. Which of the following are invalid file-handling statements? Why?

   a. 100 OPEN FOR OUTPUT "B:SAL.DAT" AS #1
   b. 200 OPEN FILE$ FOR APPEND AS #3
   c. 300 PRINT #1,
   d. 400 PRINT #1, A,
   e. 500 PRINT #1 USING "####.##"; COST
   f. 600 CLOSE
   g. 700 WHILE NOT EOF(#2)
   h. 800 INPUT #2, AMOUNT,

7. Consider the valid programs below. What is displayed if each program is executed?

   a.
   ```
   100 ' Exercise 6.7a
   110 COUNT = 0
   120 GOSUB 300
   130 PRINT COUNT
   140 GOSUB 300
   150 PRINT COUNT
   160 GOSUB 300
   170 PRINT COUNT
   180 COUNT = COUNT - 3
   190 PRINT COUNT
   200 END
   300 ' ** Increment Count **
   310 COUNT = COUNT + 1
   320 RETURN
   330 ' *** End of Program **
   ```

   b.
   ```
   1000 ' Exercise 6.7b
   1010 A = 1
   1020 PRINT A
   1030 WHILE A > 0
   1040    IF A - 2 < 0
              THEN A = 2
              ELSE GOSUB 1200
   1050    PRINT A
   1060 WEND
   1070 END
   1200 ' *** Subroutine 1 ***
   1210 IF A - 2 = 0
           THEN A = 3
           ELSE GOSUB 1400
   1220 RETURN
   1400 ' *** Subroutine 2 ***
   1410 IF A - 4 < 0
           THEN A = 4
           ELSE GOSUB 1600
   1420 RETURN
   1600 ' *** Subroutine 3 ***
   1610 IF A - 4 = 0
           THEN A = 5
           ELSE A = 1
   1620 RETURN
   1630 ' ** End of Program **
   ```

6.8 BASIC PROGRAMMING PROBLEMS

1. Creating a Master File

Purpose: To become familiar with creating a sequential file that is consistent with the format required by the INPUT statement. Use of the OPEN, CLOSE, and WRITE #n statements is required.

Problem: Construct a program to create a sequential file named EX61PAY.DAT that represents the payroll master file for the PUC Company. A **master file** is one that is for the most part permanent or includes data that is required each time an application such as payroll is processed. Each record in the file describes an employee, including the year-to-date (YTD) payroll information, as shown under the Input Data.

Write the data to the file in the format required by the INPUT #n statement. As part of the end-of-job routine, display a message indicating that the file was created as well as the total number of records written to the file. (**Hint:** See Program 6.2 on page 143 or PRG6–2 on the Student Diskette.)

Input Data: Prepare and use the following sample data. Do not enter the commas.

Employee No.	Employee Name	Dependents	Marital Status	Rate of Pay	Year-to-Date Gross Pay	Year-to-Date Federal With. Tax	Year-to-Date Social Security
123	Col, Joan	2	M	12.50	25,345.23	10,256.45	1,812.18
124	Fiel, Don	1	S	18.00	41,725.00	8,546.45	2,983.34
125	Dit, Lisa	1	S	13.00	42,115.23	11,035.78	3,003.00
126	Snow, Joe	9	M	4.50	11,510.05	854.34	822.97
134	Hi, Frank	0	M	8.75	9,298.65	2,678.25	664.85
167	Bri, Edie	3	S	10.40	8,190.45	17.50	585.62
210	Liss, Ted	6	M	8.80	7,098.04	2,120.55	507.51
234	Son, Fred	2	M	6.75	0.00	0.00	0.00

Output Results: The sequential file EX61PAY.DAT is created in auxiliary storage on the default drive. The results are shown for the first payroll record on the left. The results on the right are displayed prior to the termination of the program.

```
Payroll File Build
-------------------

Employee Number ========> 123

Employee Name ==========> Col Joan

No. of Dependents ======> 2

Marital Status =========> M

Rate of Pay ============> 12.50

YTD Gross Pay ==========> 25345.23

YTD Withholding Tax ===> 10256.45

YTD Social Security ===> 1812.18

Enter Y to add record, else N ===> Y

Enter Y to add ANOTHER record, else N ===> Y
```

```
Creation of Sequential Data File Is Complete

Total Number of Records in EX61PAY.DAT ===> 8

Job Complete
```

2. Master File List

Purpose: To become familiar with reading records in a sequential file and printing the records on the printer. Use of the `OPEN`, `CLOSE`, `INPUT #n`, `LPRINT`, and `LPRINT USING` statements and the `EOF` function is required.

Problem: Write a program that prints the data items found in each employee record of the sequential file EX61PAY.DAT created in BASIC Programming Problem 1. Double-space the detail lines and single-space the total lines. As part of the end-of-job routine, display the following totals: employee-record count, YTD gross pay, YTD federal withholding tax, and YTD social security tax. Define the YTD gross pay accumulator as a double-precision variable. (**Hint:** See Program 6.3 on page 149 or PRG6–3 on the Student Diskette.)

Input Data: Use the sequential file EX61PAY.DAT created in BASIC Programming Problem 1. If you did not complete BASIC Programming Problem 1, then use EX61PAY.DAT found on the Student Diskette.

Output Results: The following results are displayed.

```
                     Payroll File List

Employee            Marital Rate of  <--------Year-to-Date-------->
No. Name      Dep.  Status  Pay      Gross Pay With. Tax  Soc. Sec.
---  -------- ----  ------- -------  --------- ---------  ---------
123 Col Joan    2     M      12.50   25,345.23 10,256.45  1,812.18

124 Fiel Don    1     S      18.00   41,725.00  8,546.45  2,983.34

125 Dit Lisa    1     S      13.00   42,115.23 11,035.78  3,003.00

126 Snow Joe    9     M       4.50   11,510.05    854.34    822.97

134 Hi Frank    0     M       8.75    9,298.65  2,678.25    664.85

167 Bri Edie    3     S      10.40    8,190.45     17.50    585.62

210 Liss Ted    6     M       8.80    7,098.04  2,120.55    507.51

234 Son Fred    2     M       6.75        0.00      0.00      0.00

Total Number of Records ========>       8
Total YTD Gross Pay =============> 145,282.65
Total YTD Wihtholding Tax =======>  35,509.32
Total YTD Social Security =======>  10,379.47
Job Complete
```

3. A Menu-Driven Program with Multifunctions

Purpose: To become familiar with a multifunction program and with the use of a menu.

Problem: Use top-down programming techniques to write a menu-driven program to compute the volume of a box, a cylinder, a cone, and a sphere. The program should display the menu that is shown under Output Results. Once a code is entered, it must be validated. After the selection of the proper function, the program should prompt the operator for the necessary data, then compute the volume and display it accordingly. The displayed results are to remain on the screen until the Enter key on the keyboard is pressed. After that, the program should redisplay the menu. (**Hint:** See Program 6.5 on page 160 or PRG6–5 on the Student Diskette.)

Use the following formulas for the volumes V:

1. Volume of a box: V = L * W * H, where L is the length, W is the width, and H is the height of the box.
2. Volume of a cylinder: V = π * R * R * H, where π equals 3.141593, R is the radius, and H is the height of the cylinder.
3. Volume of a cone: V = (π * R * R * H)/3, where π equals 3.141593, R is the radius of the base, and H is the height of the cone.
4. Volume of a sphere: V = 4 * π * R * R * R, where π equals 3.141593, and R is the radius of the sphere.

Input Data: Use the following sample data.

    Code: 3, Radius = 7, Height = 9
    Code: 4, Radius = 10
    Code: 1, Length = 4.5, Width = 6.7, Height = 12
    Code: 2, Radius = 8, Height = 15
    Code: 7 (This code should return a diagnostic message.)
    Code: 5 (This code ends the program.)

Output Results: The following menu is displayed.

```
Menu For Computing Volumes
--------------------------

Code    Function
----    --------
  1     Compute Volume of a Box
  2     Compute Volume of a Cylinder
  3     Compute Volume of a Cone
  4     Compute Volume of a Sphere
  5     End Program

Enter a Code 1 through 5 ======>
```

4. Computing the Average Age of Employees with a Minor Control Break

Purpose: To become familiar with a method of testing for a control break in a file. Use of the OPEN, CLOSE, and INPUT #n statements and the EOF function is required.

Problem: Construct a top-down program that will find the average age of those employees less than 40 years old and the average age of those greater than or equal to 40 years old. The program should do the following:

1. Read a department number and a person's age from the sequential file EX64EMP.DAT on the Student Diskette. The employee records in EX64EMP.DAT are shown under Input Data on the next page.
2. Test to see whether the department number is the same as the previous one.
3. If it is the same department number, determine whether the age is greater than or equal to 40 or less than 40. Use an IF statement to transfer control so that the age is added to an appropriate total and a variable representing a counter has its value incremented by 1.

4. If the department number changes (control break occurs), transfer control to determine the average ages of those employees below 40 and of those 40 and above; display a summary line; then reset counters and the control variable and continue processing the next department. (**Hint:** See Program 6.6 on page 169 or PRG6-6 on the Student Diskette. Note that a department line is printed only when there is a control break.)

Input Data: The sequential file EX64EMP.DAT contains the following sample data:

Dept. No.	Age	Dept. No.	Age	Dept. No.	Age	Dept. No.	Age
1	26	1	64	2	65	2	25
1	38	1	19	2	18	3	21
1	22	1	38	2	37	3	23
1	40	2	46	2	41	3	34
1	51	2	48	2	43	3	56

Output Results: The following results are displayed.

```
                     Employee Average Age
                Below    Average Age    40 and    Average Age
 Dept. No.       40      Below 40       Above     40 and Above
 ---------      -----    -----------    ------    ------------
     1            5         28.6          3           51.7
     2            3         26.7          5           48.6
     3            3         26.0          1           56.0

Employee Age Analysis Report Complete
```

FOR LOOPS, ARRAYS, SORTING, AND TABLE PROCESSING

■ 7.1
INTRODUCTION

In earlier chapters, loops were implemented (coded) with the WHILE and WEND statements. This chapter presents a second method for implementing certain types of loops by means of the FOR and NEXT statements.

Also in this chapter, we will discuss a technique that can make a program shorter, easier to code, and more general by the use of arrays. In MS BASIC, an **array** is a variable that is allocated a specified number of storage locations, each of which can be assigned a unique value. Arrays are commonly used in programming for sorting and table processing, in which related data items are organized into rows and columns.

A report is usually easier to work with and more meaningful if the information is generated in some sequence, such as first to last, largest to smallest, or oldest to newest. Arranging data according to order or sequence is called **sorting**.

In data processing terminology, a **table** is a collection of data in which each item is uniquely identified by a label, by its position relative to other items, or by some other means. Income-tax tables, insurance tables, airline schedules, and telephone directories are examples of tables.

Upon successful completion of this chapter, you will be able to code certain types of loops more efficiently. Furthermore, you will be able to develop programs that demand that large amounts of data, stored in an orderly fashion, be available to the PC during the entire execution of the program.

■ 7.2
THE FOR AND NEXT STATEMENTS

The FOR and NEXT statements make it possible to repeatedly execute a section of a program, with automatic changes in the value of a variable between repetitions.

In Chapters 4, 5, and 6, the WHILE and WEND statements were used to implement a loop structure that executed a section of a program repeatedly. Whenever you have to develop a **counter-controlled loop** (a loop that is to be executed a specified number of times), the coding requires statements for initializing, incrementing, and testing of a counter. Any loop that involves this type of coding may also be written with the FOR and NEXT statements. When these two statements are used to establish a counter-controlled loop, we call it a **For loop**.

The While Loop Versus the For Loop

Programs 7.1 and 7.2 illustrate the similarity between the use of the WHILE and WEND statements and the FOR and NEXT statements. Both programs compute the sum of the integers from 1 to 10.

PROGRAM 7.1

```
100 ' Program 7.1
110 ' Looping Using WHILE
120 ' and WEND Statements
130 ' *******************
140 SUM = 0
150 COUNT = 1
160 WHILE COUNT <= 10
170     SUM = SUM + COUNT
180     COUNT = COUNT + 1
190 WEND
200 PRINT "The sum is"; SUM
210 END

RUN

The sum is 55
```

While Loop: lines 160–180

PROGRAM 7.2

```
100 ' Program 7.2
110 ' Looping Using FOR
120 ' and NEXT Statements
130 ' *******************
140 SUM = 0
150 FOR COUNT = 1 TO 10 STEP 1
160     SUM = SUM + COUNT
170 NEXT COUNT
180 PRINT "The sum is"; SUM
190 END

RUN

The sum is 55
```

For Loop: lines 150–170

Program 7.1 uses the WHILE and WEND statements. Lines 140 and 150 initialize the running total (SUM) to 0 and the counter (COUNT) to 1. Line 160 tests to determine whether the value of COUNT is less than or equal to 10. If the condition is true, SUM is incremented by COUNT, and the counter COUNT is incremented by 1 before control transfers back to line 160. When the condition in the WHILE statement is false, the program terminates the loop, and line 200 displays the value of SUM.

Program 7.2 incorporates the FOR and NEXT statements to define the For loop (lines 150 through 170). Read through Program 7.2 carefully and note how compact it is and how superior it is to Program 7.1. Using a single FOR statement, as in line 150 of Program 7.2, we can consolidate the functions of lines 150, 160 and 180 of Program 7.1. Besides using less main storage and being easier to read than Program 7.1, Program 7.2 is also more efficient; it executes faster than Program 7.1.

The Execution of a For Loop

The execution of the For loop in Program 7.2 involves the following important points:

1. When the FOR statement is executed for the first time, the For loop becomes *active* and COUNT is initialized to 1.
2. The statements in the For loop, in this case line 160, are executed.
3. Control returns to the FOR statement, where the value of COUNT is incremented by a value of 1, which follows the keyword STEP.
4. If the value of COUNT is less than or equal to 10, execution of the For loop continues.
5. When the value of COUNT is greater than 10, control transfers to the statement (line 180) following the NEXT COUNT statement.

The general forms of the FOR and NEXT statements are given in Tables 7.1 and 7.2.

TABLE 7.1 The FOR Statement

General Form:	FOR k = *initial value* TO *limit value* STEP *increment value* or FOR k = *initial value* TO *limit value* where **k** is a simple numeric variable called the **loop variable**, and the **initial value**, **limit value**, and **increment value** are numeric expressions.
Purpose:	Causes the statements between the FOR and NEXT statements to be executed repeatedly until the value of k exceeds the limit value. When k exceeds the limit value, control transfers to the line just after the corresponding NEXT statement. If the increment value is negative, the test is reversed. The value of k is decremented each time through the loop, and the loop is executed until k is less than the limit value.
Keyword Entry:	Hold down the Alt key and press the F key on your keyboard.
Examples:	100 FOR ITEM = 1 TO 20 200 FOR AMOUNT = -5 TO 15 STEP 2 400 FOR COUNT = 10 TO -5 STEP -3 450 FOR TAX = 0 TO 10 STEP 0.1 500 FOR TOTAL = START TO FINISH STEP INCREMENT 550 FOR S = A + 5 TO C/D STEP F * B 600 FOR I = 20 TO 20 650 FOR J = 20 TO 1
Note:	If the keyword STEP is not used, then the increment value defaults to 1.

TABLE 7.2 The NEXT Statement

General Form:	NEXT k where **k** is the same variable as the loop variable in the corresponding FOR statement.
Purpose:	Identifies the end of a For loop.
Keyword Entry:	Hold down the Alt key and press the N key on your keyboard.
Examples:	300 NEXT AMOUNT 380 NEXT ITEM

The terminology used to describe the FOR statement is shown below:

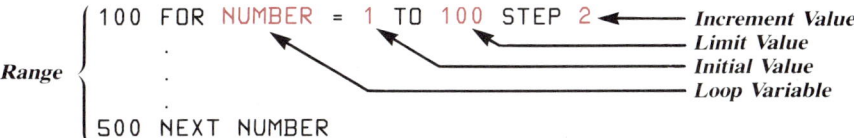

```
        ⎧ 100 FOR NUMBER = 1 TO 100 STEP 2  ←── Increment Value
        ⎪         .                             ── Limit Value
Range  ⎨         .                              ── Initial Value
        ⎪         .                             ── Loop Variable
        ⎩ 500 NEXT NUMBER
```

The **range** of a For loop is the set of repeatedly executed statements beginning with the FOR statement and continuing up to and including the NEXT statement that has the same loop variable.

Flowchart Representation of a For Loop

The flowchart representation for a For loop corresponds to a Do-While structure (see Figure 7.1). In the first process symbol, the loop variable is assigned the initial value. Next a test is made. If the condition is true, the loop is terminated and control transfers to the statement that follows the Do-While structure.

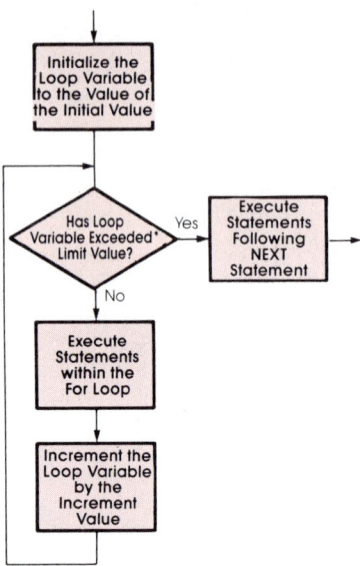

* The mathematical expression of this statement is:
  (Loop Variable Value − Limit Value) · (Sign of Increment Value) > 0
  where Sign of Increment Value is +1 or −1.

FIGURE 7.1 *General flowchart representation of a For loop.*

If the condition is false, control passes into the body of the For loop. After the statements in the For loop are executed, the loop variable is incremented by the increment value and control transfers back up to the decision symbol again to test whether the loop variable exceeds the limit value.

If the increment value is negative, the test is reversed. The value of the loop variable is decremented each time through the loop, and the loop is executed until the loop variable is less than the limit value.

Figure 7.2 illustrates a flowchart that corresponds to Program 7.2.

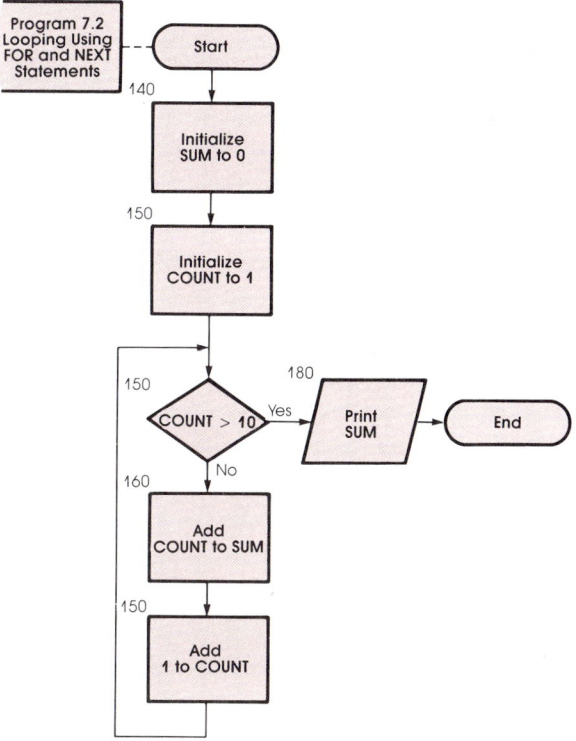

FIGURE 7.2 *A flowchart for Program 7.2.*

Nested For Loops

When the statements of one For loop lie within the range of another For loop, the loops are said to be **nested** or **embedded**. Furthermore, the outer For loop may be nested in the range of still another For loop, and so on.

When one For loop is nested within another, the name of the control variable for each For loop must be different.

As an example of a program with nested For loops, consider Program 7.3 on the next page which generates the multiplication table. Each time the loop variable in the outer For loop (lines 160 through 220) is assigned a new value, the inner For loop (lines 180 through 200) computes and displays one row of the table. Note that the two loop variables, ROW and COLUMN, are multiplied together in line 190 to form the various products in the multiplication table.

The PRINT statements in lines 170 and 190 end with the semicolon separator. You'll recall from Chapter 4 that when a PRINT statement ends with a semicolon, the cursor remains on the same line. Each time the inner loop is satisfied, the PRINT statement in line 210 prints blanks and moves the cursor to the beginning of the next line.

PROGRAM 7.3

```
100 ' Program 7.3
110 ' Generating the Multiplication Table
120 ' ***********************************
130 CLS : KEY OFF  ' Clear Screen
140 PRINT "  x  !   0   1   2   3   4   5   6   7   8   9  10  11  12"
150 PRINT "-----+--------------------------------------------------------"
160 FOR ROW = 0 TO 12
170    PRINT USING "###   _!"; ROW;
180    FOR COLUMN = 0 TO 12
190       PRINT USING "####"; ROW * COLUMN;
200    NEXT COLUMN
210    PRINT
220 NEXT ROW
230 PRINT
240 PRINT "End of Multiplication Table"
250 END

RUN
  x  !   0   1   2   3   4   5   6   7   8   9  10  11  12
-----+--------------------------------------------------------
  0  !   0   0   0   0   0   0   0   0   0   0   0   0   0
  1  !   0   1   2   3   4   5   6   7   8   9  10  11  12
  2  !   0   2   4   6   8  10  12  14  16  18  20  22  24
  3  !   0   3   6   9  12  15  18  21  24  27  30  33  36
  4  !   0   4   8  12  16  20  24  28  32  36  40  44  48
  5  !   0   5  10  15  20  25  30  35  40  45  50  55  60
  6  !   0   6  12  18  24  30  36  42  48  54  60  66  72
  7  !   0   7  14  21  28  35  42  49  56  63  70  77  84
  8  !   0   8  16  24  32  40  48  56  64  72  80  88  96
  9  !   0   9  18  27  36  45  54  63  72  81  90  99 108
 10  !   0  10  20  30  40  50  60  70  80  90 100 110 120
 11  !   0  11  22  33  44  55  66  77  88  99 110 121 132
 12  !   0  12  24  36  48  60  72  84  96 108 120 132 144

End of Multiplication Table
```

Outer For Loop encompasses lines 160–220. *Inner For Loop* encompasses lines 180–200.

Listed below and on the top of the next page are rules that summarize the FOR statement.

FOR Rule 1: If the increment value following the keyword STEP is positive, or if the keyword STEP is not used, then the PC executes the For loop until the loop variable exceeds the limit value. If the increment value is negative, the test is reversed. The value of the loop variable is decremented each time through the loop, and the loop is executed until the loop variable is less than the limit value.

FOR Rule 2: The value of the increment value must not be zero.

FOR Rule 3: A valid initial entry into a For loop can be accomplished only by transferring control to the FOR statement.

FOR Rule 4: A normal exit from a For loop leaves the current value of the loop variable equal to the sum of its value the last time the `NEXT` statement was executed plus the increment value.

FOR Rule 5: No statement that is located in the range of a For loop can change the initial, limit, and increment values.

7.3 ARRAYS VERSUS SIMPLE VARIABLES

Arrays permit a programmer to represent many values with one variable name. The variable name assigned to represent an array is called the **array name**. The elements in the array are distinguished from one another by subscripts. In MS BASIC, the subscript is written inside a set of parentheses and is placed immediately to the right of the array name. While simple variables are used to store and reference values that are independent of one another, **subscripted variables** are used to store and reference values that have been grouped into an array.

Consider the problem of writing a program that is to manipulate the 12 monthly sales for a company and generate a year-end report. Figure 7.3 illustrates the difference between using an array to store the 12 monthly sales and using simple variables.

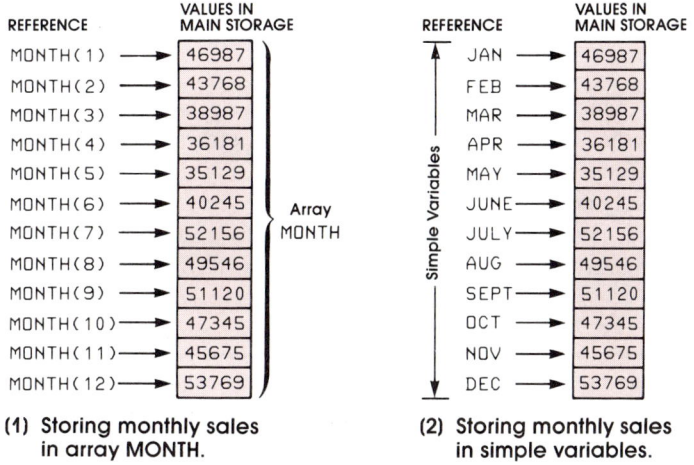

(1) Storing monthly sales in array MONTH.

(2) Storing monthly sales in simple variables.

FIGURE 7.3 *Utilizing an array (1) versus simple variables (2).*

The monthly sales stored in an array require the same storage allocation that the sales represented as independent variables do. The difference lies in the programming techniques that can access the different values. For example, the programmer may assign the values of simple variables in a `READ` statement in this manner:

```
150 READ JAN, FEB, MAR, APR, MAY, JUNE, JULY, AUG, SEPT, OCT, NOV, DEC
```

Each simple variable must explicitly appear in a LET or PRINT statement if the monthly sales are to be summed or displayed. Not only is the programming time consuming, but the variables *must* be properly placed in the program.

The same function can be accomplished by entering all 12 values into array MONTH:

```
170 FOR NUM = 1 TO 12
180    READ MONTH(NUM)
190 NEXT NUM
```

In line 170, the value of NUM is initialized to 1. In line 180, the first value in the data-holding area is assigned to MONTH(1) (read "MONTH sub 1"). Then NUM is incremented to 2, and the next value is assigned to MONTH(2). This continues until MONTH(12) is assigned the 12th value in the data-holding area.

MONTH2 and MONTH(2) are different from each other. MONTH2 is a simple variable, no different from SALE, INC, DIG, or COST. On the other hand, MONTH(2) is a subscripted variable. It is the second element in array MONTH. The manner in which it is called upon in a program differs from the fashion in which a simple variable is referenced.

7.4 DECLARING ARRAYS

Before arrays can be used, the amount of main storage to be reserved must be declared in the program. This is the purpose of the DIM statement. The keyword DIM is an abbreviation of **dimension**. The DIM statement also declares explicitly the **upper-bound value** and implicitly the **lower-bound value** of the subscript. The upper- and lower-bound values define the range of permissible values that a subscript may be assigned.

The DIM Statement

The main function of the DIM statement is to declare to the PC the necessary information regarding the allocation of storage locations for arrays used in a program. Good programming practice dictates that every program that utilizes array elements should have a DIM statement that properly defines the arrays.

The general form of the DIM statement is given in Table 7.3. Note that commas are required punctuation between the declared array elements.

TABLE 7.3 The DIM Statement

General Form:	DIM array name(size), . . . , array name(size)
	where **array name** represents a numeric or string variable name, and **size** represents the upper-bound value of each array. The size may be an integer or numeric variable for one-dimensional arrays. The size may be a series of integers or a series of numeric variables separated by commas for multidimensional arrays.
Purpose:	To reserve storage locations for arrays.
Examples:	100 DIM BAL(4) 200 DIM PICK(6), JOB$(200), LOAN(N), TIME(20, 20) 300 DIM COST(10, 45), K$(X, Y, Z), AMT(2, 25, 7)
Note:	In MS BASIC, the maximum number of dimensions an array may have is 255.

To ensure the proper placement of DIM statements, most programmers put them at the beginning of the program.

> **DIM Rule 1:** The DIM statement may be located anywhere before the first use of an array element in a program.

In Table 7.3, line 100 reserves storage for a one-dimensional array BAL, which consists of 5 elements or storage locations. These elements — BAL(0), BAL(1), BAL(2), BAL(3) and BAL(4) — can be used in a program in much the same way that a simple variable can be used. For this DIM statement, elements BAL(5) or BAL(6) or BAL(–4) are considered invalid.

Line 200 declares three one-dimensional arrays, PICK, JOB$, and LOAN, and one two-dimensional array, TIME. Line 200 reserves storage locations for 7 elements for array PICK; 201 elements for array JOB$; N + 1 elements for array LOAN; and 441 elements for array TIME.

Line 300 in Table 7.3 declares three arrays. The first array, COST, is a two-dimensional array. The last two, K$ and AMT, are three-dimensional arrays. Multi-dimensional arrays like COST, K$, and AMT are discussed in Section 7.6.

The OPTION BASE Statement

Unless otherwise specified, MS BASIC allocates the zero element for each one-dimensional array. For two-dimensional arrays, an extra row — the zero row — and an extra column — the zero column — are reserved. Thus,

```
130 DIM MONTH(12), TIME(20, 20)
```

actually reserves 13 elements for the array MONTH and 21 rows and 21 columns for the array TIME. The extra array element is MONTH(0) for array MONTH and the extra row and column is the 0th (read "zeroth") row and the 0th column for the array TIME. Although an additional element, row, or column will not present a problem to your program, the OPTION BASE statement allows you to control the lower-bound of arrays that are declared. The OPTION BASE statement can be used to set the lower-bound value to 1 instead of the default 0, and this will avoid wasting main storage on unused array elements. The OPTION BASE statement can be used only once in a program and it must precede any DIM statement. The general form of the OPTION BASE statement is found in Table 7.4.

TABLE 7.4 The OPTION BASE Statement

General Form:	OPTION BASE *n*
	where ***n*** is either 0 or 1.
Purpose:	To assign a lower bound of 0 or 1 to all arrays in a program.
Examples:	100 OPTION BASE 0
	120 OPTION BASE 1
Note:	If the OPTION BASE statement is not used, the lower-bound value for all arrays is set to zero, the default value.

7.5 MANIPULATING ARRAYS

In this section, a sample program that manipulates the elements of arrays will be discussed. Before the program is presented, however, it is important that you understand the syntax and limitations of subscripts.

Subscripts

As indicated in Section 7.3, the elements of an array are referenced by assigning a subscript to the array name. The subscript is written within parentheses and is placed immediately to the right of the array name. The subscript may be any valid nonnegative number, variable, or numeric expression within the **range** of the array. The lower and upper bounds of an array should never be exceeded. For example, if an array TAX is declared as follows:

```
100 DIM TAX(50)
```

it is invalid to reference TAX(–3), TAX(51), or any others that are outside the lower and upper bounds of the array. Noninteger subscripts are rounded to the nearest integer.

Summing the Elements of an Array

Many applications call for summing the elements of an array. In Program 7.4, the monthly sales are summed, an average is computed, and the sales are displayed, four to a line.

PROGRAM 7.4

```
100 ' Program 7.4
110 ' Monthly Sales Analysis
120 ' **********************
130 OPTION BASE 1
140 DIM MONTH(12)
150 CLS : KEY OFF   ' Clear Screen
160 TOTAL.SALES = 0
170 FOR NUM = 1 TO 12
180    READ MONTH(NUM)
190    TOTAL.SALES = TOTAL.SALES + MONTH(NUM)
200 NEXT NUM
210 AVG.SALES = TOTAL.SALES / 12
220 PRINT USING "The average monthly sales is $$##,###.##"; AVG.SALES
230 PRINT
240 FOR NUM = 1 TO 12 STEP 4
250    PRINT MONTH(NUM), MONTH(NUM + 1), MONTH(NUM + 2), MONTH(NUM + 3)
260 NEXT NUM
270 PRINT
280 PRINT "Job Complete"
290 ' ************ Data Follows ****************
300 DATA 46987, 43768, 38987, 36181, 35129, 40245
310 DATA 52156, 49546, 51120, 47345, 45675, 53769
320 END

RUN

The average monthly sales is   $45,075.67

    46987         43768         38987         36181
    35129         40245         52156         49546
    51120         47345         45675         53769

Job Complete
```

In Program 7.4, line 190 is used to sum the values of the array elements. For example, when line 170 activates the For loop, NUM is assigned the value of 1. Line 180 reads the first data item, 46987, and assigns it to MONTH(1). Line 190 increments TOTAL.SALES by MONTH(1). NUM is incremented to 2, and line 200 returns control to the FOR statement in line 170.

After the READ statement, TOTAL.SALES is assigned the sum of TOTAL.SALES and MONTH(2). This process continues until the 12th element is added to the sum of the first 11 elements of the array S. Line 210 computes the average, and line 220 displays it.

The For loop found in lines 240 through 260 displays the monthly sales, four to a line. The first time through the loop, NUM is equal to 1, and MONTH(1), MONTH(2), MONTH(3), and MONTH(4) display on one line. The next time through the loop, NUM is equal to 5, and MONTH(5), MONTH(6), MONTH(7), and MONTH(8) display on the next line. Finally, NUM is set equal to 9 and MONTH(9), MONTH(10), MONTH(11), and MONTH(12) display on the third line. The subscripts in line 250 are in the form of numeric expressions.

■ 7.6 MULTI-DIMENSIONAL ARRAYS

The dimension of an array is the number of subscripts required to reference an element in an array. Up to now, all the arrays were one dimensional, and an element was referenced by an integer, a variable, or a single expression in the parentheses following the array name. MS BASIC allows arrays to have up to 255 dimensions. One- and two-dimensional arrays are the most commonly used arrays. Three-dimensional arrays are used less frequently in business applications, and arrays with more than three dimensions are rarely used except in scientific and engineering applications.

Manipulating Two-Dimensional Arrays

As illustrated in Table 7.3 on page 184, the number of dimensions is declared in the DIM statement. For example,

```
140 DIM COST(2, 5)
```

declares an array to be two-dimensional. A two-dimensional array usually takes the form of a table. The first subscript tells how many rows there are, and the second subscript tells how many columns. Figure 7.4 shows a 2 × 5 array (read "2 by 5 array"). COST(1, 1) — read "COST sub one one" — references the element found in the first row and first column. COST(2, 3) — read "COST sub two three" — references the element found in the second row and third column. Although Figure 7.4 does not show the zero row and zero column, they always exist unless the OPTION BASE statement is used to set the lower bound to 1.

		COLUMNS				
		1	2	3	4	5
ROWS	1	COST(1, 1)	COST(1, 2)	COST(1, 3)	COST(1, 4)	COST(1, 5)
	2	COST(2, 1)	COST(2, 2)	COST(2, 3)	COST(2, 4)	COST(2, 5)

FIGURE 7.4 *Conceptual view of the storage locations reserved for a 2 × 5 two-dimensional array called COST, with the name of each element specified.*

	COLUMNS				
ROWS	1	2	3	4	5
1	6	12	-52	3.14	0.56
2	8	2	5	6	2

FIGURE 7.5 *A 2 × 5 array with each element assigned a value.*

Assuming that the elements of array COST are assigned the values shown in Figure 7.5, the following statements are true:

COST(1, 2) is equal to 12
COST(2, 4) is equal to 6
COST(2, 2) is equal to 2
COST(3, 5) is outside the range of the array; it does not exist.
COST(-2, -5) is outside the range of the array; it does not exist.

Initializing Arrays

Excluding the zeroth row and column, you may write the following code to initialize to 0, row by row, all the elements in a 4 × 3 array called AREA:

```
200 DIM AREA(4, 3)
210 FOR ROW = 1 TO 4
220     FOR COLUMN = 1 TO 3
230         AREA(ROW, COLUMN) = 0
240     NEXT COLUMN
250 NEXT ROW
```

To initialize to 1 all elements on the main diagonal of a 5 × 5 array called TABLE, you may write the following:

```
300 DIM TABLE(5, 5)
310 FOR ROW = 1 TO 5
320     TABLE(ROW, ROW) = 1
330 NEXT ROW
```

As a result, elements TABLE(1, 1), TABLE(2, 2), TABLE(3, 3), TABLE(4, 4), and TABLE(5, 5) are assigned the value of 1.

If a company makes 5 models of a particular product and the production of each model involves a certain amount of processing time on 6 different machines, the processing time can be summarized in a table of 5 rows and 6 columns, as illustrated in Figure 7.6.

PRODUCT PROCESSING TIME IN MINUTES		MACHINE					
		1	2	3	4	5	6
MODEL NUMBER	1	13	30	5	17	12	45
	2	23	12	13	16	0	20
	3	45	12	28	16	10	13
	4	21	16	15	22	19	26
	5	23	50	17	43	15	18

FIGURE 7.6 *A table of the processing time each model spends on a machine.*

To sum all the elements in row 4 of the table in Figure 7.6 into a running total SUM4 and to sum all the elements in column 2 into a running total SUM2, you can write the following:

```
500 DIM TIME(5, 6)
510 SUM2 = 0
520 SUM4 = 0
530 FOR MODEL = 1 TO 5
540     SUM2 = SUM2 + TIME(MODEL, 2)
550 NEXT MODEL
560 FOR MACHINE = 1 TO 6
570     SUM4 = SUM4 + TIME(4, MACHINE)
580 NEXT MACHINE
```

The last three short partial programs should give you an idea of how to handle elements that appear in various rows and columns of two-dimensional arrays.

■ 7.7 SORTING

Sorting data into alphabetical or numerical order is one of the more frequently executed operations in a business data processing environment. It is also a time-consuming operation, especially when large amounts of data are involved. Computer professionals have spent a great deal of time developing algorithms to speed up the sorting process. Usually, the faster the process, the more complex the algorithm. In this section, we will discuss the **bubble sort** algorithm. Data can be sorted in ascending or descending sequence. Data that is in sequence from lowest to highest in value is in **ascending sequence**. Data that is in sequence from highest to lowest in value is in **descending sequence**.

The Bubble Sort

The bubble sort is a straightforward method of sorting data items that have been placed in an array. To illustrate the logic of a bubble sort, we will sort the data found in Figure 7.7 into ascending sequence. Assume that the data has been assigned to array B, as illustrated below:

FIGURE 7.7 *Data in no particular sequence.*

The bubble sort involves comparing adjacent elements and **swapping** (i.e., interchanging) the values of those elements when they are out of order. For example, B(1) is compared to B(2). If B(1) is less than or equal to B(2), no swap occurs. If B(1) is greater than B(2), the values of the 2 elements are swapped. B(2) is then compared to B(3), and so on, until B(4) is compared to B(5). One complete time through the array is called a **pass**. At the end of the first pass, the largest value is in the last element of array B, as illustrated in Figure 7.8 on the next page. Its box has been shaded to show that it is in its final position and will not move again.

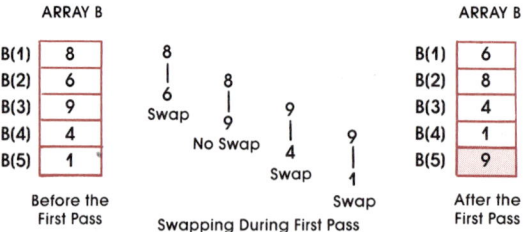

FIGURE 7.8 *First pass through array B.*

The maximum number of passes necessary to sort the elements in an array is equal to the number of elements in the array less 1. Since array B has 5 elements, at most four passes are made on the array. Figures 7.9, 7.10, and 7.11 illustrate the second, third, and fourth passes made on array B. On the fifth pass, no elements are swapped. The swapping pushes the larger values down in the illustrations, and as a side effect, the smaller numbers "bubble" up to the top of the array.

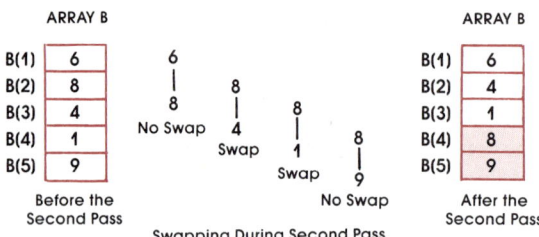

FIGURE 7.9 *Second pass through array B.*

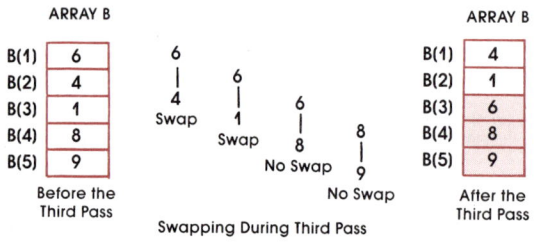

FIGURE 7.10 *Third pass through array B.*

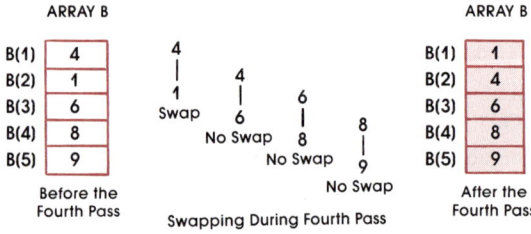

FIGURE 7.11 *Fourth pass through array B, which is now in ascending sequence.*

The SWAP Statement

To exchange the values of two storage locations in a program, we use the SWAP statement. The general form of the SWAP statement is shown in Table 7.5.

TABLE 7.5 The SWAP Statement

General Form:	SWAP variable$_1$, variable$_2$ where **variable$_1$** and **variable$_2$** are of the same type.
Purpose:	Exchanges the values of two variables or two elements of an array.
Examples:	1000 SWAP OLDBAL, NEWBAL 2000 SWAP ARR(SUB), ARR(SUB + 1) 3000 SWAP CODE1$(I, I), CODE2$(I, I)

In Table 7.5, line 1000 exchanges the values of the two simple variables OLDBAL and NEWBAL. Prior to the execution of line 1000, if OLDBAL is equal to 500 and NEWBAL is equal to 600, then after its execution, OLDBAL is equal to 600 and NEWBAL is equal to 500.

In line 2000 of Table 7.5, the values of the two subscripted variables ARR(SUB) and ARR(SUB + 1) are exchanged. Exchanging the values of two adjacent elements of an array is a common practice with sort algorithms. Finally, line 3000 in Table 7.5 exchanges the values of the two corresponding string elements of tables CODE1$ and CODE2$.

Implementing the Bubble Sort

The following partial program will effectively sort the elements of array B as described in Figures 7.7 through 7.11 into ascending sequence.

```
250 ' ********* Bubble Sort ********
260 SWITCH$ = "ON"
270 WHILE SWITCH$ = "ON"
280    SWITCH$ = "OFF"
290    FOR I = 1 TO 4
300       IF B(I) > B(I + 1)
             THEN SWAP B(I), B(I + 1) :
                  SWITCH$ = "ON"
310    NEXT I
320 WEND
```

The variable SWITCH$ controls whether another pass will be done on the array. Line 260 assigns SWITCH$ a value of ON. Since SWITCH$ equals ON, line 270 passes control into the body of the While loop. Line 280 assigns SWITCH$ a value of OFF just before the For loop makes a pass on the loop. If SWITCH$ is not modified later in the loop (line 300), the values in the array are in sequence and the next time that line 270 is executed, control transfers to the line following 320.

The FOR statement in line 290 initializes I to 1. The first element B(1) is then compared to B(2). If B(1) is greater than B(2), the THEN clause swaps the values of the two elements and assigns SWITCH$ a value of ON. Next, B(2) is compared to B(3) and so on. The number of comparisons per pass is equal to the number of elements to compare minus 1. Since the number of data items to sort is 5, the limit parameter in the FOR statement is set to 4.

Program 7.5 incorporates the logic found in this partial program to sort 8, 6, 9, 4, and 1. Line 170 reserves storage for array B. The For loop made up of lines 190 through 220 loads and displays the unsorted elements of the array. Lines 260 through 320 sort the numeric array. Lines 350 through 380 display the elements after the array has been sorted.

PROGRAM 7.5

```
100 ' Program 7.5
110 ' Sorting Numeric Data Using the
120 ' Bubble Sort Technique
130 ' *****************************
140 '
150 ' ******* Initialization *******
160 OPTION BASE 1
170 DIM B(5)
180 PRINT "Unsorted -";
190 FOR I = 1 TO 5
200    READ B(I)
210    PRINT B(I);
220 NEXT I
230 PRINT : PRINT
240 '
250 ' ********* Bubble Sort ********
260 SWITCH$ = "ON"
270 WHILE SWITCH$ = "ON"
280    SWITCH$ = "OFF"
290    FOR I = 1 TO 4
300       IF B(I) > B(I + 1)
              THEN SWAP B(I), B(I + 1) :
                   SWITCH$ = "ON"
310    NEXT I
320 WEND
330 '
340 ' **** Display Sorted Array ****
350 PRINT "Sorted   -";
360 FOR I = 1 TO 5
370    PRINT B(I);
380 NEXT I
390 '
400 ' ******** Data Follows ********
410 DATA 8, 6, 9, 4, 1
420 END

RUN

Unsorted - 8  6  9  4  1

Sorted   - 1  4  6  8  9
```

7.8 SEARCHING TABLES

Many applications call for the use of data that is arranged in tabular form. Rates of pay, tax brackets, parts cost, and insurance rates are examples of tables that contain systematically arranged data. Arrays make it easier to write programs for applications involving tables.

Table Organization

Tables are organized on the basis of how the data items (also called **table functions**) are to be referenced. In **positionally organized tables**, table functions can be accessed by their position in the table. In **argument-organized tables**, table functions are accessed by the value that corresponds to the desired table function.

Positionally Organized Tables

To illustrate a positionally organized table, a program can be written that displays the name of the month in response to a month number, 1 through 12. Figure 7.12 shows the basic concept behind accessing a table function in a positionally organized table.

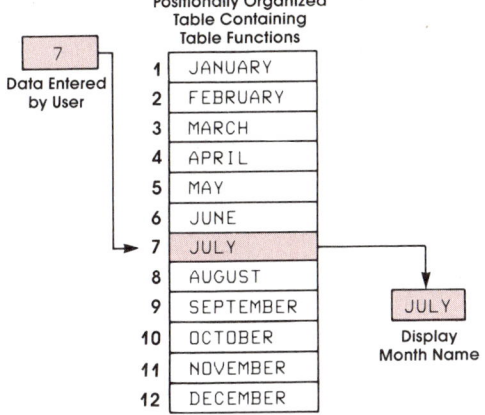

FIGURE 7.12 *Accessing a table function in a positionally organized table.*

In Figure 7.12, the month name is selected from the table on the basis of its location. A value of 1, entered by the user, equates to January, 2 to February, and so on. To write a program that uses table processing techniques, you must do the following:

1. define the table by declaring an array;
2. load the table functions into the array; and
3. write statements to access the table entries.

Program 7.6 on the next page illustrates how to declare, load, and access the table of month names described in Figure 7.12. Line 2040 defines the table by declaring the one-dimensional array MONTH$ to 12. Lines 2050 through 2070 load the table functions — in this case, the month names — into the array. Line 3440 in the Access the Table Function Module accesses the desired table function.

The routine to access the table function in Program 7.6 is rather straightforward. The user enters a value for NUM, and line 3440 references the corresponding element of the array that contains the table functions. Figures 7.13 and 7.14 show the results displayed by Program 7.6 as a result of entering the month numbers 7 and 12.

PROGRAM 7.6

```
1000 ' Program 7.6
1010 ' Accessing Functions in a Positionally Organized Table
1020 ' ********************************************************
1030 ' *                    Main Module                       *
1040 ' ********************************************************
1050 GOSUB 2000     ' Call Initialization
1060 GOSUB 3000     ' Call Process a Request
1070 GOSUB 4000     ' Call Wrap-up
1080 END
1090 '
2000 ' ********************************************************
2010 ' *                   Initialization                     *
2020 ' ********************************************************
2030 OPTION BASE 1
2040 DIM MONTH$(12)              ' Declare the Table
2050 FOR NUM = 1 TO 12
2060    READ MONTH$(NUM)         ' Load the Table
2070 NEXT NUM
2080 KEY OFF   ' Clear 25th Line
2090 RETURN
2100 '
3000 ' ********************************************************
3010 ' *                Process a Request                     *
3020 ' ********************************************************
3030 CONTROL$ = "Y"
3040 WHILE CONTROL$ = "Y" OR CONTROL$ = "y"
3050    GOSUB 3200   ' Call Accept Operator Input
3060    GOSUB 3400   ' Call Access the Table Function
3070 WEND
3080 RETURN
3090 '
3200 ' ********************************************************
3210 ' *               Accept Operator Input                  *
3220 ' ********************************************************
3230 CLS   ' Clear Screen
3240 LOCATE 5, 15
3250 INPUT "Month Number (Enter 1 through 12) =====> ", NUM
3260 WHILE NUM < 1 OR NUM > 12
3270    LOCATE 6, 15 : PRINT "Month Number Invalid, Please Reenter"
3280    LOCATE 5, 56 : PRINT SPC(15)
3290    LOCATE 5, 56 : INPUT "", NUM
3300    LOCATE 6, 15 : PRINT SPC(40)
3310 WEND
3320 RETURN
3330 '
3400 ' ********************************************************
3410 ' *             Access the Table Function                *
3420 ' ********************************************************
3430 LOCATE 7, 15
3440 PRINT "Month Name ============================> "; MONTH$(NUM)
3450 LOCATE 9, 15
3460 INPUT "Enter Y to process another month number, else N... ", CONTROL$
3470 RETURN
3480 '
```

(continued)

```
4000 ' ************************************************************
4010 ' *                        Wrap-up                           *
4020 ' ************************************************************
4030 CLS  ' Clear Screen
4040 PRINT : PRINT "Job Complete"
4050 RETURN
4060 '
4070 ' *************** Table Entries Follow ****************
4080 DATA January, February, March, April, May, June, July
4090 DATA August, September, October, November, December
4100 ' **************** End of Program ********************

RUN
```

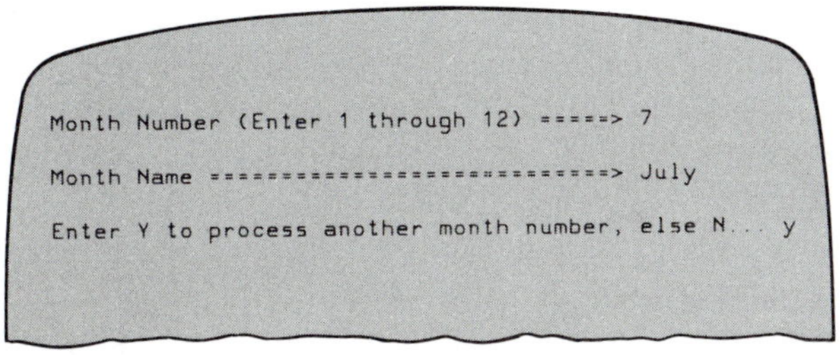

```
Month Number (Enter 1 through 12) =====> 7

Month Name ==============================> July

Enter Y to process another month number, else N... y
```

FIGURE 7.13 *The display by Program 7.6 due to entering the month number 7.*

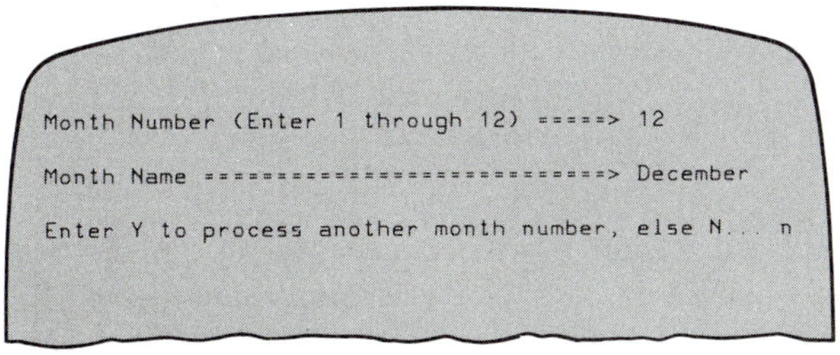

```
Month Number (Enter 1 through 12) =====> 12

Month Name ==============================> December

Enter Y to process another month number, else N... n
```

FIGURE 7.14 *The display by Program 7.6 due to entering the month number 12.*

Positionally organized tables such as MONTH$ in Program 7.6 are not difficult to understand. Unfortunately, few tables can be constructed on the basis of the relative position of the table functions. Months, days of the week, and job classes are examples of systematic data that can be organized into positional tables.

Argument-Organized Tables

In most applications, tables are characterized by entries made up of multiple functions. Multiple-function entries are accessed by means of a **search argument**. The search argument is entered by the user much as the month number was in Program 7.6. The search argument is compared to the **table argument**, a table entry, to retrieve the corresponding table function. Figure 7.15 on the next page illustrates the composition of a table that is organized by arguments.

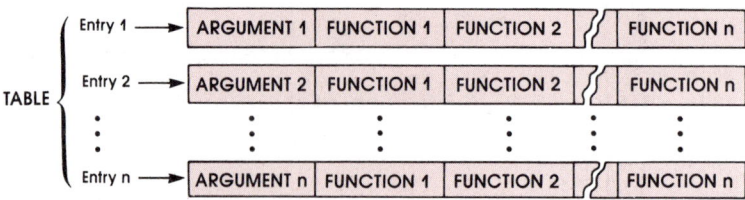

FIGURE 7.15 *Conceptual view of an argument-organized table.*

The table argument is assigned to a one-dimensional array. Functions are assigned to **parallel arrays** which are two or more arrays that have corresponding elements. Unlike a positionally organized table, in which the value entered is used to obtain the table function, an argument-organized table must be searched until the search argument agrees with one of the table arguments. This search is a **table search** or a **table lookup**.

There are two methods for searching a table: the **serial search** and the **binary search**. A serial search begins by comparing the search argument to the first table argument. If the two agree, the search is over. If they do not agree, then the search argument is compared to the second table argument, and so on. In the serial search, the table arguments may be either in sorted or unsorted order.

In general, a binary search begins the search in the middle of the table and determines whether the table argument that agrees with the search argument is in the upper half or the lower half of the table. The half that contains this table argument is then halved again. This process continues until there is nothing left to divide in half. At that point, the binary search is complete. The binary search, which requires that the table arguments be in ascending or descending sequence, will be discussed in greater detail later.

Serial Search

A serial search is a procedure that all of us use in everyday life. Suppose, for example, that you have a parts list that contains the part numbers and corresponding part descriptions and part costs. If you have a part number, one method for finding the part description and cost is to read through the part number list until you find the part number you are searching for. You can then read off the description and cost that correspond to the part number. Figure 7.16 illustrates the basic concept of a serial search.

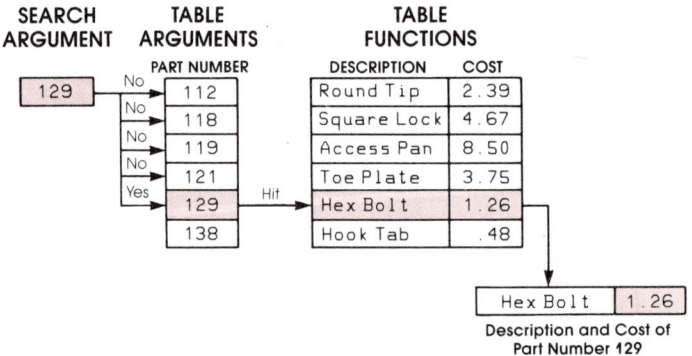

FIGURE 7.16 *Conceptual view of a serial search.*

The search argument is tested against each of the table arguments, beginning with the first, until a *hit* is made. At that point, the corresponding part description and part cost are selected from the table.

A program that completes the serial search illustrated in Figure 7.16 first needs to have the table defined. Since each entry is made up of a table argument and two functions, we declare three parallel arrays — PART, DESC$, and COST, as shown in line 2050. The variable ENTRIES is assigned the number of parts in the parts list.

```
2030 OPTION BASE 1
2040 READ ENTRIES
2050 DIM PART(ENTRIES), DESC$(ENTRIES), COST(ENTRIES) 'Declare the Table
```

Array PART is assigned the part numbers, array DESC$ the part descriptions, and array COST the part costs. A For loop is used to load the table, as follows:

```
2060 FOR NUM = 1 TO ENTRIES
2070    READ PART(NUM), DESC$(NUM), COST(NUM)          ' Load the Table
2080 NEXT NUM
```

Each time the READ statement is executed, one entry is loaded into the parallel arrays. Each entry in the table consists of an argument and two functions.

The following partial program searches the argument table and causes either the part description and part cost or a diagnostic message to be displayed. Assume that the user has assigned the part number that is to be looked up to the variable PART.NUM, the search argument.

```
3400 ' ***********************************************************
3410 ' *               Access the Table Function                *
3420 ' ***********************************************************
3430 SWITCH$ = "OFF"
3440 FOR NUM = 1 TO ENTRIES
3450    IF PART.NUM = PART(NUM)
            THEN GOSUB 3600 :
                 SWITCH$ = "ON" : NUM = ENTRIES   ' Process a Table Hit
3460 NEXT NUM
3470 IF SWITCH$ = "OFF"
        THEN PRINT "** Error **"; PART.NUM; "is an Invalid Part Number"
3480 LOCATE 11, 15
3490 INPUT "Enter Y to look up another part number, else N... ", CONTROL$
3500 RETURN
3510 '
3600 ' ***********************************************************
3610 ' *               Display Table Function                    *
3620 ' ***********************************************************
3630 PRINT "Description =====> "; DESC$(NUM)
3640 LOCATE 9, 15
3650 PRINT USING "Cost ============> $$#.##"; COST(NUM)
3660 RETURN
3670 '
```

A For loop (lines 3440 through 3460) is used to implement the serial search algorithm. Prior to the For loop, a switch (SWITCH$) is assigned a value of OFF. The switch is assigned a value of ON within the loop when a hit is made. If the switch is not on when the For loop terminates, then there is no part number in the table which corresponds to the part number entered by the user, and a diagnostic message is displayed by line 3470.

The IF statement in line 3450 compares the part number entered by the user against the part numbers in the table. If a search is successful, the subscript value is used in lines 3630 and 3650 to display the corresponding part description and part cost found in the parallel arrays. Furthermore, when a search is successful, line 3450 assigns SWITCH$ a value of ON and the loop variable a value equal to the limit value, that is, NUM = ENTRIES, which causes the For loop to terminate immediately following a successful lookup.

Ordering the Table Arguments for a Serial Search

For a serial search, it is not necessary that the table arguments be in sequence. If it is known that some table entries are requested more often than others, then the table entries requested most often should be placed at the beginning of the table to reduce search time. For example, assume that a frequency analysis uncovered the following pattern of requests regarding the part-number table entries illustrated earlier in Figure 7.16:

Part Number	% Requested
112	10
118	4
119	15
121	40
129	25
138	6

According to the frequency analysis, the description and cost for part number 121 are requested 40% of the time, and the description and cost for part number 118 are requested only 4% of the time.

If we load the table according to the frequency analysis, then the table entry for part number 121 is at the beginning of the table and the table entry for part number 118 is at the end of the table. This is shown in Figure 7.17. Note that in contrast to the search done earlier in Figure 7.16, the same search takes three fewer comparisons in Figure 7.17. Furthermore, if we load the table according to the frequency analysis, 65% of the requests will require at most two comparisons.

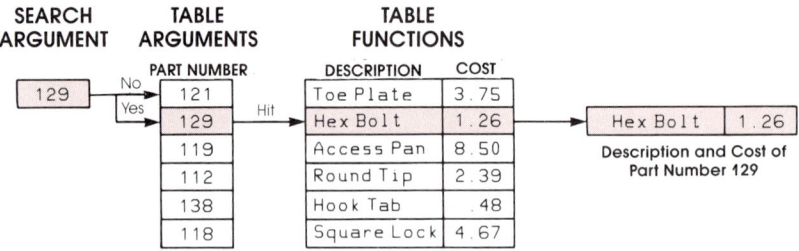

FIGURE 7.17 *A serial search of a table loaded according to a frequency analysis.*

Binary Search

A serial search is useful for short tables but not for long ones. For example, suppose the names in a telephone book were not listed alphabetically. If there were 15,000 names, it would take, on the average, 7,500 comparisons to find a specific telephone number. Some numbers might require only a few comparisons to find, while others might require nearly 15,000 comparisons.

Because telephone books are arranged alphabetically, any name listed therein can be located quickly and easily. When the arguments in a table are in alphabetical or numerical order, an efficient algorithm known as the binary search can be used. A binary search begins the search in the middle of the table. If the search argument is less than the middle table argument, the search continues by halving the lower-valued half of the table. If the search argument is greater than the middle table argument, the search continues by halving the higher-valued half of the table. If the search argument is equal to the middle table argument, the search is over. The binary search algorithm continues to narrow the table until it either finds a match or determines that there is no match.

Figure 7.18 illustrates how the binary search algorithm works with a table of part numbers and corresponding part costs. Follow carefully the arrows numbered 1 to 4.

Part number 182 is first compared against the 9th element of the 17-element array. Since 182 is greater than 157, the match is located in the higher-valued half of the table. Part number 182 is next compared to the 13th element (halfway between 10 and 17). The part number is less than 192, and the confined area between 10 and 13 is halved again. On the next comparison, 182 is greater than 178 and the area is reduced by half. On the fourth comparison, a match is found. A serial search for part number 182 would have taken 12 comparisons before a match was found. The difference in the number of comparisons between the two algorithms becomes even greater as the size of the table increases.

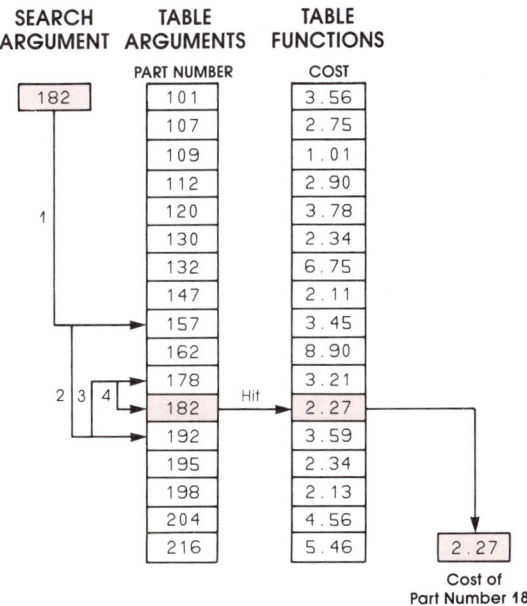

FIGURE 7.18 *A conceptual view of a binary search.*

The following partial program illustrates a binary search using the search argument PART.NUM.

```
3400 ' *********************************************************
3410 ' *                  Access the Table Function            *
3420 ' *********************************************************
3430 LOW = 1
3440 HIGH = ENTRIES
3450 NUM = 1
3460 WHILE PART.NUM <> PART(NUM) AND LOW <= HIGH
3470    NUM = INT((LOW + HIGH) / 2)   ' Find the INTeger Value of the Quotient
3480    IF PART.NUM < PART(NUM)
           THEN HIGH = NUM - 1
3490    IF PART.NUM > PART(NUM)
           THEN LOW  = NUM + 1
3500 WEND
3510 IF PART.NUM = PART(NUM)
        THEN PRINT USING "Cost ==============> $$#.##"; COST(NUM)
        ELSE PRINT "** Error **"; PART.NUM; "is an Invalid Part Number"
3520 LOCATE 11, 15
3530 INPUT "Enter Y to look up another part number, else N... ", CONTROL$
3540 RETURN
3550 '
```

The variables LOW and HIGH point to the beginning and end of that part of the array PART to which the search is confined. Line 3430 initializes LOW to 1. Line 3440 initializes HIGH to ENTRIES, which is equal to the number of entries in the table. Line 3450 initializes NUM to 1 to ensure that PART(NUM), in line 3460, is within the range of the array.

Lines 3400 through 3550 carry out the actual search. The compound condition in line 3460 terminates the While loop when PART.NUM is equal to PART(NUM) or when LOW exceeds HIGH. If the search ends because PART.NUM is equal to PART(NUM), the search is successful. If the search ends because LOW exceeds HIGH, the search is unsuccessful. Immediately following the While loop, line 3510 tests to determine which of the two conditions caused the loop to terminate.

■ 7.9 TEST YOUR BASIC SKILLS (Even-numbered answers are in Appendix B.)

1. Consider the valid programs listed below. What is displayed if each program is executed?

```
a. 100 ' Exercise 7.1a
   110 CLS : KEY OFF   ' Clear Screen
   120 OPTION BASE 1
   130 DIM A(5), B(5), C(5)
   140 FOR I = 1 TO 5
   150    READ A(I), B(I)
   160 NEXT I
   170 FOR I = 1 TO 5
   180    C(I) = A(I) * B(I)
   190    PRINT C(I);
   200 NEXT I
   210 DATA 1, 4, 2, 3, 4, 4, 2, 4, 3, 5
   220 END
```

```
b. 100 ' Exercise 7.1b
   110 F = 0
   120 FOR I = 1 TO 3
   130    G = 0
   140    F = F + 1
   150    FOR J = 1 TO 4
   160       G = G + F
   170       PRINT F, G
   180    NEXT J
   190 NEXT I
   200 END
```

2. Assume that the lower bound is 1 and that array L is declared to have 5 rows and 5 columns. The elements of array L are assigned the following values:

ARRAY L

2	5	14	30	50
7	12	21	70	10
5	15	70	60	0
19	20	30	10	20
22	45	20	40	50

Write the subscripted variable name that references the following values found in array L.

a. 12   b. 70   c. 15   d. 45   e. 60   f. 7   g. 14   h. 22

3. Assume that array A has 4 rows and 4 columns and that the elements of array A are assigned the following values:

ARRAY A

1	2	3	4
5	6	7	8
9	10	11	12
13	14	15	16

Note: A(1, 1) = 1 and A(3, 2) = 10.

What will be the final arrangement of array A after the following partial program is executed? Select your answer from the choices below.

```
100 ' Exercise 7.3
110 FOR I = 1 TO 4
120    FOR J = 1 TO 4
130       A(I, J) = A(J, I)
140    NEXT J
150 NEXT I
```

a. 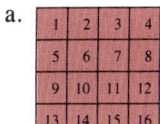   b. 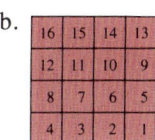   c. 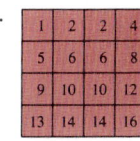   d. 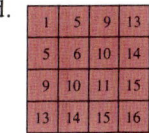   e. None of these.

4. Refer to the initial array A given in Exercise 3. What will be the final arrangement of array A after each of the following partial programs is executed? Select your answers from the choices given in Exercise 3.

```
a. 100 ' Exercise 7.4a
   110 FOR I = 1 TO 4
   120    A(I, 3) = A(I, 2)
   130 NEXT I
```

```
b. 100 ' Exercise 7.4b
   110 J = 2
   120 FOR I = 1 TO 4
   130    A(I, J + 1) = A(I, J)
   140 NEXT I
```

```
c. 100 ' Exercise 7.4c
   110 FOR I = 1 TO 4
   120    A(I, I) = A(I - 2, I + 2)
   130 NEXT I
```

```
d. 100 ' Exercise 7.4d
   110 FOR I = 1 TO 4
   120    FOR J = 1 TO 4
   130       A(I, J) = A(I, J)
   140    NEXT J
   150 NEXT I
```

5. Given an array F that has been declared to have 100 elements, assume that each element of array F has been assigned a value. Write a partial program to shift all the values up one location. That is, assign the value of F1 to F2, F2 to F3, and F100 to F1. Do not use any array other than array F. Be careful not to destroy a value before it is shifted.

6. Given the three arrays A, B, and C, each declared to have 50 elements, assume that the elements of arrays A and B have been assigned values. Write a partial program that compares each element of array A to its corresponding element in array B. Assign a 1, 0, or –1 to the corresponding element in array C, as follows:

   1 if A is greater than B
   0 if A is equal to B
   –1 if A is less than B

7. Identify the error(s), if any, in each of the following partial programs:

   a. ```
      100 ' Exercise 7.7a
      110 DIM X(300)
      120 FOR I = 1 TO 500
      130   READ X(I)
      140 NEXT I
      ```

   b. ```
      100 ' Exercise 7.7b
      110 DIM X(700)
      120 FOR K = 700 TO 1 STEP -1
      130     READ X(K)
      140 NEXT K
      ```

8. Identify the error(s), if any, in each of the following variables and their subscripts.

   a. SUM(8)   b. AMT(6 - 8)   c. BAL(K)   d. F(I(K))
   e. X(3.7)   f. DESC$(5, 6, 7)   g. QUIT(K, A)   h. PAY(3)
   i. LOAN(6.6, 9)   j. Y(I * 3 / J, K + M ^ P)

9. A program utilizes four arrays, B(I), K(J), L(I), and M(Q, J), where the maximum value of I, J, and Q are 15, 36, and 29. Write a correct DIM statement.

■ 7.10 BASIC PROGRAMMING PROBLEMS

1. Sum of a Series of Numbers

Purpose: To become familiar with the implementation of counter-controlled loops by means of the FOR and NEXT statements.

Problem: Write five different programs, as described below.

> **Part A:** Construct a program using a For loop to compute and display the sum of the following series: 1 + 2 + 3 + . . . + 100. Use a For loop to create these integers, and sum them. (**Hint:** See Program 7.2 on page 178 or PRG7-2 on the Student Diskette.)
>
> **Part B:** Same as Part A except sum all the even numbers from 2 to 100, inclusive.
>
> **Part C:** Same as Part A except input the lower and upper limits.
>
> **Part D:** Same as Part C except include a variable step.
>
> **Part E:** Same as Part A except construct a one-statement BASIC program to compute directly, instead of iteratively, the sum of the numbers from 1 to 100.

Input Data: For Parts A, B, and E, there is no input. For C, input a lower limit of 15 and an upper limit of 42. For Part D, input a lower limit of 20, an upper limit of 75, and a step of 5.

Output Results: Display the result of each program in sentence form. For Parts A and E, the sum is 5050; for Part B, the sum is 2550; for Part C, the sum is 798; for Part D, the sum is 570.

2. Credit Card Verification

Purpose: To become familiar with declaring, loading, and serially searching a table.

Problem: Write a top-down program that will accept a 6-digit credit card number and verify that this number is in a table. If the credit card number is in the table, display a message indicating that the credit card number is valid. If the credit card number is not in the table, display a message indicating that the credit card is invalid and to alert the manager. Declare the credit card-number table to N elements. Use the following 15 credit card numbers.

```
131416  238967  384512  583214  172319
345610  410001  672354  194567  351098
518912  691265  210201  372198  562982
```

Input Data: Use the following sample data.

```
372198  518912  102002  672354  210200
```

The 15 credit card numbers are stored in the sequential file EX72CARD.TBL on the Student Diskette.

Output Results: The following results are shown for credit card numbers 372198 and 210200.

```
             Credit Card Verification

Credit Card Number =====> 372198
Credit Card Number is valid
Enter Y to verify another Credit Card Number, else N   Y
```

```
             Credit Card Verification

Credit Card Number =====> 210200
** Error ** Credit Card Number is invalid - Alert Your Manager
Enter Y to verify another Credit Card Number, else N   N
```

3. Week-Ending Department and Store Receipts

Purpose: To become familiar with the use of arrays for determining totals.

Problem: Businesses are usually subdivided into smaller units for the purpose of better organization. The Tri-Quality retail store is subdivided into four departments. Each department submits its receipts at the end of the day to the store manager. Using an array consisting of 5 rows and 6 columns, write a program that is assigned the daily sales. Use the 5th row and 6th column to accumulate the totals. After accumulating the totals, display the entire array.

Input Data: Use the following sample data in DATA statements or use the sequential file EX73SAL.DAT on the Student Diskette.

Dept.	Monday	Tuesday	Wednesday	Thursday	Friday
1	$2,146	$6,848	$8,132	$8,912	$5,165
2	8,123	9,125	6,159	5,618	9,176
3	4,156	5,612	4,128	4,812	3,685
4	1,288	1,492	1,926	1,225	2,015

Output Results: The following results are displayed.

```
              Week-Ending Store Receipts

 Dept    Mon.      Tues.      Wed.      Thur.      Fri.      Total
 ------------------------------------------------------------------
   1     2,146     6,848     8,132     8,912     5,165     31,203
   2     8,123     9,125     6,159     5,618     9,176     38,201
   3     4,156     5,612     4,128     4,812     3,685     22,393
   4     1,288     1,492     1,926     1,225     2,015      7,946
   T    15,713    23,077    20,345    20,567    20,041     99,743

 Job Complete
```

4. Sorting Customer Numbers

Purpose: To become familiar with sorting data into ascending or descending sequence and to gain a better understanding of the bubble sort algorithm.

Problem: Write a program that requests the selection from a menu of functions for sorting the customer numbers into ascending or descending sequence. Print the sorted customer numbers on the printer. Declare the customer number array to have 100 elements. Note that there are only 15 customer numbers. Assume that the number of customers varies from 1 to 100.

Input Data: Use the following customer numbers in DATA statements or use the sequential file EX74CUS.DAT on the Student Diskette.

```
45621   42171   38971   36182   18431
35128   41961   52146   14192   21687
51120   45345   45756   53726   14891
```

Output Results: The following is displayed on the screen.

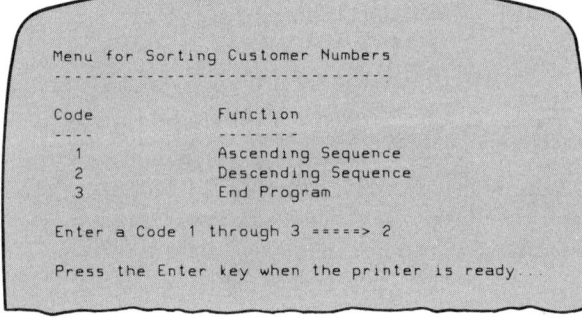

MORE ON STRINGS AND FUNCTIONS

■ 8.1
INTRODUCTION

Computers were originally built to perform mathematical calculations. Today, they are still used for that purpose; however, more and more applications require computers to process string (text) data as well. Section 3.5 briefly introduced four string functions — LEFT$, MID$, RIGHT$ and LEN — giving some indication of the ability of MS BASIC to manipulate string data. As you shall see in this chapter, MS BASIC includes several additional string functions, string statements, and special variables that place it among the better programming languages for manipulating letters, numbers, words, and phrases.

MS BASIC also includes numeric functions to handle common mathematical calculations. For example, it is often necessary in programming to obtain the square root or the logarithm of a number. In this chapter, we will discuss the two numeric functions that handle these two calculations, as well as fourteen others.

A second type of function that will be discussed in this chapter is the **user-defined function**. With a function that is defined by the user, numeric or string functions can be created to perform a task that is often needed by the programmer.

■ 8.2
STRING FUNCTIONS, STRING STATEMENTS, AND SPECIAL VARIABLES

A list of the string functions and a list of the special variables that are available in MS BASIC, along with their areas of use, are shown on the next page, in Tables 8.1 and 8.2, respectively. To be used, these functions and special variables need only be referred to by name in a LET, PRINT, or IF statement.

The major difference between functions and special variables is that functions require a built-in routine to be executed in order to generate the value returned to your program, whereas special variables don't. Special variables point to addresses in main storage that already contain the desired information.

TABLE 8.1 MS BASIC String Functions

FUNCTION	FUNCTION VALUE
ASC(X$)	*Returns a two-digit numeric value that is equivalent in ASCII code to the first character of the string argument X$.*
CHR$(N)	*Returns a single string character that is equivalent in ASCII code to the numeric argument N.*
INPUT$(N)	*Suspends execution of the program until N number of characters from the keyboard are entered.*
INSTR(P,X$,S$)	*Returns the beginning position of the substring S$ in string X$. P indicates the position the search begins in X$ and may be omitted from the argument list. If the search for S$ in X$ is unsuccessful, INSTR returns a value of zero.*
LEFT$(X$, N)	*Extracts the leftmost N characters of the string argument X$.*
LEN(X$)	*Returns the length of the string argument X$.*
MID$(X$, P, N)	*Extracts N characters of the string argument X$ beginning at position P.*
RIGHT$(X$, N)	*Extracts the rightmost N characters of the string argument X$.*
SPACE$(N)	*Returns N number of spaces.*
SPC(N)	*Displays N spaces. May be used only in an output statement.*
STR$(N)	*Returns the string equivalent of the numeric argument N.*
STRING$(N, X$)	*Returns N times the first character of X$.*
VAL(X$)	*Returns the numeric equivalent of the string argument X$.*

TABLE 8.2 MS BASIC Special Variables

SPECIAL VARIABLE	SPECIAL VARIABLE USE
CSRLIN	*Equal to the vertical (row) coordinate of the cursor.*
DATE$	*Equal to the current date as a string in the form mm-dd-yyyy.*
ERL	*Equal to the line number of the last error. Used for error trapping.*
ERR	*Equal to the error code of the last error. Used for error trapping.*
INKEY$	*Equal to the last character entered through the keyboard.*
TIME$	*Equal to the current time of day in 24-hour notation as a string in the form hh:mm:ss.*

Concatenation, Substrings and Character Counting Revisited — +, LEN, LEFT$, RIGHT$, and MID$

The extraction of substrings from a large string and the combining of two or more strings are important in manipulating nonnumeric data. In Section 3.5, on page 57, the concatenation operator + and the LEN, LEFT$, RIGHT$, and MID$ functions were briefly introduced. You'll recall that concatenation is the only string operation allowed in MS BASIC. It joins two strings to form a new string. For example,

```
500 JOIN$ = "ABC" + "DEF"
```

assigns JOIN$ the value ABCDEF. The second string is joined to the right end of the first string to form the result, which is then assigned to JOIN$.

The LEN function returns the length of the argument. The argument may be a string constant, a string variable, or a string expression. Program 8.1 illustrates the use of the LEN function.

PROGRAM 8.1

```
100 ' Program 8.1
110 ' Examples of the use of the LEN function
120 ' *****************************************
130 WORD1$ = "Structured"
140 WORD2$ = "Programming"
150 LENGTH = LEN(WORD1$)
160 PRINT WORD1$; " has"; LENGTH; "characters."
170 PRINT WORD2$; " has"; LEN(WORD2$); "characters."
180 PRINT WORD1$ + " " + WORD2$; " has";
          LEN(WORD1$ + " " + WORD2$); "characters."
190 END

RUN

Structured has 10 characters.
Programming has 11 characters.
Structured Programming has 22 characters.
```

In Program 8.1, LEN(WORD1$) in line 150 assigns the variable LENGTH a value of 10. In line 170, LEN(WORD2$) is displayed as 11. In line 180, the LEN function returns the length of the string expression WORD1$ + " " + WORD2$ as 22.

The LEFT$, MID$, and RIGHT$ string functions may be used to extract substrings from a string constant, a string variable, or a string expression. A **substring** is a part of a string. For example, some substrings of Return of the Jedi are Return, Jedi, of t, and ed. All three functions reference substrings on the basis of the position of characters within the string argument, where the leftmost character of the string argument is position 1, the next is position 2, and so on. For example, in the string Return of the Jedi, the substring Return begins in position 1, and the substring Jedi begins in position 15.

LEFT$(X$, N) extracts a substring starting with the leftmost character (position 1) of the string X$. The length of the substring is determined by the integer value of the length argument N. For example, the following statement assigns SUB1$ the value Return

```
300 SUB1$ = LEFT$("Return of the Jedi", 6)
```

Return begins in position 1 and has a length of 6. The quotation marks are not part of the string.

RIGHT$(X$, N) extracts a substring starting with the rightmost character of the string argument X$. The length of the substring is determined by the value of the length argument N. For example, if MOVIE$ is equal to the string Raiders of the Lost Ark, then the following statement assigns SUB2$ the substring Ark

```
400 SUB2$ = RIGHT$(MOVIE$, 3)
```

MID$(X$, P, N) extracts a substring beginning with the character in position P of X$. The length of the substring is determined by the value of the length argument N. For example, if PHRASE$ is equal to the string Every dog must have his day, then the following statement assigns SUB3$ the substring dog must have

```
500 SUB3$ = MID$(PHRASE$, 7, 13)
```

If the length argument is not included in the list for the MID$ function, then the PC returns a substring that begins with the position argument and ends with the last character in the string argument. For example, if PHRASE$ is equal to the string Today is the tomorrow I worried about yesterday, then the following statement assigns SUB4$ the substring I worried about yesterday

```
600 SUB4$ = MID$(PHRASE$, 23)
```

Program 8.2 makes use of the LEN and MID$ functions. The basic purpose of the program is to search for words in a sentence. Each time a word is found, the program displays it on a separate line. The program assumes that each word, except for the last, is followed by a space.

PROGRAM 8.2

```
100 ' Program 8.2
110 ' Displaying Each Word in a Sentence
120 ' ************************************
130 PRINT "Enter the sentence without punctuation:"
140 PRINT : INPUT "", SENTENCE$
150 BEG = 1
160 PRINT : PRINT "Words in the sentence:"
170 FOR CHAR = 1 TO LEN(SENTENCE$)
180     IF MID$(SENTENCE$, CHAR, 1) = " "
            THEN PRINT TAB(23); MID$(SENTENCE$, BEG, CHAR - BEG) :
                BEG = CHAR + 1
190 NEXT CHAR
200 ' ****** Display the Last Word *****
210 PRINT TAB(23); MID$(SENTENCE$, BEG)
220 PRINT "Job Complete"
230 END

RUN

Enter the sentence without punctuation:

If an experiment works something has gone wrong

Words in the sentence:
                      If
                      an
                      experiment
                      works
                      something
                      has
                      gone
                      wrong
Job Complete
```

When Program 8.2 is executed, line 130 displays a prompt message. Line 140 accepts the sentence and assigns it to the variable SENTENCE$. In line 150, the variable BEG is assigned a value of 1. This variable is used later, in line 180 to indicate the beginning position of each word and in line 210 to display the last word in the sentence.

Line 180 in the For loop tests each character in the sentence to determine whether it is a space. If a character is a space, then the word beginning at position BEG with length of CHAR - BEG is displayed and BEG is set equal to a value that is equivalent to the beginning position of the next word. Since the last word in the sentence does not end with a space, line 210 instead of line 180 is used to display the last word.

Substring Searching and Replacement — INSTR Function and MID$ Statement

MS BASIC includes the INSTR function to search a string argument for a particular substring. INSTR(P, X$, S$) returns the beginning position of the substring S$ in X$. The search begins at position P of X$. For example, the following partial program causes the variable CNT1 to be assigned the value 4:

```
490 PHRASE$ = "To be or not to be"
500 CNT1 = INSTR(1, PHRASE$, "be")
```

Line 500 assigns CNT1 the position of the first character of the substring be in string PHRASE$. If there are no occurrences of the substring, INSTR returns the value zero. Table 8.3 illustrates some additional examples of the INSTR function.

TABLE 8.3 Examples of the INSTR Function

THE STATEMENT	RESULTS IN
Assume that S$ is equal to Rally 'round the flag, boys, rally once again	
100 POS1 = INSTR(1, S$, ",")	POS1 = 22
200 POS2 = INSTR(START, S$, "rally")	POS2 = 30 *(assume START = 22)*
300 POS3 = INSTR(S$, " ' ")	POS3 = 7 *(search begins at position 1 by default)*

The MID$ statement is used for substring replacement. Do not confuse the MID$ statement with the MID$ function. The MID$ function returns a substring, but the MID$ statement replaces a series of characters within a string with a designated substring. The general form of the MID$ statement is given in Table 8.4 on the next page.

As illustrated by the general form in Table 8.4, a substring of X$, specified by the beginning position P and the length N, is replaced by the substring S$. For example, if PHRASE$ is equal to Inprocment and SUBSTR$ is equal to vest, then the following statement,

```
100 MID$(PHRASE$, 3, 4) = SUBSTR$
```

assigns PHRASE$ the value Investment. The substring vest replaces the substring proc.

TABLE 8.4 The MID$ Statement

General Form:	`MID$(X$, P, N) = S$`
	*where **X$** is the string in which the replacement takes place;*
	P *is the position at which the replacement begins;*
	N *is the number of characters to replace; and*
	S$ *is the replacement substring.*
Purpose:	*Replaces a substring within a string.*
Examples:	`100 MID$(PHRASE$, 3, 4) = SUBSTR$`
	`200 MID$(WORD1$, 1, 5) = "Y"` *(1 character replaced)*
	`300 MID$(WD1$, 30, 2) = "abcde"` *(2 characters replaced)*
	`400 MID$(E$, 4, 5) = A$ + B$`

Program 8.3 modifies a line of text through the use of the `INSTR` function and the `MID$` statement. The program searches for all occurrences of the substring `ne`. Each time the substring is found, it is replaced with the substring `in`.

PROGRAM 8.3

```
100 ' Program 8.3
110 ' Searching and Replacing Strings
120 ' *******************************
130 PHRASE$ = "The rane in Spane stays manely in the plane"
140 PRINT "Old text ===> "; PHRASE$
150 POSITION = INSTR(PHRASE$, "ne")
160 WHILE POSITION <> 0
170    MID$(PHRASE$, POSITION, 2) = "in"
180    POSITION = INSTR(POSITION + 2, PHRASE$, "ne")
190 WEND
200 PRINT
210 PRINT "New text ===> "; PHRASE$
220 END

RUN

Old text ===> The rane in Spane stays manely in the plane
New text ===> The rain in Spain stays mainly in the plain
```

Line 150 in Program 8.3 assigns the variable POSITION the value 7, which is the beginning position of the first occurrence of the substring `ne`. Line 170 replaces the substring `ne` that begins in position 7 with the substring `in`. Line 180 searches for the next occurrence of the substring `ne`. The search begins one position to the right of the previous occurrence. The next occurrence of the substring `ne` begins at position 16. Therefore, the `INSTR` function assigns POSITION a value of 16. The loop continues, with line 170 making the next replacement.

This process continues until all the occurrences of `ne` have been changed to `in`. At this point, line 180 assigns POSITION a value of zero and the loop terminates. The modified value of PHRASE$ is then displayed by line 210.

Converting Character Codes — ASC and CHR$

The ASC and CHR$ functions facilitate the manipulation of individual characters. ASC(X$) returns a two-digit numeric value that corresponds to the ASCII code for the first character of the string argument X$. The ASCII code is what the PC uses for storing a character in main storage or on auxiliary storage. For example, the character A has an ASCII code of 65, the character B has an ASCII code of 66, and so on (see Table A.1 in Appendix A). The following statement displays the result 67:

```
PRINT ASC("C")
67
```

CHR$(N) can be described as the reverse of the ASC function. It returns a single string character that is equivalent in ASCII code to the numeric argument N. For example, the following statement displays the character B:

```
PRINT CHR$(66)
B
```

A total of 256 different characters are represented by the ASCII code. The CHR$ function allows you to enter any of the 256 characters by using the corresponding ASCII code as the argument. For example, the following partial program,

```
300 FOR I = 1 TO 10
310    PRINT CHR$(7);
320 NEXT I
330 PRINT CHR$(12)
```

causes the PC to beep ten times and clear the first 24 lines of the screen because the ASCII code 7 corresponds to the character BEL (Bell) and the ASCII code 12 corresponds to the character FF (Form Feed) as shown in Table A.1 in Appendix A.

The ASC function is used to convert a single character string into a numeric value, which can later be manipulated arithmetically. Programming Case Study 12, below, makes use of the CHR$ and ASC functions to decipher a coded message.

PROGRAMMING CASE STUDY 12: *Deciphering a Coded Message*

Messages are often coded by having one letter represent another. The coded message is called a **cryptogram**, and an algorithm is used to decipher the message into readable form.

The objective here is to take a coded message and have the PC display the corresponding deciphered message. The algorithm calls for subtracting 3 from the numeric code that represents each character in the coded message. Obviously, the algorithm can be, and usually is, more complex.

The coded message is

WKH#VKDGRZ#NQRZV

Following is a list of program tasks; a program solution; and a discussion of the program solution.

Program Tasks

1. Clear the screen.
2. Accept a message from the user.
3. Use a For loop to process each character in the message. The For loop includes the following:

    a. an initial parameter of 1
    b. a limit parameter of LEN(message)
    c. the MID$ function to extract each character
    d. the ASC function to determine the numeric value that is equivalent to the ASCII code of the extracted character
    e. subtraction of 3 from the numeric value determined in 3d
    f. the CHR$ function to change the numeric value in 3e to a character
    g. display the character

Program Solution

The following program corresponds to the preceding tasks.

PROGRAM 8.4

```
100 ' Program 8.4
110 ' Deciphering a Coded Message
120 ' ***************************
125 CLS : KEY OFF   ' Clear Screen
130 PRINT : INPUT "Coded message ========> ", CODE$
140 PRINT : PRINT "The message is ========> ";
160 FOR CHAR = 1 TO LEN(CODE$)
170    NUM = ASC(MID$(CODE$, CHAR, 1))
180    NUM = NUM - 3
190    LETTER$ = CHR$(NUM)
200    PRINT LETTER$;
210 NEXT CHAR
220 PRINT
230 END

RUN

Coded message ========> WKH#VKDGRZ#NQRZV

The message is ========> THE SHADOW KNOWS
```

Discussion of the Program Solution

Program 8.4 accepts a coded message, deciphers it one character at a time, and displays the corresponding message one character at a time.

In line 160, LEN(CODE$) is the limit value for the For loop. Line 170 determines the numeric value that corresponds to the ASCII code for the character selected by the MID$ function. It is valid for a string function to be part of the argument for another string function. Line 180 subtracts 3 from the value of NUM, and in line 190 the CHR$ function returns the corresponding character.

Modifying Data Types — STR$ and VAL

The PC cannot add a string value to a numeric value. The STR$ and VAL functions allow this restriction to be circumvented. The STR$(N) function returns the string equivalent of the numeric value N. VAL(X$) returns the numeric equivalent of the string X$.

Table 8.5 gives examples of both the STR$ and VAL functions. These two functions are used primarily in instances where a substring of numeric digits within an identification number — like a credit card number or an invoice number — need to be extracted for computational purposes and the result has to be transformed back as a string value.

TABLE 8.5 Examples of the STR$ and VAL Functions

VALUE OF	THE STATEMENT	RESULTS IN
	100 A$ = STR$(34)	A$ = 34
B = 64.543	200 S$ = STR$(B)	S$ = 64.543
C = -3.21	300 Z$ = STR$(C)	Z$ = -3.21
	400 F = VAL("766.321")	F = 766.321
K$ = 12E-3	500 Q = VAL(K$)	Q = 12E-3
P$ = ABC	600 W = VAL(P$)	W = 0

Note: Any numeric value that is assigned to a string variable is actually a string, not a number.

Duplicating Strings — SPACE$ and STRING$

The SPACE$ and STRING$ functions are used to duplicate string data. SPACE$(N) returns N spaces or blank characters. It is similar to the SPC function which was discussed in Chapter 4. For example, the two statements

        700 PRINT "DEC"; SPC(4); "Micro VAX"

and

        710 PRINT "DEC"; SPACE$(4); "Micro VAX"

display identical results. The advantage of the SPACE$ function over the SPC function is that SPACE$ may be used in statements other than the PRINT statement. For example, the following statement,

        720 SP$ = SPACE$(25)

assigns SP$ a string value of 25 spaces. If the argument is equal to or less than zero, the function returns the null string.

The STRING$(N, X$) function returns N times the first character of the string X$. The STRING$ function may be used to duplicate any character. For example, the following statement,

        730 PRINT STRING$(72, "*")

displays a line of 72 asterisks.

Accessing the System Time and Date — The Special Variables DATE$ and TIME$

The special variables DATE$ and TIME$ are automatically equal to the system date and system time, respectively. The special variable DATE$ is equal to the current system date as a string value in the form mm-dd-yyyy. The first two characters, mm, represent the month. The fourth and fifth characters, dd, represent the day. The last four characters, yyyy, represent the year.

The special variable TIME$ is equal to the system's time of day, in 24-hour notation, as a string value in the form hh:mm:ss. The first two characters, hh, represent the hours (range 00–23). The fourth and fifth characters, mm, represent the minutes (range 00–59). The last two characters, ss, represent the seconds (range 00–59).

Table 8.6 gives examples of both special variables DATE$ and TIME$.

TABLE 8.6 Examples of the Special Variables DATE$ and TIME$

THE STATEMENT	RESULTS IN
Assume DATE$ = 09-15-1993 *and* TIME$ = 15:26:32	
100 TD$ = DATE$	TD$ = 09-15-1993
200 TT$ = TIME$	TT$ = 15:26:32
300 MONTH$ = MID$(DATE$, 1, 2)	MONTH$ = 09
400 DAY$ = MID$(DATE$, 4, 2)	DAY$ = 15
500 YEAR$ = MID$(DATE$, 9, 2)	YEAR$ = 93
600 HOUR$ = MID$(TIME$, 1, 2)	HOUR$ = 15
700 MINUTE$ = MID$(TIME$, 4, 2)	MINUTE$ = 26
800 SECOND$ = MID$(TIME$, 7, 2)	SECOND$ = 32

Note: Any numeric value that is assigned to a string variable is actually a string, not a number.

Accepting String Data — LINE INPUT Statement, INKEY$ Variable, and INPUT$ Function

The LINE INPUT statement accepts a line entered from the keyboard as a string value and assigns it to a string variable. The LINE INPUT statement ignores the usual delimiters, namely, the quotation mark and the comma.

The general form of the LINE INPUT statement is shown in Table 8.7.

TABLE 8.7 The LINE INPUT Statement

General Form:	LINE INPUT *string variable*
	or
	LINE INPUT *"input prompt message"*; *string variable*
	or
	LINE INPUT #n, *string variable*
Purpose:	*Provides for the assignment to a string variable of an entire line (up to 255 characters), including commas and quotation marks, entered from an external source, such as the keyboard or auxiliary storage.*
Examples:	**LINE INPUT Statement** — ***Data from an External Source***
	100 LINE INPUT CUS.REC$ — "123","Adams Joe",44,0520
	200 LINE INPUT "What? "; STAT$ — "Don't do it", Amanda Said
	300 LINE INPUT "Weight ===> "; WGT$ — 126.5 lbs.
	400 LINE INPUT #2, LIN$ — "John Smith", 46, "3", 12
Note:	*A question mark is not displayed as part of the prompt unless it is included in the input prompt message.*

When executed, an INPUT or LINE INPUT statement instructs the PC to suspend execution of the program until the Enter key is pressed. That is, with these two statements, we must always signal the PC by pressing the Enter key when we have finished entering the requested data. The special variable INKEY$ and the INPUT$ function do not require that the Enter key be pressed for the PC to accept input.

The special variable INKEY$ *does not* suspend execution of the program; instead, it checks the keyboard to determine whether a character is pending — that is, whether a key was recently pressed. The following statement,

```
100 PENDING$ = INKEY$
```

assigns PENDING$ the character that corresponds to the last key pressed. If no character is pending, then INKEY$ assigns the null string to PENDING$.

Consider the following example, in which the INKEY$ function is used to control a looping process. The values of NUM and NUM MOD 7 are displayed until the user presses a key or until an overflow condition occurs in line 530.

```
500 NUM = 1
510 WHILE INKEY$ = ""
520     PRINT NUM, NUM MOD 7
530     NUM = NUM + 1
540 WEND
```

In this partial program, the INKEY$ function is used in the WHILE statement to control the loop. As long as there is no character pending from the keyboard, the PC continues to execute the loop.

The special variable INKEY$ is useful for applications that require that a program not be interrupted and yet accept responses from the keyboard. This method of processing is essential for video game programs, like Nintendo's Duck Hunt or Super Mario Bros. In these games, objects on the monitor are in constant motion, and at the same time the games must check for user input, like the firing of a phaser or torpedo.

The INPUT$(N) function is more sophisticated than the variable INKEY$, because it accepts N characters from the keyboard. However, unlike INKEY$, INPUT$ suspends execution of the program until the user has pressed N number of keys. For example, the statement

```
300 CHAR$ = INPUT$(1)
```

causes the PC to suspend execution of the program and wait until a key is pressed.

The characters entered in response to the INPUT$ function are not displayed on the screen. To display the response, the statement that contains the function should be followed with a PRINT statement. For example,

```
400 CHAR$ = INPUT$(5)
410 PRINT CHAR$
```

displays the five characters entered by the user.

A common use of the `INPUT$` function is to suspend the execution of a program at the conclusion of a task so that the information on the screen may be read before it disappears. For example, if a program is displaying a long list of items, you may want to suspend execution of the program after every 20 or so lines are displayed. The message

```
Press any key to continue...
```

is often used in this context. The `INPUT$` simplifies the entry by not requiring that the Enter key be pressed. The following partial program shows how to incorporate this technique into a BASIC program.

```
1000 PRINT "Press any key to continue..."
1010 CHAR$ = INPUT$(1)
```

Line 1000 displays the message, and line 1010 suspends execution of the program. Execution continues when the user presses any key on the keyboard except Ctrl-Break.

8.3

The numeric functions that are part of MS BASIC are listed in Table 8.8. In the discussion that follows, several examples of each numeric function are presented.

TABLE 8.8 MS BASIC Numeric Functions

FUNCTION	FUNCTION VALUE
ABS(N)	Returns the absolute value of the argument N.
ATN(N)	Returns the angle in radians whose tangent is the value of the argument N.
COS(N)	Returns the cosine of the argument N where N is in radians.
EXP(N)	Returns e (2.718281...) raised to the argument N.
FIX(N)	Returns the value of N truncated to an integer.
FRE(N)	Returns the number of unused bytes within BASIC's data space.
INT(N)	Returns the largest integer that is less than or equal to the argument N.
LOG(N)	Returns the natural log of the argument N where N is greater than 0.
POS(N)	Returns the current cursor column position.
RND	Returns a random number between 0 (inclusive) and 1 (exclusive).
SCREEN(R, C)	Returns the ASCII code for the character at the specified row (R) and column (C) on the screen.
SGN(N)	Returns the sign of the argument N: –1 if the argument N is less than 0; 0 if the argument N is equal to 0; or +1 if the argument N is greater than 0.
SIN(N)	Returns the sine of the argument N where N is in radians.
SQR(N)	Returns the square root of the positive argument N.
TAN(N)	Returns the tangent of the argument N where N is in radians.
TIMER	Returns a value equal to the number of seconds elapsed since midnight.

Arithmetic Functions — ABS, FIX, INT, and SGN

The functions classified as **arithmetic** include ABS (absolute value), FIX (fixed integer), INT (integer), and SGN (sign).

The ABS function takes any numeric expression and returns its positive value. For example, if N is equal to –4, then ABS(N) is equal to 4. Additional examples of the ABS function are shown in Table 8.9.

The FIX(N) function returns the integer portion of the argument N. When the argument is positive, the FIX function is identical to the INT function. For example, if N is equal to 13.45, then FIX(N) returns 13. However, when the argument is negative, the two functions return a different result. For example, if N is equal to –4.45, then FIX(N) returns –4 and INT(N) returns –5. The INT function returns an integer that is less than or equal to the argument. Additional examples of the FIX and INT functions are shown in Table 8.9.

The SGN(N) function returns a value of +1 if the argument N is positive, 0 if the argument is 0, and –1 if the argument N is negative. Table 8.9 shows examples of the SGN function.

TABLE 8.9 Examples of the ABS, FIX, INT, and SGN Functions

VALUE OF VARIABLE	THE STATEMENT	RESULTS IN
NUM = -3	100 P = ABS(NUM)	P = 3
CNT = 4.5	200 C = ABS(CNT)	C = 4.5
C = 4, D = -6	300 A = C + ABS(D)	A = 10
G = 25.567	400 F = FIX(G)	F = 25
G = -25.567	500 F = FIX(G)	F = -25
G = -25.567	600 I = INT(G)	I = -26
G = -25.567	700 K = INT(ABS(G))	K = 25
D = 4	800 E = SGN(D)	E = 1
P = -5	900 F = 5 + SGN(P)	F = 4

Exponential Functions — SQR, EXP, and LOG

The functions classified as **exponential** include the SQR (square root), EXP (exponential), and LOG (logarithmic).

The SQR(N) function computes the square root of the positive argument N. Table 8.10 shows several examples of computing the square root of a number.

TABLE 8.10 Examples of the SQR Function

VALUE OF VARIABLE	THE STATEMENT	RESULTS IN
	100 ROOT = SQR(9)	ROOT = 3
VALUE = 0	200 R1 = SQR(VALUE)	R1 = 0
CUBE = 625	300 R2 = SQR(SQR(CUBE))	R2 = 5
SUB(1) = 1.15129	400 R3 = SQR(SUB(1))	SUB = 1.072982
X = 3, Y = 4	500 HYP = SQR(X ^ 2 + Y ^ 2)	HYP = 5
NEG = -49	600 POSI = SQR(ABS(NEG))	POSI = 7
NUM = -25	700 ROOT = SQR(NUM)	Illegal Function Call

The symbol **e** in mathematics represents 2.718281..., where the three dots show that the fractional part of the constant is not a repeating sequence of digits. In MS BASIC, the keyword `EXP` is used to represent this constant, which is raised to the power given as the argument in parentheses following the function name. The `EXP` function can be used, for example, to determine the value of $e^{1.14473}$. The following statement,

```
210 PI = EXP(1.14473)
```

results in the variable PI being assigned a value of 3.141593, which is a close approximation of π. If the value of the argument for the `EXP` function exceeds 88.02968, then an overflow condition occurs.

The natural log ($\log_e$ or ln) of a number can be determined by using the `LOG` function. For example, the value of X in the equation $e^x = 3.141593$ can be determined by using the following statement:

```
310 X = LOG(3.141593)
```

The resulting value of X is 1.14473 and, therefore, $e^{1.14473} = 3.141593$.

This function can also be used to determine the logarithm to the base 10 by multiplying the `LOG` function by 0.434295. For example, in the statement

```
410 LOG10 = 0.434295 * LOG(3)
```

LOG10 is assigned the value 0.4771219, the base 10 logarithm of 3.

The following Programming Case Study is an example of the use of the `LOG` function.

PROGRAMMING CASE STUDY 13: Determining the Time It Takes to Double an Investment

The formula for computing the amount of an investment compounded annually for a given number of years is $A = P(1 + J)^N$ where A is the total amount, P is the initial investment, J is the annual rate of interest, and N is the number of years.

This formula can be rewritten to solve for the number of years N:

$$N = \frac{\log \frac{A}{P}}{\log(1 + J)}$$

If the number of years it takes to double an investment is to be determined, then the amount A is equal to twice the investment P, or $A = 2P$. The formula for determining the number of years to double an investment can further be simplified to the following:

$$N = \frac{\log 2}{\log(1 + J)}$$

The ensuing problem uses the `LOG` function to compute the number of years it takes to double an investment.

Problem: The WESAVU National Bank requests that a program be written to display a table of annual interest rates and the corresponding years it will take to double an investment compounded annually for integer interests rates from 8 through 18, inclusive. Display the number of years to the nearest tenths place.

Following are an analysis of the problem; a program solution; and a discussion of the program solution.

Program Tasks

1. Initialization
   a. Clear the screen.
   b. Call the Print Report and Column Headings Module.

2. Generate Table
   a. Set NUMERATOR equal to LOG(2).
   b. Use a For loop to generate the annual interest rates (INTEREST) from 8 through 18. Within the loop perform the following tasks:
      (1) Determine the number of years (TIME) it takes to double an investment at INTEREST percent, using the statement:

      TIME = NUMERATOR / LOG(1 + INTEREST / 100).

      (2) Display the interest rate (INTEREST) and the number of years it takes to double an investment (TIME) to the nearest tenths place.

3. Wrap-up — display an end-of-job message.

Program Solution

The following program corresponds to the preceding tasks.

PROGRAM 8.5

```
1000 ' Program 8.5
1010 ' Determining the Time to Double an Investment
1020 ' *********************************************
1030 ' *              Main Module                  *
1040 ' *********************************************
1050 GOSUB 2000    ' Call Initialization
1060 GOSUB 3000    ' Call Generate Table
1070 GOSUB 4000    ' Call Wrap-up
1080 END
2000 ' *********************************************
2010 ' *              Initialization               *
2020 ' *********************************************
2030 CLS : KEY OFF  ' Clear Screen
2040 GOSUB 2200     ' Call Print Report and Column Headings
2050 RETURN
2060 '
```

(continued)

```
2200 ' ****************************************************
2210 ' *       Print Report and Column Headings            *
2220 ' ****************************************************
2230 PRINT     "Doubling an Investment"
2240 PRINT     "----------------------"
2250 PRINT
2260 PRINT     "Interest    Number"
2270 PRINT     "Rate in %   of Years"
2280 PRINT     "---------   --------"
2290 FORMAT$ = "    ##         ##.#"
2300 RETURN
2310 '
3000 ' ****************************************************
3010 ' *                 Generate Table                    *
3020 ' ****************************************************
3030 NUMERATOR = LOG(2)
3040 FOR INTEREST = 8 TO 18
3050     TIME = NUMERATOR / LOG(1 + INTEREST / 100)
3060     PRINT USING FORMAT$; INTEREST, TIME
3070 NEXT INTEREST
3080 RETURN
3090 '
4000 ' ****************************************************
4010 ' *                    Wrap-up                        *
4020 ' ****************************************************
4030 PRINT : PRINT "End of Report"
4040 RETURN
4050 ' ************** End of Program **************
RUN

Doubling an Investment
----------------------

Interest    Number
Rate in %   of Years
---------   --------
    8         9.0
    9         8.0
   10         7.3
   11         6.6
   12         6.1
   13         5.7
   14         5.3
   15         5.0
   16         4.7
   17         4.4
   18         4.2

End of Report
```

Discussion of the Program Solution

With slight modifications to the values in the FOR statement in Program 8.5, the number of years it takes to double an investment that is compounded annually can be determined for a variety of interest rates. The argument in the first reference to the LOG function in line 3030 may be changed to other numbers, like 3 or 4, to determine how long it takes to triple or quadruple an investment that is compounded annually. See BASIC Programming Problem 2 at the end of this chapter to determine the number of years it takes to double an investment that is compounded quarterly.

Trigonometric Functions — SIN, COS, TAN, and ATN

In MS BASIC, the SIN, COS, and TAN functions can be used to determine the sine, cosine, and tangent of an angle X. For these functions to work correctly, the angle X *must* be expressed in radians. Since angles are usually expressed in degrees, the following statements relating angles and radians should prove helpful:

$$1 \text{ radian} = 180 / \pi \text{ degrees} = 180 / 3.141593 \text{ degrees}$$
$$1 \text{ degree} = \pi / 180 \text{ radians} = 3.141593 / 180 \text{ radians}$$

When using these three functions, remember that if the argument is in units of degrees, it must first be multiplied by 3.141593 / 180 in order to convert it into units of radians before the function can evaluate it. In mathematics, if the equation $X = \sin 30°$ is evaluated, then $X = 0.5$. Evaluating the same equation in MS BASIC requires the following:

```
510 RADS = 30 * 3.141593 / 180
520 X = SIN(RADS)
```

or:

```
510 X = SIN(30 * 3.141593 / 180)
```

MS BASIC does not have corresponding functions for the cosecant, the secant and the cotangent. These three trigonometric functions must be evaluated by combinations of the SIN, COS, and TAN functions. Table 8.11 illustrates the combinations.

TABLE 8.11 Determining the Cosecant, Secant and Cotangent

TO FIND THE	USE
Cosecant	1 / SIN(X)
Secant	1 / COS(X)
Cotangent	1 / TAN(X)

The fourth trigonometric function that is available in MS BASIC is the arctangent. The ATN function returns a value that is the angle (in units of radians) that corresponds to the argument. For example,

```
610 ANGLE = ATN(1)
```

results in ANGLE being assigned the value of 0.7853982 radians. Multiplying this number by 180/3.141593 yields an angle of 45°.

Utility Functions — FRE, POS, SCREEN, and the Special Variable CSRLIN

When the argument is any numeric value, the FRE function returns the number of unused bytes within **BASIC's data space**. BASIC's data space is defined as that part of main storage which is allocated to MS BASIC by the PC, less the reserved portion of the interpreter work area. The following statement

```
700 BYTES = FRE(0)
```

assigns the variable BYTES the amount of available data space.

When the argument is any string, the function causes the PC to collect and compress any fragmented string data that is stored in BASIC's data space before returning the number of free bytes. The end result is more data space available to a program. For example, the statement

```
710 FREE.SPACE = FRE("X")
```

performs housekeeping on BASIC'S data space and then assigns FREE.SPACE the number of free bytes.

This function can be useful with programs that manipulate large amounts of string data and terminate owing to a lack of main storage. Note that the argument within parentheses following the keyword FRE is required even though it is not used.

The POS function returns the current column position of the cursor relative to the left edge of the display screen. The value returned is an integer in the range 1 to 40 or 1 to 80, depending on the current screen-width setting. For example,

```
800 WIDTH 80
810 PRINT TAB(15);
820 PRINT POS(0)
```

causes the PC to display the value 15. The value of the argument plays no role in the value returned by the POS function.

The special variable CSRLIN is equal to the current row (line) the cursor is on relative to the top of the display screen. The value of CSRLIN varies in the range 1 to 25. For example, the following statement entered in the immediate mode,

```
LOCATE 5, 6 : PRINT CSRLIN
 5
```

displays the current line position.

The special variable CSRLIN and the POS function are used in applications where a value must be displayed at a position on the screen other than the current one, followed by the return of the cursor to the former position. Consider the following partial program.

```
820 ROW = CSRLIN
830 COL = POS(0)
840 LOCATE 1, 20 : PRINT "Aim the arrow carefully"
850 LOCATE ROW, COL
```

Line 820 assigns ROW the line the cursor is on. Line 830 assigns COL the column the cursor is in. Line 840 moves the cursor to column 20 of line 1 and displays the message. Line 850 returns the cursor to its former position on the screen.

The SCREEN function allows you to determine what character is currently displayed at the intersection of a row and a column on the screen. The function returns the ASCII code for the character found at the specified location. For example, the following partial program assigns CHAR the value 66, since that is the ASCII code for the character B.

```
900 WIDTH 80
910 LOCATE 15, 16 : PRINT "B"
920 CHAR = SCREEN(15, 16)
```

Performance Testing — The TIMER Function

The TIMER function returns a single-precision numeric value that represents the number of seconds that have elapsed since midnight. The For loop below illustrates values returned by the TIMER function.

Line 100 resets the system time to 12:00 noon (43,200 seconds past midnight). In the For loop, line 120 displays both the system time and the number of seconds elapsed since midnight. A close look at the results shows that, on the average, it takes 0.11 seconds to make a pass on the For loop defined by lines 110 through 130.

```
100 TIME$ = "12:00:00"
110 FOR I = 1 TO 10
120     PRINT "Time = "; TIME$, "Timer ="; TIMER
130 NEXT I

RUN

Time = 12:00:00          Timer = 43200.1
Time = 12:00:00          Timer = 43200.21
Time = 12:00:00          Timer = 43200.32
Time = 12:00:00          Timer = 43200.43
Time = 12:00:00          Timer = 43200.54
Time = 12:00:01          Timer = 43200.6
Time = 12:00:01          Timer = 43200.71
Time = 12:00:01          Timer = 43200.82
Time = 12:00:01          Timer = 43200.93
Time = 12:00:01          Timer = 43201.04
```

The time it takes to make a pass on a given loop will vary slightly between runs. For this reason, when **benchmarking** an algorithm, you should take the average duration of time it takes to accomplish the same task over many runs of the program under the same conditions. Benchmarking is the activity of comparing the performance of algorithms or applications that are running under similar conditions on one or more computer systems.

Random Number Function and the RANDOMIZE Statement

The RND function is important to the programmer who is involved in the development of programs that simulate situations described by a random process. The owners of a shopping mall, for example, might want a program written to simulate the number of cars that would enter their parking lots during a particular period of the day. Or, the manager of a grocery store might want a program to model unpredictable values that represented people standing in line waiting to check out. The unpredictable values could be supplied by the RND function. Actually, the random numbers generated by the PC are provided by a repeatable process, and for this reason they are often called **pseudo-random numbers**.

The RND function returns an unpredictable decimal fraction number between 0 (inclusive) and 1 (exclusive). Each time the function is referenced, any number between 0 and < 1 has an equal probability of being returned by the function. For example, the statement

```
200 NUM = RND
```

assigns NUM a random number. Program 8.6 on the next page illustrates the generation of five random numbers.

PROGRAM 8.6

```
100 ' Program 8.6
110 ' Generating Random Numbers
120 ' *************************
130 FOR I = 1 TO 5
140    PRINT RND,
150 NEXT I
160 END
```

RUN

.7151002   .683111   .4821425   .9992938   .6465093

Each time the RND function is referenced in line 140 of the loop, a random number between 0 and <1 is displayed.

The INT (or FIX) and RND functions can be combined to create random digits over a specified range. The following expression allows for the generation of random digits over the range $C \leq n \leq D$:

INT((D - C + 1) * RND + C)

For example, to generate random digits over the range 1 to 10, inclusive, change line 140 in Program 8.6 to:

140 PRINT INT((10 - 1 + 1) * RND + 1)

or:

140 PRINT INT(10 * RND + 1)

Program 8.7 simulates tossing a coin 20 times. The expression INT (2 * RND) returns a zero (heads) or a one (tails). The expression in line 160 returned 13 zeros (heads) and 7 ones (tails).

PROGRAM 8.7

```
100 ' Program 8.7
110 ' Simulation of Coin Tossing
120 ' 0 is a Head and 1 is a Tail
130 ' The Coin is Tossed 20 Times
140 ' ***************************
150 FOR I = 1 TO 20
160    PRINT INT(2 * RND);
170 NEXT I
180 END
```

RUN

1 0 1 0 0 0 1 1 0 1 0 0 0 0 1 0 0 1 0 0

Every time Program 8.7 is executed, it will display the same results, because the PC generates random numbers from a starting value called the **seed**. Unless the seed is changed, the PC continues to generate the same set of random numbers in the same sequence each time the same program is executed. Once a program containing the RND function is ready for production, the RANDOMIZE statement can be used to instruct the PC to generate random numbers from a different seed each time the program is executed. The general form of the RANDOMIZE statement is shown in Table 8.12.

TABLE 8.12 The RANDOMIZE Statement

General Form:	RANDOMIZE or RANDOMIZE *numeric expression*
Purpose:	To supply a new seed for the generation of random numbers by the RND function.
Example:	100 RANDOMIZE 200 RANDOMIZE TIMER 300 RANDOMIZE 396.5 400 RANDOMIZE VAL(RIGHT$(TIME$,2))
Note:	If you do not include a parameter following the keyword RANDOMIZE, then the PC suspends execution of the program and requests a value between −32768 and 32767. You may also reseed the random-number generator by using a negative argument with the RND function, as in RND(-1). This method is not used in this book.

The rule for the execution of the RANDOMIZE statement in a program is as follows:

> **RANDOMIZE Rule 1:** The RANDOMIZE statement must be executed prior to any reference to the RND function.

PROGRAMMING CASE STUDY 14: *Computer Simulation*

Program 8.8 on the next page simulates a popular guessing game, in which the player attempts to guess a number between 1 and 100. The RANDOMIZE statement is included so that the RND function will return a new set of random numbers each time the program is executed.

When the RUN command is issued for Program 8.8, line 2040 in the Initialization Module ensures that the program does not generate the same set of random numbers it generated the last time the program was executed. The seed is based on the value returned by the TIMER function. The chances of generating the same set of random numbers from one run of Program 8.8 to the next is very rare.

Line 2050 assigns RANDOM the number to be guessed (94). Lines 2070 through 2130 display the instructions for the game. Line 3030 in the Guess a Number Module accepts a guess (GUESS) from the user. Line 3040 sets the guess counter (GUESS.COUNT) to 1. If GUESS is equal to RANDOM in line 3050, the program terminates after 1 guess. If GUESS does not equal RANDOM, the PC executes the While loop and displays an appropriate message before requesting the next guess and incrementing GUESS.COUNT. When the user finally guesses the number, control passes to line 4000 and a message and the value of GUESS.COUNT are displayed.

PROGRAM 8.8

```
1000 ' Program 8.8
1010 ' Guess a Number Between 1 and 100
1020 ' **********************************************
1030 ' *              Main Module                   *
1040 ' **********************************************
1050 GOSUB 2000  ' Call Initialization
1060 GOSUB 3000  ' Call Guess a Number
1070 GOSUB 4000  ' Call Wrap-up
1080 END
1090 '
2000 ' **********************************************
2010 ' *             Initialization                 *
2020 ' **********************************************
2030 CLS : KEY OFF  ' Clear Screen
2040 RANDOMIZE TIMER
2050 RANDOM = INT(100 * RND + 1)
2060 CNT = 1
2070 PRINT "**********************************************"
2080 PRINT "*                                            *"
2090 PRINT "* Guess a number between 1 and 100.          *"
2100 PRINT "* I will tell you if your guess is           *"
2110 PRINT "* too high or too low.                       *"
2120 PRINT "*                                            *"
2130 PRINT "**********************************************"
2140 PRINT
2150 RETURN
2160 '
3000 ' **********************************************
3010 ' *             Guess a Number                 *
3020 ' **********************************************
3030 INPUT "Guess a number ====> ", GUESS
3040 GUESS.COUNT = 1
3050 WHILE GUESS <> RANDOM
3060    IF GUESS > RANDOM
            THEN PRINT "Too High"
            ELSE PRINT "Too Low"
3070    INPUT "Guess a number ====> ", GUESS
3080    GUESS.COUNT = GUESS.COUNT + 1
3090 WEND
3100 RETURN
3110 '
4000 ' **********************************************
4010 ' *                Wrap-up                     *
4020 ' **********************************************
4030 PRINT : PRINT "Your guess is correct."
4040 PRINT "It took you"; GUESS.COUNT; "guesses."
4050 ' *********** End of Program *************
RUN
```

(continued

```
*****************************************
*                                        *
* Guess a number between 1 and 100.      *
* I will tell you if your guess is       *
* too high or too low.                   *
*                                        *
*****************************************
Guess a number ====> 50
Too Low
Guess a number ====> 75
Too Low
Guess a number ====> 87
Too Low
Guess a number ====> 95
Too High
Guess a number ====> 93
Too Low
Guess a number ====> 94

Your guess is correct.
It took you 6 guesses.
```

8.4 USER-DEFINED FUNCTIONS

In addition to numeric and string functions, MS BASIC allows you to define new string or numeric functions that relate to a particular application. This type of function, known as a **user-defined function**, is written directly into the program as a one-line statement. MS BASIC recognizes a user-defined function by the keywords DEF FN (for "define function"), which are incorporated in the function statement just to the right of the line number. For example, the DEF FN statement

```
150 DEF FNY(X) = X * (X + 1) / 2
```

defines a function, $x(x + 1) / 2$, whose name is FNY. The parentheses following the name of the function surround a simple variable known as a **function parameter**. The expression to the right of the equal sign indicates the operations that are to be performed with the value of X when the function is referenced in such statements as LET, PRINT, ON-GOSUB, and IF. For example, either

```
200 RESULT = FNY(VALUE) + 5
```

or

```
210 PRINT FNY(PT / 3)
```

found in the same program with the previous line 150 will reference the FNY function.

Defining your own function reduces programming effort and makes your program "compact" and efficient. Instead of writing a common formula over and over again, you simply define it once as a function, give it a name, and then reference it by that name whenever you need it.

The DEF FN Statement

Table 8.13 shows that the DEF FN statement permits the creation of user-defined functions. The name of the function follows DEF, and it must begin with the two letters FN, followed by a variable name that is consistent with the rules used for naming variables.

TABLE 8.13 The DEF FN Statement

General Form:	DEF FNx(p_1, ..., p_n) = expression
	where **x** is a simple variable that must agree in type with the expression, and p_1 through p_n are simple variables. A function may be defined with a null list of function parameters.
Purpose:	To define a function that is relevant to a particular application that can be referenced as frequently as needed in the program in which it is defined.
Examples:	100 DEF FNCUBE(Y, Z) = Y ^ 3 + Z ^ 3
	200 DEF FNPI = 3.141593
	300 DEF FNSUB$(STNG$, P, N) = MID$(STNG$, P, N)
	400 DEF FNRADIAN%(DEG) = DEG * (FNPI / 180)
	500 DEF FNRANDOM(X) = INT(10 * RND)
	600 DEF FNVOL#(L#, W#, H#) = L# * W# * H#

The parameters in a user-defined function are sometimes called **dummy variables**, since they are assigned the values of the corresponding arguments when reference is made to the function. For example, the following partial program contains two user-defined functions. The first one, in line 200, rounds the value assigned to NUM to the nearest cent. The second one, in line 210, truncates the value assigned to NUM to the nearest cent.

Dummy variable — value of GROSS is assigned to NUM.

```
200 DEF FNROUND(NUM)    = FIX(NUM * 100 + SGN(NUM) * .5) / 100
210 DEF FNTRUNCATE(NUM) = FIX(NUM * 100) / 100
   .
   .
400 PRINT FNROUND(GROSS), FNTRUNCATE(GROSS)
```
Argument

The value of the variable GROSS in line 400 is used in place of the variable NUM in line 200 when the user-defined function FNROUND is called. The same applies when the user-defined function FNTRUNCATE is called by the second item in the list in line 400.

The dummy variable(s) assigned as the parameter in a DEF FN statement are local to the function definition. That is, they are distinct from any variable with the same name outside of the function definition.

A function with no parameters may be defined. Such functions may be used to define constants or expressions that do not require a variable, as shown below.

```
100 DEF FNPI#     = 3.14159265
200 DEF FNCENTI   = 2.54
300 DEF FNRANDOM  = INT(10 * RND + 1)
```

Line 100 defines FNPI# equal to pi (π). Line 200 defines FNCENTI equal to the number of centimeters in an inch. Line 300 defines FNRANDOM so it returns a random number between 1 and 10.

The rules regarding DEF FN statements in a program are:

> **DEF FN Rule 1:** A user-defined function may be located anywhere before the first reference in a program.

> **DEF FN Rule 2:** The same function may be defined as often as required. The most recently stated definition is always used.

> **DEF FN Rule 3:** A function definition cannot reference itself.

■ 8.5 TEST YOUR BASIC SKILLS (Even-numbered answers are in Appendix B.)

1. Consider the valid programs below. What is displayed if each program is executed?

   a.
   ```
   100 ' Exercise 8.1a
   110 CLS : KEY OFF   ' Clear Screen
   120 STATE$ = "Mississippi"
   130 FOR I = 1 TO LEN(STATE$)
   140    LOCATE I, I : PRINT LEFT$(STATE$, I)
   150 NEXT I
   160 END
   ```

   b.
   ```
   100 ' Exercise 8.1b
   110 CODE$ = "08<NC74N0AA>FN20A45D;;H"
   120 PRINT "Coded message ======> "; CODE$
   130 PRINT : PRINT "The message is =====> ";
   140 FOR I = 1 TO LEN(CODE$)
   150    MESG = ASC(MID$(CODE$, I, 1))
   160    MESG = MESG + 17
   170    CHAR$ = CHR$(MESG)
   180    PRINT CHAR$;
   190 NEXT I
   200 END
   ```

2. Evaluate each of the following. Assume that PHR$ is equal to the following string:

   ```
   If I have seen further it is by standing upon the shoulders of giants
   ```

   a. LEN(PHR$)
   b. RIGHT$(PHR$, 100)
   c. LEFT$(PHR$, 5)
   d. MID$(PHR$, 11, 4)
   e. VAL("36.8")
   f. ASC(MID$(PHR$, 4, 1))
   g. CHR$(71)
   h. STRING$(14, "A")
   i. STR$(-13.691)
   j. INSTR(10, PHR$, "i")
   k. MID$(PHR$, 64, 7) = "midgets"
   l. SPACE$(4)

3. Evaluate each of the following. Assume that NUM is equal to 2 and that PHR$ is equal to the following string:

   ```
   GOTO is a four letter word
   ```

   a. LEN(PHR$)
   b. RIGHT$(PHR$, 4)
   c. RIGHT$(PHR$, 30)
   d. LEFT$(PHR$, 50)
   e. LEFT$(PHR$, 1.5)
   f. LEFT$(PHR$, NUM)
   g. MID$(PHR$, NUM, 3)
   h. MID$(PHR$, NUM ^ 3, 2)
   i. MID$(PHR$, 1, 5 * NUM)
   j. INSTR(PHR$, "is")
   k. INSTR(NUM, PHR$, "t")
   l. INSTR(2 * NUM, PHR$, "r ")

4. Evaluate each of the following.

   a. VAL("99")
   b. ASC("+")
   c. CHR$(63)
   d. STR$(48.9)
   e. CLS : PRINT CSRLIN
   f. CLS : ? "B" : ? SCREEN(1, 1)
   g. CHR$(37)
   h. ASC(":")
   i. PRINT , POS(0)
   j. LOCATE 23, 46 : ? POS(0) + CSRLIN

5. What is the numeric value of each of the following?

   a. INT(-18.5)
   b. ABS(-3)
   c. INT(16.9)
   d. ABS(6.7)
   e. EXP(1)
   f. LOG(0)

6. Write separate BASIC statements for each of the following.

   a. determine the sign of $2X^3 + 3X + 5$
   b. determine the integer part of $4X + 5$

7. Write a program that displays the values for X and SIN X where X varies between 0° and 180°. Increment X in steps of 5.

8. Write a single BASIC statement for each of the following. Use numeric functions wherever possible. Assume that the value of X is a real number.

   a. $p = \sqrt{a^2 + b^2}$
   b. $b = \sqrt{|\tan X - 0.51|}$
   c. $q = 8 \cos^2 X + 4 \sin X$
   d. $y = e^x + \log_e (1 + X)$

9. Characterize the four methods of accepting input through the keyboard—INPUT, LINE INPUT, INKEY$, and INPUT$(N) — in terms of suspension of program execution; type and length of data that may be assigned; and whether the Enter key must be pressed.

10. Write a program that will generate and display 100 random numbers between 1 and 52, inclusive.

11. Explain the purpose of the RANDOMIZE statement. Why is the TIMER function a good choice for determining the seed?

12. Write a user-defined function that will determine a 10% discount on the amount of purchase PUR in excess of $200.00. The discount applies to the excess, not the entire purchase.

8.6 BASIC PROGRAMMING PROBLEMS

1. Palindromes

Purpose: To become familiar with the manipulation of strings through the use of the LEN and MID$ functions.

Problem: A palindrome is a word or phrase that is the same when read either backward or forward. For example, *noon* is a palindrome, but *moon* is not. Write a program that requests the user to enter a string of characters (uppercase) and that determines whether the string is a palindrome.

Input Data: Use the following sample data.

```
9876556789
ABLE WAS I ERE I SAW ELBA
I
BOB DID BOB
WOW LIL DID POP
OTTO
RADAR
!@#$$@#!
( )
A PROGRAM IS A MIRROR IMAGE OF THE MIND
```

Output Results: The following partial results are shown.

```
String? 9876556789
9876556789 is a palindrome.

Enter Y to continue, else N... Y
         .
         .
         .
String? WOW LIL DID POP
WOW LIL DID POP is not a palindrome.

Enter Y to continue, else N... Y
```

2. Time to Double an Investment Compounded Quarterly

Purpose: To become familiar with the use of numeric functions and user-defined functions, and the concepts of rounding and truncation.

Problem: Write a program that will determine the time it takes to double an investment compounded quarterly for the following annual interest rates: 6%, 7%, 8% and 9%. The formula for computing the time is:

$$N = \frac{\log 2}{M(\log(1 + J/M))}$$

where N = time in years
       J = annual interest rate
       M = number of conversion periods

Once the time has been determined for a given interest rate, use the following expressions:

```
ROUNDED.YEARS  = FIX(N * 100 + SGN(N) * .5) / 100
TRUNCATE.YEARS = FIX(N * 100) / 100
```

to round and truncate the answer (N) to two decimal places. Define both expressions as user-defined functions in your program.

Input Data: None.

Output Results: The following results are displayed.

```
          Time to Double an Investment
                Compounded Quarterly
          -------------------------------

                  Years            Years
  Annual        to Double       to Double
 Interest       (Rounded)       (Truncated)
 --------       ---------       -----------
    6%            11.64            11.63
    7%             9.99             9.98
    8%             8.75             8.75
    9%             7.79             7.78

Job Complete
```

3. The Check Digit Problem

Purpose: To illustrate the concepts of generating check digits.

Problem: Construct a program to verify a six-digit part number by validating the units position for a check digit. A check digit is an addition to a number that requires validation; this addition can be used to verify the rest of the digits. A check digit is effective for catching the most common mistakes made in entering a number.

The computation of the check digit for this problem involves multiplying every other digit of the original number by 2 and then adding these values and the remaining digits of the number together. The units digit of the result obtained is then subtracted from 10 to obtain the check digit.

To illustrate the process, let's form the part number by computing the check digit for the number 72546. The alternate digits are first multiplied by 2:

```
    7    5    6
       ×  2
   --------------
   14   10   12
```

Then the remaining digits (2 and 4) are included and all above digits are added:

$$1 + 4 + 1 + 0 + 1 + 2 + 2 + 4 = 15$$

The check digit is the units position of the sum, or 5. The part number 72546 becomes 725465. This algorithm is quite sophisticated, since it can detect invalid part numbers that have digits reversed, such as 752465 instead of 725465.

Hint: The 6 digits must be separated. You may separate digits through the use of the INT function. For example, the leftmost digit (D6) can be determined from the following, where PART is the 6-digit value:

    D6 = INT(PART / 100000)

and the second leftmost digit (D5) is equal to:

    D5 = INT((PART - D6 * 100000) / 10000)

Continue in this fashion until all 6 digits have been extracted.

Input Data: Prepare and use the following part numbers. Check to see whether the rightmost digit is the correct check digit.

725465, 752465, 033332, 098792, 098798
089798, 000000, 000001, 999999, 999995

Output Results: The following results are displayed for 725465.

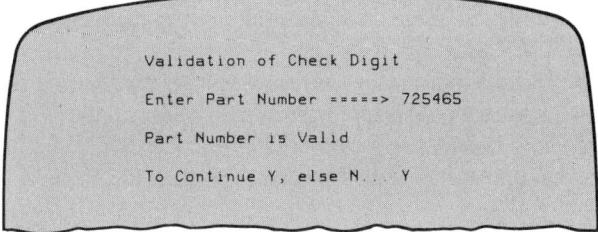

```
         Validation of Check Digit

     Enter Part Number =====> 725465

     Part Number is Valid

     To Continue Y, else N... Y
```

4. Payroll Problem V: Spelling Out the Net Pay

Purpose: To become familiar with table utilization, use of the zero element of an array, the INT and STR$ functions, and spelling out numbers.

Problem: Construct a program that spells out the net pay for check-writing purposes. For example, the net pay $5,078.45 is written out on a check as follows:

   Five Thousand Seventy-Eight Dollars and 45 Cents

Assume that the net pay does not exceed $9,999.99.

Hint: Use the INT function to separate the integer portion of the net pay into single digits. Use the single digits to access the words from one of two positionally organized tables. If the digit represents the thousands, hundreds, or units position, then access the word from the following table:

Digit	Word	Digit	Word
0	Null	10	Ten
1	One	11	Eleven
2	Two	12	Twelve
3	Three	13	Thirteen
4	Four	14	Fourteen
5	Five	15	Fifteen
6	Six	16	Sixteen
7	Seven	17	Seventeen
8	Eight	18	Eighteen
9	Nine	19	Nineteen

If the digit represents the tens position, then access the word from the following table:

Digit	Word	Digit	Word
0	Null	5	Fifty
1	Ten	6	Sixty
2	Twenty	7	Seventy
3	Thirty	8	Eighty
4	Forty	9	Ninety

The word entries for both tables are found in the sequential file EX84TAB.TBL on the Student Diskette. The entries for the thousands, hundreds, and units tables are first in the sequential file, followed immediately by the entries for the tens table.

Use the INT and STR$ functions to determine the fraction portion of the net pay. Use the concatenation operator to string the words together. If there are no dollars or cents, display the word "No" accordingly.

Input Data: Use the sequential file EX84DATA.DAT found on the Student Diskette. The data file includes the following sample data.

Employee Number	Net Pay	Employee Number	Net Pay
123	$8,462.34	127	$1,003.00
124	987.23	128	4,037.00
125	78.99	129	4.67
126	6,000.23	130	0.02

Output Results: The following results are displayed.

```
Employee
Number     Net Pay    Net Pay Spelled Out
--------   -------    -------------------
   123     8,462.34   Eight Thousand Four Hundred Sixty-Two Dollars and 34 Cents
   124       987.23   Nine Hundred Eighty-Seven Dollars and 23 Cents
   125        78.99   Seventy-Eight Dollars and 99 Cents
   126     6,000.23   Six Thousand  Dollars and 23 Cents
   127     1,003.00   One Thousand Three Dollars and No Cents
   128     4,037.00   Four Thousand Thirty-Seven Dollars and No Cents
   129         4.67   Four Dollars and 67 Cents
   130         0.02   No Dollars and 2 Cents

Job Complete
```

COMPUTER GRAPHICS AND SOUND

9.1 INTRODUCTION

The value of the computer for displaying information in the form of charts, figures, and graphs as opposed to printed characters, has long been recognized. For many years, however, the cost of equipment kept most users from incorporating **computer graphics** into their programs. With the advent of the PC, more and more users are displaying the results from their programs pictorially, and sometimes with sound.

As you will see in this chapter, MS BASIC has statements that provide a considerable graphics capability. Although no attempt is made here to present sophisticated graphics, at the conclusion of this chapter you will have enough knowledge of the graphics features of MS BASIC to start using them in the programs you write. This chapter also explores the MS BASIC statements that allow you to play music and create sound effects.

PC Graphics Modes

The PC provides three graphics modes. They are **text**, **medium resolution**, and **high resolution**. As described in Table 9.1, the text mode is available on all PCs. Medium-resolution and high-resolution graphics are available only if you have a **color/graphics interface board** in your PC.

TABLE 9.1 Graphics Capabilities with Different Hardware Configurations

DISPLAY DEVICE	DISPLAY INTERFACE BOARD	GRAPHICS CAPABILITIES
1. IBM Compatible Monochrome (Black and White) Display	IBM Compatible Monochrome Display Interface	Only text mode with a width of 40 or 80 characters. Black and white character graphics.
2. IBM Compatible Monochrome (Black and White) Display	Color/Graphics Interface	Shades of black and white graphics in text, medium resolution, and high resolution.
3. IBM Compatible Color Monitor	Color/Graphics Interface	Color graphics in text and medium resolution. Black and white graphics in high resolution.

The text mode is the one used throughout this book. In this mode, the screen is divided into either 25 rows and 80 columns or 25 rows and 40 columns. At the intersection of each row and column, the PC can display any one of the 256 characters shown in Table A.1 in Appendix A. Each intersection of a row and column is called a **character position**. In this mode, the PRINT statement and the ASCII character set are used to display figures and graphs as well as nongraphic information such as words and sentences. If you have the proper hardware, you can also display the characters in 16 different colors. The text mode is often used to create logos and simple animated designs.

With medium-resolution graphics, the screen is divided into 200 rows and 320 columns. Each intersection of a row and column represents a small dot, also called a **pixel** (picture element). The total number of pixels is 64,000 (200 × 320). Forty characters per line are displayed in this mode. If you have a color monitor, each pixel can be assigned any one of 16 colors. In medium resolution you can plot points, draw figures, and create high-quality animated designs.

The high-resolution graphics mode divides the screen into 200 rows and 640 columns. The total number of pixels is 128,000 (200 × 640). The larger number of pixels across the screen allows you to draw figures that require finer detail than is available with medium resolution. Eighty characters per line are displayed in this mode. Only monochrome colors are available in high resolution — black and white or amber or green.

All the programs presented thus far can be executed in any one of the three modes as long as you recognize the different default width settings (80 for text and high resolution, 40 for medium resolution).

The SCREEN Statement

When MS BASIC is started, the PC is in the text mode. The SCREEN statement may then be used to select among the three modes as follows:

```
SCREEN 0  (text mode)
SCREEN 1  (medium-resolution graphics mode)
SCREEN 2  (high-resolution graphics mode)
```

The statement may be entered without a line number or as part of a program. Each time the SCREEN statement is executed, the screen is erased and the color is set to white on black. However, nothing is changed on the screen if the mode in the SCREEN statement is the same as the current one. If there is a BASIC program in main storage, it is not erased when you switch from one mode to another. The general form of the SCREEN statement is shown in Table 9.2.

TABLE 9.2 The SCREEN Statement

General Form:	SCREEN mode, color switch, active page, visual page
	where **mode** is 0 (text), 1 (medium resolution) or 2 (high resolution);
	color switch is 0 (disables color) or any other number (enables color) in the text mode. With medium resolution, 0 enables color and any other number disables color;
	active page is an integer expression (in the range 0 to 7 for width 40 characters, and 0 to 3 for width 80) which specifies the page to be written to by output statements; and
	visual page is an integer expression in the same range as active page that selects the page to be displayed.
Purpose:	Selects the screen attributes to be used by subsequent output statements.
Keyword Entry:	Press the F10 key or hold down the Alt key and press the S key on your keyboard.
Examples:	2030 SCREEN 1 3030 SCREEN ,,2, 3 4030 SCREEN 0, 1, 1, 0 5030 SCREEN 0,, 0, 1 6030 SCREEN 1, 1 7030 SCREEN 2
Note:	The parameters active page and visual page are valid only in the text mode, i.e., mode = 0.

Line 2030 in Table 9.2 clears the screen and switches to the medium-resolution mode. If any parameter is omitted in the SCREEN statement, the PC maintains the current status for the omitted parameter.

In line 3030, the mode remains the same, and all future output statements are directed to page 2. Page 3 is immediately displayed. Here, the term *page* refers to a 2K (width = 40) or 4K (width = 80) byte area of the 16K display buffer. Note that in this example we are preparing to have the PC build one page (page 2) while displaying another (page 3). This form of flip-flopping the screens may be used in the text mode to create animations.

In line 4030 of Table 9.2, the mode is switched to text; color is enabled; all future output statements are directed to page 1; and page 0 is displayed. In line 5030, the mode is switched to text; color maintains its status; future output statements are directed to page 0; and page 1 is displayed. Line 6030 switches the PC to medium resolution and the color is disabled. Finally, line 7030 switches the PC to high resolution.

■ 9.2 TEXT-MODE GRAPHICS

You can produce interesting and useful graphics on any PC with the PRINT and PRINT USING statements, the CHR$ function, and the ASCII character set. Program 9.1 on the next page, shows how you can access additional graphics characters (ASCII codes 128 through 255, also called the **USA character set**) through the use of the CHR$ function. You'll recall from Chapter 8 that the CHR$ function returns a character that is equivalent in ASCII code to the numeric argument.

PROGRAM 9.1

```
100 ' Program 9.1
110 ' Displaying the Last Half of the ASCII Character Set
120 ' ******************************************************
130 CLS : KEY OFF   ' Clear Screen
140 FOR CODE = 128 TO 255
150    PRINT USING "###  !"; CODE, CHR$(CODE)
160 NEXT CODE
170 END
```

When the RUN command is issued for Program 9.1, the For loop (lines 140 through 160) causes the PC to display the last half of the ASCII character set, as shown in Table A.1 in Appendix A. Through the use of the CHR$ function, these characters may be used in the text mode to draw various figures. Besides characters made up of curved lines, you can choose characters that range from a solid dark color (codes 219 through 223) to a lighter shade (code 176, 177, and 178) for drawing bar graphs.

PROGRAMMING CASE STUDY 15: Logo for the Bow-Wow Dog Food Company

The following Programming Case Study pertains to the display of a logo that employs some of the graphics characters that make up the last half of the ASCII character set.

Problem: On a recent tour through the main office, Mr. Beagle, president of the Bow-Wow Dog Food Company, noticed the large number of PCs in use. To brighten the office area, he has requested that the Data Processing Department display the company logo, shown in Figure 9.1, on all idle PCs.

The program that displays the logo must **chain to** (call) a menu-driven program called MAINMENU when the operator presses any key. For a discussion of how a program chains to another program, see an MS BASIC manual.

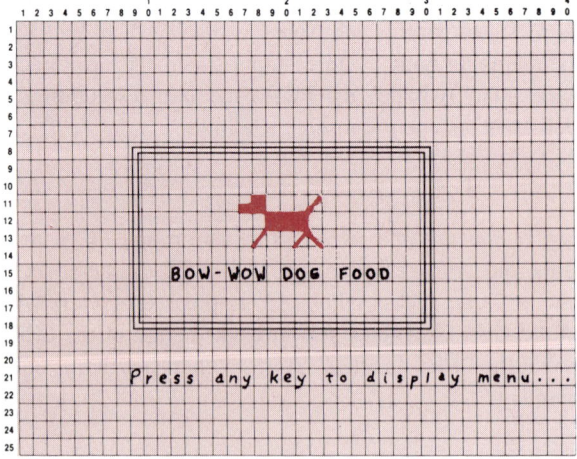

FIGURE 9.1 The Bow-Wow Dog Food Company logo designed on a screen layout form with a width of 40 characters.

Following are a top-down chart (Figure 9.2); a list of the program tasks in outline form; a program solution; and a discussion of the program solution.

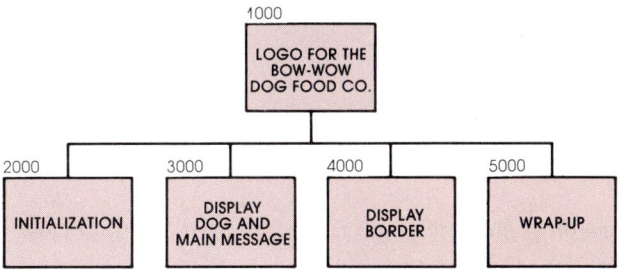

FIGURE 9.2 *A top-down chart for Program 9.2.*

Program Tasks

The following program tasks correspond to the top-down chart in Figure 9.2.

1. Initialization

   a. Clear the screen.
   b. Use the `WIDTH` statement to set the display mode of the screen to 40 characters per line.

2. Display Dog and Main Message

   Use the `LOCATE` and `PRINT` statements to position the dog and main message on the screen. Use the `CHR$` function and the following ASCII character codes for the dog's body parts:

Body Part	ASCII Code	Body Part	ASCII Code
Nose	220	Tail	47
Head	219	Legs pointing left	47
Body	219 (three)	Leg pointing right	92

3. Display Border

   Use the `LOCATE` and `PRINT` statements to display the border surrounding the dog and the main message. Use the `CHR$` function and the following ASCII character codes for the border:

Border Part	ASCII Code	Border Part	ASCII Code
Upper-left corner	201	Lower-right corner	188
Lower-left corner	200	Vertical border	186
Upper-right corner	187	Horizontal border	205

CHAPTER NINE — COMPUTER GRAPHICS AND SOUND

    4. Wrap-up

        a. Display the message `Press any key to display menu...`
        b. Use the `INPUT$` function to suspend execution until a key is pressed by the operator.
        c. Set the display mode of the screen to 80 characters per line.

Use the following statement in place of the END statement in the Main Module to chain to MAINMENU:

```
CHAIN "MAINMENU"
```

Program Solution   The following program corresponds to the top-down chart in Figure 9.2 and to the preceding program tasks.

PROGRAM 9.2

```
1000 ' Program 9.2
1010 ' Logo for Bow-Wow Dog Food Company
1020 ' *********************************
1030 ' *           Main Module         *
1040 ' *********************************
1050 GOSUB 2000    ' Call Initialization
1060 GOSUB 3000    ' Call Display Dog and Main Message
1070 GOSUB 4000    ' Call Display Border
1080 GOSUB 5000    ' Call Wrap-up
1090 CHAIN "MAINMENU"    ' Call Program MAINMENU
1100 '
2000 ' *********************************
2010 ' *        Initialization         *
2020 ' *********************************
2030 CLS : KEY OFF    ' Clear Screen
2040 WIDTH 40         ' Switch to 40-Column Display
2050 RETURN
2060 '
3000 ' *********************************
3010 ' *   Display Dog and Main Message *
3020 ' *********************************
3030 LOCATE 11, 17 : PRINT CHR$(220); CHR$(219); SPC(3); CHR$(47)
3040 LOCATE 12, 19 : PRINT STRING$(3, 219)
3050 LOCATE 13, 18 : PRINT CHR$(47); SPC(2); CHR$(47); CHR$(92)
3060 LOCATE 15, 12 : PRINT "BOW-WOW DOG FOOD"
3070 RETURN
3080 '
4000 ' *********************************
4010 ' *         Display Border        *
4020 ' *********************************
4030 LOCATE 8, 9 : PRINT CHR$(201); STRING$(20, 205); CHR$(187)
4040 FOR I = 9 TO 17
4050    LOCATE I,  9 : PRINT CHR$(186)
4060    LOCATE I, 30 : PRINT CHR$(186)
4070 NEXT I
4080 LOCATE 18, 9 : PRINT CHR$(200); STRING$(20, 205); CHR$(188)
4090 RETURN
4100 '
```

(continued)

```
5000 ' ***********************************
5010 ' *              Wrap-up             *
5020 ' ***********************************
5030 LOCATE 21, 9 : PRINT "Press any key to display menu...";
5040 HALT$ = INPUT$(1)
5050 WIDTH 80   ' Switch to 80-Column Display
5060 RETURN
5070 ' ********* End of Program *********
RUN
```

Discussion of the Program Solution

When Program 9.2 is executed, the Initialization Module clears the screen and switches the screen to the 40-column display mode. The Display Dog and Main Message Module uses the CHR$ function to display the various graphics characters. Note that in line 3040, the STRING$ function causes three solid dark characters to display.

The Display Border Module, lines 4000 through 4100, uses a For loop to display the vertical lines. In the Wrap-up Module, the INPUT$ function is used to suspend execution until the operator wants to display the main menu. Line 1090 of the Main Module chains to MAINMENU before Program 9.2 terminates execution. The logo displayed by Program 9.2 is shown in Figure 9.3.

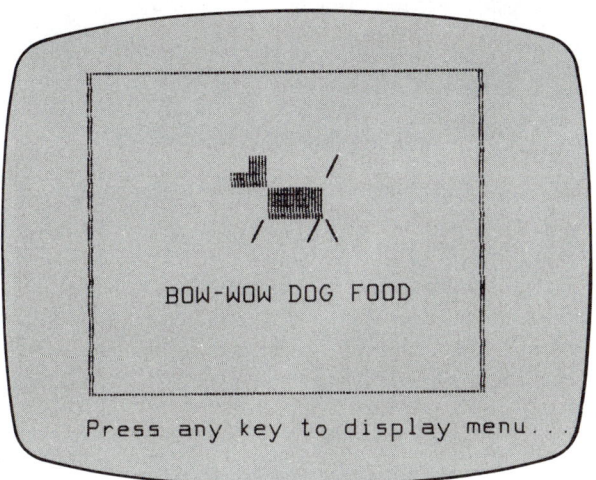

FIGURE 9.3 *The logo displayed through the execution of Program 9.2.*

The COLOR Statement for Text Mode

If your PC has a color monitor and color/graphics interface board, then you can enhance your screen displays with color. There are two COLOR statements, one for the text mode and another for the medium-resolution graphics mode. In this section, we will discuss the COLOR statement for the text mode.

The COLOR statement allows you to select colors for the foreground, background, and border of the screen. As illustrated in Figure 9.4, the **background** is that part of the screen against which the characters are displayed. Displayed characters are the **foreground**. The **border** is the edge of the screen.

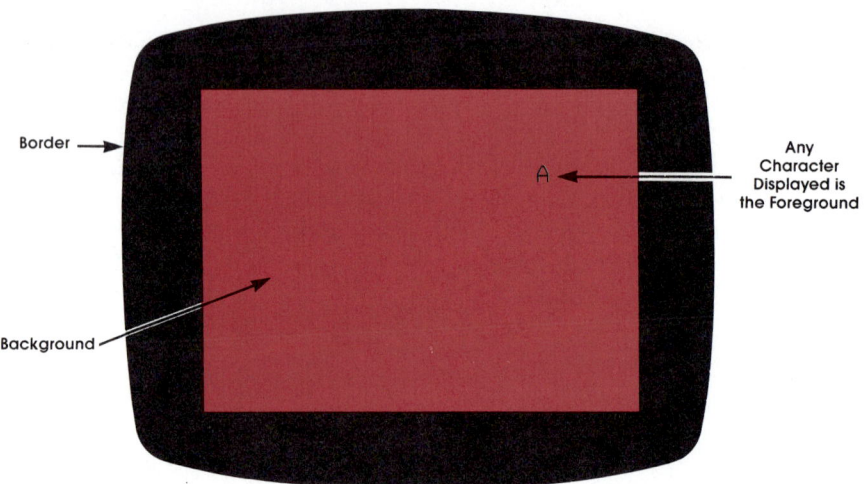

FIGURE 9.4 *The background, foreground, and border of the screen.*

When the system command BASICA is first keyed in, the color is set to white on black; that is, the foreground is set to white and the background and border are set to black. The COLOR statement may then be used in the immediate mode or as a statement in a program to change colors as often as desired. The general form of the COLOR statement for the text mode is shown in Table 9.3.

TABLE 9.3 The COLOR Statement for the Text Mode

General Form:	COLOR foreground, background, border
	where **foreground** is a numeric expression in the range 0 to 31; **background** is a numeric expression in the range 0 to 7; and **border** is a numeric expression in the range 0 to 15.
Purpose:	Sets the color for the foreground, background, and border of the screen. The foreground and border may be set equal to any of the 16 colors described in Table 9.4. Adding the number 16 to the foreground value causes the characters to blink in that color. Only the colors with numbers 0 through 7 may be selected for the background.

(continued)

(continued)

Keyword Entry:	Hold down the Alt key and press the C key on your keyboard.	
Examples:	`300 COLOR 14, 2, 6`	`' Yellow on Green with a Brown Border`
	`350 COLOR 12`	`' Light Red Foreground`
	`400 COLOR ,, 14`	`' Yellow Border`
	`450 COLOR 7, 0, 0`	`' White on Black`
	`500 COLOR 0, 7`	`' Black on White`
	`550 COLOR 0, 0, 0`	`' Black on Black`

TABLE 9.4 The 16 Colors Available with a Color Monitor and Color/Graphics Interface Board

COLOR	NUMBER	COLOR	NUMBER	COLOR	NUMBER
Black	0	Brown	6	Light Red	12
Blue	1	White	7	Light Magenta	13
Green	2	Grey	8	Yellow	14
Cyan	3	Light Blue	9	Bright White	15
Red	4	Light Green	10		
Magenta	5	Light Cyan	11		

Line 300 in Table 9.3 sets a yellow foreground, a green background, and a brown border screen. Line 350 changes the foreground to light red; the background and border colors remain as they were. Line 400 changes only the border color to yellow. Line 450 resets the colors to the normal white on black. In this case, the background and border are the same. Line 500 reverses the colors; that is, it changes them to black on white. With line 550, the foreground, background, and border are the same color, and, therefore, character images sent to the screen will not display.

When the `COLOR` statement is executed, all previously displayed characters remain in the original color. The new colors are used for future displays. For this reason, the `COLOR` statement is often followed by the `CLS` statement. The `CLS` statement causes the entire background and border to immediately display in the newly assigned colors. For example,

```
COLOR 14, 7, 2 : CLS
```

instructs the PC to change the screen immediately to a white background and green border. All characters displayed as a result of listing or executing a program will display in the color yellow.

You may instruct the PC to blink characters by adding the number 16 to the foreground color. For example,

```
COLOR 31, 4 : CLS
```

causes the PC to blink bright white characters on a red background.

If you have a monochrome display (black and white or green or amber color) and a color/graphics interface board, the color settings in Table 9.4 are still useful, but the different colors will appear in various patterns of shading on your screen.

The COLOR statement improves substantially the quality of the results displayed by a program. For example, if the following statement,

```
2035 COLOR 15, 1, 4
```

is added to any of the previous menu-driven programs, then the main menu displays in bright white on a blue background with a red border. Other color combinations can be considered for submenus and the results displayed by a program.

9.3 MEDIUM-RESOLUTION AND HIGH-RESOLUTION GRAPHICS

To change to the medium-resolution graphics mode, enter the statement SCREEN 1. In this mode, the screen is divided into 200 rows and 320 columns. To change to the high-resolution graphics mode, the statement SCREEN 2 is entered. In the high-resolution graphics mode, the screen is divided into 200 rows and 640 columns.

Here are some important points regarding the medium-resolution and high-resolution graphics modes:

1. These two graphics modes are available only if your PC has a color/graphics interface board.
2. To send graphical designs to the printer, you must have one that emulates the IBM graphics printer. Also, you must enter the PC command GRAPHICS before you enter the PC command BASICA. For example, if you have changed the default drive to B, then after the B> prompt enter

   ```
   B> A:GRAPHICS
   B> A:BASICA
   ```

3. With a color monitor, medium-resolution graphics allow us to color objects on the screen. High-resolution graphics allow displays only in black and white, but with much greater detail.
4. In either of the two graphics modes, the intersection of a row and column is a point, or pixel. We plot points and draw lines and curves by instructing the PC to turn on selected pixels.
5. We give the PC information about the points, lines, and curves to draw in the form of coordinates like (x, y), where x is the column (horizontal axis) and y is the row (vertical axis).
6. Coordinates are specified with the column first, then the row. This is different from the LOCATE statement in the text mode, which requires the row first, then the column.
7. Rows and columns are numbered beginning with 0, rather than 1.
8. There are two ways to indicate the coordinates of a point on the screen: absolute form and relative form. Coordinates of the form (x, y) are absolute in relation to the origin (0, 0). Coordinates of the form STEP(x, y) are relative to the last point referenced by the last graphics statement executed.
9. If you enter WIDTH 80 in the medium-resolution graphics mode, the PC will switch to the high-resolution graphics mode. If you enter WIDTH 40 in the high-resolution graphics mode, the PC will switch to the medium-resolution graphics mode.

In the sections that follow, several graphics statements and examples are presented.

The COLOR Statement for the Medium-Resolution Graphics Mode

The general form of the COLOR statement for the medium-resolution graphics mode is given in Table 9.5. Be aware that this COLOR statement is different from the one in Table 9.3.

TABLE 9.5 The COLOR Statement for the Medium-Resolution Graphics Mode

General Form:	COLOR background, palette
	where **background** is a numeric expression in the range 0 to 15, and **palette** is a numeric expression. If the expression is an even number, then palette 0 is selected for the foreground; otherwise, palette 1 is selected.
Purpose:	Sets the background color of the screen and selects one of two palettes of color for the foreground. The background may be set equal to any of the 16 colors described in Table 9.4 on page 243. The choice of palettes for the foreground is as follows:

Palette 0	Palette 1	Number
Background Color	Background Color	0
Green	Cyan	1
Red	Magenta	2
Brown	White	3

Keyword Entry:	Hold down the Alt key and press the C key on your keyboard.
Examples:	500 COLOR 9, 1 600 COLOR , 0 700 COLOR BACK, PAL
Note:	The COLOR statement selects the palette (0 or 1) for the foreground. Graphics statements that follow the COLOR statement select the color number from the palette. If no color number is selected, then the default color number 3 is used for medium resolution and the color number 1 is used for high resolution. In medium resolution the border is always the same color as the background.

In Table 9.5, line 500 sets the background color to light blue and selects palette 1 for the foreground. Graphics statements that follow line 500 may select cyan (color number 1 in Table 9.5), magenta (2), white (3), or the background color (0) for the foreground. Selecting the background color turns off the referenced pixel(s).

Line 600 leaves the background color the same and palette 0 is selected for the foreground. Graphics statements that follow line 600 may select the foreground color from green (1), red (2), brown (3), or the background color (0). Finally, line 700 in Table 9.5 selects the background color on the basis of the value of BACK and a palette on the basis of whether PAL is odd (palette 1) or even (palette 0).

The PSET and PRESET Statements

The `PSET` (point set) and `PRESET` (point reset) statements can be used to set a point (pixel) on the screen to one of the four colors on the active palette. The general forms of the `PSET` and `PRESET` statements are given in Table 9.6.

TABLE 9.6 The PSET and PRESET Statements

General Form:	`PSET` *(x, y), color*
	and
	`PRESET` *(x, y), color*
	where **(x, y)** are the coordinates of the point to be plotted (turned on), and **color** is an integer expression in the range 0 to 3. The color number selects the color from the active palette (see Table 9.5).
Purpose:	*Draws a point on the screen.*

Examples:	`700 PSET (34, 72), 2`
	`750 PSET (COL, ROW)`
	`800 PSET STEP (X, 5), 0`
	`850 PRESET STEP (40, 90), KOLOR`
	`900 PRESET (34, 72)`

Note:	1. The coordinates *(x, y)* may be absolute or relative. 2. The PC ignores points referenced outside the range of the screen. 3. `PSET` and `PRESET` are identical statements except for the default color number when the color parameter is not included. With the `PSET` statement, the color number defaults to 3. With the `PRESET` statement, the color number defaults to 0, the background color. Thus, `PSET (X, Y), 0` is identical to `PRESET (X, Y)`.

Line 700 in Table 9.6 plots the point at the intersection of column 34 and row 72. Depending on which palette is active, the point is colored red or magenta. Line 750 plots the point (COL, ROW), using the default color number 3 on the active palette. Lines 800 and 900 in Table 9.6 erase the point defined by the specified coordinates. You'll recall that a color number of 0 or a lack of the color parameter in the `PRESET` statement instructs the PC to use the background color (i.e., the pixel is turned off). Line 850 plots the point that is 40 columns and 90 rows from the last point referenced. The color of the point is based upon the value of KOLOR and the active palette.

Consider Program 9.3 and the results due to its execution in Figure 9.5. Line 140 switches the PC to the medium-resolution graphics mode and clears the screen. Line 150 sets the background color to yellow and selects palette 0. The For loop (lines 160 through 180) draws a green vertical line. The color number in line 170 selects the color green from palette 0. Lines 190 and 200 plot two points, using the color red on the left and right sides of the green vertical line. Finally, the second For loop (lines 210 through 230) erases part of the line drawn by the first For loop.

As we shall see in the next section, MS BASIC has a `LINE` statement that simplifies drawing lines like the one drawn by Program 9.3 in Figure 9.5.

PROGRAM 9.3

```
100 ' Program 9.3
110 ' Plotting a Line and Points
120 ' and Erasing Part of a Line
130 ' **************************
140 SCREEN 1 : CLS : KEY OFF
150 COLOR 14, 0
160 FOR Y = 50 TO 150
170     PSET (160, Y), 1
180 NEXT Y
190 PSET (150, 100), 2
200 PSET (170, 100), 2
210 FOR I = 90 TO 110
220     PRESET (160, I)
230 NEXT I
240 END

RUN
```

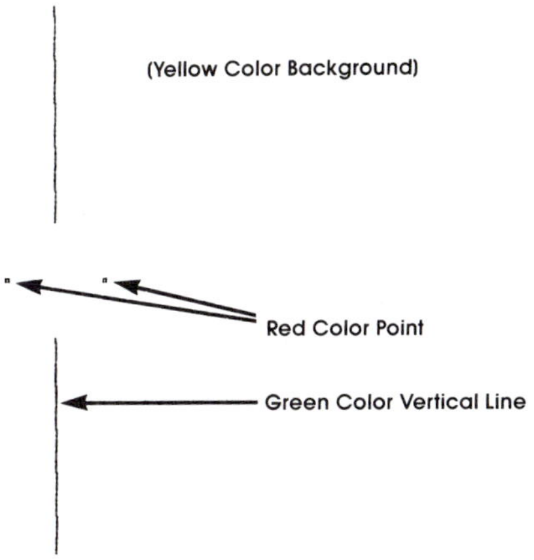

FIGURE 9.5 *Plotting a line and points.*

The LINE Statement

The LINE statement can be used to draw a line or a box on the screen. The general form of the LINE statement is given in Table 9.7.

TABLE 9.7 The LINE Statement

General Form: LINE $(x_1, y_1) - (x_2, y_2)$, color, box, style

where (x_1, y_1) is the starting point;
(x_2, y_2) is the ending point;
color selects the color for the line from the active palette;
box is B or BF,
where **B** instructs the PC to draw a box, rather than a line, with
(x_1, y_1) and (x_2, y_2) as opposite coordinates; and
BF is similar to B, except that the box is filled with color; and
style determines the type of line (dashed or solid) to be drawn. (The style parameter is optional and will not be used in this book.)

(continued)

(continued)

Purpose:	Connects two points with a line or draws a box (filled or unfilled) on the screen.
Examples:	100 LINE (50, 70) - (90, 100), 2 200 LINE - (65, 90) 300 LINE (0, 0) - (319, 199), 3 400 LINE (0, 199) - (319, 0), 1, B 500 LINE (COL1, ROW1) - (COL2, ROW2),, BF
Note:	Lines that extend beyond the range of the screen are **clipped**; that is, the PC determines the intersection of the line with the edge of the screen and draws the line up to the edge.

In Table 9.7, line 100 draws a line from the point defined by the intersection of column 50 and row 70 to the point defined by the intersection of column 90 and row 100. The color of the line is either red (palette 0) or magenta (palette 1). Line 200 draws a line from the last point referenced to the point (65, 90) in the default color on the active palette.

Line 300 in Table 9.7 draws a diagonal line from the upper left-hand corner to the lower left-hand corner of the screen. If palette 0 is active, then the color of the line is brown. Line 400 draws a box around the outer edge of the screen. If palette 0 is active, then the lines making up the box are colored green. Otherwise, the lines of the box are colored cyan. Line 500 also draws a box. The location of the box on the screen is dependent on the values assigned to COL1, ROW1, COL2, and ROW2. The parameter BF instructs the PC to fill the box with the default color for the active palette.

Consider Program 9.4 in Figure 9.6 and the right triangle displayed as a result of its execution. In Program 9.4, line 130 switches the PC to the medium-resolution graphics mode and clears the screen. Line 140 changes the background of the screen to blue and selects palette 1. Line 150 draws the base of the triangle. Line 160 draws the altitude, and line 170 draws the hypotenuse. Since none of the LINE statements includes a color number, the default color number 3 (white for palette 1) is used. Note also that lines 160 and 170 both draw lines from the last point referenced.

PROGRAM 9.4

```
100 ' Program 9.4
110 ' Drawing a Right Triangle
120 ' ***********************
130 SCREEN 1 : CLS : KEY OFF
140 COLOR 1, 1
150 LINE (20, 75) - (100, 75)
160 LINE - (100, 25)
170 LINE - (20, 75)
180 END
```

RUN

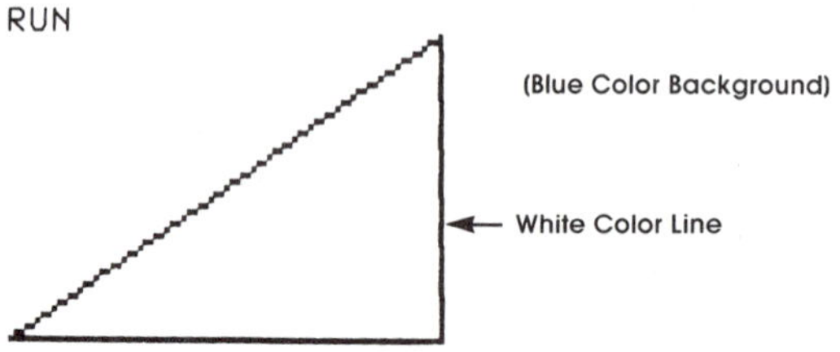

FIGURE 9.6 *Drawing a right triangle.*

As another example of the use of the LINE statement, consider Program 9.5 in Figure 9.7. This program instructs the PC to draw 5 boxes (one of which is inside another). Line 130 switches the PC to the medium-resolution graphics mode and clears the screen. Line 140 selects a black background and palette 0.

The first LINE statement in Program 9.5 draws the small, unfilled, square box with opposite coordinates of (20, 10) and (40, 30), using the color green. Line 160 draws a filled large square box, using the color red. Next, line 170 draws a filled square within the square drawn by line 160. Because the background color is used in line 170, the red pixels are turned off to leave an unfilled square within the large red square.

Line 180 in Program 9.5 draws the filled vertical box, using the color green. Finally, line 190 draws the filled horizontal box, using the default color brown on palette 0.

PROGRAM 9.5

```
100 ' Program 9.5
110 ' Drawing Boxes
120 ' *************
130 SCREEN 1 : CLS : KEY OFF
140 COLOR 0, 0
150 LINE (20, 10) - (40, 30), 1, B
160 LINE (20, 40) - (60, 80), 2, BF
170 LINE (30, 50) - (50, 70), 0, BF
180 LINE (70, 0) - (90, 80), 1, BF
190 LINE (110, 20) - (170, 40),, BF
200 END

RUN
```

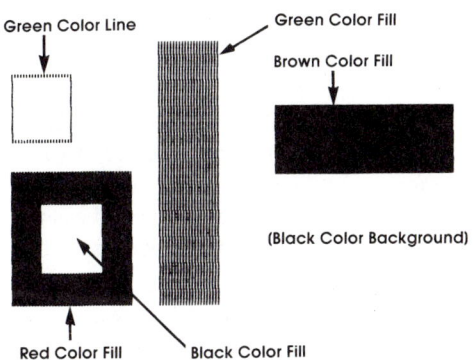

FIGURE 9.7 *Drawing boxes.*

The CIRCLE Statement

The `CIRCLE` statement draws circles, ellipses, arcs, and wedges. The general form of the `CIRCLE` statement is given in Table 9.8.

TABLE 9.8 The CIRCLE Statement

General Form:	CIRCLE (x, y), radius, color, start, end, shape
	where **(x, y)** is the center of the curved figure;
	radius is the distance from the center to the outer edge of the curved figure, as measured in points (pixels);
	color selects the color for the curved figure from the active palette;
	start and **end** are the two ends of the arc to be drawn (The measures are angles in radians and can range between –2*PI and 2*PI where PI = 3.141593. Negative values [–0 is not allowed] cause a wedge or pie slice to be drawn. If these two parameters are omitted, the PC draws the entire curved figure.); and
	shape is the ratio of the radius in the y direction to the radius in the x direction (height/width). This parameter is used to draw ellipses. If this parameter is omitted, the PC draws a partial or complete circle, depending on the start and end parameters.
Purpose:	Draws circles, ellipses, arcs, and wedges.
Examples:	200 CIRCLE (160, 100), 20
	300 CIRCLE (60, 40), 30, 1
	400 CIRCLE (20, 20), 50
	500 CIRCLE (X, Y), RAD, KOLOR
	600 CIRCLE (120, 120), 35,, 0, 1.5708
	700 CIRCLE (160, 100), 50, 1, -3.141593, -4.7124
	800 CIRCLE (100, 100), 40,,,,5/18
Note:	The last point referenced after the CIRCLE statement is executed is the center point (x, y).

In Table 9.8, line 200 instructs the PC to draw a circle with a center at column 160 and row 100 and with a radius of 20 points. The default color number 3 on the active palette is used to draw the circle. In line 300, a circle with a center at (60, 40) with a radius of 30 points is drawn in green or cyan.

Line 400 in Table 9.8 draws a circle that is clipped, because part of the circle goes beyond the screen. Line 500 causes a circle to be drawn, using the color number KOLOR, with center at (X, Y) and a radius of RAD points.

Line 600 in Table 9.8 draws an arc from 0° to 90°, with a center at (120, 120) and a radius of 35 points. The default color on the active palette is used to color the curved figure. Line 700 draws a wedge. The negative start and end parameters instruct the PC to connect the center to the ends of the arc to form a wedge. The wedge extends from 180° to 270°. Figure 9.8 shows the relationship between radians and slices of a circle.

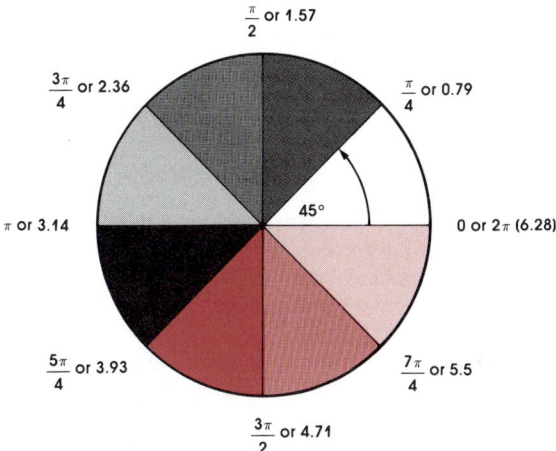

FIGURE 9.8 *A circle is composed of 2π or 6.28 radians, or 360°. (Note that the decimal fraction values are rounded to the nearest hundredths place.)*

Line 800 in Table 9.8 draws a horizontal (flatter) ellipse. The center of the ellipse is at (100, 100). Because the shape is less than 1, the radius parameter is the x radius. The product of the shape (5/18) and the radius parameter is the y radius.

In mathematics, when the shape is equal to 1, a circle is defined. A shape that is less than 1 causes the ellipse to be horizontal (flatter). A shape greater than 1 causes the ellipse to be vertical (taller).

Because the pixel length for the PC screen is not the same in both the x and y direction (320 × 200 for medium resolution), the default value of the shape that draws a circle is 5/6 (5 rows for every 6 columns) in medium resolution and 5/12 (5 rows for every 12 columns) in high resolution. With this in mind, you must adjust slightly the mathematical definition of the term *shape*. For example, the following statement,

```
900 CIRCLE (160, 100), 50,,,, 1
```

does not result in a circle, even though the shape is 1. Line 900 draws an ellipse that is slightly taller than it is wide. The following statement draws a circle because the PC uses a *default value* of 5/6 for the shape.

```
950 CIRCLE (160, 100), 50
```

See Program 9.6 in Figure 9.9 on page 253 for additional examples of CIRCLE statements that draw ellipses.

The PAINT Statement

Another color statement that is available with MS BASIC is the PAINT statement. This statement paints (fills) an area on the screen with the selected color. The general form of the PAINT statement is given in Table 9.9.

TABLE 9.9 The PAINT Statement

General Form:	PAINT (x, y), paint, boundary
	where **(x, y)** are the coordinates of a point within the area to be filled with color;
	paint is a numeric expression or a string expression (If paint is a numeric expression, then it must be within the range 0 to 3 for medium resolution and 0 or 1 for high resolution. The numeric expression determines the color the PC uses to paint the area on the screen. The default for medium resolution is 3 and for high resolution 1. If paint is a string expression, then it describes a tiling pattern for the area.); and
	boundary is a numeric expression that defines the color of the edges of the area to be filled.
Purpose:	Paints an area defined by the boundary color on the screen with the selected color.
Examples:	600 PAINT (50, 25), 2, 1 700 PAINT (COL, ROW), KOLOR, EDGE 800 PAINT (200, 100) 900 PAINT (100, 150), TILE$
Note:	1. The area defined by the boundary color must be completely enclosed or the entire screen is painted. 2. In high resolution, the paint parameter should not be different from the boundary parameter.

Assuming that in medium resolution palette 0 is active, line 600 in Table 9.9 paints the area with the color red that is bounded by the color green in which the point with coordinates (50, 25) is located. If there is no green boundary surrounding (50, 25), then the entire screen is painted red. Line 600 is invalid in high resolution because the paint parameter is not 0 or 1.

In either medium resolution or high resolution, line 700 paints the area encompassing the point with coordinates (COL, ROW) and bounded by the color number EDGE with the color associated with KOLOR. Line 800 colors the area that includes the point with coordinates (200, 100) with the default color (3 in medium resolution and 1 in high resolution). If the edge of the area is not equal to the default color, then the entire screen is painted. Line 900 causes the area to be tiled rather than painted. Tilling involves covering a specified area on the screen with a pattern which is uniformly repeated over the entire area.

Consider Program 9.6 and the results due to its execution, which are shown in Figure 9.9.

PROGRAM 9.6

```
100 ' Program 9.6
110 ' Drawing Circles, Arcs,
120 ' Wedges, and Ellipses
130 ' ********************
140 PI = 3.141593
150 SCREEN 1 : CLS : KEY OFF
160 COLOR 1, 0
170 ' **** Draw Circle ****
180 CIRCLE (40, 40), 20, 1
190 PAINT (40, 40), 3, 1
200 ' ****** Draw Arc *****
210 CIRCLE (80, 40), 20, 1, 0, PI/2
220 ' **** Draw Wedge *****
230 CIRCLE (120,40),20,3,-2*PI,-PI/2
240 PAINT (125, 35), 1, 3
250 ' ** Draw Horizontal Ellipse **
260 CIRCLE (40, 100), 30, 3,,,7/18
270 PAINT (40, 100), 2, 3
280 ' ** Draw Vertical Ellipse **
290 CIRCLE (90, 100), 30, 3,,,18/7
300 PAINT (95, 95), 1, 3
310 ' ** Draw Circle Within Box **
320 LINE (120, 70)-(180, 130), 3, B
330 CIRCLE (150,100), 20, 3
340 PAINT (125, 75), 2, 3
350 END
```

RUN

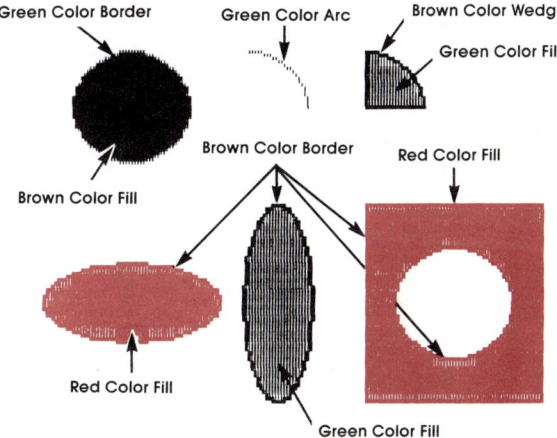

FIGURE 9.9 *Examples of the COLOR and PAINT statements.*

In Figure 9.9, line 150 switches the PC to the medium-resolution graphics mode. The color statement in line 160 selects a blue background and activates palette 0. Line 180 draws the circle in the upper-left corner of the output results. Line 190 paints the circle brown. Note that the boundary parameter in line 190 is equal to the color number used to draw the circle in line 180.

Line 210 in Program 9.6 draws an arc from $0°$ to $90°$ with a center at (80, 40). Line 230 draws the wedge illustrated in Figure 9.9. Line 240 paints the wedge green. You'll recall that the negative start and end parameters instruct the PC to draw lines from the center point to the end points of the arc to form a wedge. A start parameter of $-2 * PI$, which is the same as $0°$, is used (–0 is invalid).

Line 260 draws a horizontal ellipse. Line 290 draws a vertical ellipse. Both ellipses are shown in the output results in Figure 9.9. Each of the two CIRCLE statements is followed by a PAINT statement that paints the ellipses. Line 270 paints the horizontal ellipse the color red, and line 300 paints the vertical ellipse the color green.

The lower-right figure in Figure 9.9 is displayed because of lines 320 through 340. Line 320 draws the box. Line 330 draws the circle within the box. Both figures are drawn using the color brown (palette 0, color 3). Line 340 uses the color red to paint the area within the box and outside the circle. Painting continues in all directions until the brown border is reached.

The DRAW Statement

The DRAW statement instructs the PC to draw an object defined by a string expression. The string expression is made up of a series of easy-to-code commands (see Table 9.11). The commands can be used to draw lines, plot points, set colors, and perform other special operations — all within one statement.

The general form for the DRAW statement is shown in Table 9.10. The list of commands that can be assigned to the string expression in the DRAW statement is given in Table 9.11.

TABLE 9.10 The DRAW Statement

General Form:	DRAW *string expression*
	where ***string expression*** *is a command or series of commands as described in Table 9.11.*
Purpose:	*Draws an object as specified in the string expression.*
Examples:	300 DRAW "BM75,120 M200,50 M100,150 M75,120" 400 DRAW "U100 R100 D100 L100" 500 DRAW "E=S1; F=S2; L=S3" 600 DRAW DESIGN$
Note:	*The commands within the string expression may be separated from each other by a blank character or a semicolon.*

TABLE 9.11 DRAW Commands

COMMAND	FUNCTION	EXAMPLES
M x,y	Move and draw to (x,y).	M20,50
M ±x, ±y	Move and draw to (X + x, Y + y), where (X,Y) is the last referenced point.	M+30,+50
Un	Move and draw up n rows.	U70
Dn	Move and draw down n rows.	D35
Rn	Move and draw right n columns.	R45
Ln	Move and draw left n columns.	L27
En	Move and draw diagonally up and right, where n = diagonal distance.	E40
Fn	Move and draw diagonally down and right, where n = diagonal distance.	F90
Gn	Move and draw diagonally down and left, where n = diagonal distance.	G10
Hn	Move and draw diagonally up and left, where n = diagonal distance.	H36
B	Causes the next move command to move without drawing.	BM20,50
N	Instructs the PC to return to the current point after the next move command.	NR75
An	Set angle n, where n ranges from 0 to 3. 0 = 0 degrees, 1 = 90 degrees, 2 = 180 degrees, and 3 = 270 degrees. Rotates next object drawn through the specified angle.	A2
Tn	Turn angle n for subsequent drawings, where n is in the range –360 to 360; n > 0 turns angle counterclockwise, n < 0 turns angle clockwise.	T30
Sn	Scale subsequent drawings, where n varies between 1 and 255 (all line lengths are multiplied by n/4).	S24
Cn	Selects color from active palette.	C2
Pp,b	Fills area, using color number p to boundary b.	P1,2
Xv	Execute a subcommand, where v is a string variable containing additional commands. Allows a series of commands to exceed the string expression limit of 255 characters.	XDESIGN2$

Programs 9.7 and 9.8 in Figure 9.10 illustrate the use of the DRAW statement to instruct the PC to draw two simple figures — a bicycle wheel and a sailboat.

PROGRAM 9.7

```
100 ' Program 9.7
110 ' Draw a Bicycle Wheel
120 ' ******************
130 SCREEN 2 : CLS : KEY OFF
140 CIRCLE (320, 100), 60
150 FOR ANGLE = 0 TO 360 STEP 10
160    DRAW "TA=ANGLE; NU25"
170 NEXT ANGLE
180 END

RUN
```

PROGRAM 9.8

```
100 ' Program 9.8
110 ' Draw a Sailboat
120 ' **************
130 SCREEN 1 : CLS : KEY OFF
140 COLOR 9, 1
150 DRAW "C2 L10 F10 R20 E10 L30 BU1 C3 U40 F30 L30"
160 PAINT (160, 105), 2, 2
170 PAINT (165, 85), 3, 3
180 END

RUN
```

FIGURE 9.10 *Examples of the DRAW statement.*

■ 9.4 SOUND AND MUSIC

A speaker is located in the system unit of the PC. Though this speaker is small, it is capable of producing a variety of sounds. For example, in Chapter 6 we used the BEEP statement to produce a high-pitched sound to draw the operator's attention to data-entry errors. In this section, we will explore two additional statements that can activate the speaker under program control. They are the SOUND and PLAY statements.

The SOUND Statement

The SOUND statement is used to create a sound of variable frequency and duration. The general form of the SOUND statement is given in Table 9.12. Program 9.9 illustrates the use of the SOUND statement to generate a siren sound. Line 130 clears the screen. Line 140 selects a blinking red foreground on a black background with a blue border. Lines 150 and 160 display messages. The While loop (lines 170 through 210) executes until the user presses a key on the keyboard.

The For loop (lines 180 through 200) in Program 9.9 generates a siren-like sound, using the PC's speaker. Each time through the For loop, the frequency increases until it reaches 1100 Hertz (cycles per second).

TABLE 9.12 The SOUND Statement

General Form:	SOUND frequency, duration
	where **frequency** is a numeric expression between 37 and 32767; and **duration** is a numeric expression in the range 0 to 65535. The expression represents the duration in clock ticks, and there are 18.2 clock ticks per second. A duration of zero turns off the current sound.
Purpose:	Generates sound through the PC's speaker.
Examples:	500 SOUND 1000, 85 600 SOUND 32767, 0 700 SOUND FREQ, DUR
Note:	The frequency is measured in Hertz (cycles per second).

PROGRAM 9.9

```
100 ' Program 9.9
110 ' Using the Speaker as a Siren
120 ' ****************************
130 WIDTH 40 : KEY OFF
140 COLOR 20, 0, 1
150 LOCATE 13, 8 : PRINT "EMERGENCY!!   EMERGENCY!!"
160 LOCATE 24, 4 : PRINT "Press any key to stop the siren...";




220 WIDTH 80 : COLOR 7, 0, 0 : KEY ON
230 END
RUN
```

The PLAY Statement

The PLAY statement converts your PC into a piano. Like the DRAW statement, the PLAY statement instructs the PC to play music that is defined by a string expression. The string is made up of a series of easy-to-code commands (see Table 9.14 on the next page). The music you compose may be as simple as a single note or as complex as the counterpoint in Bach or a symphony by Beethoven. The general form of the PLAY statement is shown in Table 9.13.

TABLE 9.13 The PLAY Statement

General Form:	PLAY string expression
	where **string expression** is a command or series of commands, as described in Table 9.14.
Purpose:	Plays music as specified in the string expression.
Examples:	100 PLAY "C D E F G A B >C C< B A G F E D C" 200 PLAY "L4 C D E2 L4 E D L2 C D E C" 300 PLAY MUSIC$ 400 PLAY "L=LENGTH; XCHORUS$; XBRIDGE$; XCHORUS$;"
Note:	The commands within the string expression may be separated from each other by blank characters or a semicolon, except that a semicolon is not allowed after MF, MB, MN, ML, or MS.

As a sample program that uses the PLAY statement, consider Program 9.10. This program plays the tune "Twinkle Twinkle Little Star" over and over again until the user presses a key on the keyboard. Both the chorus and the bridge are defined prior to the PLAY statement in lines 160 and 180. In line 210, the PLAY statement employs the X command to reference the subcommands assigned to CHORUS$ and BRIDGE$.

PROGRAM 9.10

```
100 ' Program 9.10
110 ' Twinkle Twinkle Little Star
120 ' ***************************
130 'CLS : KEY OFF
140 'LOCATE 13, 25 : PRINT "Press any key to stop the song..."
150 ' ****** Define Chorus ******
160 CHORUS$ = "L4 C C G G A A L2 G L4 F F E E D D L2 C"
170 ' ****** Define Bridge ******
180 BRIDGE$ = "L4 G G F F E E L2 D L4 G G F F E E L2 D"
190 ' ******** Play Song ********
200 WHILE INKEY$ = ""
210     PLAY "XCHORUS$; XBRIDGE$; XCHORUS$;"
220 WEND
230 END

RUN
```

TABLE 9.14 PLAY Commands

COMMAND	FUNCTION	EXAMPLES
A to G with optional #, +, or −	Plays the specified note in the current octave. A number sign (#) or plus sign (+) appended to the letter indicates a sharp; a minus sign (−) indicates a flat.	C A+ D−
On	Sets the octave for the notes that follow. There are 7 octaves, numbered 0 to 6. Octave 4 is the default. Each octave goes from C to B, and octave 3 starts with middle C.	O2
>n or <n	The greater than sign (>) instructs the PC to climb to the next octave and play note n. The less than sign (<) lowers the octave by 1. Either sign affects all notes that follow.	>C <D−
Nn	Play note n, where n ranges from 0 to 84. This serves as an alternative to using the O command followed by the note name. N0 is a "rest."	N27 N0
Ln	Sets the length of the notes that follow. The parameter n can range from 1 to 64. The PC interprets n as 1/n. The length of a note may also follow the note. For example, C4 is the same as L4C.	L4 L=S;
Pn	Pause. The parameter n can range from 1 to 64. As with the L command, the PC interprets n as 1/n.	P16 P=R;
	Dot. Placed after a note, the dot causes the note to be played as a dotted note. Multiple dots are valid.	A. C+..

(continued)

(continued)

Tn	Tempo. Defines the number of quarter notes per minute. The parameter n can range from 32 to 255. The default is 120.	T110 T=NU;
MF	Music foreground. The music created by the SOUND or PLAY statement runs in the foreground. The program is put into a wait state until the music statement is finished. A note does not start until the previous note is finished. MF is the default.	MF
MB	Music background. The music created by the SOUND or PLAY statement runs in the background. That is, the BASIC program continues to execute while the music plays in the background.	MB
ML	Music legato. Each note that follows plays the full period set by L.	ML
MN	Music normal. Each note that follows plays 7/8 of the time specified by L. Default between MN, ML, and MS.	MN
MS	Music staccato. Each note that follows plays 3/4 of the time specified by L.	MS
Xv;	Execute a subcommand, where v is a string variable containing additional commands. Allows a series of commands to exceed the string expression limit of 255 characters.	XMUSIC$;

■ 9.5 TEST YOUR BASIC SKILLS (Even-numbered answers are in Appendix B.)

1. Evaluate each of the following. Assume that the statements are executed in the high-resolution graphics mode.

    a. `100 PSET (320, 100)`
    b. `400 CIRCLE (50, 50), 15,, -3, -4`
    c. `500 CIRCLE (320, 160), 30,,,, 5/8`
    d. `600 LINE - (40, 30)`
    e. `700 LINE (0, 0)-(160, 100)`
    f. `800 DRAW "BM320,160 NR45 D45"`
    g. `900 SOUND 200, .03`
    h. `950 PLAY "XMUS$;"`

2. Use PSET, LINE, and CIRCLE statements to draw the figures below and on the next page. Assume that the PC is in the medium-resolution graphics mode.

    a.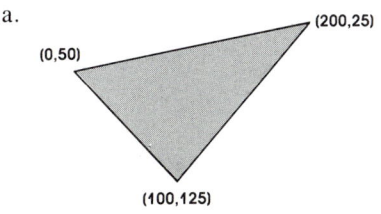
    b.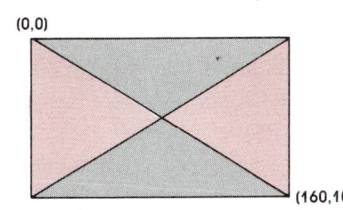

c. 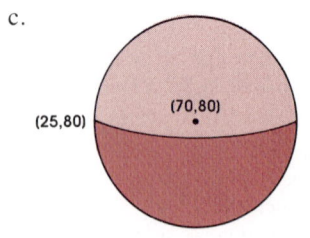 d.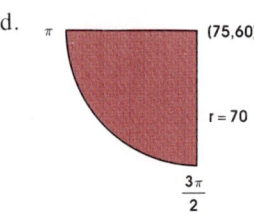

3. Identify each of the following DRAW commands.

   a. BM 10, 20   b. M+3, +5   c. C1   d. F5   e. E20
   f. A3   g. U75   h. H5   i. L20   j. NL20

4. Identify each of the following PLAY commands.

   a. A-   b. L8   c. >C   d. XM$;   e. N0
   f. T100   g. P8   h. MS   i. ML   j. O3

■ 9.6 BASIC PROGRAMMING PROBLEMS

1. Horizontal Bar Graph of Annual Sales for the Past Ten Years

Purpose: To become familiar with graphing in the text mode.

Problem: A graph gives the user of a report a pictorial view of the information. Consider the following problem, which has as its defined output a horizontal bar graph. The Sales Analysis Department of the PUC Company requests from the Data Processing Department a report in the form of a horizontal bar graph representing the company's annual sales trend for the ten-year period 1981 through 1990. The annual sales are as follows:

Year	Sales (in millions)	Year	Sales (in millions)
1981	$22	1986	$43
1982	26	1987	40
1983	28	1988	45
1984	35	1989	50
1985	40	1990	48

Include the following characteristics in the graph:

1. Display the bar graph horizontally in the 80-column display mode.
2. Display vertically the column that represents the years.
3. Use a series of asterisks to represent the sales for each year.
4. Mark off the horizontal axis in increments of 5, beginning with 0 and ending with 55. Each unit represents a million dollars.

Input Data: Use the ten-year PUC Company data shown above. The data (year and sales) for each year is in the sequential file EX91SAL.DAT on the Student Diskette.

Output Results: The following results are displayed.

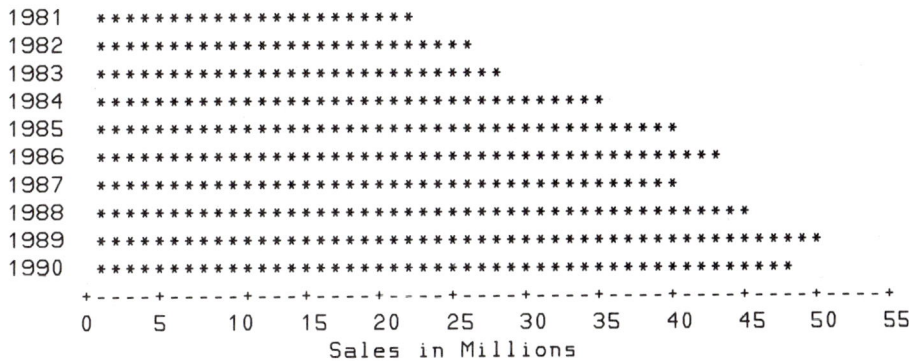

2. Drawing a Design

Purpose: To become familiar with the LINE, CIRCLE, and PAINT statements.

Problem: Construct a program that draws the design shown in the Output Results. Draw the design in the medium-resolution graphics mode. Use the PAINT statement to color the various sections of the design.

Input Data: None.

Output Results: The following results are displayed.

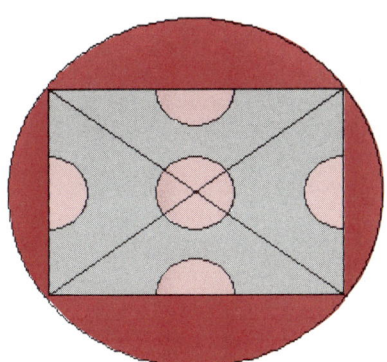

3. Playing the Musical Score "Yankee Doodle" on the PC

Purpose: To become familiar with the PLAY statement.

Problem: Obtain a song sheet of "Yankee Doodle." Use a For loop to play the song seven times, starting at octave 0 and ending at octave 6.

Input Data: None.

Output Results: The PC plays the song "Yankee Doodle" seven times, each time at a higher octave.

DEBUGGING TECHNIQUES AND THE ASCII CHARACTER CODES

APPENDIX A

A.1 DEBUGGING TECHNIQUES

Although the top-down approach and structured programming techniques help minimize errors, they by no means guarantee error-free programs. Owing to carelessness or insufficient thought, program portions can be constructed which do not work as anticipated and which give erroneous results. When such problems occur, techniques are needed to isolate the errors and correct the erroneous program statements.

MS BASIC can detect many different grammatical errors and can display appropriate diagnostic messages. However, no BASIC system can detect all errors, since literally hundreds of possible coding errors can be made. Some of these errors can go undetected by MS BASIC until either an abnormal end occurs during execution or the program terminates with erroneous results.

There are several techniques for attempting to discover the portion of the program that is in error. These methods are called **debugging techniques**. The errors themselves are **bugs**, and the activity involved in their detection is **debugging**.

Tracing (TRON and TROFF)

The TRON (TRace ON) instruction in MS BASIC provides a means of tracing the path of execution through a program in order to determine which statements are executed. The instruction TROFF (TRace OFF) turns off the tracing. These instructions may be inserted into a program as BASIC statements, or they may be used as system commands before the RUN command is issued. Pressing the F7 key enters the instruction TRON, and pressing the F8 key enters the instruction TROFF.

The TRON instruction activates tracing, and the PC displays the line number of each statement executed. The line numbers appear enclosed in square brackets to prevent them from being confused with other results the program may produce.

For example, if a PC with tracing activated executes a program portion consisting of lines 250, 260, 270, and 280, the output displayed will be as follows:

```
[250] [260] [270] [280]
```

The `TROFF` instruction deactivates tracing. Both the `TRON` and `TROFF` instructions may be used any number of times in a BASIC program.

Program A.1 has the `TRON` and `TROFF` statements in lines 125 and 195. When the RUN command is issued, all statements between lines 125 and 195 are traced, and their line numbers and corresponding output are displayed accordingly.

PROGRAM A.1

```
100 ' Program A.1
110 ' Illustrating Use of the
115 ' TRON and TROFF Instructions
120 ' ***************************
125 TRON
130 SUM = 0
140 I = 1
150 WHILE I < 4
160     SUM = SUM + I
170     I = I + 1
180     PRINT I; SUM
190 WEND
195 TROFF
200 END

RUN

[130] [140] [150] [160] [170] [180] 2  1
[190] [160] [170] [180]  3  3
[190] [160] [170] [180]  4  6
[190] [195]
```

Program A.2 is similar to Program A.1. When this program is executed, the PC displays the value of 1 for I over and over. The program has a bug, which results in an endless loop when the program is run.

PROGRAM A.2

```
100 ' Program A.2
110 ' This Program Contains a Bug
120 ' ***************************
130 SUM = 0
140 I = 1
150 WHILE I < 4
160     SUM = SUM + I
170     T = I + 1          ' This line contains an error
180     PRINT I; SUM
190 WEND
200 END
```

If the TRON instruction is used as a system command, the following output occurs during tracing:

```
TRON
RUN

[100] [110] [120] [130] [140] [150] [160] [170] [180] 1  1
[190] [160] [170] [180]  1  2
[190] [160] [170] [180]  1  3
[190] [160] [170] [180]  1  4
[190]...
```

From the output, we can see the repetition of the following sequence of line numbers:

```
[190][160][170][180]
```

This output reveals that the program executes lines 160, 170, 180, and 190 repeatedly in the While loop.

The condition in the WHILE statement in line 150 cannot be satisfied, since the value of I will always be less than 4. Line 170 has been incorrectly written. In order to satisfy the condition in the WHILE statement, use:

```
170     I = I + 1      instead of:      170     T = I + 1
```

Examining Values (STOP, PRINT, and CONT)

Another useful debugging technique is to stop a program, examine the values of various variables within the program, and then continue the execution of the program. All this can be accomplished through the use of the STOP and PRINT statements and the system command CONT (continue). Consider partial Program A.3.

PROGRAM A.3

```
100 ' Program A.3
110 ' Illustrating the Use of STOP, PRINT, and CONT
120 ' ***********************************************
130 .
    .
    .
300 V1 = 10 * 12.15
310 A1 = 2 * 24.3
320 S1 = 36.9 / 3
325 STOP
    .
    .
    .
RUN
Break in 325                    (displayed when STOP statement is executed)
PRINT V1                        (entered by user)
 121.5                          (displayed result from PRINT statement)
PRINT A1; S1                    (entered by user)
 48.6  12.3                     (displayed result from PRINT statement)
CONT                            (entered by user)
```

When the `STOP` statement is executed in line 325, the program will stop and the message `Break in 325` will be displayed. Now the values of various variables can be examined by using a `PRINT` statement without a line number.

After the values of V1, A1, and S1 are displayed, the `CONT` is issued and the remaining program is executed. `CONT` should not be placed directly into a BASIC program; instead, it should be entered as a command from the keyboard by the user.

Intermediate Output

In some instances, including intermediate `PRINT` statements as a part of the program may be preferable to using `STOP` statements and displaying the values of variables in the immediate mode.

Appropriate `PRINT` statements may be inserted after each statement or series of statements involving computations. This technique is called **source language debugging** or the **intermediate output method**. Intermediate results are displayed until the specific portion of the program that is in error can be deduced.

If a program produces little output to begin with, the intermediate-output method should be used, since the outputs from the intermediate `PRINT` statements will be easy to distinguish from the regular output. If a program produces a great deal of output, then the technique involving the `STOP`, `PRINT`, and `CONT` statements should be utilized to minimize the amount of output to the display unit.

■ A.2 ASCII CHARACTER CODES

Table A.1 lists all 256 ASCII decimal codes and their corresponding characters. Each time you press a key, the *character* is displayed on the screen and the associated *decimal code* is transmitted to main storage. Special characters may be displayed on the screen by using `PRINT CHR$(n)`, where n is the corresponding decimal code. See Program 9.1 on page 238.

ASCII decimal codes 126 to 255 represent the USA character set. However, foreign character sets may also be represented by these decimal codes.

TABLE A.1 ASCII Character Set

DECIMAL CODE	CHARACTER	DECIMAL CODE	CHARACTER	DECIMAL CODE	CHARACTER	DECIMAL CODE	CHARACTER	DECIMAL CODE	CHARACTER
000	(null)	052	4	104	h	156	£	208	⊥
001	☺	053	5	105	i	157	¥	209	╤
002	☻	054	6	106	j	158	Pt	210	╥
003	♥	055	7	107	k	159	ƒ	211	╙
004	♦	056	8	108	l	160	á	212	╘
005	♣	057	9	109	m	161	í	213	╒
006	♠	058	:	110	n	162	ó	214	╓
007	(beep)	059	;	111	o	163	ú	215	╫
008	■	060	<	112	p	164	ñ	216	╪
009	(tab)	061	=	113	q	165	Ñ	217	┘
010	(line feed)	062	>	114	r	166	ª	218	┌
011	(home)	063	?	115	s	167	º	219	█
012	(form feed)	064	@	116	t	168	¿	220	▄
013	(carriage return)	065	A	117	u	169	⌐	221	▌
014	♪	066	B	118	v	170	¬	222	▐
015	☼	067	C	119	w	171	½	223	▀
016	►	068	D	120	x	172	¼	224	α
017	◄	069	E	121	y	173	¡	225	β
018	↕	070	F	122	z	174	«	226	Γ
019	‼	071	G	123	{	175	»	227	π
020	¶	072	H	124	|	176	░	228	Σ
021	§	073	I	125	}	177	▒	229	σ
022	▬	074	J	126	~	178	▓	230	μ
023	↨	075	K	127	⌂	179	│	231	τ
024	↑	076	L	128	Ç	180	┤	232	Φ
025	↓	077	M	129	ü	181	╡	233	Θ
026	←	078	N	130	é	182	╢	234	Ω
027	→	079	O	131	â	183	╖	235	δ
028	(cursor right)	080	P	132	ä	184	╕	236	∞
029	(cursor left)	081	Q	133	à	185	╣	237	Ø
030	(cursor up)	082	R	134	å	186	║	238	∈
031	(cursor down)	083	S	135	ç	187	╗	239	∩
032	(space)	084	T	136	ê	188	╝	240	≡
033	!	085	U	137	ë	189	╜	241	±
034	"	086	V	138	è	190	╛	242	≥
035	#	087	W	139	ï	191	┐	243	≤
036	$	088	X	140	î	192	└	244	⌠
037	%	089	Y	141	ì	193	┴	245	⌡
038	&	090	Z	142	Ä	194	┬	246	÷
039	'	091	[	143	Å	195	├	247	≈
040	(	092	\	144	É	196	─	248	°
041	)	093	]	145	æ	197	┼	249	●
042	*	094	^	146	Æ	198	╞	250	•
043	+	095	_	147	ô	199	╟	251	√
044	,	096	`	148	ö	200	╚	252	ⁿ
045	-	097	a	149	ò	201	╔	253	²
046	.	098	b	150	û	202	╩	254	■
047	/	099	c	151	ù	203	╦	255	(blank)
048	0	100	d	152	ÿ	204	╠		
049	1	101	e	153	Ö	205	═		
050	2	102	f	154	Ü	206	╬		
051	3	103	g	155	¢	207	╧		

ANSWERS TO THE TEST YOUR BASIC SKILLS EXERCISES (EVEN-NUMBERED)

APPENDIX B

■ **CHAPTER 1**

2. The basic subsystems of a computer are input, main storage, central processing unit, auxiliary storage, and output.

   Input — a device that allows programs and data to enter into the computer system.

   Main Storage — a subsystem that allows for the storage of programs and data for the CPU to process at a given time.

   Central Processing Unit (CPU) — the unit that controls and supervises the entire computer system and performs the arithmetic and logical operations on data that is specified by the stored program.

   Auxiliary Storage — a subsystem that is used to store programs and data for immediate recall.

   Output — a device that allows the computer system to communicate the results of a program to the user.

4. A floppy diskette unit and a hard disk unit both serve as input and output devices.
6. Hardware is the physical equipment of a computer system. The subsystems as described in 2 above are hardware. Software refers to the programs, languages, written procedures, and documentation concerned with the operation of a computer system.

8.

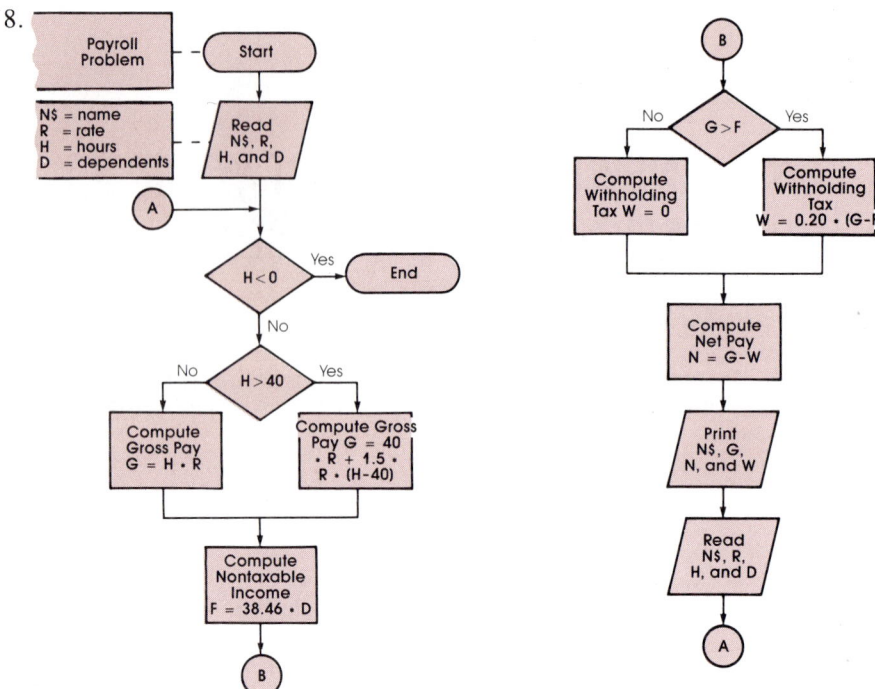

CHAPTER 2

2.

Line	W	X	Y	Displayed
100	4	0	0	
110	4	2	0	
120	4	2	6	
130	4	2	6	6
140	5	2	6	
150	5	30	6	
160	5	30	6	30
170	5	9	6	
180	5	9	4	
190	5	9	4	4
200	5	0	4	
210	5	0	4	0
220	5	0	4	

4. a. 100 T = 3   b. 200 X = T - 2   c. 300 P = T * X
    d. 400 T = 3 * T   e. 500 A = P / X   f. 600 X = X + 1
    g. 700 R = R ^ 3
         or
        700 R = R * R * R

6. (1) Insert the data as constants in the LET statement that is used to calculate a result.
    (2) Assign each data item to a variable. Use these variables in the LET statement to calculate a result.
    (3) Use the INPUT statement to assign the data items to variables. Use these variables in the LET statement to calculate a result.

8. AUTO — automatically starts a BASIC program with a line number.
   FILES — instructs the PC to list the names of the programs and data files on the default drive.
   LIST — instructs the PC to list the source statements of the current program.
   NEW — instructs the PC to delete the current program from main storage.
   RUN — instructs the PC to execute the current program in main storage.
   RENUM — renumbers the entire program uniformly.

■ CHAPTER 3

2. a. −6.333334   b. 23   c. 8
4. c: INT is a reserved word (keyword). A list of the MS BASIC reserved words is on page R.5 of the reference card at the back of this book.
   e: First character is not a letter.
   f: PRINT is a reserved word.
   g: First character is not a letter.
   h: FOR is a reserved word.

6. a. 110 Q = (D + E) ^ (1 / 3)
   b. 120 D = (A ^ 2) ^ 3.2
   c. 130 B = 20 / (6 - S)
   d. 140 Y = A1 * X + A2 * X ^ 2 + A3 * X ^ 3 + A4 * X ^ 4
   e. 150 H = X + X / (X - Y)
   f. 160 S = 19.2 * X ^ 3
   g. 170 V = 100 - (2 / 3) ^ (100 - B)
   h. 180 T = (76234 / (2.37 + D)) ^ (1 / 2)
   i. 190 V = 1234E-4 * M - (.123458 ^ 3 / (M - N))
   j. 200 Q = ((F - M * 1000) ^ (2 * B)) / (4 * M) - 1 / E

8. a, b, c, d, e, f, g, i
10. a. D = −1, A and B do not change in value.
    b. A = −2.2, B = 2, E1 = 1, E2 = 3.2, E3 = 5

■ CHAPTER 4

2. d, f, h

4. 2050 PRINT USING "The amount is **$####.##+"; AMOUNT
6. 2050 CLS : KEY OFF
   2060 LOCATE 6, 6 : PRINT 6

8. Assume that ƀ represents a blank character.

   a. ƀ25
   b. ƀƀƀ38.40
   c. ƀƀƀ$22.60−
   d. $ƀƀ425.89
   e. *****88.76
   f. %637,214.0
   g. ƀ3.98ƀ
   h. %-123.80
   i. ƀƀƀƀ12.614
   j. ƀ2.66E+02
   k. A
   l. ABCD
   m. AB
   n. ABCD

CHAPTER 5

2.
```
100 X = 0         a. 130 X = X + 1      b. 150 X = X + 7
110 T = 10           140 T = T + 1         160 T = T + 7
```
```
c. 170 X = X + 2      d. 190 X = 2 * X      e. 210 X = X - 1
   180 T = T + 2         200 T = 2 * T         220 T = T - 1
```

4.
    a. Q value greater than 8 or Q value equal to 3.
    b. Q value greater than or equal to 0.
    c. Q value less than 27.
    d. Q may be equal to any value that is within the limits of the PC.

6.
```
a. 200 IF AGE >= 21              b. 300 IF SEX.CODE$ = "M"
          THEN C = C + 1                    THEN M = M + 1
   210 S = S + 1                            ELSE F = F + 1
```

8.
```
100 ' Exercise 5.8 Solution
110 NEGA = 0
120 ZERO = 0
130 POSI = 0
140 READ NUM
150 WHILE NUM <> -1E37
160    IF NUM < 0 THEN NEGA = NEGA + 1
              ELSE IF NUM = 0
                      THEN ZERO = ZERO + 1 ELSE POSI = POSI + 1
170    READ NUM
180 WEND
190 PRINT NEGA, ZERO, POSI
200 ' ********** Data Follows **********
210 DATA 4, 2, 3, -9, 0, 0, -4, -6, -8, 3
220 DATA 2, 0, 0, 8, -3, 4, -1E37
230 END
```

10.
```
100 ' Exercise 5.10 Solution
110 CLS : KEY OFF   ' Clear Screen
120 INPUT "Number of Fibonacci Numbers ===> ", X
130 FIB1 = 1
140 FIB2 = 1
150 PRINT
160 PRINT FIB1;
170 PRINT FIB2;
180 NUM = 3
190 WHILE NUM <= X
200    FIB3 = FIB2 + FIB1
210    PRINT FIB3;
220    FIB1 = FIB2
230    FIB2 = FIB3
240    NUM = NUM + 1
250 WEND
260 PRINT : PRINT : PRINT "Job Complete"
270 END
```

12. ```
    190 ' Exercise 5.12 Solution
    200 IF U < V
            THEN IF U < W THEN S = U ELSE S = W
            ELSE IF V < W THEN S = V ELSE S = W
    ```

14. ```
    3040 ' Exercise 5.14 Solution
    3050 IF C = 0 AND D = 0
            THEN A = -1
            ELSE IF C <> 0 AND D <> 0 THEN A = -2 ELSE A = -3
    ```

■ CHAPTER 6

2. a. OPEN, OUTPUT, APPEND   b. OPEN, INPUT
   c. closed   d. EOF(n)
   e. APPEND

4. ```
   2050 OPEN "B:SALES1.DAT" FOR INPUT AS #1
   2060 OPEN "B:SALES2.DAT" FOR INPUT AS #2
   2070 OPEN "B:SALES3.DAT" FOR INPUT AS #3
   ```

6. a: Filespec must precede the mode.
   e: Comma must immediately follow filenumber.
   g: Filenumber must not be preceded by a number sign (#).
   h: Comma at the end of the list is invalid.

■ CHAPTER 7

2. a. L(2, 2)   b. L(3, 3) or L(2, 4)   c. L(3, 2)
   d. L(5, 2)   e. L(3, 4)   f. L(2, 1)
   g. L(1, 3)   h. L(5, 1)

4. a. c   b. c   c. e   d. a

6. ```
   2000 ' Exercise 7.6 Solution
   2010 OPTION BASE 1
   2020 DIM A(50), B(50), C(50)
           .
           .
           .
   3030 FOR I = 1 TO 50
   3040    IF A(I) < B(I) THEN C(I) = -1
                      ELSE IF A(I) = B(I) THEN C(I) = 0
                                          ELSE C(I) = 1
   3050 NEXT I
   ```

   Line 3040 may also be written as follows:

   ```
   3040     IF A(I) < B(I) THEN C(I) = -1
   3042     IF A(I) = B(I) THEN C(I) =  0
   3045     IF A(I) > B(I) THEN C(I) =  1
   ```

8. Assuming that the variable names that represent subscripts are positive values, all are valid except for b, which has a negative subscript.

CHAPTER 8

2. a. 69
   b. The entire string.
   c. IfᵇIᵇ (where ᵇ indicates a blank character)
   d. seen
   e. 36.8
   f. 73
   g. G
   h. AAAAAAAAAAAAAA
   i. "-13.691"
   j. 24
   k. The word giants is replaced by the word midgets in the string assigned to PHR$.
   l. ᵇᵇᵇᵇ (where ᵇ indicates a blank character)

4. a. 99   b. 43   c. ?   d. "48.9"   e. 1
   f. 66   g. %   h. 58   i. 15   j. 69

6. a. 500 SIGN = SGN(2 * X ^ 3 + 3 * X + 5)
   b. 600 INTEGER = INT(4 * X + 5)

8. a. 100 P = SQR(A ^ 2 + B ^ 2)
   b. 200 B = SQR(ABS(TAN(X) - .51))
   c. 300 Q = 8 * (COS(X)) ^ 2 + 4 * SIN(X)
   d. 400 Y = EXP(X) + LOG(1 + X)

10. ```
    100 ' Exercise 8.10 Solution
    110 RANDOMIZE TIMER
    120 FOR R = 1 TO 100
    130     PRINT INT(52 * RND + 1)
    140 NEXT R
    150 END
    ```

12. `100 DEF FNDISCOUNT(PURCHASE.AMT) = .10 * (PURCHASE.AMT - 200)`

CHAPTER 9

2. a.
   ```
   100 ' Exercise 9.2a Solution
   110 SCREEN 1 : CLS : KEY OFF
   120 PSET (0, 50)
   130 LINE -(200, 25)
   140 LINE -(100, 125)
   150 LINE -(0, 50)
   160 END
   ```

   b.
   ```
   100 ' Exercise 9.2b Solution
   110 SCREEN 1 : CLS : KEY OFF
   120 LINE (0, 0) - (160, 100),, B
   130 LINE -(0, 0)
   140 LINE (160, 0) - (0, 100)
   150 END
   ```
   ```

c. ```
100 ' Exercise 9.2c Solution
110 SCREEN 1 : CLS : KEY OFF
120 PI = 3.141593
130 CIRCLE (70, 80), 45
140 PSET (70, 80)
150 CIRCLE (70, 80), 45,, PI, 2 * PI, 1/6
160 END
```

d. ```
100 ' Exercise 9.2d Solution
110 SCREEN 1 : CLS : KEY OFF
120 PI = 3.141593
130 CIRCLE (75, 60), 70,, -PI, -3 * PI / 2
140 END
```

4. a. Causes the note A-flat to be played.
   b. Sets all notes that follow to lengths of 1/8.
   c. Sets all notes that follow to the next octave and causes the C note to be played.
   d. Executes the subcommand M$, which contains additional commands.
   e. Rest.
   f. Sets the tempo to 100 quarter notes per minute.
   g. Pause a length of 1/8.
   h. Music staccato—each note that follows plays 3/4 of the time specified by L.
   i. Music legato—each note that follows plays the full period set by L.
   j. Sets the octave to 3.

INDEX

ABS function, 216–217
Accumulator, 106–107
Address, 3
Algorithm, 11
AND operator, 121, 124–126
Appending records, 135–136
Argument-organized tables, 195–200
Arithmetic
   functions, 216–223
   operators, 20–21, 58–59
Arithmetic-logic section, 3
Array, 177, 183–189
   declaring, 184–185
   lower bound of, 184
   manipulating an, 186–187
   multi-dimensional, 187–189
   name, 183
   one-dimensional, 184
   parallel, 196
   range of, 186
   summing elements of, 189
   upper bound of, 184
ASC function, 206, 211
ASCII code, 211, 237, 266–267
Ascending sequence, 189
Assignment statement, 20
ATN function, 216
AUTO command, 36
Auxiliary storage, 2–3, 6

Background of screen, 242
BASIC, 9
   commands, R.2–R.3
   data space, 221–222
   statements, R.1–R.2

BASICA command, 30–31
BEEP statement, 156
Benchmarking, 223
Binary search, 196, 199–200
Booting the PC, 30–31
Bubble sort, 189–192
Bugs in a program, 263
Byte, 3

Calling a subroutine, 151–154
Case structure, 103, 155
Central processing unit, 2–3
Chip, 6
CHR$ function, 206, 211
CIRCLE statement, 250–251
Clear screen, 27–28, 36
CLOSE statement, 136–137
CLS, 26–28
Coding techniques, 28–30
Color/graphics board, 235
COLOR statement
   medium resolution, 245
   text mode, 243–244
Comma separator, 69, 78–80
Compound condition, 120
Computer, 1
   advantages, 1
   disadvantages, 1
   graphics, 235
   hardware, 2
   music, 256–259
   simulation, 225–227
   software, 8–9
   sound, 256–259
Concatenation operator, 57, 60, 206–207

Condition, 71–72, 104
  compound, 120
Constant, 46
  numeric, 20, 46–48
  string, 49
CONT command, 265
Control break, 164
Control-break processing, 164–171
Control fields, 164
Control variable, 164
COS function, 216, 221
Counter, 106–107
Counter-controlled loop, 177–178
CPU, 2–3
CSRLIN variable, 206, 221–222
Cursor control keys, 32

Data-sequence holding area, 73
DATA statement, 72–74
DATE$ variable, 206, 214
Debugging techniques, 83, 263–266
Decision making, 102
DEF FN statement, 228–229
DELETE command, R.2
DeMorgan's laws, 127
Descending sequence, 189
Descriptor field, 84–89
Desk checking, 40
Detail line, 91
DIM statement, 184–185
Diskette, 6–7
Documentation, 28
DOS, 10
Double precision, 47–48, 52
Do-Until logic structure, 101, 103, 112–113
Do-While logic structure, 101, 103, 112–113
DRAW statement, 254–256

Editing a program, 32–33
Empty string, 49
END statement, 21
End-of-file, 71, 146
  detection, 146–147
  mark, 146
  routine, 71

EOF function, 146–147
EQV, 123–124
EXP function, 216–218
Exponential form, 46, 48
Expressions
  evaluation of, 58–59
  formation of, 57
  numeric, 57
  string, 57, 60

File, 133–134
  appending records to, 136
  creating a, 135, 142–145
  extension, 33–34
  handling statements, 133–134
  name, 33–34
  opening a, 135
  organization, 134
  sequential, 134
FILES command, 36
Filespec, 33–34, 135
Filler, 82
FIX function, 216–217
Fixed-point constant, 46
Floating-point constant, 46
Flowcharting, 11–13
For loop, 177–183
  execution of, 178
  flowchart representation, 180–181
  nested, 181–182
  range of, 179
  versus While loop, 178
FOR statement, 177–179
Foreground of screen, 242
Format diskette, 17
FRE function, 216, 221–222
Function, 61, 205–206, 216
  arithmetic, 217
  exponential, 217–218
  keys, 35
  numeric, 216
  random numbers, 223–227
  string, 206
  user-defined, 227–229

GOSUB statement, 152–154
GOTO statement, 117

Graphics, 235
    high-resolution, 244
    medium-resolution, 244
    text-mode, 237–244
GRAPHICS DOS command, 244

Hard-copy output, 36–37
Hard disk, 3, 7
Hardware, 2
Hierarchy
    chart, 150–151
    of operations, 58–59, 124–125, R.4
High-resolution graphics, 244

IBM PC, 4–8
    AT, 4
    compatibles, 4
    family, 4
    graphics, 235–236
    keyboard, 5
    peripherals, 6–7
    portable, 4
    speaker, 156
    start-up procedures, 30–31
IBM Personal System/2, 2, 4
IF statement, 104–106
    nested, 119
If-Then-Else
    logic structure, 101–102, 114–118
    nested forms, 117–118
    simple forms, 114–116
Immediate mode, 28, 83
IMP operator, 123–124
Initialization Module, 151
INKEY$ variable, 206, 215
INPUT mode for files, 135–136
Input prompt, 24–25
INPUT statement, 23–26
INPUT #n statement, 145–146
INPUT$ function, 206, 214–216
INSTR function, 206, 209–210
INT function, 216–217
Integer
    constant, 46–47
    variable, 52
Iteration, 70

Internal
    comments, 28
    subroutine, 151

K, 6
KEY statement, 35–36
Keyboard, 5
    function keys, 5, 35
    numeric keypad, 5, 32
    typewriter keys, 5
Keyword, 20
KILL command, 36

LEFT$ function, 60–61, 206–207
Left-justify, 93
LEN function, 60–61, 206–207
LET statement, 20, 54–57
LINE INPUT statement, 214–215
Line number, 20, 22
LINE statement, 247–249
List, 25
LIST command, 34–35
LLIST command, 35
LOAD command, 36
LOCATE statement, 93–94
LOG function, 216–220
Logic structure, 102
    Case, 103
    If-Then-Else, 102
    Do-Until, 103
    Do-While, 103
    Sequence, 102
Logical line, 105–106
Loop
    counter-controlled, 177
    Do-Until, 112–113
    Do-While, 101, 112–113, 180–181
    endless, 72
    variable, 179
Lower-bound value, 184
LPRINT statement, 83
LPRINT USING statement, 90

Magnetic
    disk, 3, 6
    tape, 3

Main storage, 2
Mechanical Man problem, 14–15
Medium-resolution graphics, 244–245
Menu-driven program, 156–164
Microsoft BASIC, 19
   creating a program, 19
   editor, 32–33
   files, 133–134
   general characteristics, 19
   reserved words, R.5
MID$
   function, 60–61, 206, 208
   statement, 209–210
MOD operator, 21, 57
Module, 151
Modulo, 21, 57
Monitor, 3
MS BASIC. *See* Microsoft BASIC
MS DOS, 9
Multiple statements per line, 30
Music, 256–259

NAME command, 36
Nested
   For loops, 181–183
   IF statements, 119
   If-Then-Else structures, 114–118
   parenthetical expressions, 60, 125–126
   While loops, 69
Network, 7
NEW command, 35
NEXT statement, 179
Nonexecutable statement, 29, 74
NOT operator, 120
Null
   ELSE, 115
   list, 28
   string, 49
   THEN, 115
Numeric
   comparison, 106
   constant, 46–49
   function, 216–225
   output, 27, 79
   variable, 50
Numeric expressions. *See* Expressions

ON-GOSUB statement, 155–156
OPEN statement, 135–136
Operators, R.4
   arithmetic, 21, 58–59
   concatenation, 57, 60, 206–207
   logical, 120–126
   relational, 72
OPTION BASE statement, 185
OR operator, 122–124
Order of operations, 58–59, 124, R.4
OUTPUT mode for file, 135–136

PAINT statement, 252–254
Pass, on a loop, 70
Parallel arrays, 196
Parameters, 93, 227
Parentheses, 59, 125
PC. *See* IBM PC
PC DOS. *See* MS DOS
PF keys, 35
Physical line, 105–106
Pixel, 236
PLAY statement, 257–259
Pointer
   for data-holding area, 75
   for sequential file, 146
POS function, 216, 221
Positionally organized tables, 193–195
Precision, 47–48
PRESET statement, 246–247
Print
   item, 78
   position, 78
   zones, 78–79
PRINT statement, 78–83
PRINT #n statement, 137–138
PRINT #n, USING statement, 137–138
PRINT USING statement, 83–93
Program, 2, 8–10
   editing a, 32–33
   flowchart, 11–13
   menu-driven, 133, 156
   specifications, 37
Prompt, 24
PSET statement, 246–247
Pseudocode, 11, 13–14
Pseudo-random members, 223

Question mark
  input prompt, 24
  PRINT statement, 78

RAM, 6
Random
  file, 134
  numbers, 223-227
RANDOMIZE statement, 225
Range
  of For loop, 179
  of array, 186
READ statement, 75-77
Relational operators, 72
Relative file, 134
REM statement, 28-29
Remark lines, 28
RENUM command, 36
Reserved word, 20, 50
RESTORE statement, 77
RETURN statement, 152
RIGHT$ function, 60-61, 206-207
Right-justify, 93
RND function, 216, 223-227
ROM, 6
Rules of precedence, 58-59, 124
RUN command, 34
Running total, 107

SAVE command, 36
Scientific notation, 48
Screen, 3, 244
  background, 242
  border, 242
  foreground, 242
SCREEN
  statement, 236-237
  function, 216, 222
Search argument, 195
Seed for random number, 225
Semicolon separator
  INPUT statement, 26
  PRINT statement, 80-81
Sentinel
  record, 71
  value, 71

Separator
  comma, 79-80
  semicolon, 80-81
  space, 80-81
Sequence logic structure, 101-102
Sequence file
  creating, 141-145
  organization, 134
  writing a report to, 137-141
Serial search of table, 196-198
SGN function, 216-217
SIN function, 216, 221
Single precision, 47, 52
Software, 8-10
Sort, 177, 189-192
SOUND statement, 256-257
Space separator, 80-81
SPC function, 82
Speaker, 156, 256
SQR function, 216-217
Statements, 19
  multiple per line, 30
  non-executable, 29, 74
STEP parameter, 179
STOP statement, 265-266
Stored program, 8
STR$ function, 206, 213
STRING$ function, 206, 213
String, 50
  comparing, 106
  constant, 49
  displaying, 54
  expression, 57
  function, 60-61, 206
  values, 45
  variable, 50
Structure terminator, 114
Structured programming, 101-103
Subroutine, 151
Subscripted variable, 183
Subscripts, 186-189
Substrings, 207
  extracting, 61, 207-209
  replacement, 209-210
  searching for, 209-210
SWAP statement, 191

System
  command, 20, 33
  diskette, 9
SYSTEM command, 35–37

TAB function, 81–82
Table, 177
  argument, 195
  argument-organized, 195–200
  binary search, 199–200
  function, 193, 196
  lookup, 193, 196, 198–199
  organization, 193
  positionally organized, 193–195
  searching, 193–200
  serial search, 196–198
TAN function, 216, 221
Text-mode graphics, 237–244
TIME$ variable, 206, 214
TIMER function, 223
Tips, debugging, 263–266
Top-down
  approach, 150–151
  chart, 150–151
Trailer record, 71
Trigonometric functions, 221
TROFF command, 263–265
TRON command, 263–265
Truth tables, 124

Upper-bound value, 184
USA character set, 237, 266
User-defined function, 205, 227–229
Utility functions, 221–222

VAL function, 206, 213
Variable, 20, 49–54
  declaring types, 52
  dummy, 228
  names, 20, 50–52
  numeric, 50–51
  selection of names, 50–52
  string, 50–51
  subscripted, 183
VTOC, 150

WEND statement, 70–71
While loop, 69
  versus For loop, 178
WHILE statement, 70–71
WRITE #n statement, 141

XOR operator, 123–124

3 1/2-inch diskette, 6
5 1/4-inch diskette, 6–7

MICROSOFT BASIC REFERENCE CARD

Legend: *Uppercase letters are required keywords. You must supply items within < >s. You must select one of the entries within { }s. Items within [ ]s are optional. Three ellipsis points (...) indicate that an item may be repeated as many times as you wish. The symbol b represents a blank character.*

Summary of BASIC Statements

BEEP
Causes the speaker on the PC to beep for a quarter of a second.

CHAIN <"filespec"> [,line number] [,ALL]
Instructs the PC to stop executing the current program, then load another program from auxiliary storage and start executing it.

CIRCLE <(x, y), radius> [,color [,start,end [,shape]]]
Causes the PC to draw an ellipse, circle, arc, or wedge with center at (x, y).

CLOSE [#] [filenumber] [,[#] [filenumber]]...
Closes specified files.

CLS
Erases the information on the first 24 lines of the screen and places the cursor in the upper-left corner of the screen.

COLOR [background] [,palette]
In medium-resolution graphics mode, sets the color for the background and palette of colors.

COLOR [foreground] [,background] [,border]
In the text mode, defines the color of the foreground characters, background, and border around the screen.

COM(n) {ON / OFF / STOP}
Enables or disables trapping of communications activity on adaptor n.

COMMON <variable> [,variable]...
Passes specified variables to a chained program.

DATA <data item> [,data item]...
Provides for the creation of a sequence of data items for use by the READ statement.

DATE$ = mm{ / - }dd{ / - }yy[yy]
Sets the system date, where mm = month, dd = day, yy = year, yyyy = 4-digit year.

DEF FN <name> [(variable [,variable]...)] = <expression>
Defines and names a function that can be referenced in a program as often as needed.

DIM <array name(size)> [,array name(size)]...
Reserves storage locations for arrays.

DRAW <string expression>
Causes the PC to draw the object that is defined by the value of the string expression.

END
Terminates program execution and closes all opened files.

ERASE <array name> [,array name]...
Eliminates previously defined arrays.

FIELD <#filenumber, width AS string variable> [,width AS string variable]...
Allocates space for variables in a random file buffer.

FOR numeric variable = initial TO limit [STEP increment]
Causes the statements between the FOR and NEXT statements to be executed repeatedly until the value of the numeric variable exceeds the value of the limit.

GET <(x₁, y₁) − (x₂, y₂), array name>
Reads the colors of the points in the specified area on the screen into an array.

GET <[#][filenumber] [,record number]
Reads the specified record from a random file and transfers it to the buffer that is defined by the corresponding FIELD statement.

GOSUB <line number>
Causes control to transfer to the subroutine represented by the specified line number. Also retains the location of the next statement following the GOSUB statement.

GOTO <line number>
Causes an unconditional branch to the line number.

IF <condition> THEN [clause]
Causes execution of the THEN clause if the condition is true.

IF <condition> THEN [clause] ELSE [clause]
Causes execution of the THEN clause if the condition is true. Causes execution of the ELSE clause if the condition is false.

INPUT [;]["prompt message" {; / ,}] <variable> [,variable]...
Provides for the assignment of values to variables from a source external to the program, like the keyboard.

INPUT <#filenumber, variable> [,variable]...
Provides for the assignment of values to variables from a sequential file in auxiliary storage.

KEY {ON / OFF}
Turns the display of the ten function keys on line 25 of the screen to on or off.

KEY(n) {ON / OFF / STOP}
Activates or deactivates trapping of the specified key n.

[LET] <variable> = <expression>
Causes the evaluation of the expression, followed by the assignment of the resulting value to the variable to the left of the equal sign.

LINE [(x₁, y₁)] <−(x₂, y₂)> [,color] [,B[F]] [,Style]
Draws a line or a box on the screen.

LINE INPUT [;]["prompt message";] <string variable> or LINE INPUT [;]["prompt message";] <string variable>
Provides for the assignment of a line of up to 255 characters from a source external to the program, like the keyboard or a sequential file.

LINE INPUT <#filenumber, > <string variable>
Provides for the assignment of a line of up to 255 characters from a source external to the program, like the keyboard or a sequential file.

LOCATE [row] [,column] [,cursor] [,start] [,stop]
Positions the cursor on the screen. Can also be used to make the cursor a block or underscore.

LPRINT [item] [item]... Provides for the generation of output to the printer.

LPRINT USING <string expression;> <item> [{; / ,} { item }]...
Provides for the generation of formatted output to the printer.

LSET <string variable> = <string expression>
Moves string data left-justified into an area of a random file buffer that is defined by the string variable.

MID$ <(string var, start position [,number]> = <substring>
Replaces a substring within a string.

NEXT [numeric variable] [,numeric variable]...
Identifies the end of the For loop(s).

ON COM(n) GOSUB <line number>
Causes control to transfer to the line number when data is filling the communications buffer (n).

ON ERROR GOTO <line number>
Enables error trapping and specifies the first line number of an error-handling routine that the PC is to branch to in the event of an error. If the line number is zero, error trapping is disabled.

ON <numeric expression> GOSUB <line number> [,line number]...
Causes control to transfer to the subroutine represented by the selected line number. Also retains the location of the next statement following the ON-GOSUB statement.

ON <numeric expression> GOTO <line number> [,line number]...
Causes control to transfer to one of several line numbers according to the value of the numeric expression.

ON KEY(n) GOSUB <line number>
Causes control to transfer to the line number when the function key or cursor control key (n) is pressed.

ON PEN GOSUB <line number>
Causes control to transfer to the line number when the light pen is activated.

ON PLAY(n) GOSUB <line number>
Plays continuous background music. Transfers control to the line number when a note (n) is sensed.

(BASIC Statements continued on page R.2 in left column)

R.1

MICROSOFT BASIC REFERENCE CARD

Summary of BASIC Statements (continued)

ON STRIG(n) GOSUB <line number>
Causes control to transfer to the line number when one of the joystick buttons (n) is pressed.

ON TIMER(n) GOSUB <line number>
Causes control to transfer to the line number when the specified period of time (n) in seconds has elapsed.

OPEN <filespec> FOR <mode> AS <[#]filenumber> [LEN = record length] or
OPEN <mode, [#]filenumber, filespec> [,record length]
Allows a program to read or write records to a file. If record length is specified, then the file is opened as a random file. If the record length is not specified, then the file is opened as a sequential file.

OPTION BASE {0 | 1}
Assigns a lower bound of 0 or 1 to all arrays.

PAINT <(x, y)> [[,paint] [,boundary]]
Paints an area on the screen with the selected color.

PEN(n) {ON | OFF | STOP}
Enables or disables the PEN read function used to analyze light pen activity.

PLAY <string expression>
Causes the PC to play music according to the value of the string expression.

PRESET <(x, y)> [,color]
Draws a point in the color specified at (x, y). If no color is specified, it erases the point.

{PRINT | ?} [item] [{, | ; | b} item]...
Provides for the generation of output to the screen.

{PRINT | ?} <#filenumber,> [item] [{, | ; | b} item]...
Provides for the generation of output to a sequential file.

PRINT USING <string expression;> <item> [{, | ; | b} item]...
Provides for the generation of formatted output to the screen.

PRINT <#filenumber,> USING <string expression;>
<item> [{, | ; | b} item]...
Provides for the generation of formatted output to a sequential file.

PSET <(x, y)> [,color]
Draws a point in the color specified at (x, y).

PUT <(x₁, y₁), array name> [,action]
Writes the colors of the points in the array onto an area of the screen.

PUT <[#]filenumber> [,record number]
Writes a record to a random file from a buffer defined by the corresponding FIELD statement.

RANDOMIZE [numeric expression]
Reseeds the random number generator.

READ <variable> [,variable]...
Provides for the assignment of values to variables from a sequence of data items created from DATA statements.

{REM | '} [comment]
Provides for the insertion of comments in a program.

RESTORE [line number]
Allows the data items in DATA statements to be reread.

RESUME {line number | NEXT | 0 | b}
Continues program execution at the line number, or the line following that which caused the error, after an error-recovery procedure.

RETURN [line number]
Causes control to transfer from a subroutine back to the statement that follows the corresponding GOSUB or ON-GOSUB statement.

RSET <string variable> = <string expression>
Moves string data right-justified into an area of a random file buffer that is defined by string variable.

SCREEN [mode] [,color switch] [,active page] [,visual page]
Sets the screen attributes for text mode, medium-resolution graphics, or high-resolution graphics.

SOUND <frequency, duration>
Causes the generation of sound through the PC speaker.

STOP
Stops execution of a program. Unlike the END statement, files are left open.

STRIG(n) {ON | OFF | STOP}
Enables or disables trapping of the joystick buttons.

SWAP <variable, variable₂>
Exchanges the values of two variables or two elements of an array.

TIME$ = hh[:mm[:ss]]
Sets the system time where hh = hours, mm = minutes, and ss = seconds.

TIMER {ON | OFF | STOP}
Enables or disables trapping of timed events.

VIEW [[SCREEN] (x₁, y₁) – (x₂, y₂)] [,color] [,boundary]
Defines a viewport.

WEND
Identifies the end of a While loop.

WHILE <condition>
Identifies the beginning of a While loop. Causes the statements between WHILE and WEND to be executed repeatedly while the condition is true.

WIDTH {40 | 80}
Erases the information on the first 24 lines of the screen, sets the width of the line on the screen to 40 or 80 characters, and places the cursor in the upper-left corner of the screen.

WINDOW <[SCREEN] (x₁, y₁) – (x₂, y₂)>
Redefines the coordinates of the viewport. Allows you to draw objects in space and not be bounded by the limits of the screen.

WRITE [expression list]
Writes data to the screen. Identical to the PRINT statement except that it causes commas to be inserted between items displayed; causes strings to be delimited with quotation marks; and positive numbers are not preceded by blanks.

WRITE <#filenumber,> [item] [{, | ; | b} item]...
Writes data to a sequential file. Causes the PC to insert commas between the items written to the file.

Summary of BASIC Commands

AUTO [line number] [,increment]
Automatically starts a BASIC line with a line number. Each new line is assigned a systematically incremented line number.

CLEAR
Assigns all numeric variables the value zero and all string variables the null value.

CONT
Resumes a system activity, like the execution of a program, following interruption due to pressing the Control and Break keys simultaneously or execution of the STOP or END statement.

DELETE [lineno₁] [–lineno₂]
Deletes line numbers lineno₁ through lineno₂ in the current program.

EDIT <line number>
Displays a line for editing purposes.

FILES ["device name:]
Lists the names of all programs and data files in auxiliary storage as specified by the device name.

(BASIC Commands *continued on page R.3 in left column*)

MICROSOFT BASIC REFERENCE CARD

R.3

Summary of BASIC Commands (continued)

KILL <"filespec">
Deletes a previously stored program or data file from auxiliary storage.

LIST [line number₁] [−line number₂] [,"filespec"]
Causes all or part of the BASIC program currently in main storage to be displayed on the screen. The LIST command can also be used to copy lines to a file in auxiliary storage.

LLIST [line number₁] [−line number₂]
Causes all or part of the BASIC program currently in main storage to be displayed on the printer.

LOAD <"filespec">
Loads a previously stored program from auxiliary storage into main storage.

MERGE <"filespec">
Merges the lines from a program in auxiliary storage with the program in main storage. The program in auxiliary storage must have been saved using the A (ASCII) parameter.

NAME <"old filespec"> AS <"new filespec">
Changes the name of a program or data file in auxiliary storage to a new name.

NEW
Causes the BASIC program currently in main storage to be erased and indicates the beginning of a new program to be created in main storage.

RENUM [new line number] [,[old line number] [,increment]]
Renumbers the program uniformly with a new line number and increment.

RUN { line number / "filespec" [",R] } $_B$
Causes the BASIC program currently in main storage to be executed. This command can also be used to begin execution at a specified line number of the program in main storage or to load and execute a program from auxiliary storage.

SAVE <"filespec"> [,A]
Saves the current program into auxiliary storage for later use. The parameter A instructs the PC to save the file in character format (ASCII) rather than binary format.

SHELL
Places the current BASICA session in a temporary wait state and returns control to the operating system MS DOS. When the operating system prompt appears, you can enter MS DOS commands. To return to the BASICA session, type EXIT.

SYSTEM
Causes the PC to permanently exit BASICA and return control to the operating system MS DOS.

TROFF
Turns off the program trace feature.

TRON
Turns on the program trace feature.

Summary of BASIC Functions

ABS(N)
Returns the absolute value of the argument N.

ASC(X$)
Returns a two-digit numeric value that is equivalent in ASCII code to the first character of the string argument X$.

ATN(N)
Returns the angle in radians whose tangent is the value of the argument N.

CHR$(N)
Returns a single string character that is equivalent in ASCII code to the numeric argument N.

COS(N)
Returns the cosine of the argument N where N is in radians.

CVI(X$), CVS(X$), CVD(X$)
Returns the integer, single-precision, or double-precision numeric value equivalent to the string X$. Used with random files.

EOF(filenumber)
Returns −1 (true) if the end of file has been sensed on the sequential file associated with filenumber. Returns 0 (false) if the end of file has not been sensed.

EXP(N)
Returns e (2.718281...) raised to the argument N.

FIX(N)
Returns the value of N truncated to an integer.

FRE(N)
Returns the number of unused bytes within BASIC's data space. N is a dummy argument.

INPUT$(N)
Suspends execution of the program until a string of N characters is received from the keyboard.

INSTR(P, X$, S$)
Returns the beginning position of the substring S$ in string X$. P indicates the position at which the search begins in the string X$.

INT(N)
Returns the largest integer that is less than or equal to the argument N.

LEFT$(X$, N)
Returns the leftmost N characters of the string argument X$.

LEN(X$)
Returns the length of the string argument X$.

LOC(#filenumber)
With a random file, it returns the number of the last record read or written. With a sequential file, it returns the number of records read from or written to the file.

LOF(#filenumber)
Returns the number of bytes allocated to a file.

LOG(N)
Returns the natural log of the argument N where N is greater than 0.

MID$(X$, P, N)
Returns N characters of the string argument X$ beginning at position P.

MKI$(N), MKS$(N), MKD$(N)
Returns the string equivalent of an integer, single-precision or double-precision value. Used with random files.

PEN(n)
Reads the light pen.

PLAY(n)
Returns the number of notes currently in the music background buffer.

PMAP (c, n)
Returns the world coordinate of the physical coordinate c or vice versa. The parameter n varies between 0 and 3 and determines whether c is an x or y coordinate and whether the coordinate is to be mapped from the physical to the world coordinate or vice versa.

POINT { (x, y) / (n) }
With the argument (x, y), the PC returns the foreground color attribute of the point (x, y). With the argument n, the PC returns the physical or world x or y coordinate of the last point referenced. The parameter n varies in the range 0 to 3.

POS(N)
Returns the current position of the cursor on the screen. N is a dummy argument.

RIGHT$(X$, N)
Returns the rightmost N characters of the string argument X$.

RND(N)
Returns a random number between 0 (inclusive) and 1 (exclusive). If N is positive or not included, the next random number is returned. If N is 0 (zero), the previous random number is returned. If N is negative, the random number generator is reseeded before a random number is returned.

SCREEN(row, column)
Returns the ASCII code for the character at the specified row (line) and column on the screen.

(BASIC Functions *continued on page R.4 in left column*)

MICROSOFT BASIC REFERENCE CARD

Summary of BASIC Functions (continued)

SGN(N)
Returns the sign of the argument N: −1 if the argument N is less than 0; 0 if the argument N is equal to 0; or +1 if the argument N is greater than 0.

SIN(N)
Returns the sine of the argument N where N is in radians.

SPACE$(N)
Returns a string of N spaces.

SPC(N)
Displays N spaces. Can be used only in an output statement, like PRINT or LPRINT.

SQR(N)
Returns the square root of the positive argument N.

STR$(N)
Returns the string equivalent of the numeric argument N.

STRIG(n)
Returns the status of the joystick buttons.

STRING$(N, X$)
Returns N times the first character of X$.

TAB(N)
Causes the PC to tab over to position N on the output device. Can be used only in an output statement, like PRINT or LPRINT.

TAN(N)
Returns the tangent of the argument N where N is in radians.

TIMER
Returns a value that is equal to the number of seconds elapsed since midnight.

VAL(X$)
Returns the numeric equivalent of the string argument X$.

Summary of Special Variables

CSRLIN
Equal to the vertical (row) coordinate of the cursor.

DATE$
Equal to the current date (mm-dd-yyyy).

ERL
Equal to the line number of the last error. Used for error trapping.

ERR
Equal to the error code of the last error. Used for error trapping.

INKEY$
Equal to the last character entered from the keyboard.

TIME$
Equal to the current time (hh:mm:ss).

Summary of All Operators

ORDER OF PRECEDENCE	OPERATOR	SYMBOL
Highest	Arithmetic	^
		* or / (Unary + or − sign)
		* or /
		MOD
		+ or − (Binary + or − sign)
	Concatenation	+
	Relational	=, >, >=, <, <=, or <>
	Logical	NOT
		AND
		OR or XOR
		EQV
Lowest		IMP

Summary of Keyword Entries Using the Alt Key

PRESS	KEYWORD ENTERED	PRESS	KEYWORD ENTERED	PRESS	KEYWORD ENTERED
Alt A	AUTO	Alt I	INPUT	Alt R	RUN
Alt B	BSAVE	Alt K	KEY	Alt S	SCREEN
Alt C	COLOR	Alt L	LOCATE	Alt T	THEN
Alt D	DELETE	Alt M	MOTOR	Alt U	USING
Alt E	ELSE	Alt N	NEXT	Alt V	VAL
Alt F	FOR	Alt O	OPEN	Alt W	WIDTH
Alt G	GOTO	Alt P	PRINT	Alt X	XOR
Alt H	HEX$				

Summary of Keyword Entries Using Special Characters

SPECIAL CHARACTER	KEYWORD ENTERED
?	PRINT
'	REM

Summary of Function Keys in BASIC

F1 — LIST	F2 — RUN Enter
F3 — LOAD"	F4 — SAVE"
F5 — CONT Enter	F6 — "LPT1:" Enter
F7 — TRON Enter	F8 — TROFF Enter
F9 — KEY	F10 — SCREEN 0, 0, 0 Enter

Summary of Special Keys

KEYS	FUNCTION
Caps Lock	Acts as a toggle switch for changing the keyboard to the uppercase or lowercase mode. Nonletter keys are not affected.
Ctrl Alt Del	Resets the PC. Used to "warm start" (i.e. reboot) the PC.
Ctrl Break	Terminates a PC activity, like the execution of a program, automatic line numbering or the listing of a program.
Ctrl End	Erases from the cursor position to the end of the current line.
Ctrl Enter	Inserts blanks through the end of the current line.
Ctrl Home	Clears the screen and places the cursor in the upper-left corner of the screen.
Ctrl Num Lock	Stops the PC. Press any key (except Shift, Break, or Ins) to resume.
Ctrl PrtSc	Acts as a toggle on/off switch. Directs output to the printer as well as the screen.
Del	Deletes the character at the cursor position on the screen.
End	Moves the cursor to the end of the line.
Esc	Cancels any changes to the current line.
Home	Moves the cursor to the upper-left corner of the screen.
Ins	Enters or exits the Insert mode.
Num Lock	Acts as a toggle switch to turn the numeric keypad on or off.
Shift PrtSc	Prints the contents of the screen onto a printer.
Space Bar	Transmits a blank character and advances the cursor one position to the right.
⇧ (Shift)	Causes characters pressed while this key is held down to be displayed in uppercase form (lowercase if the keyboard is in the uppercase mode).
←	Backspaces the cursor one position and erases the character that was to the left of the cursor.
↵	Used to enter a line and place the cursor in position 1 of the next line.
← ↑ ↓ →	These four keys are used to move the cursor in the indicated directions.
↹	Moves the cursor to the next tab position. Inserts 8 blanks in the Insert mode.

R.4